THE FLORA AND FAUNA
OF
EXMOOR NATIONAL PARK

THE FLORA AND FAUNA OF EXMOOR NATIONAL PARK

A NATURAL HISTORY CHECK-LIST

Edited by
CAROLINE GIDDENS – FLORA
JOHN ROBBINS – INVERTEBRATES
NOEL ALLEN – VERTEBRATES

EXMOOR NATURAL HISTORY SOCIETY

Foreword by
Keith Bungay, Exmoor National Park Officer

EXMOOR BOOKS

First published in Great Britain in 1996 by Exmoor Books

Copyright © 1996 Exmoor Natural History Society

All rights reserved. No part of this publication may be reproduced, stored in a retrieval system, or transmitted in any form or by any means electronic, mechanical, photocopying, recording or otherwise, without the prior permission of the copyright holder.

British Library Cataloguing-in-Publication Data
A CIP Catalogue Record for this book is available from the British Library

ISBN 0 86183 307 4

EXMOOR BOOKS
Dulverton, Somerset

Trade sales enquiries
Westcountry Books
Halsgrove House
Lower Moor Way
Tiverton, EX16 6SS

Telephone: 01884 243242
Facsimile: 01884 243325

Printed and bound in Great Britain by
Longdunn Press Ltd

FOREWORD

By Keith Bungay, Exmoor National Park Officer

In 1994 we celebrated the fortieth anniversary of the designation of Exmoor as a National Park. The same year the Exmoor Natural History Society marked its twentieth anniversary. These twin commemorations provided the spur for the Society and the National Park Authority to agree to work together to produce this new, comprehensive version of the check-list of the flora and fauna of Exmoor. It incorporates a great deal of new information painstakingly collected since the first edition was published back in 1988.

Since that time wildlife conservation has assumed an ever increasing importance in the work of National Park Authorities. The National Park Plan for Exmoor published in 1991 sets out two specific objectives for wildlife conservation on Exmoor, namely, to improve knowledge and understanding of wildlife, its distribution and value; and to protect, conserve, enhance and, where appropriate, to interpret the natural and semi-natural habitats and native species of the National Park.

This check-list makes a major contribution to the achievement of these objectives. It is a truly remarkable achievement by the Exmoor Natural History Society and, in particular, by its Chairman, Noel Allen, Editor of Vertebrates; its Secretary, Caroline Giddens, Editor of the Flora; John Robbins, Lepidopterist and Editor of the Invertebrates, and by its highly skilled and dedicated band of volunteer recorders. All who care for, and about, this very special place owe them all an immense debt of gratitude.

January, 1996.

ACKNOWLEDGEMENTS

We thank the following for their assistance with the first and second edition:

EXMOOR NATURAL HISTORY SOCIETY MEMBERS who faithfully send in their wildlife records and the RECORDERS for writing the reports.
The EXMOOR NATIONAL PARK AUTHORITY, Dulverton.
The EXMOOR SOCIETY, Dulverton.
ENGLISH NATURE.
The FIELD STUDIES CENTRE, Nettlecombe Court.
The FRESHWATER BIOLOGICAL ASSOCIATION, Wareham.
The NATIONAL TRUST, Holnicote Estate.
The SOMERSET WILDLIFE TRUST, Fyne Court.
SOMERSET ENVIRONMENTAL RECORD CENTRE

Other acknowledgements are made in the appropriate sections of this book.

****

THE RECORDERS

N.V. Allen (Chairman)	Preface; Introduction; Pisces (Fish) and Bibliography
D.C. Boyce	Coleoptera (Beetles)
R.J. Butcher	Aves (Birds) and Odonata (Dragonflies & Damselflies)
Tina Cattley	Mammals
Thelma M. Cheek	Isopoda (Woodlice)
A.E. Cooper	Arachnida (Spiders and allies)
J.A. Edwards	Fungi
Caroline Giddens	Flowering Plants and Ferns
J.A. Hollier	Hemiptera (Bugs) and Neuroptera (Lacewings)
E.J. Houghton	Terrestrial Mollusca (Land Slugs and Snails)
Beryl Lappage	Reptiles and Amphibians
C. Owen	Conifers
Rene Perry	Bryophytes (Mosses and Liverworts)
H.E. Porter	Maritime Life
H. Prudden	Soils of Exmoor
T.J. Richards	Orthoptera (Grasshoppers and Bushcrickets)
J.I. Robbins	Lepidoptera (Butterflies and Moths) and Diptera (Flies)
Olive Russell	Freshwater Life
P. Webley	Climate

ILLUSTRATIONS specially drawn for this edition by ENHS member Jonathan White.

COVER PHOTOGRAPHS: Early-purple Orchids, Noel Allen; Heath Fritillary butterfly, Roger Butcher; Red Deer calf, Noel Allen.

EXMOOR NATURAL HISTORY SOCIETY: Secretary, 12 King George Road, Minehead, Somerset, TA24 5JD.

CONTENTS

	PAGE
Foreword	v
Acknowledgements	vi
The Recorders	vi
Preface	ix
Introducing Exmoor National Park - A Brief Survey	ix
An Introduction to the Soils of Exmoor	1
Exmoor's Climate	4

THE FLORA:

Algae (Freshwater, Marine and Terrestrial)	7
Fungi: Introduction	17
Myxomycotina (Slime Moulds)	18
Ascomycotina (Sac Fungi)	19
Uredinales (Rust Fungi)	21
Ustilaginales (Smut Fungi)	24
Basidiomycetes (Cap, Bracket, etc. fungi)	25
Lichenes (Lichens, Lichenized Fungi & Non-Lichenized Fungi)	43
Bryophyta: Hepaticae (Liverworts)	61
Anthocerotae (Hornworts)	65
Musci (Mosses)	65
Lycopodiopsida (Clubmosses)	75
Equisetopsida (Horsetails)	75
Pteropsida (Ferns)	76
Pinopsida (Conifers)	78
Flowering Plants: Magnoliopsida (Dicotyledons)	80
Liliidae (Monocotyledons)	110

THE FAUNA - INVERTEBRATES

Invertebrates along the Coast	122
Freshwater Life	143
Mollusca (Snails and Slugs)	154
Oligochaeta (Earthworms)	157

Continued over......

Isopoda (Woodlice)	158
Myriapoda (Centepedes, Millipedes, etc.)	159
Insecta: Apterygota (Wingless Insects)	160
Odonata (Damselflies and Dragonflies)	161
Orthoptera (Crickets and Grasshoppers)	163
Blattodea to Anoplura (Cockroach, Earwig, Lice)	164
Hemiptera (Bugs)	166
Thysanoptera to Megaloptera (Thrips, Snake Flies, Alder Flies)	177
Neuroptera to Mecoptera (Lacewings and Scorpion Flies)	177-178
Lepidoptera (Butterflies and Moths)	179
Diptera (Flies)	221
Siphonaptera (Fleas)	241
Hymenoptera (Wasps, Ants and Bees)	242
Coleoptera (Beetles)	250
Arachnida (Spiders, Harvestmen, Pseudoscorpions, Ticks and Mites)	285

VERTEBRATES:

Fish	295
Amphibians and Reptiles	301
Birds	303
Mammals	317
Appendix I. Additions to Diptera	320
Maps SSSI'S on Exmoor	321
Rivers and Waters	322
Principal Woodlands	323
Geology	324
Bibliography	325
Summary of numbers of species recorded	326
Index of Scientific Names	327
Index of English Names	332

PREFACE

EXMOOR NATURAL HISTORY SOCIETY: Founded in 1974 to study and record the flora and fauna of Exmoor National Park. This led to the publication of an annual magazine *Exmoor Naturalist*, to booklets on the wild flowers, the birds, the butterflies and moths of Exmoor and, in 1988 to the 272 page work, *The Flora and Fauna of Exmoor National Park, a Provisional Check-List*. Since 1988 eight supplements to the book have been issued, and there is now the need to publish an up-dated edition of the whole work. This has been made possible by the generous offer from Exmoor National Park Authority to underwrite the cost of printing this new edition.

The check-list now covers all of Exmoor's plant and animal groups. Fortunately we have among our members a few professional biologists who have given unstinted help and advice, plus a number of excellent and enthusiastic amateur naturalists. Also we have been able to incorporate the knowledge and suggestions of various 'outside' experts.

The Society has been required to prepare the text camera-ready, and this exacting task has been carried out by our secretary and botanical recorder Caroline Giddens. This new edition lists over 8,000 species of flora and fauna occuring within Exmoor National Park plus the adjoining area of Minehead and Dunster Beach, compared with 5,064 in the 1988 book. We have removed the word 'Provisional' from the sub-title, for though such a work can never be definitive, most Orders are now very fully recorded. We are especially grateful to John Robbins our Invertebrate Editor with his extensive knowledge of technical and scientific terms, for checking through the whole work, and to Dr. Graham Wills, Head of National Park Management, for his ready support at all times.

INTRODUCING EXMOOR NATIONAL PARK
A BRIEF SURVEY

The Park was established by Act of Parliament in 1954 with 71% of the land in West Somerset and 29% in North Devon. It is administered by a National Park Committee comprised of members of Somerset County Council and the West Somerset and North Devon District Councils, and of members appointed by the Secretary of State for the Environment. However, the Government has plans for a new National Park Authority from April 1997, which will more closely involve local people. The day-to-day running of the Park is carried out by the National Park Officer and his staff from Exmoor House, Dulverton. Primarily, they have the dual task, but each with many ramifications, of (i) preserving and enhancing the natural beauty of Exmoor and (ii) promoting the enjoyment of the Park by the public, while having due regard to the needs of agriculture and forestry, and to social and economic interests. The total area of the National Park is 693 square kilometres (267 square miles) or 69,100 hectares (170,900 acres), half of which lies between 304 and 488 metres (1,000 and 1,600 feet) above sea level. The underlying rock consists mainly of sandstones and grits, with some small outcrops of limestone, of the Devonian period.

The Park Authority owns some 4,654 hectares (11,500 acres) of Exmoor; the National Trust 6,800 hectares (17,000 acres); the Forestry Commission 1,200 hectares (3,000 acres) and the Crown Estate 2,420 hectares (5,980 acres). The balance of 54,000 hectares (133,500 acres) is privately owned. There are 1,100 kilometres (700 miles) of footpaths and bridleways, plus the traditional freedom to roam over much of the 16,000 hectares (40,000 acres) of open moorland.

The moorland area is about equally divided between heather and grass, with sheep and beef cattle the usual stock. The grass moorland covers much of the ancient Royal Forest of

Exmoor which remained with the Crown from the time of William the Conqueror until its sale in 1818. Many acid tolerant plants flourish on the peaty soil of the moors and these include heath-spotted orchid, ivy-leaved bellflower, eyebright, bog pimpernel, bog asphodel, round-leaved sundew and bogbean. Ring ouzel, whinchat, stonechat, wheatear, snipe, curlew, cuckoo, merlin, raven, tree and meadow pipits, and skylark are the chief breeding birds of the high moor. Hen harrier, great grey shrike, short-eared owl and golden plover are regular winter visitors.

6,500 hectares (16,500 acres) of woodland, half broad-leaved, form a vital component of Exmoor, enhancing the beauty of the landscape, providing a refuge for the wild red deer, and a breeding habitat for many birds. These include three kinds of woodpeckers, nuthatch, treecreeper, goldcrest, tawny owl, buzzard, wood warbler, pied flycatcher and redstart. The wooded parts of the Horner, Hawkcombe, Lyn and Barle valleys consist largely of old oaks with a rich variety of ferns, mosses, lichens, fungi, and insects. Some 2,000 hectares (5,000 acres) are considered to be 'ancient woodland', that is, continuously wooded since 1600, and are of national importance. Conifers predominate on the Brendon Hills, and harbour fallow and roe deer, and the nightjar regularly nests in the clearings.

The Chains, a bleak, windswept tableland 457 metres (1,500 feet) high with an average rainfall of 2,300mm (90 inches) a year, is the source of many Exmoor rivers and streams. Here begin the Exe, Barle, Bray, West Lyn, Hoaroak and Farley Waters. In total there are 471 kilometres (300 miles) of major waters on Exmoor, home to the dipper, grey wagtail, heron, the alien mink and more frequently over the past few years, the elusive otter. The waters which all run quickly over beds of boulders and stones, are full of brown trout, plus salmon and sea trout in season. Exmoor has three main impounding reservoirs, but only the latest and largest, Wimbleball Lake, 148 hectares (370 acres), attracts wintering duck, geese, grebes and coots in good numbers.

Exmoor's coastline extends for 55 kilometres (34 miles) from the outskirts of Minehead to Combe Martin. Its cliffs are among the finest and highest in Britain in places falling a thousand feet or more to the sea. These cliffs are very unstable with periodical landslips, dangerous to climb, and the beach difficult of access and boulder strewn most of the way. There are important salt marshes around Porlock Bay with specialised plants and where redshank, lapwing and shelduck nest. This is an area which regularly attracts unusual birds and recent visitors have been little egret, spoonbill, Wilson's phalarope, bittern, bean and pink-footed geese, little gull and Iceland gull. Between Lynmouth and Heddon's Mouth are some of the best seabird colonies in South West England. These include razorbill, guillemot, fulmar, kittiwake, cormorant, shag, herring gull and great black-backed gull.

Finally, there are the villages of Exmoor, more than fifty altogether, all with a history founded in Domesday Book, and most probably extending back into the Saxon period. Here are all the expected birds: tits, finches, thrushes, buntings, and crows. By the sides of the linking roads and lanes grow masses of spring flowers attracting frogs, toads and newts in ponds and ditches, and patrolling dragonflies. House martins, swallows and swifts enliven the summer skies with more than thirty species of butterflies and hundreds of moths. Beyond the villages lie scattered farmsteads set in a varied pattern of fields divided by hedges with a rich flora and always a haven for foxes, badgers, weasels, stoats, dormice and invertebrates.

The pages which follow will show that over the past twenty years we have recorded a great deal of Exmoor's rich flora and fauna. For certain, there is much more to be discovered, identified, and recorded, and as the task continues there are sure to be many happy days ahead for naturalists within Exmoor National Park.

Noel Allen, Chairman,
Exmoor Natural History Society

AN INTRODUCTION TO THE
SOILS OF EXMOOR

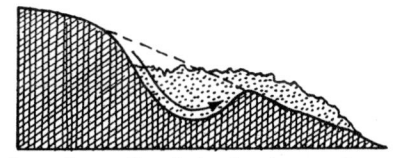

Soils sum up the character of habitats in so much as they reflect bedrock, slopes, climate, biological as well as human activity. It is probably true to say that the latter has had an important influence on Exmoor soils. The aim of what follows is first to paint a broad picture of the soils, and secondly to encourage the reader to go out and get to know them.

CLASSIFICATION OF SOILS

The variations in soil type are influenced by the following factors:

  a. Bedrock e.g. sandstone or slate.
  b. Steepness of slopes.
  c. Altitude i.e. increasing height above sea level results in greater rainfall, lower temperatures and less evapo-transpiration.

Soils are classified according to the observable characteristics of their profiles and the physical, chemical and biological processes which have helped to form the profiles. The lowest category in soil classificatioin is the soil series and these are the basis of the types of soils shown on soil maps.

Since soil types can change within very short distances, several types are grouped together as a soil association and named after the dominant soil series in the group. The descriptions below concentrate on the dominant soil type in any particular association.

ROCKS AND SOILS IN EXMOOR NATIONAL PARK

The slates were formerly muds deposited on the sea floor and break down into a stony, silty clay loam. The sandstones tend to be largely composed of quartz sands and are inherently less fertile and more acidic. At lower altitudes the slates are associated with the Milford association and the sandstones with the Rivington association. Both associations are in the Brown Earth Group.

Sandstones, such as the Pickwell Down Beds between the coast at Morte Bay and Haddon Hill, are associated with the Podzol Group of soils. The latter tend to develop on non-calcareous, well drained quartz sands.

The high rainfall and low evaporation rates are reflected by extensive areas of Podzol soils where the already low content of bases is leached out thus intensifying the naturally acidic nature of the soils. The Chains have an annual rainfall of over 1600mm and the consequent waterlogging has led to the slow decay of organic matter and the formation of peat.

There are calcareous rocks in Exmoor National Park. The Permo-Triassic red sands and the silty clays usually give a reaction when tested with weak hydrochloric acid (Worcester association). The Selworthy inlier consists of limestones and shales (Evesham 2 association), similar to the rocks seen along the coast from Watchet to Lilstock. Further south there is a narrow belt of Devonian age limestones extending from Withycombe to Roadwater, Treborough, Luxborough, Luckwell Bridge and Newland, west of Exford. The impact of these outcrops is lessened by their association with adjacent silt stones and slates. They supported lime kilns and quarries which are no longer worked and which are becoming overgrown with a natural succession of shrubs and trees.

GEOLOGY

FIELD STUDY OF SOIL ASSOCIATIONS ON EXMOOR - SOIL DESCRIPTION

The best way to get to know soils is to note how they differ one from another. A useful exercise is to collect samples and photograph any soil seen in profile and then to compare samples and profiles.

There are abundant opportunities to examine soil profiles on Exmoor in old quarries, eroding gullies, trackways and so forth. Some suggestions are made below of localities where visitors can familiarise themselves with the various soil types. Remember that soil associations may include patches of ground with soil series (types) that differ from the dominant soil series.

The soil groups and soil associations that follow, together with their associated numbers, are those shown on the 1:250,000 scale map *Soils of England and Wales; Sheet 5 South West England*. Fuller details can be found in the accompanying volume listed in the references.

PELOSOLS (Group 4)
4.11b Evesham 2 association - Slowly permeable calcareous clay soils, which support mixed farming. Found immediately south of Selworthy on an inlier of Lower Lias limestones and clays. (SS920 465)

4.31 Worcester association - Calcareous red clayey soils which can suffer seasonal waterlogging. Most under permanent grassland owing to problems of cultivation and surface wetness. Found around Wootton Courteney on reddish, often calcareous, Permo-Triassic mudstones. (SS937 430)

BROWN SOILS (Group 5)
5.41a Milford association - Well drained fine reddish-brown loams over slates or Head (disturbed bedrock). Mixed farming with grassland on higher slopes; coniferous and deciduous woodland. May be seen around Rodhuish on outcrops of Ilfracombe Beds, slates and siltstones. (ST 01 49)

5.41g Rivington association - Stony sandy, non-calcareous, well drained loam. Permanent pasture, rough grazing and woodland, especially on steep slopes. 'Unenclosed land near the Bristol Channel affords poor grazing of bristle-agrostis grassland and dry western heath. On high moorland further inland, the soils are under either acid bent-fescue grassland of high rough grazing value or poorer heath moor, often with bracken and gorse' *(Findlay et. al 1984)*. Occurs along the toll road on the north side of Porlock Hill on Hangman Sandstones. (SS 85 47)

5.41i Munslow association - Well drained silty, non-calcareous soils. Mixed farming; deciduous woodland on steep slopes. Found around Exton on Pickwell Down Beds. (SS 92 33)

PODZOLIC SOILS (Group 6). Tend to develop under acid conditions.
611c Manod association - Dark brown, well drained, shallow clay loam over ochreous irony subsoil on rock or rock debris. No bleached subsoil horizon. Soils are naturally acid. Most is permanent grass, leys and rough grazing. Woodlands on steeper slopes. These are very extensive along the B3224 on the Brendon Hills (e.g. SS 00 34) on slates, siltstones of the Brendon Hill Beds (Morte Slates). Also between Withypool and Exford and a large area around Blackmoor Gate. (SS646 433)

633 Larkbarrow association - A well drained, coarse, loamy, very acid podzol. A thin organic surface layer and a bleached, very stony subsurface horizon overlie a brightly coloured subsoil. 'Near the Bristol Channel...dry western heath is developed, comprising ling, bell heather, western furze and bristle-leaved bent' *(Findlay et al 1984)*. On either side of the A39 between Culbone Hill and County Gate on rubbly sandstones of the Hangman

GEOLOGY

Grits and Head e.g. disused quarry at SS 812 478.

654a Hafren association - Loamy acid soils which have a wet peaty surface horizon over bleached subsoil and ironpan which hinders drainage. Early nineteenth century reclamation improved the drainage in some areas. Much is permanent pasture; many areas are conserved as semi-natural vegetation e.g. moist atlantic heather moor, mostly of ling and purple moorgrass. Found along the B3223 on Winsford Hill e.g. at Wambarrow (SS 876 343) on slates and siltstones of the Morte Slates. Also on the slates and sandstones of the Kentisbury Slates (Ilfracombe Slates) along the footpath from the B 3358 (SS 724 405) to Pinkworthy Pond (SS 723 423); note how peat forms on gentler slopes along the minor valley leading up to Pinkworthy Pond. A superb exposure of peaty gleyed podzol is seen 2.5 km south west of Simonsbath (Burcombe Series) (SS751 382).

654b Lydcott association - The sandstones result in a very acid, peaty top surface with strongly leached stony subsoil derived from bedrock or sandstone Head. The association covers much of the distinctive unimproved 'Exmoor' moorland landscape: atlantic heather moor with some drier heathy patches of ling and whortleberry. Some grass and bracken on steep slopes. Occurs on Dunkery on sandstones of the Hangman Sandstones (SS 90 41) and around Anstey Gate on Pickwell Down Beds (SS 83 29).

SURFACE WATER GLEY SOILS (Group 7). 'Gleying' is the process by which ferric iron is reduced to more mobile, colourless or grey ferrous iron complexes, by micro-organisms or products of decomposing organic matter. Subsoils show mottling which is an indicator of intermittent wetness and an important diagnostic property for assessing soil condition.

721d Wilcocks 2 association - Loamy upland soil with very acid, peaty surface horizon. Seasonally waterlogged wet moorland. Mainly open moorland and rough grazing. Occurs on hilltops underlain by Morte Slates south west of Simonsbath (SS 74 37).

GROUND-WATER GLEY SOILS (Group 8)
813f Wallasea 1 association - Non-calcareous, deep, stoneless, clayey gley soils. Groundwater may cause severe waterlogging. Mostly permanent grassland. Developed on marine alluvium at Porlock Bay and Dunster Marsh (SS99 45)

PEAT SOILS (Group 10) - Mainly organic soils derived from partially decomposed plant remains that accumulated under waterlogged conditions. Groups differ from one another because of varying combinations of parent material, wetness, texture and the layers or horizons making up the soil.
1011b Winter Hill association - Very thick, fibrous raw peat soils. Permanently wet with ph <4.0. Wet moorland habitat with blanket bog. Occurs on The Chains in SS 73 41.

1013b Crowdy 2 association - Thick, very acid amorphous raw peat soils permanently wet. Extensive area west of The Chains e.g. Exe Plain in SS 76 42.

H.C. PRUDDEN
Geological Recorder, ENHS

References:
D.C. Findlay, et al. *Soils and their use in South West England* (1984) Soil Survey of England and Wales Bulletin No. 14. Harpenden. This volume has been used extensively for the present account.

L.F. Curtis, *Soils of the Exmoor Forest* (1971) Soil Survey of England and Wales.

D.V. Hogan, *Soils in Devon* VII (Sheet SS74 Lynton).

EXMOOR'S CLIMATE

A study of this Check-list will confirm the overall friendliness of Exmoor's climate towards the Flora and Fauna within our National Park. Springtime rarely delays its arrival, the months of March, April, and May seldom allowing winter to retain its grip. Summertime is mostly able to satisfy farmer, grower, and holiday-maker alike. Autumn can often bring an early foretaste of hazardous weather ahead but these threats seldom materialise. The winter months of December, January, and February can bring periods of snowfall and intense cold to the higher moors, but such conditions are not often prolonged.

The coastal areas are milder and tend to escape with only minor inconvenience during those periods of hostile weather on the hills. Coastal storms occasionally create havoc and sea defences are then fully tested.

Exmoor rainfall is heaviest on the bleak wild moorland called The Chains, average 2030-2300mm (80-90 inches), but during a very wet 1994 annual rainfall amounted to 2735mm (107.6 inches). Around Dunkery Beacon a rainfall of 1730-1830mm (68-72 inches) is normal. In 1994 a figure of 2122mm (83.5 inches) was attained. The coastal area of Minehead varies between 800-900mm (32-35 inches) annually.

Westerly winds prevail. Wind speeds above 70 mph are rarely encountered.

Sunshine hours at Minehead average 1660 annually.

For the naturalist, walker, and rider it is wise to treat Exmoor's weather with respect and weather observations are always worthwhile.

P.A. WEBLEY
WEATHER RECORDER, E.N.H.S.

WEST SOMERSET WEATHER STATISTICS (AVERAGE FIGURES FOR 20 years 1974-94)

Month	Rainfall mm	Sunshine hours	Mean Max. Daily Temp.°C	Mean Min. Daily Temp.°C
January	86	56	9	5
February	73	72	8- 9	3
March	65	130	10-11	5-6
April	58	165	12	6
May	53	220	15	8
June	55	210	18-19	11
July	60	214	20-21	13
August	62	204	21	13
September	64	128	18	11
October	97	100	15	8
November	88	66	13-14	9
December	98	46	10-11	5-6

THE FLORA

Division: ALGAE
(FRESHWATER, MARINE and TERRESTRIAL)

In the list which follows, the majority of Marine algae (Seaweeds) were recorded between 1974 and 1986 by Mr H.E. Porter and Mr J. Hill, Maritime Recorders, Exmoor Natural History Society. Some of the Freshwater algae were listed by Miss Olive Russell, ENHS Freshwater Recorder, but for many of the microscopic marine, freshwater and terrestrial algae, we can trace no more recent work than that carried out in the 1950's by Dr. W. Watson, whose findings were published in *Proceedings,* Somerset Archæological and Natural History Society. For the sake of completeness, these are included in the following list, prefixed § – with due acknowledgements. It has not been possible to include the status for every species but this is inserted where known.

Class: CHLOROPHYCEAE (GREEN ALGAE)

The largest group of algae; very diverse and widely distributed, containing terrestrial, saltwater and freshwater species.

Order: VOLVOCALES

SPHAERELLACEAE

Chlamydomononas pulvisculus Ehrenb.   Round swimming cells in freshwater.   Common

Volvox aureus Ehrh.   Colonies of hundreds of cells may be visible in puddles and ponds

Order: TETRASPORALES

PALMELLACEAE

§Palmella mucosa Kütz.   Moorland combes

§Coccomyxa subellipsoides Acton

§Gloeocystis gigas (Kütz.) Lagerh.

§G. vesiculosa Naeg.

§Dactylococcus braunii Lagerh.

§Botrydina vulgaris Bréb.

Order: CHLOROCOCCALES

CHLOROCOCCACEAE

§Characium heterorphum Reinsch.   Freshwater.   Common

OOCYSTACEAE

§Oocystis solitaria With.   Ponds and slow moving rivers

§O. elliptica West.   Slow moving water

7

ALGAE

SELENASTRACEAE
Ankistrodesmus falcatus (Corda) Ralfs.	Slow, still and fast waters	Common

DICTYOSPHAERIACEAE
§Westella botyroides De Wildem.

PLEUROCOCCACEAE
Pleurococcus vulgaris Naeg.	Tree trunks	Very common

DESMIDIACEAE (DESMIDS)
Closterium lunula s.l.	Ponds, slow rivers, bogs	Common

There are many more unrecorded species of desmid which occur.

ZYGNEMACEAE
Zygnema spp.	Puddles and pools	Common
Spirogyra tenuissima (Hass.) Kütz.	Standing water	Common
§Spirogyra cataeniformis (Hass.) Kütz.	Standing water	

Order: SIPHONALES

VAUCHERIACEAE
§Vaucheria sessilis (Vauch.) DC.	Stagnant or slow water	Common
§V. ornithocephala Ag.	Stagnant or slow water	
§V. hamata (Vauch.) Lyngb.		

BRYOPSIDACEAE
§Bryopsis plumosa C.Ag.		Maritime

Order: SIPHONOCLADALES

CLADOPHORACEAE
Cladophora fracta (Dillw.) Kütz.	BLANKET WEED	Ponds and pools	Very common
C. rupestris Kütz.		On rocks	Maritime
§C. utriculosa Kütz.			Maritime
§C. hirta Kütz.			Maritime
§Chaetomorpha aerea Kütz.			Maritime
§C. melagonia Kütz.			Maritime
§Rhizoclonium hieroglyphicum Kütz.			Maritime

TRENTEPOHLIACEAE
Trentepohlia aurea (L.) Mart.	Damp rocks	Locally common

Although a green algae, this grows in patches which have the appearance of orange velvet

Phycopeltis arundinacea (Mont.) De Toni	Trees and shrubs	Locally abundant

MICROSPORACEAE
Microspora sp.	Running or still water

ALGAE

ULOTHRICACEAE

Ulothrix zonata (W. and M.) Kütz.	Running or still water	Common
§U. subtilis Kütz.		Common
§U. aequalis Kütz.	Pools	
§U. moniliformis Kütz.		
§Binuclearia tatrana Wittr.	Pools	

Order: ULVALES (GREEN MARINE ALGAE)

ULVACEAE

Ulva lactuca L. SEA LETTUCE	Rocks and rock pools	Frequent
Monostroma grevillei (Thuret) Wittrock	Rock pools	Uncommon
Enteromorpha intestinalis (L.) Link	Brackish water	Common
§E. compressa (L.) Greville	Brackish water, rocks & pilings	Uncommon
§E. prolifera J. Agardh		
E. linza (L.) J. Agardh	Rocks	Sometimes washed up on shore

Order: SCHIZOGONIALES (FRESHWATER)

PRASIOLACEAE

§Prasiola crispa (Light.) Menegh.   Rocks frequented by birds, in streams

Order: OEDOGONIALES (FRESHWATER)

OEDOGONIACEAE

§Oedogonium vaucherii (Le Cl.) A.Br.	Still water
§O. obsoletum Wittr.	Still water
§O. itzigsohnii DB	Still water
§O. rufescens Wittr.	Still water

Order: HETEROTRICHIALES (FRESHWATER)

TRIBONEMACEAE

§Tribonema bombycinum (Ag.) Derb. & Sol.   Pools

Class: CHAROPHYCEAE (STONEWORTS)

CHARACEAE

Nitella flexilis (L.) Agardh	Ponds and rivers	Records from 1930's only
N. translucens (Persoon) Agardh	Pinkworthy Pond	Local

ALGAE

Class: BACILLOPHYCEAE (DIATOMS)

Order: DISCOIDALES

MELOSIRACEAE
§Melosira varians Ag.   Ditches, ponds   (has brown chloroplasts)

Order: FRAGILARIALES

FRAGILARIACEAE
Fragilaria sp.   Chain-forming diatoms
§Synedra ulna (Nitz.) Ehren.   A non-chain forming diatom

Class: MYXOPHYCEAE (CYANOPHYCEAE) (BLUE-GREEN ALGAE)

Order: GLAUCOCYSTIDALES

GLAUCOCYSTACEAE
§Glaucocystis nostochinearum Itzig.   In pools

Order: CHAMAEOSIPHONALES

CHAMAEOSIPHONACEAE
§Chamaeosiphon incrustans Grun.   Attached to other algae

Order: COCCOGONALES

CHROOCOCCACEAE
§Gloeothece confluens Naeg.
§G. granosa Rabh.
§Aphanothece microscopica Naeg.   Wet rocks; bogs
§Gloecapsa coracina Kütz.   Wet rocks
§Chroococcus macrococcus (Kütz.) Rab.   Boggy pools

Order: HORMOGONALES

OSCILLATORIACEAE
§Oscillatoria irrigua Kütz.   Wet rocks, soil and in water

ALGAE

§Oscillatoria rubiginosa Carm.	Wet rocks and stones
§O. tenuis Ag.	Wet rocks etc.
§Phormidium autumnale (Ag.) Gom.	Wet rocks and soil etc.
§Symploca muscorum (Ag.) Gom.	Wet places
NOSTOCACEAE	
§Nostoc commune Vauch.	Wet soil – colony forming
§N. sphaericum Vauch.	
§N. coeruleum Lyngb.	On mosses and submerged plants
§N. verrucosum Vauch.	
§Anabaena variabilis Kütz.	Brackish water and bogs
§A. torulosa Lagerh.	Brackish waters
SCYTONEMACEAE	
§Scytonema mirabile (Dillw.) Born.	Wet rocks and soil
STIGONEMACEAE	
§Stigonema minutum (Ag.) Hass.	Damp rocks
§S. ocellatum (Dillw.) Thur.	Damp rocks
RIVULARIACEAE	
§Calothrix pariatine (Naag.) Thur.	Upland streams
§Rivularia crustacea Carm.	Waterfalls and upland streams

Class: EUGLENOPHYCEAE

Order: EUGLENALES (GREEN FLAGELLATES)

EUGLENACEAE
Euglena sp.   Most water, particularly ponds.

Class: RHODOPHYCEAE – RED ALGAE

Order: NEMALIONALES

HELMINTHOCLADIACEAE		
§Batrachospermum moniliforme Roth	Upland waters	
CHAETANGIACEAE		
§Scinaia forcellata Bivona	Sublittoral, on stones	Maritime
LEMANEACEAE		
§Sacheria fluviatilis (Ag.) Sirod.	Freshwater	
§S. mammilosa Sirod.	Freshwater	

ALGAE

Order: BANGIALES

BANGIACEAE

Porphyra umbilicalis (L.) Kütz.	LAVER	Stones on sandy beaches	Locally common

Order: GELIDIALES (RED MARINE ALGAE)

GELIDIACEAE
§Gelidium pusillum Le Jol.   On rocks
WRANGELIACEAE
§Naccaria wigghii Endl.   Stony shores

Order: CRYPTONEMIALES

GRATELOUPIACEAE
§Grateloupia filicina (OC.) Ag.   Sandy shores
§G. dichotoma J.Ag.   Sandy shores
DUMONTIACEAE
§Dumontia incrassata (Müller) Lamouroux   Rockpools, on pebbles & seaweeds
§Dilsea edulis Stackh. *(D. carnosa (Schmid.) Kuntze)*   Rocks
NEMASTOMACEAE
Halarachnion ligulatum (Woodward) Kütz.   On stones in shallow water
§Furcellaria fastigiata (L.) Lamour.   Shallow water
RHIZOPHYLLIDACEAE
§Polyides rotundus (Hudson) Grev.   Stones and pools on lower shore
CORALLINACEAE
§Melobesia farinosa Lamour.   A coralline which encrusts other seaweeds
§M. corticiformis Kütz.   As above
§M. verrucata Lamour.   As above
§Hapalidium roseolum Rabh.   Parasitic on other seaweeds
Corallina officinalis L.   Rockpools

Order: CERAMIALES

DELESSERIACEAE
Delesseria sanguinea (Huds.) Lamour.   Shallow water   Occasionally washed up
§Membranoptera alata (Hudson) Stackhouse   Rockpools and shallow water
§Myriogramme bonnemaisonii Kylin.   Kelp stipes, other algae, rocks
Phycodrys rubens (L.) Batters   Rocks, kelp stipes and mussels
§Nitophyllum punctatum (Stackhouse) Grev.   On seaweeds in pools

ALGAE

§Polyneuria gmelini Kylin.	Lower shore
§Hypoglossum woodwardii Kützing	Rocks and pools
§Apoglossum ruscifolium (Turner) J.Agardh	Rocks, pools and on kelp
§Cryptopleura ramosa (Hudson) Newton	Rocks, kelp stipes

RHODOMELACEAE

§Rhodomela confervoides (Hudson) Silva *(R. subfusca)*	Rocks and seaweeds
§Laurencia pinnatifida (Hudson) Lamour. PEPPER DULSE.	Rocks on lower shore
§Polysiphonia urceolata (Dillw.) Grev.	Rocks, shells and other algae
P. lanosa (L.) Tandy *(P. fastigiata)*	On other seaweeds
§P. nigrescens (Huds.) Grev.	Rockpools
Brongniartella byssoides (Good.et Woodw.) Schm.	Rocks on lower shore
Heterosiphonia plumosa (Ellis) Batters	Rocks etc. in shallow water

CERAMIACEAE

§Spondylothamnion multifidum (Huds.) Naeg.	Pools on lower shore
§Griffithsia flosculosa (Ellis) Batters	On rocks in pools on lower shore
§Plenosporium borreri Naeg.	Lower shore
§Rhodochorton rothii Naeg.	
§Callithamnion byssoides Arn.	
§C. polyspermum C.Ag.	
§C. tetragonum (With.) C.Ag.	On other seaweeds
§C. tetricum C.Ag.	Rock pools
§Plumaria elegans (Bonnemaison) Schmitz	On shaded side of rocks
§Antithamnion plumula (Ellis) Thur.	Muddy rocks
§Ceramium diaphanum (Lightfoot) Roth.	On other seaweeds
§C. deslongchampsii Chauv.	
§C. circinatum J.Ag.	
§C. rubrum (Hudson) C.Agardh	Rocks and other seaweeds
§C. flabelligerum J.Ag.	On other seaweeds
§C. echionotum J.Ag.	Rocks and rockpools
§C. ciliatum (Ellis) Ducluz.	Littoral zone
§C. acanthonotum Harv.	Rocks and shells

Order: GIGARTINALES

GIGARTINACEAE

Chondrus crispus (L.) Stackhouse IRISH MOSS or CARRAGHEEN
                                          Stones and rocks on lower shore   Frequent
Gigartina stellata (Stackhouse) Batters   Rocks on lower shore   Local
§Phyllophora crispa (Huds.) Dixon *(P.epiphylla)* Vertical rocks in shallow water

ALGAE

§Phyllophora membranifolia (Good. & Woodw.) J.Ag.   Vertical rock faces in shallow water
§Stenogramme interrupta Mont.   Stones in sand   Rare
§Gymnogongrus norvegicus (Gunn.) J.Ag.   Rocks on lower shore
§Ahnfeltia plicata (Hudson) Fries   Rocks in pools
§Callophyllis laciniata (Hudson) Kütz.   Rocks in shallow water
RHODOPHYLLIDACEAE
§Catenella caespitosa (Withering) Dixon *(C. repens; C. opuntia)*
                                                    Rocks on upper shore
§Cystoclonium purpureum (Hudson) Batters   Rocks and seaweeds on lower shore

Order: RHODYMENIALES

SPHAEROCOCCACEAE
§Gracilaria verrucosa (Hudson) Papenfuss *(G. confervoides)*
                                                    Stones on middle shore
§Calliblepharis ciliata (Hudson) Kütz.   Rocks and rockpools
§C. jubata Grev. *(C. lanceolata Batt.)*   Rockpools
RHODYMENIACEAE
Palmaria palmata (L.) Kuntze *(Rhodymenia p.)* DULSE   Rocks and on kelp stipes
Lomentaria articulata (Hudson) Lyngbye   Rocks and seaweeds
§L. clavellosa (Turner) Gaillon   Rocks and seaweeds
Plocamium cartilagineum (L.) Dixon *(P.coccineum)*   On rocks in shallow water

Class: PHAEOPHYCEAE (BROWN MARINE ALGAE)

Order: ECTOCARPALES

ECTOCARPACEAE
§Ectocarpus siliculosus (Dillwyn) Lyngbye   Rocks and stones. This species represents an aggregation of several formerly separated species of Ectocarpus and Pilayella.
ELACHISTACEAE
§Elachista fucicola Fr.   On Fucus species
CORYNOPHLOEACEAE
§Leathesia difformis (L.) Areschoug   On other seaweeds
MYRIONEMACEAE
§Ralfsia verrucosa (Areschoug) Agardh   On rocks and shells
DESMARESTIACEAE
§Desmarestia aculeata (L.) Lamour.   On rocks on lower shore
§D. ligulata (Lightfoot) Lamour.   Rocks in pools
§Arthrocladia villosa (Hudson) Duby   Rocks and stones

ALGAE

PUNCTARIACEAE
§Punctaria latifolia Greville   Rocks, stones and shells

Order: SPHACELARIALES

SPHACELARIACEAE
Sphacelaria spp.   Often on other algae
CLADOSTEPHACEAE
§Cladostephus spongiosus (Huds.) J.Ag.   On rocks in pools
STYPOCAULACEAE
§Halopteris filicinas (Grat.) Kütz.   Rocks, seaweeds, shells on lower shore

Order: LAMINARIALES

LAMINARIACEAE
Laminaria digitata (Hudson) Lamouroux   OARWEED   Often washed up
              Attached to rocks on lower shore, seldom uncovered by tide
L. saccharina (L.) Lamouroux   SEA BELT/POOR MAN'S WEATHERGLASS   Frequent
              Attached to rocks and stones on lower shore
Saccorhiza polyschides (Lightfoot) Batters *(S. bulbosa)* FURBELOWS
              Rocks on lower shore   Frequent
Alaria esculenta (L.) Greville DABBERLOCKS Rockpools and shallow water   Uncommon

Order: DICTYOTALES

DICTYOTACEAE
§Dictyota dichotoma (Hudson) Lamouroux   Rocks and seaweeds
§Taonia atomaria (Woodward) J.Agardh   Rocks and stones
§Dictyopteris membranacea (Stackh.) Batters   Rocks on lower shore

Order: FUCALES

FUCACEAE
Fucus vesiculosus L.   BLADDER WRACK   Rocks on middle shore   Common
F. serratus L.   TOOTHED WRACK   Rocks on lower middle shore   Common
F. spiralis L.   SPIRAL WRACK   Rocks on upper shore   Local
§F. ceranoides L.   Areas of reduced salinity
Ascophyllum nodosum (L.) Le Jolis KNOTTED/EGG WRACK
                                           Upper and middle shore   Common
Pelvetia canaliculata (L.) Decaisne & Thur. CHANNELLED WRACK
                                           Rocks on upper shore   Local

15

ALGAE

§Halidrys siliquosa (L.) Lyngbye   SEA-OAK   Rocks, middle shore
§Cystoseira baccata (Gmelin) Silva *(C. fibrosa)* Rocks and pools on lower shore

References:
Belcher & Swale, *Beginners Guide to Freshwater Algae* (3rd Imp. 1978) H.M.S.O.
Watson, W. *The Algae of Somerset* (1952) SANHS Taunton *Proceedings* Vol.XCVII.
Hiscock, Sue, *A Field Key to the British Red Seaweeds* (1986) Field Studies Council
Campbell, A.C. *Guide to the Seashore and Shallow Seas of Britain and Europe* (1979) Hamlyn.
Moore, J.A. *Charophytes of Great Britain and Ireland* (1986) BSBI Handbook No 5.
Exmoor Natural History Society Records (1974-1995)

Division: FUNGI (MYCOTA)

Since the first check-list of species of fungi occuring on Exmoor was published some eight years ago, we have been fortunate in adding several hundreds to the list. The varied terrain of Exmoor provides suitable habitats for a good selection of fungi. In particular, the considerable areas of ancient woodland are ideal sites for many which thrive on decaying wood and in undisturbed surroundings.

Although mycology has been one of the more neglected branches of the natural sciences, there has been increasing interest in the last decade or two. One factor which may have stimulated this is the widespread use of colour photography and the more accurate reproduction of coloured plates in publications, which makes initial identification a less formidable task for the amateur. There are some 3,000 species of larger fungi to be found in the British Isles but many of these are rare. Once the observer has familiarised himself with the commoner genera, naming the species is less difficult.

Fungi contain a wide variety of chemical substances including deadly poisons, hallucinogenics and substances used in the drug industry such as Antabuse which causes acute discomfort if consumed with alcohol. Whilst fungi can be compared with flowering plants in many aspects of their structure, they lack chlorophyll and thus cannot build up carbon compounds; their food is derived from living or dead plants and some are parasitic upon other species of fungi.

In Britain we do not eat a great variety of species compared with the rest of Europe. It has been suggested that this attitude may spring from our Druidic ancestors who considered that many fungi contained magical properties and were to be eaten only at certain ceremonies.

There have been many changes in the nomenclature of fungi over recent years, and space precludes the inclusion of all synonyms in this list. We are most grateful to Dr. B. Spooner and to Peter Roberts of the Royal Botanic Gardens, Kew for their assistance in checking the names used, as there is no published up-to-date check-list for fungi. Likewise, there is as yet no Red Data Book for nationally vulnerable species so the status given refers to Exmoor National Park only.

Members of the Exmoor Natural History Society have contributed many records of fungi since 1974 but there are undoubtedly more species to be added and we will always be glad to receive additional records.

J.A. Edwards
Recorder of Fungi, E.N.H.S.

Sub-Division: **MYXOMYCOTINA**
(SLIME MOULDS)

Class: **MYXOMYCETES**

In the past, there has been confusion over the placing of this group, due to the authorities being unable to agree on their status as plants or animals. At one stage in the development of Myxomycetes, they move and feed like the amœba, giving rise to their classification as *Mycetozoa* 'Fungus Animals.' At another stage however, they form reproductive bodies similar to fungi and they are in this work classed as a sub-division of that group. These fungus-like bodies are often brightly coloured and occur on damp and decaying twigs and leaves. Nobody in the ENHS has as yet taken up their study and the following list therefore relies heavily on Hadden, Norman G. *The Mycetozoa of West Somerset*. SANHS *Proceedings* Vol. lxxxviii (1942), which covered the Minehead/Porlock area. The list has been put in alphabetical order for ease of reference.

Amaurochaete fuliginosa Macbr.
Arcyria cinerea Pers.
A. denudata Wettst.
A. ferruginea Sauter
A. incarnata Pers.
A. nutans Grev.
A. oerstedtii Rost.
A. pomiformis Rost.
Badhamia affinis Ros.
B. nitens Berk.
B. panicea (Chev.) Rost.
B. rubiginosa Rost.
B. utricularis Berk.
Clastoderma debaryanum Blytt.
Colloderma oculatum Lister
Comatrichia elegans Lister
C. laxa Rost.
C. lurida Lister
C. nigra Schröt
C. pulchella Rost.
C. rubens Lister
C. tenerrima Lister
C. typhoides Rost.
Craterium aureum Rost
C. leucocephalum Ditm.
C. minutum Fr.
Cribaria argillacea Pers.
C. aurantiaca Schrad.
C. pyriformis Schrad.
C. rufa Rost.
Diachaea cerifera Lister
D. leucopoda Rost.
Dianema corticatum List.
D. depressum List.
D. harveyi Rex.
D. repens List. & Cran.
Dictydiathalium plumbeum Macb.
Dictydium cancellatum Macbr.
Diderma asteroides Lister

Diderma floriforme Pers.
D. effusum Morg.
D. hemisphericum Horn.
D. niveum Macbr.
D. ochraceum Schröt.
D. radiatum Lister
D. spumarioides Fr.
Didymium clavus Rabenh.
D. difforme Duby.
D. effusum Morg.
D. dubium Rost.
D. melanospermum Macbr.
D. nigripes Fr.
D. squamulosum Fr.

Enerthenema papillatum Ros.
Enteridium olivaceum Rost.
Fuligo cinerea Morg.
F. muscorum Alb.
F. septica Gmel.
Hemitrichia clavata Rost.
H. karstenii Lister
H. minor G.Lister
H. vesparium Macbr.
Lachnobolus congestus Lis.
Lamproderma arcyrionema
L. columbinum Rost. /Rost.
L. scintillans Morg.
L. violaceum Rost.
Leocarpus fragilis Rost.
Lepidoderma tigrinum Rost.
Leptoderma iridescens G.L.
Licea flexuosa Pers.
Lycogala epidendrum Fr.*
Margarita metallica List.
Mucilago spongiosa Morg.
Orcadella operculata Wing.
Perichaena corticalis Rost.
P. depressa Libert.

Perichaena vermicularis Rost.
Physarum bitectum List.
P. compressum Pers.Al.&Sch.
P. conglomeratum Rost.
P. contextum Pers.
P. leucopus Link.
P. luteo-album Lister
P. nucleatum Rex.
P. nutans Pers.
P. ovisporum G.Lister
P. psittacinum Ditm.
P. pusillum Lister
P. sinuosum Weinm.
P. straminipes Lister
P. vernum Somm.
P. virescens Ditm.
P. viride Pers.
Prototrichia metallica Mass.
Reticularia lycoperdon Bull.*
Stemonitis confluens Cooke
S. ferruginea Ehr.
S. flavogenita Jahn.
S. fusca Roth.
S. herbatica Peck
S. hyperopta Meyler
S. splendens Rost.
Trichia affinis De Bary
T. botrytis Pers.
T. contorta Rost.
T. decipiens Macbr.
T. favoginea Pers.
T. floriformis (Schwein.)
T. persimilis Karst./G.Lister
T. scabra Rost.
T. varia Pers.
Tubifera ferruginosa Gmel.

*Currently common.

Sub-division: ASCOMYCOTINA (SAC FUNGI)
Class: ASCOMYCETES

Acanthophiobolus chaetophorus = A. helicosporus (Berk. & Br.) Walker   Rarely recorded
Aleuria aurantia (Pers.) Fuckel *(Peziza a.)*   ORANGE PEEL FUNGUS   Common
Ascobolus denudatus Fr.   Uncommon
Ascocoryne sarcoides (Jacq.) Groves & Wilson   Common
Bisporella citrina (Batsch : Fr.) Korf & Carpenter   Common
Bulgaria inquinans Fr.   BLACK BULGAR   Common
Byssonectria fusispora (Berk.) Rogerson & Korf *(Inermisia f.)*   Uncommon
Ceratocystis ulmi (Buisman) C.Moreau   DUTCH ELM DISEASE
    All large elms on Exmoor have died
Chlorosplenium aeruginascens (Nyl.) Karst   GREEN OAK   Frequent
Claviceps purpurea (Fr.) Tul. & C.Tul.   ERGOT   Scarce on various grasses
    A variety also occurs on Purple Moor Grass (Molinia caerulea)
Cordyceps militaris (L.) Link   SCARLET CATERPILLAR FUNGUS   Fairly common
Cudoniella acicularis (Bull.: Fr.) Schröt.   Occasional
C. clavus (Alb. & Schwein.) Dennis   Scarce
Daldinia concentrica (Bolt.: Fr.) C. & de Not.   CRAMP BALL or   Common on ash
    KING ALFRED'S CAKES
Dasyscyphus virgineus = Lachnum virgineum (Batsch)   Occasional; probably under-recorded
Dasyscyphus apalus = Lachnum apalum (Berk. & Br.) Nannfeldt   Rarely recorded
Diatrype disciformis (Hoffm.: Fr.) Fr.   Common
Disciotis venosa (Pers.) Boud.   MOREL   Local
Elaphomyces granulatus Fr.   FALSE TRUFFLE   Scarce
Epichloe typhina   Cylindrical gall on grass stems, coated white
Eutypa acharii Tul. & C.Tul.   Common
Geoglossum fallax Durand   Uncommon
Geopora sumneriana (Cooke) Massee *(Sepultaria s.)*   Rare
Helvella crispa (Scop.) Fr.   COMMON WHITE HELVELLA   Common
Helvella lacunosa Afzelius : Fr.   BLACK HELVELLA   Rarely recorded
Humaria hemisphaerica (Wigg.) Fuckel   Uncommon
Hymenocyphus calyculus agg.   Uncommon, on sticks
H. epiphyllus (Pers.) Rehm   Occasional
H. fructigenus (Bull.) Gray   NUT CUP   Uncommon; on fallen hazelnuts
H. pileatus (Karst) O.Kuntze   Local
H. scutula (Pers.) Phill.   Apparently scarce but probably under-recorded
Hypoxylon confluens (Tode) Westend.   on Quercus lignum   Scarce

SAC FUNGI

Hypoxylon fragiforme (Pers.: Fr.) Kickx		Common
H. fuscum (Pers.: Fr.) Fr.		Uncommon
H. howeianum Peck		Occasional
H. multiforme (Fr.) Fr.		Common
H. rubiginosum (Pers.) Fr.		Common
Lasiosphaeria canescens (Pers.) P.Karst.		Occasional
L. spermoides (Hoffm.) Ces. & de Not.		Rare
Leotia lubrica (Scop.) Pers.	JELLY BABIES	Uncommon
Microglossum viride (Pers.: Fr.) Gillet		Uncommon
Mitrula paludosa Fr.		Uncommon
Mollisia cinerea (Batsch) Karst.		Rather uncommon
Myriosclerotinia sulcata (Whetzel) Buchwald	SEDGE FUNGUS	Uncommon
Nectria cinnabarina (Tode : Fr.) Fr.	CORAL SPOT FUNGUS	Common
Nemania serpens (Pers.) Kick. *(Hypoxylon s.)*		Frequent
Neobulgaria pura (Fr.) Petrak		Frequent
Octospora rutilans (Fr.) Fr. *(Neottiella r.)*		Uncommon
Onygena equina (Willd.) Pers.		Rare
Otidea alutacea (Pers.) Massee		Scarce
O. leporina (Batsch) Fuckel		Uncommon
Peziza badia Pers.	BROWN CUP	Common
P. repanda Pers.		Uncommon
P. succosa Berk.		Uncommon
P. vesiculosa Bull.		Uncommon
Rhizina undulata Fr.	PINE FIRE FUNGUS	Uncommon
Rhopographus filicinus (Fr.) Nitschke : Fuckel		Common
Rhytisma acerinum (Pers.) Fr.	TAR SPOT	On sycamore, locally common
Rustroemia firma (Pers.) Karst.		Frequent
Sarcoscypha coccinea Fr. *(Peziza c.)*	SCARLET ELF-CUP	Common on hazel
Scutellinia scutellata (L.) Lamb.	EYELASH FUNGUS	Uncommon
Taphrina betulina Rostr. *(T.turgida)*	WITCHES BROOM	Common gall on birch
T. deformans (Berk.) Tul.& C.Tul.		Galls on nectarine
T. pruni Tul.& C.Tul.		Galls on blackthorn
Thuemendium atropurpurea (Batsch) O. Kuntze		Uncommon
Trichoglossum hirsutum (Pers.: Fr.) Boud.	HAIRY EARTH TONGUE	Scarce
Trochila ilicina (Nees) Greenhalgh & Morgan-Jones		Common
Ustulina deusta (Fr.) Petrak		Common
Xylaria carpophila (Pers.) Fr.		Frequent
X. hypoxylon (L.) Grev.	CANDLE SNUFF FUNGUS	Common
X. polymorpha (Pers.) Grev.	DEAD MAN'S FINGERS	Fairly common

Class: BASIDIOMYCETES

Section One: SMALL PARASITIC FUNGI

Order: UREDINALES (RUST FUNGI)

Study of the Rust Fungi is a specialised subject, and the only accounts we have been able to trace are those c1920/30 compiled by the late Norman Hadden. However, Exmoor Natural History observers have been able to confirm that most of the species listed by Hadden are still present (probably all occur) so the list which follows once again relies heavily on Hadden brought up to date in nomenclature and with a few additions.

The Rust Fungi have an intricate life-cycle involving five stages or types of spore, sometimes affecting different plants in the various stages, for example in the Reed and Dock Rust *(Puccinia phragmitis)* the whitish spermogonia are followed by aecidia which have white spoor masses situated on brilliant red spots on Dock *(Rumex)* leaves. The spores discharged from these settle on Reeds *(Phragmites)* and produce brownish uredospores. Next, black teleutospores develop from which basidiospores grow and explode to float away and re-infect Docks and begin the cycle again.

The list which follows is arranged in alphabetical order.

	HOST PLANT	
Coleosporum tussilaginis (Pers.) Lev.	*sensu lato* Noted on a variety of species	
Kuhneola uredinis (Link.) Arth.	Rubus (Bramble)	Frequent
Melampsora capraearum Thum.	Salix (Willow)	Common
M. epitea Thum.	Euonymus (Spindle)	Scarce
M. euphorbiae Cast.	Euphorbia (Spurges)	Common
M. hypericorum Wint.	Hypericum androsaemum (Tutsan)	Frequent
M. lini (Ehrenb.) Lév.	Linum catharticum (Fairy Flax)	Uncommon
M. populnea (Pers.) Karst.	Mercurialis perennis (Dog's-mercury)	Frequent
Melampsorella betulinum (Fr.) Kleb.	Betula (Birch) esp. seedlings	Abundant
M. caryophyllacearum Schröt.	Teleutospores on Cirsium vul. & Stellaria hol. (NGH)	
M. symphyti Bubak	Symphytum (Comfrey)	Scarce
Milesina blechni Syd.	Blechnum spicant (Hard-fern)	Scarce
M. dieteliana Syd.	Polypody (Polypody fern)	Uncommon
M. scolopendrii (Faull) Henderson	Phyllitis vulgare (Hartstongue fern)	Scarce
Miyagia pseudosphaeria (Mont.) Jorst.	Sonchus (Sowthistle)	Rare
Phragmidium bulbosum (Str.) Schl.	Rubus (Bramble)	Uncommon
P. fragariae (DC) Rabh.	Potentilla sterilis (Barren Strawberry)	Common
P. mucronatum (Pers.) Schl.	Rosa (Roses)	Abundant
P. rubi-idaei (DC) Karst.	Rubus idaeus (Raspberry)	Common
P. sanguisorbae (DC) Schröt.	Sanguisorba minor (Salad Burnet)	Rare
P. violaceum Wint.	Rubus fruticosus (Bramble)	Abundant

RUST FUNGI

Puccinia acetosae Koern.	Rumex acetosa (Sorrel)	Frequent
P. adoxae DC	Adoxa moschatellina (Moschatel)	Frequent
P. albescens Plowr.	Adoxa moschatellina (Moschatel)	Uncommon
P. annularis (Str) Rohl.	Teucrium scorodonia (Wood Sage)	Uncommon
P. arenariae (Schum.) Wint.	Stellaria (Stitchwort) and other Caryophyllaceae	Frequent
P. brachypodii Otth.	Brachypodium (Wood false-brome)	Frequent
P. calcitrapae DC	Cirsium, Arctium (Thistles, Burdock)	Rare
P. circaeae Pers.	Circaea lutetiana (Enchanter's Nightshade)	Common
P. cnici-oleracei Pers ex Desm.	Achillea, Chrysanthemum and other Compositae	Common
P. conii Lagh.	Conium maculatum (Hemlock)	Scarce
P. coronata Corda	Uredospores on various grasses	Common
P. crepidoca crepidicola Syd.	Crepis sp. (Hawksbeard)	Frequent
P. difformis Kunze	Galium aparine (Cleavers)	Rare
P. dioicae Magn. var. silvatica (Schröt.) Hend.	Aecidia on Taraxacum (Dandelion)	
P. epilobii DC	Epilobium palustre (Bog Willowherb)	Rare
P. fergussoni B. & Br.	Viola palustris (Marsh Violet)	Rare
P. festucae Plowr.	Teleutospores on Sheep's Fescue	
P. glechomatis DC	Glechoma hederacea (Ground-ivy)	Uncommon
P. glomerata Grev.	Senecio spp. (Ragworts)	Frequent
P. graminis Pers.	Dactylis glomerata (Cocksfoot grass)	Frequent
P. hieracii Mart.	Various Composites: Taraxacum, Hieracium, Centaurea, etc.	Abundant
P. iridis Wallr.	Iris spp. (Stinking and Garden Iris)	Local
P. lagenophorae Cooke	Senecio spp. (Groundsel, Ragwort)	Frequent
P. lapsanae Fuc.	Lapsana communis (Nipplewort)	Abundant
P. luzulae Lib.	Luzula pilosa (Hairy Woodrush)	Scarce
P. maculosa (Str.) Rohl.	Mycelis muralis (Wall Lettuce)	Uncommon
P. malvacearum Mont.	Malva sylvestris (Common Mallow)	Common
P. menthae Pers.	Mentha spp. (Mints)	Common
P. moliniae Tul.	Molinia caerulea (Purple Moor-grass)	Uncommon
P. nitida (Str.) Rohl.	Aethusa cynapium (Fool's Parsley) Also on Garden Parsley	Frequent
P. obscura Schröt.	Aecidia on Bellis perennis (Daisy) Teleutospores on Luzula (Woodrush)	Uncommon
P. oxalides	Oxalis corniculata (Pink Oxalis)	Local
P. phragmitis Koern.	Aecidia on Rumex (Docks) Teleutospores on Phragmites (Reed)	Locally common
P. pimpinellae (Str.) Rohl.	Pimpinella saxifraga (Burnet Saxifrage)	Rare

RUST FUNGI

P. poarum Niels.	Aecidia on Tussilago (Coltsfoot)	
	Teleutospores on Poa (Meadow-grass)	Common; local
P. polygoni-amphibii Pers.	Persicaria (Red-leg)	Uncommon
P. primulae Duby.	Primula vulgaris (Primrose)	Frequent
P. pulverulenta Grev.	Epilobium spp. (Willowherbs)	Common
P. punctata Link.	Galium spp. (mainly Bedstraws)	Local
P. punctiformis (Str.) Rohl.	Cirsium arvense (Creeping Thistle)	Abundant
P. recondita Rob. & Desm.	Agropyrum (Couch Grass)	Common
P. saniculae Grev.	Sanicula europaea (Sanicle)	Locally frequent
P. silenes Schröt.	Silene spp. (Campions)	Rare
P. smyrnii Biv-Bernh.	Smyrnium olusatrum (Alexanders)	Locally abundant
P. tanaceti DC	Artimisia absinthium (Wormwood)	Rare
P. tumida Grev.	Aegopodium podagraria (Ground Elder)	Occasional
P. umbilici Duby.	Umbilicus rupestris (Wall Pennywort)	Frequent
P. veronicae Schröt.	Veronica montana (Wood Speedwell)	Rare
P. vincae Berk.	Vinca major (Greater Periwinkle)	Frequent
P. violae DC	Viola spp. (Violets, Pansies)	Common
P. virgaureae Libert.	Solidago virgaurea (Golden-rod)	Rare
Pucciniastrum agrimoniae (Diet) Tranz.	Agrimonia procera (Agrimony)	Uncommon
P. circaeae (Wint.) de Toni	Circaea lutetiana (Enchanter's Nightshade)	Uncommon
P. guttatum (Schröt) H.J.& N.	Sherardia arvensis (Field Madder)	Uncommon
P. vaccinii (Wint.) Jorst.	Vaccinium myrtillus (Whortleberry)	Common
Trachyspora intrusa (Grev.) Arth.	Alchemilla sp. (Lady's Mantle)	Uncommon
Tranzschelia discolor Tranz. & Litr.	Prunus spinosa (Blackthorn)	Uncommon
Triphragmium ulmariae (DC) Link.	Filipendula ulmaria (Meadowsweet)	Fairly frequent
Uredo quercus Duby.	Quercus ilex (Holm Oak)	Uncommon
Uromyces acetosae Schröt.	Rumex acetosa (Sorrel)	Frequent
U. anthyllidis Schröt.	Anthyllis vulneraria (Kidney Vetch)	Scarce
U. armeriae Kickx	Armeria maritima (Thrift)	Rare
U. betae (Pers.) Tul.	Beta (Beet)	Local
U. dactylidis Otth.	Teleutospores on grasses	
	Aecidia on Ranunculus spp. (Buttercups)	Abundant
U. dianthi (Pers.) Niessl.	Garden carnations	Local
U. ervi West.	Vicia hirsuta (Hairy Tare)	Uncommon
U. ficariae Lév.	Ranunculus ficaria (Lesser Celandine)	Frequent
U. muscari (Duby) Lév.	Hyacinthoides; Muscari (Bluebell; Grape Hyacinth)	Frequent
U. nerviphilus (Grog.) Hotson.	Trifolium repens (White Clover)	Frequent
U. pisi (DC) Otth.	Trifolium spp. (Clovers)	Not known
U. polygonii-aviculare (Pers.) Karst.	various arable weeds	Frequent

RUST FUNGI

Uromyces rumicis (Schum.) Wint.	Rumex spp. (Docks)	Common
U. salicorniae de Bary.	Salicornia spp. (Glasswort)	Rare and local
U. sparsus Lév.	Spergularia spp. (Sea Spurrey)	Uncommon and local
U. valerianae (DC) Lév.	Valeriana officinalis (Valerian)	Uncommon
U. vicia-fabae (Pers.) Schröt.	various legumes	Scarce

References:

Wilson & Henderson, *British Rust Fungi* (C.U.P. 1966)

Hadden, N.G., *The Uredineae of West Somerset* and *Uredinales of North Devon Journal of Botany* Vols. 58 (1920) 37 and 54 (1916) 52.

Order: USTILAGINALES (SMUT FUNGI)

These parasitic fungi, named from their black spores, are the cause of many plant diseases such as Bunt or Stinking Smut on wheat. The subject is still wide open for study on Exmoor and has not yet been tackled by the Exmoor N.H.S. but the following has been noted:

Ustilago violacea (Pers.) Roussel   PURPLE ANTHER SMUT   common on Silene alba (White Campion)

Reference:
Mordue & Ainsworth, *Ustilaginales of the British Isles* (1984) Commonwealth Mycological Institute, Kew.

Class: BASIDIOMYCETES

Section Two: THE LARGER FUNGI

Note: Arrangement is in alphabetical order in line with current practice.

Agaricus abruptibulbus Peck		Uncommon
A. arvensis Schaeff. S. Lange *(Psalliota arvensis (Schaeff.ex Secr.) Kumm.)*	HORSE MUSHROOM	Fairly common
A. augustus Fr.	THE PRINCE	Scarce
A. bisporus (Lange) Pilát var.albidus (J.Lange) Sing.	CULTIVATED MUSHROOM	Uncommon
A. bresadolianus Bohus *(A.campestris var.radicatus)*		Rare
A. campestris L.: Fr.	FIELD MUSHROOM	Becoming less common
A. comtulus Fr.		Scarce
A. cupreobrunneus (J.Schaeff. & Steer ex Møller) Pilát		Rare
A. essetti Bon.		Rare
A. fuscofibrillosus (Møll.) Pilát		Rare
A. haemorrhoidarius Schulz. apud Kalchbr.		Rare
A. koelerionensis Bon.		Rare
A. langei (Møll.) Møll.		Uncommon
A. luteolorufescens P.D.Orton		Rare
A. lutosus (Møll.) Møll.		Rare
A. macrosporus (Møll. & J.Schaeff.) Pilát		Scarce
A. niveolutescens Huijsm.		Rare
A. placomyces Peck		Uncommon
A. poryphyrocephalus Møll.		Scarce
A. semotus Fr.		Rare
A. silvaticus J.Schaeff.		Common
A. silvicola (Vitt.) Peck	WOOD MUSHROOM	Rare
A. stramineus (Møll. & Schaeff.) Singer		Rare
A. variegans Møll.		Rare
A. xanthodermus Genev.	YELLOW STAINER	Fairly common
Agrocybe cylindracea (DC. : Fr.) Maire		Fairly common
A. dura (Bolt.: Fr.) Sing.		Scarce
A. praecox (Pers.: Fr.) Fayod		Uncommon
Amanita citrina (Schaeff.) Gray	FALSE DEATH CAP	Common
A. crocea (Quél.) Kühn. & Romagn.		Uncommon
A. excelsa (Fr.) Kumm.		Uncommon

25

FUNGI

Amanita fulva (Schaeff.) Secr.	TAWNY GRISETTE	Common
Amanita inaurata Secr.		Uncommon
A. muscaria (L.: Fr.) Hook.	FLY AGARIC	Common
A. pantherina (DC. : Fr.) Secr.	PANTHER CAP	Uncommon
A. phalloides (Vaill. : Fr.) Secr.	DEATH CAP	Uncommon
A. rubescens (Pers.: Fr.) Gray	THE BLUSHER	Uommon
A. submembranacea Bon.		Rare
A. vaginata (Bull.: Fr.) Vitt.		Common
Antrodia xantha (Fr.: Fr.) Ryv. *(Amyloporia x.)*		Rare
Armillaria bulbosa Barla		Occasional
A. mellea (Vahl.: Fr.) Kumm.	HONEY FUNGUS	Common
A. ostoyae Romag.		Rare
A. polymyces (Pers.) Sing.		Common
Asterophora parasitica (Bull. Fr.) Sing.	PICK-A-BACK FUNGUS	Scarce On other fungi
Aurantioporus fissilis (Berk. & Curtis) Jahn	(bracket)	Rare
Aureoboletus cramesinus (Secr.) Watl.		Rare
Auricularia auricula-judae (Bull.:Fr.) Wettst.	JEW'S EAR	Common on elder
A. mesenterica (Dicks.) Pers.	TRIPE FUNGUS	Common
Auriscalpium vulgare Gray		Rare
Baeospora myosura (Fr.: Fr.) Sing.	PINECONE FUNGUS	Scarce, on pinecones
Battarraea phalloides (Dicks.) Pers.		Very rare
Bjerkandera adusta (Wild.: Fr.) Karst.	(bracket)	Common
Bolbitius aleuriatus (Fr.: Fr.) Singer		Rare
B. vitellinus (Pers.: Fr.) Fr.		Local
Boletinus cavipes (Opat.) Kalchbr.	MOCK OYSTER	Rare
Boletus aereus Bull.: Fr.		Rare
B. appendiculatus Schaeff.: Fr.		Rare
B. badius Fr.	BAY BOLETE or PANTHER CAPPED BOLETUS	Common
B. bovinus L.: Fr.		Uncommon
B. calopus Fr.		Scarce
B. chrysenteron Bull.	RED CRACKED BOLETUS	Common
B. edulis Bull.: Fr.	CEP	Common
B. elegans Schum.: Fr. *(Suillus grevillei (Klotzsch:Fr.) Sing.)*	LARCH BOLETE	Scarce
B. erythropus (Fr.: Fr.) Secr.	RED STALKED BOLETE	Common
B. lanatus Fr.		Rare
B. luteus L.: Fr.*(Suillus luteus (L.:Fr.) Gray)* SLIPPERY JACK		Common

FUNGI

Boletus parasiticus Bull.: Fr.	Scarce, parasitic on Scleroderma (Earthball)	
B. piperatus Bull.: Fr.	PEPPERY BOLETUS	
B. porosporus (Imler) Watl.		Uncommon
B. pruinatus Fr. & Hök		Rare
B. pulverulentus Opat.		Rare
B. rubellus Krombh.		Rare
Boletus scaber Fr. *(Leccinum scabrum)*	BROWN BIRCH BOLETE	Uncommon
B. subtomentosus L.: Fr.	DOWNY BOLETUS	Uncommon
B. versipellis Fr.& Hök *(Leccinum versipelle)*	ORANGE BIRCH BOLETE	Uncommon
Bovista nigrescens Pers.: Pers.	(puffball)	Uncommon
B. plumbea Pers.: Pers.	DUSKY PUFFBALL	Uncommon
Calocera cornea (Batsch: Fr.) Fr.		Common on frondose wood
C. glossoides (Pers.: Fr.) Fr.		Occasional on oak
C. viscosa (Pers.: Fr.) Fr.		Common on coniferous wood
Calocybe carnea (Bull.: Fr.) Kühn.		Rare
C. constricta (Fr.) Kühn.		Occasional
Calvatia gigantea Batsch : Pers.	GIANT PUFFBALL	Fairly common
Cantharellus cibarius Fr.	CHANTERELLE	Fairly frequent
C. cinereus (Pers.) Fr.		Uncommon
C. infundibuliformis (Scop.) Fr. *(C. tubaeformis Fr.)*		Uncommon
Ceriporia reticulata (Hoffm.: Fr.) Dom.		Occasional
Chondrostereum purpureum (Fr.) Pouz.	SILVER LEAF FUNGUS (bracket)	Common
Chroogomphus rutiluns (Schaeff.: Fr.) O.K. Miller		Uncommon
Clavaria argillacea Pers.: Fr.	FIELD or MOOR CLUB	Uncommon
C. vermicularis Fr.	WHITE SPINDLES	Scarce
Clavulina cinerea (Fr.) Schröt.	GREY CORAL FUNGUS	Fairly common
C. cristata (Fr.) Schröt.	WHITE or CRESTED CORAL	Common
C. rugosa (Fr.) Schröt.	WHITE OR WRINKLED CLUB	Common
Clavulinopsis cineroides (Atk.) Corner		Scarce
C. corniculata (Fr.) Corner	STAG'S-HORN FUNGUS	Common
C. cristata Fr. *(Clavulina c.)*	WHITE or CRESTED CORAL	Common
C. fusiformis (Fr.) Corner	GOLDEN SPINDLES	Scarce
C. helvola (Fr.) Corner		Fairly common
C. luteo-alba (Rea) Corner *(Clavaria c.)*		Fairly common
C. laeticolor (Berk. & Curt.) Petersen *(C. pulcher (Peck) Corner)*		Occasional
Clitocybe cerussata (Fr.) Gill.	WHITE LEAD CLITOCYBE	Uncommon
C. clavipes (Pers.: Fr.) Kumm.	CLUB FOOT	Uncommon
C. dealbata (Sow.: Fr.) Kumm.		Scarce
C. discolor (Pers.) Lange		Occasional

FUNGI

Clitocybe fragrans (Sow.: Fr.) Kumm.		Uncommon
C. geotropa (Bull.) Quél.		Rare
C. gibba (Pers.: Fr.) Kumm.		Occasional
C. houghtonii (Berk. & Br.) Dennis *(Omphalia roseotincta)*		Rare
C. harmajae Lamoure		Rare
C. hydrogramma (Bull.: Fr.) Kumm.		Rare
C. infundibuliformis (Schaeff.) Quél.	COMMON FUNNEL CAP	Common
C. inornata (Sow.: Fr.) Gill.		Rare
C. langei Sing.: Hora		Rare
C. nebularis (Batsch: Fr.) Kumm.	CLOUDED AGARIC	Common
C. odora (Bull.: Fr.) Kumm.	ANISEED TOADSTOOL	Scarce
C. phyllophila (Fr.) Kumm.		Rare
C. pinsitus (Fr.) Joss.		Uncommon
C. pseudoclusilis (Joss.& Konrad) P.D.Orton		Rare
C. rivulosa (Pers.: Fr.) Kumm.		Rare
C. suaveolens (Schum.: Fr.) Kumm.		Uncommon
C. vibecina (Fr.) Quél.		Common
Clitopilus prunulus (Scop.: Fr.) Kumm.	THE MILLER	Common
Collybia acervata (Fr.) Kumm.		Uncommon
C. butyracea (Bull. : Fr.) Kumm.	BUTTER CAP	Common
C. cirrhata (Schum.: Fr.) Kumm.		Scarce
C. confluens (Pers.: Fr.) Kumm.	CLUSTERED TOUGH SHANK	Common
C. cookei (Bres.) J.D.Arnold		Rare
C. dryophila (Bull.: Fr.) Kumm.		Common
C. erythropus (Pers.: Fr.) Kumm.		Rare
C. fusipes (Bull.: Fr.) Quél.	SPINDLE SHANK	Uncommon
C. maculata (Alb. & Schw.: Fr.) Kumm.	SPOTTED TOUGH SHANK	Common
C. peronata (Bolt.: Fr.) Kumm.	WOOD WOOLLY-FOOT	Common
C. tuberosa (Bull.: Fr.) Kumm.		Rare
Coniophora puteana (Schum.) Karst.		Common
Conocybe blattaria (Fr.: Fr.) Kühn.		Rare
C. filaris (Fr.) Kühn. *(Pholiota filaris (Fr.) Lange)*		Rare
C. kuehneriana Sing.		Rare
C. lactea (Lange) Métrod		Scarce
C. pseudopilosella (Kühn.) ex Kühn. & Romagn.		Uncommon
C. pubescens (Gillet) Kühn.		Uncommon
C. rickenii (Schaeff.) Kühn.		Local
C. semiglobata (Kühn.) ex Kühn. & Watling		Fairly common
C. vestita (Fr.) Kühn.		Scarce

FUNGI

Coprinus acuminatus (Romagnesi) Orton *(Clitocybe a.)*		Rare
C. atramentarius (Bull.: Fr.) Fr.	COMMON INK CAP	Common
C. bisporus J.Lange	SMALL INK CAP	Scarce
Coprinus callinus M.Lange & A.H.Smith		Scarce
C. comatus (Mull.: Fr.) Gray	SHAGGY INK CAP or LAWYER'S WIG	Common
C. disseminatus (Pers.: Fr.) Gray	FAIRIES' BONNETS	Fairly common
C. echinosporus Bull.		Uncommon
C. foetidellus P.D.Orton		Rare
C. lagopus (Fr.) Fr.		Common
C. leiocephalus P.D.Orton		Rare
C. micaceus (Bull.: Fr.) Fr.	GLISTENING INK CAP	Common
C. niveus (Pers.: Fr.) Fr.	SNOW-WHITE INK CAP	Rare
C. picaceus (Bull.: Fr.) Gray	MAGPIE FUNGUS	Scarce
C. pilcatilis (Fr.) Fr.	PLICATE INK CAP	Uncommon
C. subimpatiens M.Lange & A.H.Smith		Rare
C. truncorum Schaeff.: Fr.		Rare
Coriolellus albidus (Fr.: Fr.) Bond. *(Antrodia albida (Fr.: Fr.) Donk)*		Common
Coriolus hirsutus (Wulf.: Fr.) Pil.		(bracket) Rare
C. versicolor (L.: Fr.) Quél.	MANY-ZONED POLYPORE (bracket)	Common
C. zonatus (Nees: Fr.) Quél.		(bracket) Local
Cortinarius alboviolaceus (Pers.: Fr.) Fr.	subgenus Sericeocybe	Uncommon
C. armillatus (Fr.) Fr.	" Telamonia	Scarce
C. balteatocumatilis Henry	" Phlegmacium	Rare
C. basiliaceus		Rare
C. bulbosus Fr. s. Rick.	" Telamonia	Scarce
C. cinnamomeobadius Hry.	" Dermocybe	Scarce
C. cinnamomeus (L.: Fr.) Fr.	" Dermocybe	Scarce
C. crocolitus Quél.	" Phlegmacium	Uncommon
C. decipiens (Pers.: Fr.) Fr.	" Hydrocybe	Scarce
Cortinarius delibutus Fr.		Occasional
C. elatior Fr.	" Myxacium	Common
C. flexipes (Pers.: Fr.) Fr.		Rare
C. fulvosquamulosus in ed.		Rare
C. hemitrichus (Fr.) Fr.		Common
C. hinnuleus (Sow.) Fr.	" Telamonia	Uncommon
C. infractus (Pers.: Fr.) Fr.	" Phlegmacium	Rare
C. lepidopus Cke.	" Sericeocybe	Common
C. malachius (Fr.: Fr.) Fr. S. Kühn. & Romagn.	Sericeocybe	Rare
C. obtusus Fr.	" Telamonia	Scarce

FUNGI

Cortinarius pholideus (Fr.) Fr.	"	Sericeocybe	Rare
C. pseudocolus			Rare
C. pseudosalor Lange	"	Myxacium	Common
C. puniceus Orton	"	Dermocybe	Rare
C. purpurascens (Fr.) Fr.	subgenus	Phlegmacium	Occasional
C. sanguineus (Wulf.: Fr.) Fr.	"	Dermocybe	Scarce
C. semisanguineus (Fr.) Gillet	"	Dermocybe	Fairly common
C. subdelibutus			Rare
C. tabularis Lange	"	Phlegmacium	Rare
C. torvus (Bull.: Fr.) Fr.	"	Telamonia	Scarce

(C. triumphans Fr. s. Lange see C. crocolitus Quél.)

Craterellus cornucopioides (L.: Fr.) Pers.	HORN-OF-PLENTY	Scarce
Crepidotus applanatus (Pers.) Kumm.		Rare
C. autochthonus Lange		Uncommon
C. cesatii (Rabenh.) Sacc.		Rare
C. mollis (Schaeff.: Fr.) Staude (incl. C. calolepis (Fr.) Karst.)		Common
C. pubescens Bres.		Rare
C. subtilis Orton		Rare
C. variabilis (Pers.: Fr.) Kumm.		Common
Cyathus olla Batsch : Pers.		Rare
C. striatus Huds.: Pers.	BIRD'S-NEST FUNGUS	Rare
Cylindrobasidium evolvens (Fr.: Fr.) Jülich		Common
Cyphella galeata (Schum.) Fr.		Occasional
Cystoderma amianthinum (Fr.) Fayod		Scarce
C. carcharias (Pers.) Fayod		Scarce
C. jasonis (Cke. & Massee) Harmaja		Occasional
C. terrei (Berk. & Br.) Harmaja		Rare
Dacrymyces stillatus Nees : Fr.	(Tremellidae)	Common
Daedalea quercina L. : Fr.	MAZE FUNGUS (Bracket)	Common on oak
Daedaleopsis confragosa (Bolt.: Fr.) Schröt. *(Daedalea c.)* BLUSHING BRACKET		Common on willow
Datronia mollis (Sommerf.) Donk. *(Trametes m.; Antrodia m.)* (Bracket)		Common
Dermoloma cuneifolium (Fr.: Fr.) P.D.Orton		Uncommon
Ditiola pezizaeformis (Lév.) Reid *(Femsjonia p.)*		Occasional
Entoloma clypeatum (L.: Fr.) Kumm.		Occasional
E. conferendum (Britz.) Noord		Rare
E. nidorosum (Fr.) Quél.		Occasional
E. porphyrophaeum (Fr.) Karst.		Very local
E. prunuloides (Fr.) Quél.		Rare

FUNGI

Entoloma rhodopolium (Fr.) Kumm.		Scarce
E. sarcitulum (Kühn. & Romagn.) Arnolds		Uncommon
E. sordidulum (Kühn. & Romagn.) P.D.Orton		Rare
(Exidia albida Huds. see E. thuretiana)		
E. glandulosa Fr.	WITCHES' BUTTER	Common
E. thuretiana (Lév.) Fr. *(E. albida Huds.)*	WHITE BRAIN JELLY	Common
(Femsjonia pezizaeformis see Ditiola p.)		
Fibuloporia mollusca (Pers.) Bond & Sing.		Occasional
Fistulina hepatica Schaeff. : Fr.	BEEF-STEAK	Common bracket on oak
Flammulaster carpophiloides (Kühn.) Watl.		Uncommon
F. ferruginea (Macr. & Maire) Watl.		Rare
Flammulina velutipes (Curt.: Fr.) Karst.	VELVET SHANK or WINTER FUNGUS	Fairly common
Galerina autumnalis (Peck) Smith & Sing.		Rare
G. cinctula Orton		Rare
G. hypnorum (Fr.) Kühn.		Uncommon; on moss
G. marginata (Batsch) Kühn.		Frequent
G. mutabilis (Schaeff.: Fr.) Orton	CHANGING GALERINA	Uncommon
G. mycenopsis (Fr.: Fr.) Kumm.		Uncommon
G. paludosa (Fr.) Kühn.		Uncommon
G. vittaeformis (Fr.) Sing.		Common
Ganoderma adspersum (Schulz.) Donk.	(bracket)	Common
G. applanatum (Pers.) Pat.	ARTISTS' FUNGUS (bracket)	Fairly common
G. resinaceum Bond	LACQUERED BRACKET	Rare
Geastrum fimbriatum Fr. *(G. sessile (Sow.) Pouz.)*	EARTH STAR	Uncommon
G. fornicatum (Huds.) Fr.	LARGE EARTH STAR	Rare
G. quadrifidum Pers.: Pers.	EARTH STAR	Uncommon
G. rufescens Pers.	COMMON EARTH STAR	Uncommon
G. schmidelii Vittad. *(G.nanum Pers.)*	EARTH STAR	Rare
Gloeophyllum sepiarium (Wulf.: Fr.) Karst.		Scarce
Grifola frondosa (Dicks.: Fr.) S.F.Gray	(bracket)	Scarce
Gymnopilus hybridus (Fr.: Fr.) Sing.		Frequent
G. junonius (Fr.) Orton		Common
G. penetrans (Fr.: Fr.) Murr.		Common
Gyroporus castaneus (Bull.: Fr.) Quél.		Uncommon
Handkea excipuliformis Schaeff *(Calvatia e., Lycoperdon e.)*	PESTLE-SHAPED PUFFBALL	Frequent
H. utriformis (Bull.: Pers.) Kreisel *(Calvatia u.)*		Very local
Hebeloma crustuliniforme (Bull.) Quél.	POISON PIE	Scarce

FUNGI

Hebeloma leucosarx Orton		
H. mesophaeum (Pers.) Quél.		Occasional
H. radicosum (Bull.: Fr.) Ricken		Occasional
H. sacchariolens Quél.		Rare
H. sinapizans (Paul.: Fr.) Gill.		Scarce
Hemimycena lactea (Pers.: Fr.) Sing. *(Mycena l.)*	SNOW BONNET	Scarce
H. tortuosa (Orton) Redhead *(Mycena t.)*		Scarce
Henningsomyces candidus (Pers.: Fr.) Kuntze		
Heterobasidion annosum (Fr.) Bref.	ROOT FOMES (bracket)	Common
Heteroporus biennis (Bull.: Fr.) Laz.	(bracket)	Occasional
Hohenbuchelia cyphelliformis (Berk.) O.K.Miller		Scarce
Hydnellum scrobiculatum (Fr.) Karst.		Uncommon
H. spongiosipes (Peck) Pouz.		Uncommon
Hydnum repandum L. : Fr.	WOOD HEDGEHOG or HEDGEHOG FUNGUS	Scarce
H. rufescens Fr. *(H. repandum var rufescens (Fr.) Barla)*		Rare
H. scrobiculatum (Fr.) Karst.		Scarce
Hydropus floccipes (Fr.) Sing. *(Mycena f.)*		Local
Hygrocybe calyptraeformis (B. & Br.) Fayod	PINK WAX CAP	Scarce
H.cantharellus (Fr.) Sing.		Rare
H. coccinea (Schaeff. : Fr.) Kumm.	SCARLET HOOD	Scarce
H. conica (Scop.: Fr.) Kumm.	CONICAL WAX CAP	Frequent
H. chlorophana (Fr.) Karst.*(Hygrophorus c.)*		Frequent
H. fornicata (Fr.) Sing.		Rare
H. flavescens (Kauff.) Sing. *(Hygrophorus f.)*		Rare
H. helobia (Arnolds) Bon.		Rare
H. hypothejus (Fr.: Fr.) Fr.	YELLOW WAX CAP	Scarce
H. lacma *(Camarophyllus lacmus (Schum.) Lange)*		Frequent
H. miniata (Fr.) Kumm.	SMALL RED WAX CAP	Uncommon
H. nigrescens (Quél.) Kühn.	BLACKENING WAX CAP	Fairly common
H. nitrata (Fr.) Sing.		Rare
H. nivea (Scop.) Fr.	SNOWY WAX CAP	Common
H. ochraceopallida Orton		Rare
H. pratensis (Pers.: Fr.) Fr.	MEADOW WAX CAP	Uncommon
H. psittacina (Schaeff.: Fr.) Kumm.	PARROT WAX CAP	Uncommon
H. punica (Fr.) Kumm.	CRIMSON WAX CAP	Fairly common
H. reai (Maire) Lange		Frequent
H. strangulata Orton		Scarce
H. unguinosa (Fr.) Karst.		Scarce

FUNGI

Hygrocybe quieta (Kühn.) Sing.		Scarce
H. virginea *(Camarophyllus virgineus (Wulf.: Fr.) Kumm)*		Scarce
H. vitellina (Fr.) Karst.		Scarce
Hygrophoropsis aurantiaca (Fr.) Maire	FALSE CHANTERELLE	Common
Hygrophorus berkeleyi Orton *(= H.pratensis var. pallidus (Cke.) Lange)*		Occasional
Hymenochaete corrugata (Fr.) Lév.		Rare
H. rubiginosa (Dicks.: Fr.) Lév.		Fairly common
Hymenostilbe sphecophila (Ditm.) Petch		Rare
Hyphoderma setigerum (Fr.) Donk		Common
Hyphodontia barba-jovis (Bull.) J.Erikss.		Occasional
H. sambuci (Pers.: Fr.) J.Erikss. *(Hyphoderma s.)*		Common
Hypholoma epixanthum = H. capnoides (Fr.) Kumm.		Uncommon
H. fasiculare (Huds.: Fr.) Kumm.	SULPHUR TUFT	Common on tree stumps
H. marginatum (Pers.: Fr.) Schröt. *(H. dispersum)*		Scarce
H. sublateritium (Fr.) Quél.	BRICK CAP	Scarce; on tree stumps
H. subericaeum (Fr.) Kühn.		Scarce
H. udum (Pers.: Fr.) Kühn.		Scarce
Inocybe abjecta (Karst.) Sacc.		Uncommon
I. asterospora Quél.		Scarce
I. cookei Bres.		Scarce
I eutheles (Berk. & Br.) Quél.		Common in coniferous woods
I. geophylla (Sow.: Fr.) Kumm.		Common
var. lilacina Gillet		Scarce
I. jurana Pat.		Uncommon
I. maculata Boud.		
I. margaritispora (Berk. apud Cke.) Sacc.		Rare
I. napipes Lange		Uncommon
I. posterula (Britz.) Sacc.		Uncommon
I. pyriodora (Pers.: Fr.) Kumm.		Occasional
Inonotus dryadeus (Pers.: Fr.) Murr.	(bracket)	Scarce; on oaks
I. hispidus (Bull.: Fr.) Karst.	(bracket)	Uncommon
I. radiatus (Sow.: Fr.) Karst.	(bracket)	Uncommon; mainly on alder
Ischnoderma resinosum (Fr.) Karst.	(bracket)	Rather scarce; tree stumps
Laccaria amethystea (Bull.) Murr.	AMETHYST DECEIVER	Common
Laccaria bicolor (Maire) Orton		Scarce
L. laccata (Scop.: Fr.) Cke.	DECEIVER	Common
L. purpureo-badia Reid		Scarce
L. tortilis ([Bolt.] S.F. Gray) Cke.		Frequent
Lachnella villosa (Pers.: Fr.) Gill.		Occasional

FUNGI

Lacrymaria velutina (Pers.: Fr.) Konrad & Maubl.	WEEPING WIDOW	Common
Lactarius azonites (Bull.) Fr.	WHITE MILK CAP	Scarce
L. bertillonii (Neuh.) Bon.	A recent split of L. vellereus.	Scarce
L. blennius (Fr.: Fr.) Fr.	SLIMY MILK CAP	Common
L. camphoratus (Bull.) ex Fr.	CURRY-SCENTED MILK CAP	Frequent
L. chrysorrheus Fr.		Very local
L. cimicarius (Batsch) Gillet	WATERY MILK CAP	Occasional
L. cyathula (Fr.) Fr.		Rare
L. deliciosus (L.: Fr.) Gray	SAFFRON MILK CAP	Very local
L. deterrimus Gröger		Very local
L. flavidus Boud.		Rare
L. glyciosmus (Fr.: Fr.) Fr.	COCONUT-SCENTED MILK CAP	Local
L. hepaticus Plow. apud Boud.		Common
L. mitissimus (Fr.) Fr.		Fairly common
L. pallidus (Pers.: Fr.) Fr.		Scarce
L. piperatus (Scop.: Fr.) Gray	PEPPERY MILK CAP	Common
L. pubescens (Fr.) Fr.		Scarce
L. pyrogalus (Bull.: Fr.)		
L. quietus (Fr.) Fr.	OAK MILK CAP	Common
L. rufus (Scop.: Fr.) Fr.	RUFOUS MILK CAP	Common
L. spinosulsus Quél.		Scarce
L. subdulcis (Pers.: Fr.) Gray	BROWN MILK CAP	Common
L. tabidus Fr.		Common
L. torminosus (Schaeff.: Fr.) Gray	WOOLLY MILK CAP	Common
L. uvidus (Fr.) Fr.		Uncommon
L. vellereus (Fr.) Fr.	FLEECY MILK CAP	Common
L. vietus (Fr.) Fr.	GREY MILK CAP	Common
L. volemus Fr.		Scarce
L. turpis (Weinm.) Fr.	UGLY MILK CAP	Common
Laetiporus sulphureus (Bull.: Fr.) Murr.	SULPHUR POLYPORE or CHICKEN-OF-THE-WOODS (bracket)	Frequent
Leccinum rigidipes Orton		Rare
L. rosefractum Watling		Rare
L. variicolor Watling (L. oxydabile)		Rare
Lenzites betulina (L.: Fr.) Fr.	(bracket)	Fairly common
Lepiota brunneocingulata Orton		Rare
L. castanea Quél.		Scarce
L. clypeolaria (Fr.) Kumm.		Uncommon
L. cristata Kumm.	SHIELD LEPIOTA	Common

FUNGI

Lepiota excoriata (Schaeff.: Fr.) Kumm.		Rare
L. hystrix Lange *(L. hispida)*		Rare
L. ignivolvata Bousset-Joss		Rare
L. konradii Huijsman		Scarce
L. leucothites (Vitt.) Orton		Common
L. mastoidea (Fr.) Kumm.		Scarce
L. ochraceofulva Orton		Rare
L. procera (Scop.: Fr.) S.F.Gray	PARASOL MUSHROOM	Common
L. rhacodes (Vitt.) Quél.	SHAGGY PARASOL	Common
L. serena (Fr.) Sacc.		Rare
L. sericea (Cool) Huijsm.		Rare
L. setulosa Lange		Rare
L. sistrata (Fr.) Quél.		Rare
Lepista irina (Fr.) Big.		Rare
L. flaccida (Sow.: Fr.) Pat. *(Clitocybe f.)*	TAWNY FUNNEL CAP	Scarce
L. luscina (Fr.: Fr.) Sing.		Rare
L. nuda (Bull.: Fr.) Cooke	WOOD BLEWIT	Common
L. saeva (Fr.) Orton	FIELD BLEWIT or BLUE-LEG	Common
Leptoglossum acerosum (Fr.) Moser		Rare
Leptonia incana (Fr.) Gill.		Occasional
L. lazulina (Fr.) Quél.		Rare
L. sericella (Fr.: Fr.) Barb.		Scarce
L. serrulata (Pers.: Fr.) Kumm.		Local
Leucoprinus brebissonii (Godey apud Gill.) Locq.		
Lycoperdon foetidum Bon. = L. nigrescens Pers.		Scarce
(L. giganteum see Calvatia gigantea GIANT PUFFBALL)		
L. molle Pers.: Pers.		Occasional
L. perlatum Pers.: Pers.	PUFFBALL	Common
L. pyriforme Schaeff.: Pers.	STUMP PUFFBALL	Common
Lyophyllum decastes (Fr.: Fr.) Sing. *(Clitocybe decastes)*		Scarce
Macrocystidia cucumis (Pers.: Fr.) Heim.		Rare
Macrotyphula fistulosa (Fr.) Petersen *(Clavaria f.)*		Scarce
M. juncea (Fr.) Berthier *(Clavariadelphus j.)*		Occasional
Marasmius androsaceus (L.: Fr.) Rea	HORSE-HAIR FUNGUS	Common
M. calopus (Pers.: Fr.) Fr.		Uncommon
M. candidus (Bolt.) Fr.		Rare
M. epiphylloides (Rea) Sacc.		Rare
M. oreades (Bolt.: Fr.) Fr.	FAIRY RING CHAMPIGNON	Common
M. perforans (Fr.) Fr.		Scarce

FUNGI

Marasmius ramealis (Bull.: Fr.) Fr.		Fairly common
M. recubans Quél.		Rare
M. rotula (Scop.: Fr.) Fr.	FAIRY UMBRELLA	Fairly common on roots
M. wynnei Berk. & Br.		Uncommon
Megacollybia platyphylla (Pers.: Fr.) Kotl. & Pouz.		Rare
Melanoleuca cognata (Fr.) Konrad & Maub.		Rare
M. melaleuca (Pers.: Fr.) Murr.		Local
M. strictipes (Karst.) Schaeff.		Rare
Melanophyllum cognata (Fr.) Konrad & Maubl.		Occasional
M. echinatum (Roth.: Fr.) Sing.		
Meripilus giganteus (Pers.: Fr.) Karst.	GIANT POLYPORE (bracket)	Common
Mutinus caninus (Pers.) Fr.	DOG STINKHORN	Scarce
Mycena acicula (Schaeff.: Fr.) Kumm.		
M. aetites (Fr.) Quél.		Fairly common
M. alcalina (Fr.) Kumm. (M.stipata Maas G. & Schwöbel)		Common
M. amicta (Fr.) Quél.		Rare
M. arcangeliana Bres.		Rare
M. bulbosa (Cejp.) Kühn.		Rare
M. epipterygia (Scop.: Fr.) Gray		Uncommon
M. erubescens Höhnel		Uncommon
M. fibula (Bull.: Fr.) Kühn. (Rickenella fibula (Bull.: Fr.) Raithel)		
M. filopes (Bull.: Fr.) Kumm.		Common
M. flavescens Vel.		Rare
M. flavoalba (Fr.) Quél.		Rare
M. galericulata (Scop.: Fr.) Gray	BONNET MYCENA	Common
M. galopus (Pers.: Fr.) Kumm.		Common
M. haematopus (Pers.: Fr.) Kumm.		Uncommon
M. hiemalis (Fr.) Quél.		Common
M. inclinata (Fr.) Quél.		Fairly common
(M. lactea (Pers. ex Fr.) Kumm. see Hemimycena l.)		
M. leptocephala (Pers.: Fr.) Gillet		Common
M. leucogala (Cooke) Sacc.		Scarce
M. maculata Karst.		Local
M. metata Fr.		Local
M. mucor (Batsch: Fr.) Gill.		Uncommon
M. olida Bres. (M. minutula (Peck.) Sacc.)		Local
M. olivaceomarginata Massee		Fairly common
M. pearsoniana Dennis		Scarce
M. pelianthina (Fr.) Quél.		Common

FUNGI

Mycena polygramma (Bull.: Fr.) Gray		Occasional
M. pseudocorticola Kühn.		Common
M. pudica Hora *(Resinomycena saccharifera (Berk. & Br.) Kühn.)*		Rare
M. pura (Pers.: Fr.) Kumm.		Common
M. sanguinolenta (Alb. & Schw.: Fr.) Kumm.		Common
M. speirea (Fr.) Gillet		Scarce
M. stylobates (Pers.: Fr.) Kumm.		Scarce
M. swartzii (Fr.: Fr.) A.H.Smith *(Rickenella swartzii (Fr.) Kuyper)*		Uncommon
M. tenerrima (Berk.) Sacc. *(M. adscendens (Lasch) Maas G.)*		Scarce
M. tintinnabulum (Fr.) Quél.		Rare
M. uracea Pearson *(M. megaspora Kauff.)*		Scarce
Mycoacia uda (Fr.) Donk.		Uncommon
Myxarium nucleatum Wallr.		Uncommon
Naucoria bohemica Vel.		Common
N. escharoides (Fr.: Fr.) Kumm.		
N. luteolofibrillosa (Kühn.) Kühn. & Romagn.		Rare
N. scolecina (Fr.) Quél.		Uncommon
N. striatula Orton		Rare
Nolanea hirtipes (Schum.: Fr.) Kumm.		Scarce
N. icterina (Fr.) Kumm. *(Rhodophyllus i.)*		Uncommon
N. lucida Orton		Scarce
N. papillata Borg.		Rare
N. staurospora Bres.		Common
N. tenuipes Orton		
Omphalina ericetorum (Fr.: Fr.) Lange	HEATH FUNGUS	Fairly common
O. fibula (Fr.) Kumm.		Common
O. pyxidata (Pers.: Fr.) Quél.		Common
Oudemansiella mucida (Schrad.: Fr.) Kühn.	PORCELAIN or POACHED EGG FUNGUS	Common
O. radicata (Relh.: Fr.) Sing.	ROOTING SHANK	Common
Panaeolina foenisecii (Pers.: Fr.) Maire		Scarce
Panaeolus campanulatus (Bull.: Fr.) Quél.	BELL-SHAPED MOTTLEGILL	Scarce
P. rickenii Hors.		Common
P. semiovatus (Sow.: Fr.) Lund.		Common on dung
P. sphinctrinus (Fr.) Quél.		Rare
Panellus serotinus (Schrad.: Fr.) Kühn.		Uncommon
P. stipticus (Bull.) Karst.		Scarce
Paxillus involutus (Fr.) Fr.	BROWN ROLL-RIM	Common
Peniophora incarnata (Fr.) Karst.		Frequent

FUNGI

Peniophora limitata (Fr.) Cooke		Common
P. quercina (Pers.) Cooke		Fairly common
Phaeolus schweinitzii (Fr.) Pat.	(bracket)	Uncommon
Phallus impudicus L.:Pers.	COMMON STINKHORN	Common
Phellinus ferreus (Pers.) Bourd. & Galz. *(Polyporus f.)*		Scarce
P. ignarius (L.: Fr.) Quél.		Occasional
Phellodon niger (Fr.) Karst.		Uncommon
Phlebia radiata Fr. *(P. merismoides)*		Scarce
P. rufa (Fr.) M.P.Christ.		Frequent
P. tremellosa (Schrad.: Fr.) Nakas. & Burds. *(Merulius tremellosus)*		Scarce
Pholiota adiposa (Fr.) Kumm.		Uncommon
P. alnicola (Fr.) Sing.		Uncommon
P. cerifera (Karst.) Karst. *(P. aurivella)*		Rare
P. gummosa (Lasch) Sing.		Uncommon
P. highlandensis (Peck) Smith & Hesler		Frequent
P. inaurata (W.G.Smith) Moser apud Cams.		Scarce
P. squarrosa (Mull.: Fr.) Kumm.	SHAGGY PHOLIOTA	Fairly common
P. tuberculosa (Schaeff.: Fr.) Kumm.		
Phylloporus rhodoxanthus (Schwein.) Bres.		Rare
Physisporinus sanguineolentus (Alb. & Schw.: Fr.) Pilát *(Rigidoporus s.)*		Occasional
Piptoporus betulinus (Bull.: Fr.) Karst.	BIRCH POLYPORE or (bracket) RAZOR STROP	Very common on birch
Pleurotus cornucopiae Paul.		Scarce
P. dryinus (Pers.: Fr.) Kumm.		Scarce
P. ostreatus (Jacq.: Fr.) Kumm.	OYSTER MUSHROOM	Common
P. pulmonarius (Fr.) Quél.		Scarce
Pluteus aurantiorugosus (Trog.) Sacc.		Rare
P. cervinus (Schaeff.: Fr.) Kumm.		Common
P. galeroides P.D.Orton		Scarce
P. griseoluridus Orton		
P. hispidulus (Fr.: Fr.) Gillet		Rare
P. luteovirens Rea		Uncommon
P. lutescens (Fr.) Bres.		Uncommon
P. petasatus (Fr.) Gillet		Uncommon
P. phlebophorus (Ditm.: Fr.) Kumm.		Uncommon
P. podospileus Sacc. & Cub.		Uncommon
P. pseudorobertii Moser & Stangl		Rare
P. salicinus (Pers.: Fr.) Kumm.		Rare
P. thomsonii (Berk. & Br.) Dennis		Frequent

FUNGI

Pluteus umbrosus (Pers.: Fr.) Kumm.			Local
P. xanthophaeus P.D.Orton			Rare
Polyporus badius (Pers.: Gray) Schum.			Frequent
P. brumalis Pers.: Fr.		(bracket)	Fairly common
P. ciliatus Fr.: Fr.		(bracket)	Fairly common
P. squamosus Huds.: Fr.	DRYAD'S SADDLE or SCALY POLYPORE	(bracket)	Common On elm stumps
Poria vaillantii *(Antrodia vaillantii (D.C.: Fr..) Ryv.)*			Common
Porphyrellus pseudoscaber (Secr.) Sing. *(Boletus porphyrosporus Fr. & Hok.)*			Rare
Psathyrella candolleana (Fr.) Maire			Frequent
P. cernua (Vahl.: Fr.) Moser apud Gams.			Occasional
P. gossypina (Bull.: Fr.) Pears. & Dennis			Occasional
P. gracilis (Fr.: Fr.) Quél.			Rare
P. hydrophila (Bull.) Maire *(P. piluliformis)*			Scarce; on tree stumps
P. microrhiza (Lasch) Konrad & Maubl.			Occasional
P. obtusata (Fr.) Smith			Uncommon
P. pennata (Fr.) Pearson & Dennis			Common
P. sarcocephala (Fr.) Sing.			Common
P. spadicea (Fr.) Sing. *(Psilocybe s.)*			Occasional
P. spintrigera (Fr.) Konr. & Maubl.			Frequent
P. spintrigeroides P.D.Orton			Frequent
P. squamosa (Karst.) Moser			Scarce
Pseudoclitocybe cyathiformis (Bull.: Fr.) Sing. *(Clitocybe c.)*		THE GOBLET	Uncommon
Pseudocraterellus sinuosus (Fr.) Reid			Rare
Pseudohydnum gelatinosum (Scop.: Fr.) Karst.		JELLY TONGUE	Scarce
Pseudotrametes gibbosa (Pers.) Bond. & Sing.		(bracket)	Uncommon
Psilocybe montana (Pers.) Kumm.			Scarce
P. semilanceata (Fr.) Kumm.		LIBERTY CAP	Common One of the 'Magic Mushrooms'
Ptyochogaster albus Corda			An imperfect form of polypore - rare
Pulcherricium caerulea (Fr.) Parm.			Rare
Ramaria stricta (Fr.) Quél.		UPRIGHT RAMARIA	Scarce
Ramariopsis kunzei (Fr.) Corner			Uncommon
Rhodotus palmatus (Bull.: Fr.) Maire			Becoming common on elm stumps
Rigidoporus ulmarius (Sow.: Fr.) Imazeki		(bracket)	Fairly common at tree bases
Russula aeruginea Lind.: Fr.			
R. anatina Romagn.			Rare
R. atropurpurea (Krombh.) Britz.		BLACKISH-PURPLE RUSSULA	Common
R. betularum Hora		BIRCH RUSSULA	

FUNGI

Russula caerulea (Pers.) Fr.		Occasional
R. cyanoxantha (Schaeff.) Fr.	THE CHARCOAL BURNER	Common
R. delica Fr.	MILK-WHITE RUSSULA	Scarce
R. densifolia (Secr.) Gillet		Frequent
R. emetica (Schaeff.: Fr.) Gray	THE SICKENER	Common
R. farinipes Romell apud Britz.		Locally common
R. fellea (Fr.) Fr.	GERANIUM-SCENTED RUSSULA	Frequent
R. foetens (Pers.: Fr.) Fr.	FETID RUSSULA	Common
R. fragilis (Pers.: Fr.) Fr.	FRAGILE RUSSULA	Frequent
R. gracillima J.Schaeff.		Rare
R. grisea (Pers.) Fr.		Occasional
R. heterophylla (Fr.) Fr.		Occasional
R. ionochlora Romagn.		Rare
R. laurocerasi Melzer		Uncommon
R. lepida Fr.		
R. lutea (Huds.: Fr.) Gray		Occasional
R. mairei Sing.	MAIRE'S RUSSULA or BEECHWOOD SICKENER	Common
R. nigricans (Bull.) Fr.	BLACKENING RUSSULA	Scarce
R. nitida (Pers.: Fr.) Fr.		Common
R. ochroleuca (Pers.) Fr.	COMMON YELLOW RUSSULA	Common
R. olivacea (Schaeff.) Fr.		Uncommon
R. parazurea J.Schaeff.		Occasional
R. rosea Fr. apud Quél.		Common
R. sardonia Fr.		
R. sororia (Fr.) Romell		Fairly frequent
R. vesca Fr.	BARE-TOOTHED RUSSULA	Frequent
R. veternosa (Fr.) Romell		Local
R. virescens (Schaeff.) Fr.		Occasional
R. xerampalina (Schaeff.) Fr.	(var. barlae)	Frequent
Schizophyllum commune Fr.	SPLIT-GILL	Rare
Schizopora paradoxa (Schrad.: Fr.) Donk.		Common
Scleroderma citrinum Pers.	COMMON EARTHBALL	Common
S. verrucosum (Bull.) Pers.	DEVIL'S SNUFF-BOX or EARTHBALL	Uncommon
Simocybe centunculus (Fr.) Karst. *(Ramicola c.)*		
S. sumptuosa Orton *(Ramicola s.)*		Rare
Skeletocutis nivea (Jungh.) J.Keller		Frequent
Sparassis crispa Wulf.: Fr.	CAULIFLOWER or BRAIN FUNGUS	Fairly common

FUNGI

Steccherinum ochraceum (Pers.: Fr.) Gray		
Stereum gausaptum (Fr.) Fr.		Frequent
S. hirsutum (Willd.: Fr.) Gray	HAIRY STEREUM	Common
S. rugosum (Pers.: Fr.) Fr.	BLEEDING STEREUM	Common
S. sanguinolentum (Alb. & Schw.: Fr.) Fr.		Uncommon
Stropharia aeruginosa (Curt.: Fr.) Quél.	VERDIGRIS AGARIC	Scarce
S. coronilla (Bull.: Fr.) Quél.		Frequent
S. cyanea (Bolt.) Tuomikoski		Local
S. cyarea (Desm.) Morgan		Local
S. pseudocyanea (Desm.) Morgan		
S. semiglobata (Batsch : Fr.) Quél.	DUNG ROUNDHEAD	Common on dung
Suillus fluryi Huijsman		Rare
S. variegatus (Fr.) Kuntze		Common
Taeniolella stilbospora (Corda) Hughes		Uncommon; on Salix
Tephrocybe atrata Fr.: Fr.		Frequent
T. rancida Fr.		Frequent
Thelephora terrestris (Ehrh.) Fr.	EARTH FAN	Common
Tremella foliacea Pers.: Fr.		Occasional
T. mesenterica Retz. : Fr.	YELLOW BRAIN FUNGUS	Common
T. polyporina Reid		Rare
Trichaptum abietinum (Dicks.: Fr.) Ryv.	*(Hirschioporus abietinum)*	Common
Tricholoma album Schaeff.: Fr.		Local
T. columbetta (Fr.) Kumm.		Scarce
T. fulvum (DC.: Fr.) Sacc.		Scarce
T. gambosum (Fr.) Kumm.		
T. imbricatum (Fr.: Fr.) Kumm.		Occasional
T. lascivum (Fr.) Gillet		Local
T. melaleucum (Pers.: Fr.) Kumm.		Common
T. portentosum (Fr.) Quél.		Scarce
T. resplendens (Fr.) Quél.		Rare
T. saponaceum (Fr.) Kumm.	SOAP TRICHOLOMA	Occasional
T. sciodes (Secr.) Martin		Rare
T. sulphureum (Bull.: Fr.) Kumm.		Scarce
T. ustale (Fr.: Fr.) Kumm.		Scarce
T. ustaloides Romagn.		Occasional
T. virgatum var. sciodes (Fr. ex Fr.) Kumm.		Scarce
Tricholomopsis rutilans (Schaeff.: Fr.) Sing.	PLUMS AND CUSTARD	Common
Tubaria conspersa (Pers.) Fayod		Rare
T. furfuracea (Pers.: Fr.) Gillet		Uncommon

FUNGI

Tylopilus felleus (Fr.) Karst.	BITTER BOLETE		Uncommon
Typhula erythropus Fr.			Occasional
T. phacorrhiza Fr.			Rare
T. quisquiliaris (Fr.: Fr.) P.Henn *(Pistillaria q.)*			Occasional
Tyromyces caesius (Schrad.: Fr.) Murr. *(Polyporus c.)*		(bracket)	Frequent
T. lacteus (Fr.) Murray		(bracket)	Scarce
T. serifluis		(bracket)	Occasional
T. stipticus (Pers.: Fr.) Kot. & Pouz.		(bracket)	Scarce; in conifer woods
Utipus spinosa			Common
Vascellum pratense (Pers.) Kreisel *(Lycoperdon depressum)*			Local
Volvariella caesiotincta Orton			Uncommon
V. parvispora Reid			Uncommon
V. speciosa (Fr.: Fr.) Sing.			Scarce
Vuilleminia comedens (Nees) Maire			Common

References:
It has been necessary to consult many works on fungi in order to compile this list but a good, general book for beginners is:

Phillips, R. *Mushrooms & Other Fungi of Great Britain and Europe* (1981) Pan Books Ltd.

LICHENES (LICHENS)

The Exmoor Natural History Society's recording of Lichens was begun in 1980 when Noel Allen carried out a preliminary survey - identification of abut 200 species being confirmed by Dr Mark Seaward of Bradford University. More recently, various experts outside the Society have been looking at Lichens on Exmoor and many additional species recorded.

We are, therefore, most grateful to Pat Wolseley of Nettlecombe for her help with the first edition of this work, and particularly to Dr Francis Rose for much helpful advice and additional records based on his own intensive surveys of Exmoor woodlands from 1969 to 1986. Dr Rose has been unstinting in giving of his valuable time in checking, correcting and adding to our records. Mrs. A.M. O'Dare has also carried out a valuable survey of Porlock Beach (1986-7) and the British Lichen Society added a number of species for the Winsford Hill moorland and Hurlstone Point cliffs during their excursion in September, 1985.

Coming up to date (1995), Dr Brian Coppins and Mrs Sandy O'Dare have given freely of their expert knowledge in supplying over 200 additional records as a result of their work on Exmoor, particularly in recent years, and it is largely due to their valuable services that the current Exmoor list has reached such a high level (611). Dr Coppins has also very kindly undertaken the task of reading and correcting the initial draft and his expertise in this field will be immediately apparent to users of this Check-list.

Lichens are not a separate taxon but are integrated with the fungi, most (but with a few exceptions) belonging to the Ascomycotina. The lichen, as a combination of fungus and alga, has no individual name and it is the fungal name which is used when referring to these symbiotic associations of two distinct organisms. The present list includes species that are consistently or facultatively lichenized, a few that are non-lichenized fungi and the remainder are lichenicolous fungi. Red Data Book species are indicated (RDB).

Many lichens are indicators of unpolluted air and of ancient woodland, both of which we are fortunate to enjoy on Exmoor and these factors help to account for the excellent number of species recorded to date. Horner, East Lyn and Barle Valley woods are nationally famous hunting-grounds for woodland species. Acid moorland, coastal heath and maritime rocks provide suitable habitats for other species and the calcicoles can find a footing on walls, tombstones and roofs where lime is present in the mortar. Lichens can be readily found almost everywhere within the National Park and make a most interesting study at all times of the year.

Lichenologists now adopt an alphabetical arrangement for the listing of species and the sequence and names given follow O.W. Purvis, B.J. Coppins & P.W. James *Checklist of Lichens of Great Britain and Ireland* (1994) published by the British Lichen Society.

LICHENES, LICHENIZED FUNGI & NON-LICHENIZED FUNGI

Acarospora fuscata (Schrader) Th. Fr.	acid rocks	Locally common
A. impressula Th. Fr.	maritime rocks	Local
A. smaragdula (Wahlenb.) Massal.	maritime rocks	Locally common
Acrocordia gemmata (Ach.) Massal.	trees	Common

LICHENES

A. macrospora Massal.	maritime rocks	Rare
A. salweyi (Leighton ex Nyl.) A.L.Sm.	mortar	Local
Agonimia tristicula (Nyl.) Zahlbr.	calcicolous	Frequent
Anaptychia ciliaris (L.) Körber ex Massal.	well-lit trees	Rare
A. runcinata (With.) Laundon	maritime rocks	Common
Anisomeridium biforme (Borrer) R.Harris	trees	Common
A. nyssaegenum (Ellis & Everh.) R.Harris	trees	Common
Arthonia anombrophila Coppins & P.James	Quercus	Rare
A. arthonioides (Ach.) A.L.Sm.	old Quercus	Very rare
A. cinnabarina (DC.) Wallr.	trees, esp. Corylus	Frequent
A. didyma Körber	trees	Frequent
A. elegans (Ach.) Almq.	Corylus and Quercus	Local
A. endlicheri (Garov.) Oxner	maritime rocks	Local
A. impolita (Hoffm.) Borrer	trees	Local
A. mediella Nyl.	mossy Quercus or Fraxinus	Local
A. muscigena Th. Fr.	trees	Frequent
A. punctiformis Ach.	tree twigs	Common
A. radiata (Pers.) Ach.	smooth-barked trees	Common
A. spadicea Leighton	shaded trees	Common
A. stellaris Krempelh.	smooth-barked trees	Rare
A. vinosa Leighton	old trees	Frequent
Arthopyrenia antecellans (Nyl.) Arnold	smooth bark, esp. Ilex	Local
A cerasi (Schrader) Massal.	smooth bark	Rare
A. cinereopruinosa (Schaerer) Massal.	Fraxinus	Rare
A. fraxini Massal.	Quercus or Corylus	Local
A. lapponina Anzi	smooth-barked trees	Common
A. punctiformis Massal.	tree twigs	Common
A. ranunculospora Coppins & P.James	old trees	Local
A. salicis Massal.	Corylus	Local
A. viridescens Coppins	trees	Local
Arthrorhaphis citrinella (Ach.) Poelt	acid rocks	Rare
Aspicilia caesiocinerea (Nyl. ex Malbr.) Arnold	acid rocks	Local
A. calcarea (L.) Körber	limestone walls	Locally frequent
A. cinerea (L.) Körber	acid rocks	Local
A. contorta (Hoffm.) Krempelh.	limestone walls	Locally frequent
A. grisea Arnold	acid rocks	Local
A. leprosescens (Sandst.) Havaas	maritime rocks	Local
Bacidia arceutina (Ach.) Arnold	Sambucus	Rare
B. biatorina (Körber) Vainio	trees in old woods	Local

LICHENES

Bacidia caligans (Nyl.) A.L.Sm.	Sambucus	Rare
B. circumspecta (Norrlin & Nyl.) Malme	trees in old woods	Rare
B. coralloidea in ed.	Salix	Local
B. delicata (Larbal. ex Leighton) Coppins	Fraxinus or Sambucus	Rare
B. inundata (Fr.) Körber	rocks in streams	Local
B. laurocerasi (Delise ex Duby) Zahlbr.	trees	Local
B. naegelii (Hepp) Zahlbr.	trees	Local
B. phacodes Körber	trees	Local
B. rubella (Hoffm.) Massal.	trees	Local
B. sabuletorum (Schreber) Lettau	calcicolous	Frequent
B. scopulicola (Nyl.) A.L.Sm.	maritime	Local
B. trachona (Ach.) Lettau	riverside rocks	Rare
B. vezdae Coppins & P.James	trees	Local
B. viridifarinosa Coppins & P.James	trees, rarely rocks	Local
Bactrospora corticola (Fr.) Almq.	Quercus	Very rare
Baeomyces roseus Pers.	acid soil	Local
B. rufus (Huds.) Rebent.	rocks on damp moorland	Common
Biatora epixanthoides (Nyl.) Diederich	trees in old woods	Local
B. sphaeroides (Dickson) Körber	damp old trees or rocks	Uncommon
Bryophagus gloeocapsa Nitschke ex Arnold	decaying bryophytes	Local
Bryoria fuscescens (Gyelnik) Brodo & D.Hawksw.	conifers	Very local
B. subcana (Nyl. ex Stitzenb.) Brodo & D.Hawksw.	trees	Rare
Buellia aethalea (Ach.) Th. Fr.	acid rocks and stonework	Local
B. disciformis (Fr.) Mudd	trees	Very local
B. griseovirens (Turner & Borrer ex Sm.) Almb.	trees, rocks and walls	Common
B. ocellata (Flot.) Körber	acid rocks and walls	Local
B. punctata (Hoffm.) Massal.	trees and rocks	Common
B. schaereri de Not	old trees	Rare
B. stellulata (Taylor) Mudd	rocks	Rare
B. subdisciformis (Leighton) Jatta	maritime rocks	Local
Byssoloma marginatum (Arnold) Sérusiaux	Quercus	Local
Calicium glaucellum Ach.	dry bark of trees	Rare
C. lenticulare Ach.	Quercus wood	Very rare
C. salicinum Pers.	trees	Fairly common
C. viride Pers.	trees	Common
Caloplaca arnoldii (Wedd.) Zalhlbr.	maritime rocks	Rare
C. aurantia (Pers.) Steiner	churchyards	Rare
C. ceracea Laundon	maritime rocks	Local
C. citrina (Hoffm.) Th. Fr.	mortar & walls, occ.trees	Very common

LICHENES

Caloplaca crenularia (With.) Laundon	acid and maritime rocks	Local
C. dalmatica (Massal.) H. Olivier	limestone walls	Rare
C. flavescens (Huds.) Laundon	limestone walls and gravestones	Locally common
C. flavovirescens (Wulfen) Dalla Torre & Sarnth.	old walls	Rare
C. holocarpa (Hoffm.) Wade	calcareous rocks	Local
C. marina (Wedd.) Zahbr. ex Du Rietz	maritime rocks	Locally common
C. microthallina (Wedd.) Zahlbr.	maritime rocks	Local
C. saxicola (Hoffm.) Nordin	walls	Local
C. teicholyta (Ach.) Steiner	gravestones	Local
C. thallincola (Wedd.) Du Rietz	maritime rocks	Local
C. ulcerosa Coppins & P.James	trees	Very rare
C. verruculifera (Vainio) Zahlbr.	maritime rocks	Local
Candelaria concolor (Dickson) B.Stein	trees	Rare
Candelariella aurella (Hoffm.) Zahlbr.	basic rocks	Local
C. coralliza (Nyl.) H.Magn.	acid rocks	Rare
C. reflexa (Nyl.) Lettau	trees	Local
C. vitellina (Hoffm.) Müll. Arg.	rocks	Frequent
C. xanthostigma (Ach.) Lettau	old trees	Rare
Catapyrenium squamulosum (Ach.) Breuss	old walls	Rare
Catillaria atropurpurea (Schaerer) Th. Fr.	old trees	Locally common
C. chalybeia (Borrer) Massal.	basic walls and rocks	Local
C. pulverea (Borrer) Lettau	damp mossy trees	Local
Catinaria papillosa in ed.	Quercus	Rare
Celothelium ischnobelum (Nyl.) M.B. Aguirre	Corylus	Rare
Cetraria chlorophylla (Willd.) Vainio	trees and fences	Frequent
Cetrelia olivetorum (Nyl.) Culb. & C.Culb.	old trees in high rainfall area	Local
Chaenotheca brunneola (Ach.) Müll. Arg.	old Quercus	Rare
C. chrysocephala (Turner ex Ach.) Th. Fr.	Quercus	Rare
C. ferruginea (Turner ex Ach.) Mig.	dry bark	Common
C. furfuracea (L.) Tibell	rocks	Local
C. hispidula (Ach.) Zahlbr.	Quercus	Rare
C. stemonea (Ach.) Müll. Arg.	Quercus	Rare
C. trichialis (Ach.) Th. Fr.	old Quercus	Rare
Chaenothecopsis nigra Tibell	Quercus	Very rare
C. pusilla (Ach.) A.Schmidt	Quercus wood	Local
Chiodecton myrticola Fée **RDB3**	dry bark of Quercus, or rocks	Rare
Chromatochlamys muscorum (Fr.) H.Mayrhofer & Poelt		
	old walls	Rare

LICHENES

Chrysothrix candelaris (L.) Laundon	dry acid bark	Frequent
C. flavovirens Tønsb. *(C.chrysophthalma s.l.)*	Quercus	Rare
Cladonia arbuscula (Wallr.) Flot.	moorland	Very local
C. azorica Ahti	coastal heath	Rare
C. caespiticia (Pers.) Flörke	rocks and tree trunks	Local
C. cervicornis (Ach.) Flot.	dry moorland	Local
subsp. verticillata (Hoffm.) Ahti		Uncommon
C. chlorophaea (Flörke ex Sommerf.) Sprengel	rotting wood, damp rocks and on the ground	Common
C. ciliata Stirton var. ciliata	rocks and moorland	Frequent
var. tenuis (Flörke) Ahti	moorland	Local
C. coniocraea (Flörke) Sprengel	rotting wood and trees	Very common
C. crispata (Delise) Vainio	among rocks	Local
C. digitata (L.) Hoffm.	rotting wood and trees	Local
C. diversa Asperges *(C. coccifera s.l.)*	moorland	Common
C. fimbriata (L.) Fr.	rocks and soil	Common
C. floerkeana (Fr.) Flörke	peaty moorland	Very common
C. foliacea (Huds.) Willd.	coastal heath	Local
C. furcata (Huds.) Schrader	acid soil in moorland & woods	Common
C. glauca Flörke	coastal heath	Rare
C. gracilis (L.) Willd.	moorland and rocks	Local
C. humilis (With.) Laundon	soil by tracks	Local
C. incrassata Flörke	soil banks	Local
C. macilenta Hoffm.	trees and moorland	Common
C. ochrochlora Flörke	bark or tree stumps	Uncommon
C. parasitica (Hoffm.) Hoffm.	rotting wood	Local
C. pocillum (Ach.) Grognot	decaying moss on calcareous rocks and walls	Local
C. polydactyla (Flörke) Sprengel	peaty moorland and tree bases	Common
var. umbricola (Tønsb. & Ahti) Coppins	rotting stump	Very rare
C. portentosa (Dufour) Coem.	moorland	Very common
C. pyxidata (L.) Hoffm.	tree bases, rocks and walls	Common
C. ramulosa (With.) Laundon	on the ground	Local
C. rangiformis Hoffm.	coastal heath	Common
C. scabruiscula (Delise) Nyl.	on ground in wood	Very rare
C. squamosa Hoffm.	tree bases and rocks	Common
var. subsquamosa (Nyl.ex Leighton) Vainio	rocks	Frequent
C. subcervicornis (Vainio) Kernst.	damp rocky moorland	Local
C. subulata (L.) Weber ex Wigg.	heaths	Local

LICHENES

Cladonia sulphurina (Michaux) Fr.	moorland	Rare
C. uncialis (L.) Weber ex Wigg. subsp. biuncialis (Hoffm.) M.Choisy	moorland	Common
Clauzadea monticola (Ach.) Hafellner & Bellem.	calcareous walls	Rare
Cliostomum griffithii (Sm.) Coppins	trees	Common
Coelocaulon aculeatum (Schreber) Link	rocky coastal moorland	Local
C. muricatum (Ach.) Laundon	rocky coastal moorland	Rare
Collema auriforme (With.) Coppins & Laundon	old walls (calcareous)	Local
C. crispum (Huds.) Weber ex Wigg.	churchyard walls	Local
C. furfuraceum (Arnold) Du Rietz	old trees	Very rare
C. subflaccidum Degel.	trees	Rare
C. tenax (Sw.) Ach.	maritime rocks and walls	Rare
var. ceranoides (Borrer) Degel.	maritime soils	Rare
Cystocoleus ebeneus (Dillwyn) Thwaites	damp shady rocks	Local
Dermatocarpon luridum (With.) Laundon	rocks in streams	Locally abundant
Dimerella lutea (Dickson) Trevisan	mossy trees and rocks	Locally common
D. pineti (Ach.) Vĕzda	trees	Frequent
Diploicia canescens (Dickson) Massal.	rocks, walls, occasionally trees	Frequent
Diploschistes scruposus (Schreber) Norman	acid rocks	Local
Diplotomma alboatrum (Hoffm.) Flot.	rocks and walls	Local
D. chlorophaeum (Hepp ex Leighton) Szat.	maritime rocks	Locally frequent
Dirina massiliensis f. sorediata (Müll.Arg.) Tehler	shaded rocks and walls	Local
Enterographa crassa (DC.) Fée	shaded trees, rarely rocks	Frequent
E. hutchinsiae (Leighton) Massal.	rock underhangs by rivers	Rare
E. zonata (Körber) Källsten	shaded acid rocks	Frequent
Eopyrenula avellanae Coppins	Corylus	Local
E. grandicula Coppins	Fraxinus and Buxus	Local
Ephebe lanata (L.) Vainio	damp shady rocks	Rare
Evernia prunastri (L.) Ach.	trees, fences and occasionally rocks	Very common
Fellhanera bouteillei (Desm.) Vĕzda	Buxus leaves	Very local
Fuscidia cyathoides (Ach.) V.Wirth & Vĕzda	acid rocks	Locally common
F. kochiana (Hepp) V.Wirth & Vĕzda	acid rocks	Rare
F. lightfootii (Sm.) Coppins & P.James	trees	Frequent
F. lygaea (Ach.) V.Wirth & Vĕzda	acid rocks	Local
F. recensa (Stirton) Hertel, V.Wirth & Vĕzda	acid rocks	Local
F. viridis Tønsb.	Fagus and Quercus	Rare
Graphina anguina (Mont.) Müll. Arg.	trees	Rare
G. ruiziana (Fée) Müll. Arg.	trees	Local

LICHENES

Graphis elegans (Borrer ex Sm.) Ach.	trees	Common
G. scripta (L.) Ach. LETTER LICHEN	trees	Common
Gyalecta derivata (Nyl.) H.Olivier	Fraxinus	Rare
Gyalecta jenensis (Batsch) Zahlbr.	calcareous rocks	Rare
G. truncigena (Ach.) Hepp	Fraxinus	Uncommon
Gyalideopsis anastomosans P.James & Vězda	tree branches	Local
G. muscicola P.James & Vězda	Fagus	Rare
Haematomma ochroleucum (Necker) Laundon	acid rocks	Local
var. porphyrium (Pers.) Laundon	acid rocks and walls	Frequent
Halecania ralfsii (Salwey) M.Mayrhofer	maritime rocks	Local
H. viridescens Coppins & P.James	Fraxinus	Local
Herteliana taylorii (Salwey) P.James	maritime rocks	Local
Heterodermia obscurata (Nyl.) Trevisan	trees and ground on cliffs	Local
Hymenelia lacustris (With.) M.Choisy	rocks in streams	Local
Hyperphyscia adglutinata (Flörke) M.Mayrhofer & Poelt	shaded trees, especially Sambucus	Rare
Hypocenomyce caradocensis (Leighton ex Nyl.) P.James & G.Schneider	decorticate Quercus	Rare
H. scalaris (Ach. ex Lilj.) M.Choisy	acid bark and wood	Local
Hypogymnia physodes (L.) Nyl.	trees, rocks and walls	Very common
H. tubulosa (Schaerer) Havaas	twigs and rocks	Frequent
Japewia carrollii (Coppins & P.James) Tønsb.	Salix	Local
Lauderlindsaya acroglypta (Norman) R.Sant.	Sambucus	Very rare
Lecanactis abietina (Ach.) Körber	trees	Common
L. amylacea (Ehrh. ex Pers.) Arnold RDB2	old Quercus	Very rare
L. grumulosa (Dufour) Fr.	maritime rocks	Rare
L. latebrarum (Ach.) Arnold	maritime rocks	Rare
L. lyncea (Sm.) Fr.	old Quercus	Very local
L. premnea (Ach.) Arnold	old Quercus	Local
L. subabietina Coppins & P.James	old dry bark of Quercus	Very local
Lecania aipospila (Wahlenb.) Th. Fr.	maritime rocks	Rare
L. atrynoides Knowles	maritime rocks	Local
L. baeomma (Nyl.) P.James & Laundon	maritime rocks	Rare
L. cyrtella (Ach.) Th. Fr.	trees	Local
L. cyrtellina (Nyl.) Sandst.	rough bark	Rare
L. erysibe (Ach.) Mudd	calcareous rocks	Local
L. hutchinsiae (Nyl.) A.L.Sm.	rocks and walls	Local
Lecanora actophila Wedd.	maritime rocks	Local
L. albescens (Hoffm.) Branth & Rostrup	stone walls	Frequent

LICHENES

Lecanora campestris (Schaerer) Hue	rocks and walls	Locally common
L. carpinea (L.) Vainio	Juglans	Rare
L. chlarotera Nyl.	trees and fences	Very common
L. confusa Almb.	trees, fences and coastal heaths	Frequent
L. conizaeoides Nyl. ex Crombie	trees and rocks	Very common
L. crenulata Hook.	churchyards	Common
L. dispersa (Pers.) Sommerf.	rocks and walls	Very common
L. expallens Ach.	trees and fences	Very common
L. fugiens Nyl.	maritime rocks	Local
L. gangaleoides Nyl.	maritime rocks	Locally common
L. helicopis (Wahlenb.) Ach.	maritime rocks	Local
L. intricata (Ach.) Ach.	acid rocks	Local
L. jamesii Laundon	trees in damp woodland	Local
L. muralis (Schreber) Rabenh.	rocks and walls	Local
L. orosthea (Ach.) Ach.	acid rocks	Local
L. pallida (Schreber) Rabenh.	smooth bark	Local
L. polytropa (Hoffm.) Rabenh.	acid rocks	Locally common
L. praepostera Nyl.	maritime rocks	Locally frequent
L. pulicaris (Pers.) Ach.	trees	Rare
L. rupicola (L.) Zahlbr.	acid rocks	Locally common
L. salina H.Magn.	beach pebbles	Rare
L. subcarnea (Lilj.) Ach.	maritime rocks	Local
L. sulphurea (Hoffm.) Ach.	rocks and walls	Locally common
L. symmicta (Ach.) Ach.	Calluna and Fraxinus	Local
L. tenera (Nyl.) Crombie	maritime rocks	Locally frequent
Lecidea doliiformis Coppins & P.James	old Quercus	Local
L. erythrophaea Flörke	Fraxinus	Rare
L. fuliginosa Taylor	acid rocks	Local
L. fuscoatra (L.) Ach.	rocks and walls	Local
L. hypnorum Lib.	mossy trees	Local and rare
L. hypopta Ach.	wood	Rare
L. lactea Flörke ex Schaerer	acid rocks and pebbles	Local
L. lithophila (Ach.) Ach.	acid rocks	Rare
L. sanguineoatra auct.	Quercus	Rare
Lecidella anomaloides (Massal.) Hertel & Kilias	rocks by river	Rare
L. asema (Nyl.) Knoph & Hertel	maritime rocks	Frequent
L. elaeochroma (Ach.) M.Choisy	trees	Common
f. soralifera (Erichsen) D.Hawksw.	trees	Rare
L. meiococca (Nyl.) Leuckert & Hertel	maritime rocks	Rare

LICHENES

Lecidella scabra (Taylor) Hertel & Leuckert	shaded rocks and walls	Frequent
L. stigmatea (Ach.) Hertel & Leuckert	walls	Local
Lepraria caesioalba (B.de Lesd.) Laundon	acid rocks	Rare
L. incana (L.) Ach.	damp rocks, soil and trees	Common
L. jackii Tønsb.	Quercus	Local
L. lobificans Nyl.	trees	Frequent
L. rigidula (Hue) Tønsb.	Fraxinus	Local
L. umbricola Tønsb.	Betula stumps	Local
L. thamnolica Tønsb.	trees	Local
Leprocaulon microscopicum (Vill.) Gams ex D.Hawksw.	acid rocks	Rare
Leproloma cacuminum (Massal.) Laundon	acid rocks	Rare
L. membranaceum (Dickson) Vainio	damp rocks and trees	Local
L. vouauxii (Hue) Laundon	old walls	Local
Leproplaca xantholyta (Nyl.) Harm.	dry calcareous rock crevices	Rare
Leptogium cyanescens (Rabenh.) Körber	trees and rocks	Rare
L. gelatinosum (With.) Laundon		Very rare
L. lichenoides (L.) Zahlbr.	mossy trees, rocks and walls	Common
L. schraderi (Ach.) Nyl.	old wall	Very rare
L. teretiusculum (Wallr.) Arnold	trees	Rare
L. turgidum (Ach.) Crombie	calcareous stone walls	Rare
Leptorhaphis epidermidis (Ach.) Th.Fr.	Betula	Local
Lichina confinis (Müller) Agardh	maritime rocks	Rare
Lobaria amplissima (Scop.) Forss.	old Quercus and Fraxinus	Very rare
L. pulmonaria (L.) Hoffm. LUNGWORT	trees in old woodland	Locally common
L. scrobiculata (Scop.) DC.	old trees	Rare and decreasing
L. virens (With.) Laundon	old trees and rocks	Very local
Loxospora elatina (Ach.) Massal.	Quercus	Local
Macentina stigonemoides A.Orange	Sambucus	Rare
Megalospora tuberculoaa (Fée) Sipman	old trees in ancient woods	Rare
Melaspilea ochrothalamia Nyl.	trees	Rare
Menegazzia terebrata (Hoffm.) Massal.	Alnus	Very rare
Micarea adnata Coppins	fallen tree trunk	
M. alabastrites (Nyl.) Coppins	trees	Rare
M. bauschiana (Körber) V.Wirth & Vězda	shaded rocks	Local
M. botryoides (Nyl.) Coppins	shaded rocks and soil	Local
M. cinerea (Schaerer) Hedl.	trees	Rare
M. denigrata (Fr.) Hedl.	wood	Local
M. erratica (Körber) Hertel, Rambold & Pietschm.	Juniperus	Very rare

LICHENES

Micarea leprosula (Th.Fr.) Coppins & A.Fletcher	acid rocks	Rare
M. lignaria (Ach.) Hedl.	acid rocks and debris	Local
M. lithinella (Nyl.) Hedl.	acid rocks and stones	Rare
M. lutulata (Nyl.) Coppins	acid rocks	Local
M. melaena (Nyl.) Hedl.	dead wood of Quercus	Local
M. myriocarpa V.Wirth & Vězda ex Coppins	rocks and exposed roots	Local
M. peliocarpa (Anzi) Coppins & R. Sant.	trees	Local
M. prasina Fr.	trees, especially Salix	Common
M. pycnidiophora Coppins & P.James	old trees	Local
M. subnigrata (Nyl.) Coppins & Kilias	acid rocks	Rare
M. sylvicola (Flot.) Vězda & V.Wirth	acid rocks	Rare
Microcalicium ahlneri Tibell	Quercus	Rare
Mycoblastus caesius (Coppins & P.James) Tønsb.	trees	Local
M. sanguinarius (L.) Norman	damp tree bark	Very local
M. sterilis Coppins & P.James	trees	Frequent
Mycoporum quercus (Massal.) Müll.Arg.	Quercus twigs	Frequent
Nephroma laevigatum Ach.	old mossy trees & rocks	Locally frequent
N. parile (Ach.) Ach.	old mossy trees & rocks	Rare
Normandina pulchella (Borrer) Nyl.	trees	Frequent
Ochrolechia androgyna (Hoffm.) Arnold	upland rocks and trees	Common
O. inversa (Nyl.) Laundon	Quercus	Rare
O. parella (L.) Massal.	walls, rocks and trees near the sea	Locally common
O. subviridis (Høeg) Erichsen	trees	Frequent
O. turneri (Sm.) Hasselrot	trees	Frequent; usually sterile
Omphalina hudsoniana (Jennings) H.Bigelow	peaty soil	Local
Opegrapha areniseda Nyl.	rocks	Rare
O. atra Pers.	smooth bark of trees	Very common
O. cesareensis Nyl.	maritime rocks	Local
O. corticola Coppins & P.James	old trees	Rare
O. fumosa Coppins & P.James **RDB3**	Quercus	Local
O. gyrocarpa Flot.	shaded rocks	Local
O. herbarum Mont.	trees	Uncommon
O. lithyrga Ach.	rocks by river	Rare
O. multipuncta Coppins & P.James	shaded rocks	Local
O. niveoatra (Borrer) Laundon	trees	Frequent
O. ochrocheila Nyl.	old trees	Local
O. prosodea Ach.	Quercus and Taxus	Rare
O. rufescens Pers.	upland trees	Local

LICHENES

Opegrapha saxatilis auct., non DC.	calcareous walls	Rare
O. saxigena Tayl.	shaded maritime rocks	Local
O. sorediifera P.James	trees in old woodland	Local
O. varia Pers.	trees	Locally common
O. vermicellifera (Kunze) Laundon	dry bark crevices	Frequent
O. vulgata (Ach.) Ach.	trees	Frequent
O. xerica Torrente & Egea	Hedera and Quercus	Local
Pachyphiale carneola (Ach.) Arnold	old trees	Very local
Pannaria conoplea (Ach.) Bory	trees in old woods	Uncommon
P. mediterranea C. Tav.	old woodland	Local
P. pezizoides (Weber) Trevisan	Salix by streams	Very rare
Parmelia borreri (Sm.) Turner	trees	Very rare
P. britannica D.Hawksw. & P.James	maritime	Local
P. caperata (L.) Ach.	trees, occasionally rocks	Common
P. conspersa (Ehrh. ex Ach.) Ach.	rocks and walls	Common
P. crinita Ach.	old mossy trees	Rare
P. elegantula (Zahlbr.) Szat.	trees	Uncommon
P. endochlora Leighton	cliff-top heathland	Rare
P. exasperata de Not.	horizontal tree branches	Frequent
P. exasperatula Nyl.	trees	Rare
P. glabratula (Lamy) Nyl.	trees	Very common
P. glabratula ssp.fuliginosa (Fr.ex Duby) Laundon	rocks and walls	Locally frequent
P. laciniatula (H.Olivier) Zahlbr.	smooth bark and twigs	Local
P. laevigata (Sm.) Ach.	trees and rocks in high rainfall area	Locally common
P. mougeotii Schaerer ex D.Dietr.	scree and beach pebbles	Rare
P. omphalodes (L.) Ach.	acid rocks	Rare
P. pastillifera (Harm.) R.Schubert & Klem.	trees and rocks	Very local
P. perlata (Huds.) Ach.	trees and rocks	Common
P. pulla Ach.	maritime rocks	Local
P. quercina (Willd.) Vainio **RDB2**	branches of deciduous trees	Very rare
P. reddenda Stirton	old trees	Rare
P. reticulata Taylor	maritime rocks	Local
P. revoluta Flörke	trees and rocks	Frequent
P. saxatilis (L.) Ach.	trees, exposed rocks and walls	Common
P. subaurifera Nyl.	smaller branches of trees	Common
P. subrudecta Nyl.	trees	Common
P. sulcata Taylor	trees, rocks and walls	Very common
P. taylorensis M.E.Mitch.	trees and rocks	Rare

LICHENES

Parmelia verruculifera Nyl.	maritime rocks and churchyard stones	Rare
Parmeliella jamesii S.Ahlner & P.M.Jørg.	trees in old woods	Local
P. testacea P.M.Jørg.	trees in old woods	Very rare
P. triptophylla (Ach.) Müll. Arg.	trees in old woods	Local
Parmeliopsis ambigua (Wulfen) Nyl.	Betula	Local
Peltigera collina (Ach.) Schrader	old mossy tree-trunks	Local and rare
P. didactyla (With.) Laundon	well-drained soils	Frequent
P. horizontalis (Huds.) Baumg.	mossy rocks and trees	Frequent
P. lactucifolia (With.) Laundon	mossy rocks	Frequent
P. membranacea (Ach.) Nyl. DOG LICHEN	bare ground on moors and in woods	Common
P. praetextata (Flörke ex Sommerf.) Zopf	mossy rocks and trees	Common
P. rufescens (Weiss) Humb.	calcareous ground	Rare
Pertusaria albescens (Huds.) M.Choisy & Werner	old trees; rarely rocks	Frequent
var. corallina (Zahlbr.) Laundon	old trees	Frequent
P. amara (Ach.) Nyl.	old trees; rarely mosses	Common
P. aspergilla (Ach.) Laundon	acid rocks	Frequent
P. coccodes (Ach.) Nyl.	old trees at lower altitudes	Uncommon
P. corallina (L.) Arnold	acid rocks and stones	Local
P. coronata (Ach.) Th.Fr.	old trees	Rare
P. excludens Nyl.	maritime rocks	Rare
P. flavida (DC.) Laundon	old trees	Local
P. hemisphaerica (Flörke) Erichsen	old trees	Local
P. hymenea (Ach.) Schaerer	trees; rarely rocks	Common
P. lactea (L.) Arnold	acid rocks	Local
P. leioplaca DC.	smooth-barked trees	Common
P. multipuncta (Turner) Nyl.	trees	Common
P. pertusa (Weigel) Tuck.	trees; rarely rocks	Common
P. pseudocorallina (Lilj.) Arnold	maritime rocks	Frequent
P. pupillaris (Nyl.) Th.Fr.	trees	Rare
Phaeographis dendritica (Ach.) Müll. Arg.	trees	Frequent
P. inusta (Ach.) Müll. Arg.	Betula	Rare
P. lyellii (Sm.) Zahlbr.	Quercus	Rare
P. smithii (Leighton) B.de Lesd.	smooth bark in old woods	Local
Phaeophyscia orbicularis (Necker) Moberg	trees, fences, rocks and walls	Common
Phlyctis agelaea (Ach.) Flot.	trees	Rare
P. argena (Sprengel) Flot.	deciduous trees	Common
Phyllospora rosei Coppins & P.James	old Quercus and Fraxinus	Local

LICHENES

Physcia adscendens (Fr.) H.Olivier	trees, rocks and walls	Common
P. aipolia (Ehrh. ex Humb.) Fürnr.	upland trees	Common
P. caesia (Hoffm.) Fürnr.	nitrogenous rocks,walls & roofs	Common
P. stellaris (L.) Nyl.	Fraxinus and Salix twigs	Local
P. tenella (Scop.) DC.	trees and rocks near the sea	Common
P. tribacia (Ach.) Nyl.	tree bark & calcareous rocks	Uncommon
Physconia distorta (With.) Laundon	trees; occas. rocks & walls	Common
P. enteroxantha (Nyl.) Poelt	trees, rocks and walls	Common
P. grisea (Lam.) Poelt	trees; occas. rocks and walls	Common
P. perisidiosa (Erichsen) Moberg	trees	Local
Placopsis lambii Hertel & V.Wirth	rocks with high heavy metal content	Very rare
Placynthiella icmalea (Ach.) Coppins & P.James	old trees, wood, and acid soil	Common
P. oligotropha (Laundon) Coppins & P.James	peaty soil	Very rare
P. uliginosa (Schrader) Coppins & P.James	peaty soil	Rare
Placynthium nigrum (Huds.) Gray	stone walls; calcicolous	Local
Platismatia glauca (L.) Culb. & C.Culb.	rocks and trees	Common
Polyblastia dermatodes Massal.	limestone rocks	Rare
P. gelatinosa (Ach.) Th.Fr.	coastal heath	Local
Polysporina lapponica (Schrader) Degel.	slate	Very rare
P. simplex (Davies) Vězda	acid rocks	Rare
Porina aenea (Wallr.) Zahlbr.	smooth-barked trees	Local
P. ahlesiana (Körber) Zahlbr.	rocks by river	Very rare
P. chlorotica (Ach.) Müll. Arg.	shaded acid rocks	Locally frequent
P. lectissima (Fr.) Zahlbr.	shaded acid rocks	Local
P. leptalea (Durieu & Mont.) A.L.Sm.	trees	Rare
Porpidia cinereoatra (Ach.) Hertel & Knoph	acid rocks	Frequent
P. crustulata (Ach.) Hertel & Knoph	acid rocks, pebbles and walls	Common
P. glaucophaea (Körber) Hertel & Knoph	acid rocks	Rare
P. macrocarpa (DC.) Hertel & Schwab	moorland rocks	Common
P. platycarpoides (Bagl.) Hertel	acid rocks, especially near sea	Rare
P. soredizodes (Lamy ex Nyl.) Laundon	acid rocks and stones	Local
P. tuberculosa (Sm.) Hertel & Knoph	acid rocks and pebbles	Common
Protoblastenia rupestris (Scop.) Steiner	stone walls; calcicolous	Locally frequent
Protoparmelia montagnei (Fr.) Poelt & Nimis	maritime rocks	Rare
Pseudevernia furfuracea (L.) Knoph	acid bark, branches and walls	Local
Pseudocyphellaria crocata (L.) Vainio	Fraxinus	Very rare
Psilolechia clavulifera (Nyl.) Coppins	rocks and Fraxinus	Rare
P. lucida (Ach.) M.Choisy	walls, rocks and soil	Frequent

LICHENES

Ptychographa xylographoides Nyl.	dead wood of Quercus	Very rare
Pyrenocollema halodytes (Nyl.) R.Harris	on barnacles and limpets	Frequent
P. strontianense (Swinscow) R.Harris	rocks in streams	Rare
Pyrenula chlorospila Arnold	smooth bark in old woodland	Local
P. macrospora (Degel.) Coppins & P.James	smooth bark in old woodland	Locally frequent
P. occidentalis (R.Harris) R.Harris	Quercus	Rare
Pyrrhospora quernea (Dickson) Körber	trees	Common
Racodium rupestre Pers.	shaded rocks, especially sandstone	Local
Ramalina calicaris (L.) Fr.	trees	Rare
R. canariensis Steiner	trees	Local
R. cuspidata (Ach.) Nyl.	maritime rocks	Frequent
R. farinacea (L.) Ach.	trees	Common
R. fastigiata (Pers.) Ach.	trees; maritime	Locally common
R. fraxinea (L.) Ach.	trees	Rare
R. pollinaria (Westr.) Ach.	rock underhang	Very rare
R. siliquosa (Huds.) A.L.Sm.	maritime rocks	Common
R. subfarinacea (Nyl. ex Crombie) Nyl.	maritime rocks	Local
Ramonia chrysophaea (Pers.) Vězda	Quercus	Rare
Rhaphidicyrtis trichosporella (Nyl.) Vainio	Fraxinus and Ilex	Local
Rhizocarpon concentricum (Davies) Beltr.	basic rocks	Uncommon
R. geographicum (L.) DC.	upland rocks and walls	Locally common
R. hochstetteri (Körber) Vainio	rocks	Local
R. obscuratum (Ach.) Massal.	smooth rocks	Common
R. oederi (Weber) Körber	rocks with heavy metal content	Very rare
R. richardii (Lamy ex Nyl.) Zahlbr.	maritime rocks	Uncommon
R. simillimum (Anzi) Lettau	acid rocks	Rare
R. viridiatrum (Wulfen) Körber	acid rocks	Rare
Rimularia furvella (Nyl. ex Mudd) Hertel & Rambold	acid rocks	Local
R. gyrizans (Nyl.) Hertel & Rambold	acid rocks	Rare
R. intercedens (H.Magn.) Coppins	beach pebbles	Very rare
Rinodina aspersa (Borrer) Laundon RDB3	beach pebbles	Very rare
R. efflorescens Malme	Alnus	Rare
R. flavosoralifera Tønsb.	on moss on Quercus	Rare
R. gennarii Bagl.	rocks and walls near the sea	Common
R. griseosoralifera Coppins	Quercus	Local
R. isidioides (Borrer) H.Olivier	old Quercus	Very rare
R. lecideina H.Mayrhofer & Poelt	maritime rocks and pebbles	Frequent
R. oxydata (Massal.) Massal.	shaded rocks by river	Very rare

LICHENES

Rinodina roboris (Dufour ex Nyl.) Arnold	old Quercus	Locally frequent
R. sophodes (Ach.) Massal.	smooth twigs	Common
R. subglaucescens (Nyl.) Sheard	maritime rocks	Rare
Roccella fuciformis (L.) DC.	maritime rocks	Very rare
R. phycopsis Ach.	maritime rocks	Rare
Sarcogyne regularis Körber	limestone walls	Rare
Schaereria fuscocinerea (Nyl.) Clauzade & Roux	rocks	Local
var. sorediata (Houmeau & Roux) Coppins		Rare
Schismatomma cretaceum (Hue) Laundon	old trees; open habitat	Local
S. decolorans (Turner & Borrer ex Sm.) Clauzade & Vězda		
	dry tree bark	Common
S. graphidioides (Leighton) Zahlbr. **RDB3**	Fraxinus	Very rare
S. niveum D.Hawksw. & P.James	dry tree crevices	Rare
S. quercicola Coppins & P.James	old Quercus and Alnus	Rare
Sclerophyton circumscriptum (Taylor) Zahlbr.	maritime rocks	Local
Scoliciosporum chlorococcum (Graewe ex Stenhammar) Vězda		
	Fraxinus twigs	Local
S. pruinosum (P.James) Vězda	crevices of tree bark	Rare
S. umbrinum (Ach.) Arnold	rocks, walls and Fraxinus twigs	Rare
Solenopsora candicans (Dickson) Steiner	gravestones	Local
S. holophaea (Mont.) G.Samp.	maritime rocks	Rare
S. vulturiensis Massal.	maritime rocks	Local
Sphaerophorus globosus (Huds.) Vainio	trees; mossy rocks	Very local
Stenocybe pullatula (Ach.) B.Stein	Alnus twigs	Frequent
S. septata (Leighton) Massal.	Ilex	Frequent
Stereocaulon dactylophyllum Flörke	acid rocks	Rare
S. nanodes Tuck.	rocks with heavy metal content	
		Very rare
S. pileatum Ach.	rocks with heavy metal content	
		Very rare
S. vesuvianum Pers.	moorland	Common
Sticta dufourii Delise	rocks	Very rare
S. fuliginosa (Hoffm.) Ach.	old woodland	Local
S. limbata (Sm.) Ach.	old woodland	Local
S. sylvatica (Huds.) Ach.	old woodland	Local
Strangospora ochrophora (Nyl.) R.Anderson	trees in old woodland	Rare
Strigula taylorii (Carroll ex Nyl.) R.Harris **RDB2**	Acer pseudoplatanus	Local
Teloschistes flavicans (Sw.) Norman **RDB2**	coastal heath	Rare
Tephromela atra (Huds.) Hafellner ex Kalb	basic rocks and trees	Locally common
Thelidium decipiens (Nyl.) Krampelh.	walls in churchyards	Rare

LICHENES

Thelopsis rubella Nyl.	old Quercus	Very rare
Thelotrema lepadinum (Ach.) Ach.	trees	Frequent
Thrombium epigaeum (Pers.) Wallr.	terricolous	Rare
Tomasellia gelatinosa (Chevall.) Zahlbr.	Corylus	Locally frequent
Toninia aromatica (Sm.) Massal.	basic rocks	Locally frequent
T. lobulata (Sommerf.) Lynge	old wall; calcicolous	Very rare
T. mesoidea (Nyl.) Zahlbr.	maritime rocks	Very rare
Trapelia coarctata (Sm.) M.Choisy	stones, rocks and walls	Rare
T. corticola Coppins & P.James	Quercus and Fagus	Local
T. involuta (Taylor) Hertel	acid rocks and debris	Frequent
T. obtegens (Th.Fr.) Hertel	acid stones in scree area	Rare
T. placodioides Coppins & P.James	acid rocks and stones	Local
Trapeliopsis flexuosa (Fr.) Coppins & P.James	acid bark and wood	Frequent
T. gelatinosa (Flörke) Coppins & P.James	on the ground	Rare
T. granulosa (Hoffm.) Lumbsch	damp peat and rotten stumps	Common
T. percrenata (Nyl.) G.Schneider	dead wood	Rare
T. pseudogranulosa Coppins & P.James	Quercus and on the ground	Local
T. wallrothii (Flörke ex Sprengel) Hertel & G. Schneider	maritime turf	Rare
Tylothallia biformigera (Leighton) P.James & Kilias	acid rocks in woodland	Rare
Usnea articulata (L.) Hoffm.	trees	Local
U. ceratina Ach.	trees	Locally common
U. cornuta Körber	trees and rocks	Common
U. filipendula Stirton	trees	Local
U. flammea Stirton	rocks	Rare
U. florida (L.) Weber ex Wigg.	trees	Local
U. hirta (L.) Weber ex Wigg.	conifers	Very local
U. rubicunda Stirton	trees	Frequent
U. subfloridana Stirton	trees	Abundant
U. wasmuthii Räsänen	Quercus	Local
Verrucaria aethiobola Wahlenb.	rocks in streams	Local
V. aquatilis Mudd	rocks in streams	Local
V. baldensis Massal.	churchyard	Rare
V. dolosa Hepp	rocks in woodland	Rare
V. fusconigrescens Nyl.	maritime rocks	Frequent
V. glaucina auct.brit., non Ach.	old walls, especially churchyards	Local
V. hochstetteri Fr.	old walls, especially churchyards	Common
V. hydrela Ach.	rocks in streams	Local
V. latericola Erichsen	on Caloplaca on rocks	Rare

LICHENES

Verrucaria macrostoma Dufour ex DC.	old walls	Local
V. margacea (Wahlenb.) Wahlenb.	rocks in streams	Local
V. maura Wahlenb.	rocks by the sea	Common
V. mucosa Wahlenb.	maritime rocks below high-water mark	Common
V. muralis Ach.	old walls	Common
V. nigrescens Pers.	old walls	Common
V. praetermissa (Trevisan) Anzi	rocks in streams	Local
V. prominula Nyl.	maritime rocks	Rare
V. rheitrophila Zschacke	rocks in streams	Rare
V. striatula Wahlenb.	maritime rocks below high-water mark	Local
V. viridula (Schrader) Ach.	churchyards	Common
Vezdaea aestivalis (Ohl.) Tscherm.-Woess & Poelt	old wall	Rare
Wadeana dendrographa (Nyl.) Coppins & P.James	old Fraxinus and Quercus	Rare
Xanthoria candelaria (L.) Th.Fr.	trees, fences, walls and rocks	Frequent
X. elegans (Link) Th.Fr.	walls	Rare
X. parietina (L.) Th.Fr.	rocks, walls and roofs near farms	Very common
X. polycarpa (Hoffm.) Th.Fr. ex Rieber	branches, twigs and fences	Frequent
Xylographa vitiligo (Ach.) Laundon	dead wood of Quercus	Local
Zamenhofia coralloidea (P.James) Clauzade & Roux	old Quercus	Rare

LICHENICOLOUS FUNGI

Abrothallus bertianus de Not	on Parmelia glabratula on Fraxinus and Quercus	Local
A. parmotrematis Diederich in ed.	on Parmelia perlata on Alnus	Local
Arthonia molendoi (Heufl. ex Frauenf.) R.Sant.	on Caloplaca arnoldii on rocks	Rare
Arthropyrenia microspila Körber	on Graphis scripta on trees	Local
Arthrorhaphis aeruginosa R.Sant. & Tønsb.	on Cladonia squamules	Local
Cecidonia xenophana (Körber) Triebel & Rambold	on Porpidia cinereoatra on rocks	Rare
Cyphelium sessile (Pers.) Trevisan	on Pertusaria spp.	Rare
Endococcus alpestris D.Hawksw.	on Usnea spp. on Quercus and Sorbus	Local
E. stigma (Körber) Stizenb.	on Rhizocarpon geographicum on rocks	Local
Homostegia piggottii (Berk.& Broome) P.Karsten	on Parmelia saxatilis on trees	Frequent

LICHENES

Laeviomyces opegraphae (Nyl.) D.Hawksw.	on Opegrapha herbarum on Quercus	Local
Lichenodiplis lecanorae (Vouaux) Dyko & D.Hawksw.	on Lecanora chlarotera on trees	Local
Marchandiomyces corallinus (Roberge) Diederich & D.Hawksw.	on Pertusaria spp. on Quercus	Frequent
Milospium graphideorum (Nyl.) D.Hawksw.	on ?Opegrapha sp. on Quercus	Local
Muellerella lichenicola (Sommerf. ex Fr.) D.Hawksw.	on Toninia lobulata on old wall	Rare
M. pygmaea (Körber) D.Hawksw.	on Lecanora polytropa on rocks	Local
Phaeopyxis varia Coppins, Rambold & Triebel	on Trapeliopsis gelatinosa on ground	Rare
Polycoccum sp.	on Rinodina gennarii on rocks	Rare
Roselliniella cladoniae (Anzi) Matzer & Hafellner	on Cladonia coniocraea on trees	Rare
Roselliniopsis tartaricola (Nyl.) Matzer	on Pertusaria albescens on Fraxinus	Rare
Skyttea cruciata Sherw., D.Hawksw.& Coppins	on Diploicia canescens on rocks	Rare
S. nitschkei (Körber) Sherw., D.Hawksw. & Coppins	on Thelotroma lepadinum on Quercus	Local
Sphinctrina turbinata (Pers.) de Not	on Pertusaria pertusa	Rare
Stigmidium aggregatum (Mudd) D.Hawksw.	on Pertusaria lactea on rocks	Rare
S. peltideae (Vainio) R.Sant	on Peltigera membranacea on trees	Rare
Stigmidium sp.	on Verrucaria aquatilis on rocks in streams	Local
Tremella coppinsii Diederich & Marson	on Platismatia glauca on trees	Very rare
Tremella sp.	on Caloplaca arnoldii	Rare
Tremella sp.	on Pertusaria hymenea on trees	Rare
Vouauxiella lichenicola (Lindsay) Petrak & Sydow	on Lecanora chlarotera on Crataegus	Frequent

References:

Purvis, O.W., Coppins, B.J. & James, P.W. (1994) *Checklist of Lichens of Great Britain and Ireland* British Lichen Society.
Dobson, Frank (1979) *Lichens* Richmond Publishing.
Duncan, Ursula (1970) *Introduction to British Lichens*. T.Buncle.

Division: BRYOPHYTA
(LIVERWORTS, HORNWORTS & MOSSES)

In February 1993 I began some field work on the Bryophyta of Exmoor, following on from that previously done by Caroline Giddens as recorded in our 1988 *Flora and Fauna*. I was greatly helped with identifications by Mr Len Ellis of the Department of Biology at the British Museum (Natural History) South Kensington. Much encouraged and together with Mr Ken May, in June 1994, we began recording the mosses and liverworts of Exmoor on a 2km square basis. Once again we are tremendously indebted for all the help given by Mr Mark Pool from Torquay who is engaged in a similar project for Devon. His meticulous checking and detailed notes on identification have been invaluable. In March 1995 Mr Peter Martin agreed to assist with identification of specimens from the Somerset side of Exmoor and we do thank him for his expert help.

The varied habitats on Exmoor offer great scope for the study of Bryophytes and this list contains 243 moss species and 100 liverworts.

Nomenclature follows A.J.E. Smith (1990) for Liverworts and (1978) for Mosses.

Rene Perry
Bryophyte Recorder, ENHS

Class: HEPATICAE – LIVERWORTS
Sub-Class: JUNGERMANNIIDEAE

Order: JUNGERMANNIALES

PSEUDOLEPICOLEACEAE

Blepharostoma trichophyllum (L.) Dum.	Decaying wood	Uncommon

TRICHOCOLEACEAE

Trichocolea tomentella (Furh.) Dum.	By streams	Uncommon

LEPIDOZIACEAE

Kurzia pauciflora (Dicks.) Grolle *(Lepidozia setacea auct.)*		Rare
K. trichoclados (K. Müll.) Grolle *(L. trichoclados K.Müll.)*		Rare
Lepidozia reptans (L.) Dum.	Rotten wood and moist banks	Common
L. cupressina (Sw.) Lindenb. *(L. pinnata (Hook.) Dum.)*		Uncommon
Bazzania trilobata (L.) S.F.Gray	Tree bases	Uncommon

CALYPOGEIACEAE

Calypogeia fissa (L.) Raddi		Common
C. muelleriana (Schiffn.) K.Müll.	Wet moorland	Uncommon
C. arguta Nees & Mont.	Well sheltered loamy banks	Common

LIVERWORTS & MOSSES

CEPHALOZIACEAE

Cephalozia bicuspidata (L.) Dum.	Acid banks	Common
C. lunulifolia (Dum.) Dum. *(C. media Lindb.)*		Frequent
C. connivens (Dicks.) Lindb.	On moorland	Frequent
Nowellia curvifolia (Dicks.) Mitt.	Decayed wood	Frequent
Odontoschisma sphagni (Dicks.) Dum.	Wet heath	Rare
O. denudatum (Mart.) Dum.	Decayed wood	Rare

CEPHALOZIELLACEAE

Cephaloziella rubella (Nees) Warnst.	Heathland	Rare
C. hampeana (Nees) Schiffn.		Frequent
C. divaricata (Sm.) Schiffn.		Common
C. massalongi (Spruce) K. Müll.		Rare

LOPHOZIACEAE

Barbilophozia floerkei (Web. & Mohr) Loeske	Moist boulders	Uncommon
B. attenuata (Mart.) Loeske *(B. gracilis (Schleich.) K.Müll.)*		Rare
Lophozia ventricosa (Dicks.) Dum. var. silvicola (Buch) E.W. Jones ex Schust.		Common
L. excisa (Dicks.) Dum.	Banks and old walls	Rare
L. incisa (Schrad.) Dum.	Wet moorland	Rare
L. bicrenata (Schmid. ex Hoffm.) Dum.		Rare
Leiocolea turbinata (Raddi) Buch *(Lophozia turbinata (Raddi) Steph.)*		Uncommon
Gymnocolea inflata (Huds.) Dum.		Uncommon
Tritomaria exsectiformis (Breidl.) Loeske		Rare
T. quinquedentata (Huds.) Buch		Rare

JUNGERMANNIACEAE

Jungermannia atrovirens Dum. *(Solenostoma triste (Nees) K.Müll.)* Wet places.		Uncommon
J. pumila With. *(S. pumilum (With.) K.Müll.)*		Uncommon
J. gracillima Sm. *(S. crenulatum (Sm.) Mitt.)*		Common
J. hyalina Lyell *(Plectocolea h. (Lyell) Mitt.)*		Uncommon
J. subelliptica (Lindb. ex Kaal.) Lév.		Rare
Nardia scalaris S.F.Gray *(Alicularia s. (S.F.Gray) Corda)*		Frequent
N. geoscyphus (De Not.) Lindb.		Rare

GYMNOMITRIACEAE

Marsupella emarginata (Ehrh.) Dum.	On rocks or soil.	Frequent

SCAPANIACEAE

Diplophyllum albicans (L.) Dum.		Locally common; sometimes abundant
D. obtusifolium (Hook.) Dum.		Rather frequent
Scapania compacta (A.Roth) Dum.		Rare
S. scandica (H.Arn. & Buch) Macv.	One station only.	Very rare
S. irrigua (Nees) Nees		Uncommon

LIVERWORTS & MOSSES

Scapania undulata (L.) Dum.	Fast flowing streams	Common
S. subalpina (Nees ex Lindenb.) Dum.		Rare
S. nemorea (L.) Grolle		Frequent
S. umbrosa (Schrad.) Dum.		Rare
S. gracilis Lindb.	Boulders and tree trunks	Frequent

GEOCALYCACEAE

Lophocolea bidentata (L.) Dum. var. bidentata		Common
var. rivularis (Raddi) Warnst.		Common
L. heterophylla (Schrad.) Dum.		Frequent
L. fragrans (Moris & De Not.) Gott. et al.		Rare
Chiloscyphus polyanthos (L.) Corda var.polyanthos.	Moorland & stones in streams;	Frequent
var. pallescens (Ehrh. ex Hoffm.) Hartm.		Uncommon
Saccogyna viticulosa (L.) Dum.		Frequent

PLAGIOCHILACEAE

Plagiochila porelloides (Torrey ex Nees) Lindenb.		Frequent
P. asplenioides (L. emend. Tayl.) Dum.	Resembles a minute spleenwort fern.	Frequent
P. spinulosa (Dicks.) Dum.		Occasional
P. punctata Tayl.		Uncommon

RADULACEAE

Radula complanata (L.) Dum.	Tree trunks	Uncommon

PTILIDIACEAE

Ptilidium ciliare (L.) Hampe	Heathland	Frequent
P. pulcherrimum (G.Webb) Vainio	Trees or stumps	Rare

PORELLACEAE

Porella pinnata L.		Very rare
P. arboris-vitae (With.) Grolle *(P. laevigata (Schrad.) Pfeiff.)*		Uncommon
P. obtusata (Tayl.) Trev. *(P. thuja auct.)*		Rare
P. platyphylla (L.) Pfeiff.		Frequent

FRULLANIACEAE

Frullania tamarisci (L.) Dum.	On rocks or bark	Common
F. microphylla (Gottsche) Pears.	One station only	Very rare
F. fragilifolia (Tayl.) Gottsche et al.		Uncommon
F. dilitata (L.) Dum.	On trees	Common
Jubula hutchinsiae (Hook.) Dum.		Very rare

LEJEUNEACEAE

Lejeunea cavifolia (Ehrh.) Lindb.		Common
L. lamacerina (Steph.) Schiffn.	Shaded rocks	Frequent
L. patens Lindb.		Uncommon
L. ulicina (Tayl.) Gott. et al.	Minute, easily overlooked; on tree bark	Common

LIVERWORTS & MOSSES

Marchesinia mackaii (Hook.) S.F. Gray   Very rare

Order: METZGERIALES

CODONIACEAE
Fossombronia pusilla (L.) Nees   Uncommon
F. wondraczekii (Corda) Dum.   Uncommon
PELLIACEAE
Pellia epiphylla (L.) Corda   Damp earth banks   Common
P. neesiana (Gott.) Limpr.   Moist shaded tracks   Frequent
P. endiviifolia (Dicks.) Dum.   Frequent
BLASIACEAE
Blasia pusilla L.   Rare
ANEURACEAE
Aneura pinguis (L.) Dum. *(Riccardia pinguis (L.) S.F.Gray)*   Frequent
Riccardia multifida (L.) S.F.Gray   Uncommon
R. chamedryfolia (With.) Grolle   Common
R. latifrons (Lindb.) Lindb.   Rare

METZGERIACEAE
Metzgeria furcata (L.) Dum.   Very small; on trees   Frequent
M. temperata Kuwah.   Uncommon
M. fruticulosa (Dicks.) Evans   Frequent
M. conjugata Lindb.   On rocks   Frequent

Order: MARCHANTIALES

LUNULARIACEAE
Lunularia cruciata (L.) Dum. ex Lindb.   Near habitations.   Common
WIESNERELLACEAE
Dumortiera hirsuta (Sw.) Nees   Uncommon
CONOCEPHALACEAE
Conocephalum conicum (L.) Underw.   On wet banks.   Common
AYTONIACEAE
Reboulia hemisphaerica (L.) Raddi   Occasional
MARCHANTIACEAE
Marchantia polymorpha L.   Uncommon
RICCIACEAE
Riccia sorocarpa Bisch.   Rare

Riccia glauca L. — Rare
R. subbifurca (Warnst.) ex Crozals — Occasional

Class: ANTHOCEROTAE - HORNWORTS

Order: ANTHOCEROTALES

ANTHOCEROTACEAE

Anthoceros punctatus L. *(A. husnotii Steph.)*	Damp fallow fields	Occasional
Phaeoceros laevis (L.) Prosk.		Occasional

MUSCI - MOSSES

Class: SPHAGNOPSIDA

Order: SPHAGNALES

SPHAGNACEAE - SPHAGNUM-MOSS FAMILY

Sphagnum papillosum Lindb.	Boggy moorland	Uncommon
S. palustre L.	Wet moorland	Common
S. squarrosum Crome	Oak woods & moorland springs	Frequent
S. quinquefarium (Braithw.) Warnst.	*Betula* dominated woodland	Uncommon
S. capillifolium (Ehrh.) Hedw. var. capillifolium		Local
var. rubellum Daniels & Eddy		Local
S. subnitens Russ. & Warnst. *(S. plumulosum Röll)*	Moorland bogs	Frequent
S. molle Sull.	Near moorland streams	Rare
S. compactum DC. *(S. rigidum Schimp.)*	Damp moorland	Uncommon
S. auriculatum Schimp. var. auriculatum	Wet bogs	Frequent
var. inundatum (Russ.) Hill		Uncommon
S. cuspidatum Hoffm.	Submerged in moorland pools	Frequent
S. recurvum (Russ.) Warnst. var mucronatum		Common

Class: ANDREAEOPSIDA

Order: ANDREAEALES

ANDREAEACEAE

Andreaea rothii Web. & Mohr — Scree, cliffs and walls — Uncommon

LIVERWORTS & MOSSES

Class: BRYOPSIDA Sub-Class: POLYTRICHIDEAE

Order: TETRAPHIDALES

TETRAPHIDACEAE
Tetraphis pellucida Hedw.   Woodlands   Uncommon

Order: POLYTRICHALES

POLYTRICHACEAE - HAIR-MOSS FAMILY
Polytrichum longisetum Sw. ex Brid. *(P. aurantiacum Hoppe ex Brid.)* Woodland   Rare
P. formosum Hedw.   On acid soils   Common
P. commune Hedw.   Common
P. piliferum Hedw.   Sandy heaths   Frequent
P. juniperinum Hedw.   Acid heathland   Common
P. alpestre Hoppe   Uncommon
Pogonatum nanum (Hedw.) P.Beauv. *(Polytrichum n. Hedw.)* Dry banks   Rare
P. aloides (Hedw.) P.Beauv. *(Polytrichum a. Hedw.)*   Common
P. urnigerum (Hedw.) P.Beauv. *(Polytrichum u. Hedw.)* High ground   Common
Oligotrichum hercynicum (Hedw.) Lam. & DC.   Uncommon
Atrichum crispum (James) Sull. & Lesq.   By streams   Local
A. undulatum (Hedw.) P.Beauv.   Shady woods   Common

Sub-Class: BUXBAUMIIDEAE

Order: BUXBAUMIALES

BUXBAUMIACEAE
Diphyscium foliosum (Hedw.) Mohr   Rare

Sub-Class: EUBRYIDEAE

Order: DICRANALES

DITRICHACEAE
Pleuridium acuminatum Lindb.   Frequent
P. subulatum (Hedw.) Lindb.   Rare
Pseudephemerum nitidum (Hedw.) Reim.   Common

LIVERWORTS & MOSSES

Ditrichum cylindricum (Hedw.) Grout		Common
D. heteromallum (Hedw.) Britt.		Common
DICRANACEAE - FORK-MOSS FAMILY		
Ceratodon purpureus (Hedw.) Brid.		Very common
Rhabdoweisia fugax (Hedw.) Br. Eur.		Frequent
Cynodontium bruntonii (Sm.) Br. Eur.		Uncommon
Dichodontium pellucidum (Hedw.) Schimp.		Common
Dicranella palustris (Dicks.) Crund. ex Warb.	Moorland streams.	Frequent
D. schreberana (Hedw.) Dix.		Frequent
D. varia (Hedw.) Schimp.	Damp, heavy, basic soils	Uncommon
D. rufescens (With.) Schimp.		Frequent
D. staphylina Whitehouse		Uncommon
D. heteromalla (Hedw.) Schimp.		Common
Dicranoweisia cirrata (Hedw.) Lindb. ex Milde	Tree trunks and branches	Very common
Dicranum bonjeanii De Not.		Uncommon
D. scoparium Hedw.		Common
D. majus Sm.		Frequent
D. fuscescens Sm.		Uncommon
D. scottianum Turn.		Frequent
Campylopus fragilis (Brid.) Br. Eur.	Heathland	Uncommon
C. pyriformis (Schultz) Brid.		Common
C. introflexus (Hedw.) Brid.	Favours recently burnt areas	Frequent
C. paradoxus Wils.		Frequent
LEUCOBRYACEAE		
Leucobryum glaucum (Hedw.) Ångst.		Common
L. juniperoideum (Brid.) C. Müll.		Rare

Order: FISSIDENTALES

FISSIDENTACEAE - FERN-MOSS FAMILY

Fissidens pusillus (Wils.) Milde *(F. minutulus auct.)*		On rocks.	Uncommon
F. bryoides Hedw.	'Mungo Park's Moss'	Woods.	Common
F. curnovii Mitt.			Rare
F. rivularis (Spr.) Br. Eur.			Uncommon
F. celticus Paton			Frequent
F. osmundoides Hedw.	Single record.	Damp rocks.	Rare
F. taxifolius Hedw.			Common
F. cristatus Wils. ex Mitt.			Frequent
F. adianthoides Hedw.		Moorland bogs.	Frequent

LIVERWORTS & MOSSES

Order: ENCALYPTALES

ENCALYPTACEAE
Encalypta streptocarpa Hedw. — Uncommon

Order: POTTIALES

POTTIACEAE - SCREW-MOSS FAMILY

Tortula ruralis (Hedw.) Gaertn. ssp. ruralis		Uncommon
ssp. ruraliformis (Besch.) Dix.		Common on coastal sand dunes
T. intermedia (Brid.) De Not.		Uncommon
T. muralis Hedw. var. muralis	On walls	Common
var. aestiva Hedw.		Uncommon
T. cuneifolia (With.) Turn.		Uncommon
Aloina aloides (Schultz) Kindb. var. ambigua (Br.Eur.) Craig		Early records; none current
Pottia intermedia (Turn.) Fürnr.		Uncommon
P. truncata (Hedw.) Fürnr.		Common
P. heimii (Hedw.) Fürnr.	Salt marshes	Early records; none current
Phascum cuspidatum Hedw.		Frequent
Barbula convoluta Hedw.	Garden/cinder paths	Common
B. unguiculata Hedw.		Common
B. hornschuchiana Schultz		Uncommon
B. revoluta Brid.	Wall mortar	Uncommon
B. fallax (Hedw.)		Common
B. rigidula (Hedw.) Mitt.	Walls and rocks	Uncommon
B. nicholsonii Culm.	Lanes and driveways	Uncommon
B. trifaria (Hedw.) Mitt.	Walls and rocks	Uncommon
B. tophacea (Brid.) Mitt.		Uncommon
B. vinealis Brid.		Uncommon
B. cylindrica (Tayl.) Schimp.		Common
B. recurvirostra (Hedw.) Dix.		Uncommon
Eucladium verticillatum (Brid.) Br. Eur.	On damp mortar	Frequent
Weissia controversa Hedw. var controversa	Hedgebanks	Frequent
var. densifolia (Br. Eur.) Wils.		Rare
Oxystegus sinuosus (Mitt.) Hilp. *(Trichostomum sinuosum (Mitt.) C.Müll.)*		Uncommon
O. tenuirostris (Hook. & Tayl.) A.J.E.Smith var. tenuirostris		Rare
Trichostomum crispulum Bruch	Calcareous rocks.	Uncommon
T. brachydontium Bruch		Frequent
Tortella flavovirens (Bruch) Broth.		Rare

LIVERWORTS & MOSSES

Tortella nitida (Lindb.) Broth.		Rare
T. tortuosa (Hedw.) Limpr.		Frequent
Leptodontium flexifolium (With.) Hampe		Uncommon
Cinclidotus fontinaloides (Hedw.) P.Beauv.	In streams or lakes.	Uncommon

Order: GRIMMIALES

GRIMMIACEAE

Schistidium apocarpum (Hedw.) Br.Eur.		Uncommon
S. maritimum (Turn.) Br.Eur.		Rare
S. alpicola var. rivulare (Brid.) Limpr.		Frequent
Grimmia pulvinata (Hedw.) Sm.	On walls etc.	Common
G. trichophylla Grev.	var. trichophylla	Uncommon
	var. subsquarrosa (Wils.) Smith.	Uncommon
Racomitrium aciculare (Hedw.) Brid.		Common
R. aquaticum (Schrad.) Brid.		Uncommon
R. fasciculare (Hedw.) Brid.		Uncommon
R. heterostichum (Hedw.) Brid.	var. heterostichum	Frequent
	var. obtusum Frisvall	Uncommon
R. lanuginosum (Hedw.) Brid.		Common
R. canescens (Hedw.) Brid. var ericoides (Hedw.) Hampe		Rare

PTYCHOMITRIACEAE

Ptychomitrium polyphyllum (Sw.) Br. Eur.	Walls and rocks.	Uncommon

Order: FUNARIALES

FUNARIACEAE - CORD-MOSS FAMILY

Funaria hygrometrica Hedw.	On burnt patches.	Common

Order: SCHISTOSTEGALES

SCHISTOSTEGACEAE

Schistostega pennata (Hedw.) Web. & Mohr	LUMINOUS CAVE MOSS	Rare

Order: BRYALES

BRYACEAE - THREAD-MOSS FAMILY

Orthodontium lineare Schwaegr.	Peaty banks and rotting stumps	Frequent
Leptobryum pyriforme (Hedw.) Wils.		Uncommon

LIVERWORTS & MOSSES

Pohlia nutans (Hedw.) Lindb.		Uncommon
P. proligera (Kindb.ex Breidl.) Lindb.ex Arnell *(P. annotina (Hedw.emend Correns) Loeske)*		
		Uncommon
P. camptotrachela (Ren. & Card.) Broth.		Uncommon
P. lutescens (Limpr.) Lindb.		Uncommon
P. carnea (Schimp.) Lindb.		Frequent
P. wahlenbergii (Web. & Mohr) Andrews		Common
Epipterygium tozeri (Grev.) Lindb.	Shady banks	Uncommon
Bryum pallens var. pallens Sw.		Uncommon
B. donianum Grev.		Frequent
B. capillare Hedw.	Walls and tree trunks	Common
B. flaccidum Brid.		Uncommon
B. pseudotriquetrum (Hedw.) Schwaegr. agg.		Common
B. caespiticium Hedw. agg.		Uncommon
B. alpinum Huds. ex With.	Wet rocks, cliffs and quarries	Rare
B. bicolor Dicks.		Common
B. argenteum Hedw.	Tarmac roads	Common
B. radiculosum Brid.	Old mortar	Uncommon
B. violaceum Crundw. & Nyh.	Arable fields	Uncommon
B. sauteri Br.Eur.		Uncommon
B. microerythrocarpum C.Müll. & Kindb.		Uncommon
B. bornholmense Wink. & Ruthe	Sandy soil by the sea	Uncommon
B. rubens Mitt.		Common
Rhodobryum roseum (Hedw.) Limpr.		Uncommon

MNIACEAE

Mnium hornum Hedw.		Common
M. stellare Hedw.		Uncommon
Rhizomnium punctatum (Hedw.) Kop. *(Mnium p. Hedw.)*		Common
Plagiomnium cuspidatum (Hedw.) Kop. *(Mnium c. Hedw.)*		Early records; none current
P. affine (Funck) Kop. *(Mnium a. Funck)*		Uncommon
P. undulatum (Hedw.) Kop. *(Mnium u. Hedw.)*	Woodlands.	Frequent
P. rostratum (Schrad.) Kop. *(Mnium r. Schrad.)*		Frequent

AULACOMNIACEAE

Aulacomnium palustre (Hedw.) Schwaegr.	Boggy areas.	Common
A. androgynum (Hedw.) Schwaegr.		Uncommon

BARTRAMIACEAE - APPLE-MOSS FAMILY

Bartramia pomiformis Hedw.		Frequent
Philonotis caespitosa Wils.		Uncommon
P. fontana (Hedw.) Brid.	Springs, etc.	Common

LIVERWORTS & MOSSES

Philonotis tomentella Mol.		Rare
Breutelia chrysocoma (Hedw.) Lindb.		Rare

Order: ORTHOTRICHALES

ORTHOTRICHACEAE - BRISTLE-MOSS FAMILY

Amphidium mougeotii (Br. Eur.) Schimp.		Frequent
Zygodon viridissimus (Dicks.) R.Br. var. viridissimus	On rocks & trees.	Frequent
var. stirtonii (Schimp ex Stirt.) Hagen		Common
Z. baumgartneri Malta		Uncommon
Z. conoideus (Dicks.) Hook. & Tayl.		Uncommon
Orthotrichum striatum Hedw.	On trees.	Uncommon
O. lyellii Hook. & Tayl.	On trees.	Common
O. affine Brid.	On elders (Sambucus)	Common
O. rivulare Turn.		Frequent
O. anomalum Hedw.	Rocks and walls	Frequent
O. cupulatum Brid.		Frequent
O. diaphanum Brid.	Trees and wooden fences	Common
O. tenellum Bruch ex Brid.		Uncommon
O. pulchellum Brunt.		Uncommon
Ulota crispa (Hedw.) Brid. var. crispa	On trees	Common
var. norvegica (Grönvall) Smith & Hill		Common
U. phyllantha Brid.	Rocks and trees near coast	Uncommon

HEDWIGIACEAE

Hedwigia ciliata (Hedw.) P.Beauv.	Rocks and walls	Frequent

Order: ISOBRYALES

FONTINALACEAE - WILLOW-MOSS FAMILY

Fontinalis antipyretica Hedw.	Submerged in streams	Frequent
F. squamosa Hedw.	Submerged in streams	Uncommon

CLIMACIACEAE - TREE-MOSS FAMILY

Climacium dendroides (Hedw.) Web. & Mohr		Common

CRYPHAEACEAE

Cryphaea heteromalla (Hedw.) Mohr	On trees, particularly elder	Common

LEUCODONTACEAE

Leucodon sciuroides (Hedw.) Schwaegr.	On trees	Uncommon
Pterogonium gracile (Hedw.) Sm.		Rare

LIVERWORTS & MOSSES

NECKERACEAE

Leptodon smithii (Hedw.) Web. & Mohr		Occasional
Neckera pumila Hedw.	Woodlands.	Frequent
N. complanata (Hedw.) Hüb.		Common
Homalia trichomanoides (Hedw.) Br.Eur. *(Omalia t. auct.)*	Woodlands.	Frequent

THAMNIACEAE

Thamnobryum alopecurum (Hedw.) Nieuwl. *(Thamnium a. (Hedw.) Br.Eur.)*   Common

Order: HOOKERIALES

HOOKERIACEAE

Hookeria lucens (Hedw.) Sm.   Damp situations.   Common

Order: THUIDIALES

THUIDIACEAE. FEATHER-MOSS FAMILY

Heterocladium heteropterum (Br. ex Schw.) Br.Eur. var heteropterum		Common
	var. flaccidum Br.Eur.	Frequent
Anomodon viticulosus (Hedw.) Hook. & Tayl.		Frequent
Thuidium tamariscinum (Hedw.) Br.Eur.	Woods and hedgebanks	Common
T. delicatulum (Hedw.) Mitt.		Uncommon

Order: HYPNOBRYALES

AMBLYSTEGIACEAE

Cratoneuron filicinum (Hedw.) Spruce *(Amblystegium f. (Hedw.) De Not.)*		Common
C. commutatum (Hedw.) Roth.		Frequent
Campylium stellatum (Hedw.) J.Lange & C.Jens. *(Hypnum s. Hedw.)*		Uncommon
Amblystegium serpens (Hedw.) Br.Eur.		Common
A. fluviatile (Hedw.) Br.Eur.		Occasional
A. tenax (Hedw.) C.Jens.		Occasional
Drepanocladus fluitans (Hedw.) Warnst. *(Hypnum f. Hedw.)*	High acid ground.	Frequent
D. exannulatus (Br.Eur.) Warnst.	High ground.	Uncommon
D. revolvens (Sw.) Warnst.		Uncommon
D. uncinatus (Hedw.) Warnst.		Rare
Hygrohypnum ochraceum (Turn. ex Wils.) Loeske		Uncommon
Calliergon stramineum (Brid.) Kindb. *(Acrocladium s. (Brid.) Rich.&Wall.)*		Frequent
C. cordifolium (Hedw.) Kindb. *(Acrocladium c. (Hedw.) Rich.& Wall.)*		Uncommon
C. cuspidatum (Hedw.) Kindb. *(Acrocladium c. (Hedw.) Lindb.)*		Common

LIVERWORTS & MOSSES

BRACHYTHECIACEAE

Isothecium myurum Brid.	At the base of trees	Common
I. myosuroides Brid.	Oak woods.	Very common
I. holtii Kindb.		Rare
Homalothecium sericeum (Hedw.) Br.Eur. *(Camptothecium s. (Hedw.) Kindb.)*		Common
H. lutescens (Hedw.) Robins. *(Camptothecium l. (Hedw.) Br.Eur.)*		Uncommon
Brachythecium albicans (Hedw.) Br.Eur.		Uncommon
B. rutabulum (Hedw.) Br.Eur.		Very common
B. rivulare Br.Eur.		Frequent
B. velutinum (Hedw.) Br.Eur.		Frequent
B. populeum (Hedw.) Br.Eur.		Frequent
B. plumosum (Hedw.) Br.Eur.		Frequent
Pseudoscleropodium purum (Hedw.) Fleisch.	Acid grassland	Common
Scleropodium cespitans (C.Müll.) L.Koch		Uncommon
Cirriphyllum piliferum (Hedw.) Grout		Common
C. crassinervium (Tayl.) Loeske & Fleisch.		Frequent
Rhynchostegium riparioides (Hedw.) C.Jens. *(Eurhynchium r. (Hedw.) Rich.)*		Common
R. lusitanicum (Schimp.) A.J.E.Smith *(Eurhynchium alopecuroides (Brid.) Rich.&Wall.)*		
		Uncommon
R. murale (Hedw.) Br.Eur. *(Eurhynchium m. (Hedw.) Milde)*		Occasional
R. confertum (Dicks.) Br.Eur. *(Eurhynchium c. (Dicks.) Milde)*	Hedgerow elders	Common
Eurhynchium striatum (Hedw.) Schimp.	Woods	Common
E. pumilum (Wils.) Schimp.		Common
E. praelongum (Hedw.) Br.Eur. var praelongum		Common
var. stokesii (Turn.) Dix.		Common
E. swartzii (Turn.) Curn.		Common
E. speciosum (Brid.) Jur.		Uncommon
Rhynchostegiella tenella (Dicks.) Limpr.		Frequent
R. teesdalei (Br.Eur.) Limpr.		Uncommon

PLAGIOTHECIACEAE

Plagiothecium denticulatum (Hedw.) Br.Eur.		Common
P. curvifolium Schlieph.		Uncommon
P. succulentum (Wils.) Lindb.	Shaded banks	Common
P. nemorale (Mitt.) Jaeg. *(P. sylvaticum auct.)*		Common
P. undulatum (Hedw.) Br.Eur.		Common
Isopterygium elegans (Brid.) Lindb.		Common

HYPNACEAE

Hypnum cupressiforme Hedw.	var. cupressiforme	Common
	var. resupinatum (Tayl.) Schimp.	Common

LIVERWORTS & MOSSES

Hypnum cupressiforme Hedw. var. lacunosum Brid.		Frequent
H. mammillatum (Brid.) Loeske		Frequent
H. jutlandicum Holmen & Warncke		Common
Ctenidium molluscum (Hedw.) Mitt.		Frequent
Hyocomium armoricum (Brid.) Wijk & Marg. *(H. flagellare Br.Eur.)*	Waterfalls.	Uncommon
Rhytidiadelphus triquetrus (Hedw.) Warnst.		Common
R. squarrosus (Hedw.) Warnst.		Common
R. loreus (Hedw.) Warnst.		Common
Pleurozium schreberi (Brid.) Mitt.	Acid heaths.	Common
Hylocomium brevirostre (Brid.) Br.Eur.		Uncommon
H. splendens (Hedw.) Br.Eur.		Common

References:

Smith, A.J.E. *The Liverworts of Great Britain and Ireland* (1990) Cambridge University Press.

Smith, A.J.E. *The Moss Flora of Britain and Ireland* (1978) Cambridge University Press.

Watson, E.V. *British Mosses and Liverworts* (1968) Cambridge University Press.

Division: MICROPHYLLOPHYTA

Class: LYCOPODIOPSIDA (CLUBMOSSES)

Clubmosses have declined drastically on Exmoor in the last 50 years. The reason is uncertain; burning, picking and climate could have contributed, but it is possibly due to natural fluctuation on what is the extreme border of their distribution.

LYCOPODIACEAE

Huperzia selago (L.) Bernh. ex Schrank & C.Martius *(Lycopodium selago L.)*
FIR CLUBMOSS　　　　　　　　　　　　　　Very rare

Lycopodium clavatum L.　　　　STAG'S-HORN CLUBMOSS　　(formerly plentiful) Rare

(Lycopodiella inundata (L.) Holub MARSH CLUBMOSS - No records from Exmoor for over 100 years)

(Diphasiastrum alpinum (L.) Holub ALPINE CLUBMOSS - Recorded from Exmoor sites until 1920's)

SELAGINELLACEAE

Selaginella kraussiana (Kunze) A.Braun KRAUSS'S CLUBMOSS　　　　　　Very rare

Division: ARTHROPHYTA

Class: EQUISETOPSIDA (HORSETAILS)

Leafless, flowerless plants with jointed stems. Spores in cones which in some species are on separate, earlier stems.

EQUISETACEAE

Equisetum fluviatile L.	WATER HORSETAIL	Fairly common in wet areas
E. arvense L.	FIELD HORSETAIL	Common in dry areas
E. sylvaticum L.	WOOD HORSETAIL	Uncommon; damp shady places
E. palustre L.	MARSH HORSETAIL	Common in marshy/boggy areas
E. telmateia Ehrh.	GREAT HORSETAIL	Scarce, mainly around Selworthy

Division: PTEROPHYTA

Class: PTEROPSIDA (FERNS)

The fern flora of Exmoor is particularly good with luxuriant growth in many woodlands.

OPHIOGLOSSACEAE

Ophioglossum vulgatum L.   ADDER'S TONGUE   Rare; old upland pasture
Although very local in its distribution, in favourable years large numbers of plants may occur (as happened in 1991)

Botrychium lunaria (L.) Sw.   MOONWORT   Uncommon, similar areas to above

OSMUNDACEAE

Osmunda regalis L.   ROYAL FERN   Rare relics of introduction

ADIANTACEAE

(Cryptogramma crispa (L.) R.Br.ex Hook. PARSLEY FERN Recorded in small quantities on stone walls at Challacombe and Simonsbath in the mid 18-hundreds and on scree near Simonsbath in 1956. It continued at the latter station until the drought of 1976 but has not been seen on Exmoor since.)

Adiantum capillus-veneris L.   MAIDENHAIR FERN   Probably no truly wild stands
Old introductions persist in one or two places

HYMENOPHYLLACEAE

Hymenophyllum tunbrigense (L.) Smith TONBRIDGE FILMY-FERN   Very rare
The only recent records have been from Lynmouth and Porlock areas. There was a very old record at Martinhoe.

H. wilsonii Hook.   WILSON'S FILMY-FERN   (1 site, Devon)   Very rare

POLYPODIACEAE

Polypodium vulgare L.   POLYPODY   Common in woods and hedgerows often high up on trees, particularly oaks

P. interjectum Shivas   INTERMEDIATE POLYPODY   Uncommon

P. cambricum L.   SOUTHERN POLYPODY   Uncommon

DENNSTAEDTIACEAE

Pteridium aquilinum (L.) Kuhn   BRACKEN   Common and invasive

THELYPTERIDACEAE

Phegopteris connectilis (Michaux) Watt   BEECH FERN   Local
Known from a dozen sites on Exmoor, some with just a few plants, some with several hundred and one site contained thousands in 1993.

Oreopteris limbosperma (Bellardi ex All.) Holub   LEMON-SCENTED FERN Locally common
A typical fern by moorland streams.

ASPLENIACEAE

Phyllitis scolopendrium (L.) Newman HART'S-TONGUE Common and widespread but not on high moorland

FERNS

Asplenium adiantum-nigrum L.   BLACK SPLEENWORT Common except on high moors
  (A. obovatum ssp. lanceolatum (Fiori) P.da S. LANCEOLATE SPLEENWORT. Herbarium specimens in Exeter & Taunton Museums from Lynmouth & Selworthy, from mid 1800's.)
A. marinum L.   SEA SPLEENWORT   Uncommon, in clefts in sea-cliffs
A. trichomanes L.   MAIDENHAIR SPLEENWORT   Common, widespread
A. ruta-muraria L. WALL RUE   Common on east Exmoor; absent from central moorland
  (A. septentrionale (L.) Hoffm.   FORKED SPLEENWORT. Believed extinct on Exmoor since 1939)
Ceterach officinarum Willd.   RUSTYBACK   Frequent around villages on walls

WOODSIACEAE

Athyrium filix-femina (L.) Roth   LADY FERN   Widespread; common
Gymnocarpium dryopteris (L.) Newman   OAK FERN   Very rare
  Formerly occurred in Devon and Somerset but long gone from the Devon sites.
G. robertianum (Hoffm.) Newman   LIMESTONE FERN   Somerset only.   Very rare
Cystopteris fragilis (L.) Bernh.   BRITTLE BLADDER-FERN   Rare

DRYOPTERIDACEAE

Polystichum setiferum (Forsskål) Moor ex Woynar SOFT SHIELD-FERN   Common in woods and hedgerows on the lower ground, virtually absent above 1000 ft.
P. aculeatum (L.) Roth   HARD SHIELD-FERN   Uncommon
Cyrtomium falcatum (L.f) Presl   HOUSE HOLLY-FERN (FISH-TAIL FERN)
                               Only known in one site, on the walls of a ruined house
Dryopteris filix-mas (L.) Schott   MALE-FERN   Common
D. affinis (Lowe) Fraser-Jenkins   SCALY MALE-FERN   Common
                                                 Fronds often up to 4/5 ft.
D. aemula (Aiton) Kuntze   HAY-SCENTED BUCKLER-FERN   Uncommon
  Mainly in a band running S.E. from Porlock to Luxborough, plus a few sites in Devon.
D. carthusiana (Villars) H.P.Fuchs   NARROW BUCKLER-FERN   Rare
D. dilatata (Hoffm.) A.Gray   BROAD BUCKLER-FERN   Common

BLECHNACEAE

Blechnum spicant (L.) Roth   HARD-FERN   Common on high acid ground
B. cordatum (Desv.) Hieron. CHILEAN HARD-FERN   Rare garden escape

AZOLLACEAE

Azolla filiculoides Lam.   WATER FERN   Rare (Minehead marshes only)
  This small un-fernlike plant floats on the surface of still water. Turns red after frost.

Division: CONIFEROPHYTA (CONIFERS)

Class: PINOPSIDA

The list of coniferous trees was prepared for the first edition of the *Flora & Fauna* by ENHS member Cecil Owen, who writes: 'traditionally only three species have been regarded as British native plants, but many other species have been introduced as forestry crops or for parkland and garden ornament and now form a conspicuous part of the landscape. Species that are recorded here include only those that are readily observed in public places' and are included in *List of Vascular Plants of the British Isles* Kent, 1992. Most of these can be found self-seeded on Exmoor, where, since 1920 about 10,000 acres have been planted with conifers. This area is representative of around half of Exmoor's woodlands.
The list which follows is based on Cecil Owen's former list, realigned to conform to the nomenclature in D.H. Kent's *List*.

PINACEAE

Abies alba Miller — EUROPEAN SILVER FIR — Planted as a specimen tree

A. grandis (Douglas ex D.Don) Lindley GIANT FIR — Small forestry plantings Fine specimens at Combe Sydenham

A. procera Rehder — NOBLE FIR — Small forestry plantings

Pseudotsuga menziesii (Mirbel) Franco DOUGLAS FIR — Moderate forestry policies Noted British record specimens at Broadwood, Dunster. Many seedlings.

Tsuga heterophylla (Raf.) Sarg. — WESTERN HEMLOCK — Moderate forestry policies

Picea sitchensis (Bong.) Carrière — SITKA SPRUCE — The most widely planted forestry tree

P. abies (L.) Karsten — NORWAY SPRUCE — Extensive forestry policies

Larix decidua Miller — EUROPEAN LARCH — Frequently planted
Old introductions fit into our landscape and may look like native trees.

L. decidua x L. kaempferi = L. x marschlinsii Coaz *(L. x eurolepis Henry)*
DUNKELD LARCH — Fairly common

L. kaempferi (Lindley) Carrière — JAPANESE LARCH — Commonly planted

Cedrus deodara (Roxb. ex D.Don) Don DEODAR — Rare parkland specimen tree

C. atlantica (Endl.) Carrière — ATLAS CEDAR — Rare parkland specimen tree

Pinus sylvestris L. — SCOTS PINE — Common
Like the European Larch, this tree looks fully at home on Exmoor, and pollen analysis has shown that this species was once native in southern England. However, as stated by Capt. R.G.B. Roe in *Flora of Somerset* it is highly unlikely that any descendants of the original forests survive in Somerset. Scots Pines have been planted for at least 300 years and it is probable that present trees are derived from planted ones.

P. nigra Arnold subsp. nigra — AUSTRIAN BLACK PINE — Rare; not a forestry tree

subsp. laricio Maire CORSICAN PINE — A common forestry tree

P. contorta Douglas ex Loudon — LODGEPOLE PINE — Moderate forestry policies

P. radiata D.Don — MONTEREY PINE — Common in small forestry plantings

CONIFERS

CUPRESSACEAE

Cupressus macrocarpa Hartweg ex Gordon MONTEREY CYPRESS		Widely planted as a shelter belt tree.
Chamaecyparis lawsoniana (A.Murray) Parl. LAWSON'S CYPRESS		Commonly planted
C. pisifera (Siebold & Zucc.) Siebold & Zucc. SARAWA CYPRESS		Less common
Thuja plicata Donn ex D.Don	WESTERN RED CEDAR	A common shelter belt tree
Juniperus communis L.	JUNIPER	Rare

TAXACEAE

Taxus baccata L. YEW Widely planted in churchyards
  Self-seeded and bird sown specimens occur frequently. Very well naturalized on sea-cliffs between Woody Bay and Hunters Inn.

There are also a number of conifers which may occasionally be seen on Exmoor, planted as either landscape or specimen trees, but they are not considered to be setting seed and naturalizing. These include: Ginko biloba L. MAIDENHAIR TREE; Cephalotaxus fortuni Hooker CHINESE PLUM YEW; Araucaria araucana Koch CHILEAN PINE or MONKEY PUZZLE; Calocedrus decurrens Florin INCENSE CEDAR; x Cupressocyparis leylandii Dallimore LEYLAND CYPRESS; Cryptomeria japonica Don. JAPANESE CEDAR; Metasequoia glyptostroboides Hu Cheng DAWN REDWOOD; Sequoia sempervirens Endlicher COAST REDWOOD; Sequoiadendron giganteum Buchholz WELLINGTONIA; Abies cephalonica Loudon GRECIAN FIR; Cedrus libani Richard CEDAR OF LEBANON; Pinus ayacahuite Erhenberg MEXICAN WHITE PINE.

FLOWERING PLANTS

The first edition of this *Flora & Fauna* listed 945 flowering plants recorded by the Exmoor Natural History Society 1974-88. Since then, the number has risen to 1187. A small number (c25) of the listed species have been found only in the Minehead/Dunster Beach area, or just outside the designated National Park boundary. Mention has been made in the list where this is the case. All other species have been found within Exmoor National Park. The plants occur in both V.C.4 (Devon) and V.C.5 (Somerset) unless otherwise stated.

Of this total of over a thousand flowering plants on Exmoor, about 70 per cent are native or fully naturalized species, the remainder being made up of casuals, garden escapes or throw-outs, aliens or introductions. It is important to remember that all comments refer to Exmoor area as above and the **STATUS** given applies to this area only, thus a plant listed as 'common' may be scarce nationally, and *vice versa*. 'In the north means northern Exmoor not northern England and 'not in Devon' means the Devon section of Exmoor, not Devon as a whole. Nationally scarce plants are prefixed ¶ and Red Data Book species indicated **RDB**.

We are fortunate that Exmoor has many contrasting **HABITATS**, which result in such a variety of species. The moorland may be divided into grass moor, in the west, (approx. 20,000 acres, including about 140 acres of deergrass moor), and the heather moors, in the east (also approx. 20,000 acres). The northern boundary contains some 4500 acres of coastal heath, a very precious commodity as this colourful mixture of heathers, western gorse and bent grasses as found on Exmoor and the Quantocks is scarce world wide. Virtually all of the moorland areas are 1000 ft. or over in altitude. In the south-east, the Brendon Hills are predominantly farmland but have great botanical interest in their miles of hedgerows and around Wimbleball Lake. A network of river valleys provides boggy areas and marshes wherein grow such gems as the butterworts and sundews. There are some of the largest areas of ancient sessile oak woodlands in England, particularly around Horner in Somerset and the Lyn valleys in Devon. Gardens give rise to a great variety of plants: a survey conducted by the ENHS in 1985 produced a total of 302 garden weed species, and the approaches to villages have remnants of herbs formerly introduced for medicinal purposes e.g. Feverfew and Alkanet. Lastly, our lovely sea coast gives us a colourful cliff flora and a small number of saltmarsh and dune plants. Interspersed amongst these main habitats are small pockets providing happy hunting grounds for those interested in wild flowers: a patch of ancient grassland in water meadow or churchyard, old quarries, mine workings, lime kilns, wasteground, even car parks can prove fruitful. But we must beware of becoming complacent. Over the last 50 years an average of one species every two years has disappeared from our area and although the total continues to go up, the new records are usually alien species which may ramp and swamp our precious native flora. Such species as Rhododendron and Knotweeds immediately spring to mind and the recent mild winters have resulted in an ominous spread of Winter Heliotrope which is causing ugly blotches in an alarming number of our hedgerows. Several species occur in very small quantity and hang on only because of special protection given by National Park Authorities, the National Trust or a private individual.

NOMENCLATURE and **CLASSIFICATION** in this check-list follows D.H. Kent *List of Vascular Plants of the British Isles* (1992); **ENGLISH NAMES** are according to *English Names of Wild Flowers* 2nd Edn. Dony, Jury & Perring (1986) and *New Flora of the British Isles* Clive Stace (1991). The advent of Kent's *List* which supercedes that of J.E. Dandy means that many more alien plants are now considered established in Britain and are therefore included in this check-list. **THANKS** are due to all members of the Exmoor Natural History Society who have submitted plant records over the years, and particularly to Paul and Ian Green, Recorders for the County of Somerset.

Caroline Giddens, Botanical Recorder, E.N.H.S.

Division: ANTHOPHYTA
Sub-Division: ANGIOSPERMAE
(FLOWERING PLANTS)

Class: MAGNOLIOPSIDA (DICOTYLEDONS)
Sub-Class: MAGNOLIIDAE

LAURACEAE
Laurus nobilis L.   BAY   Garden escape, often bird-sown
NYMPHAEACEAE
Nymphaea alba L. subsp.alba   WHITE WATER LILY   Uncommon introduction
RANUNCULACEAE
Caltha palustris L.   MARSH MARIGOLD, KINGCUP   Fairly frequent
    Some reduction in quantity due to drainage of meadows etc.
Helleborus foetidus L.   STINKING HELLEBORE   Occasional garden escape
H. viridis L. subsp. occidentalis (Reuter) Schiffner
                               GREEN HELLEBORE   Rare, shady places
H. orientalis Lam.   LENTEN ROSE   Garden escape or throw-out
Nigella damascena L.   LOVE-IN-A-MIST   Garden escape
Aconitum napellus L. subsp. vulgare (DC) Rouy & Fouc. MONKSHOOD   Garden escape
A. vulparia Reichb.   WOLF'S-BANE   Uncommon garden escape; Somerset
Anemone nemorosa L.   WOOD ANEMONE   Locally plentiful in old woodlands
A. apennina L.   BLUE ANEMONE   Garden escape which may persist; Som.
A. x hybrida Paxton   JAPANESE ANEMONE   Uncommon garden escape
Clematis vitalba L.   TRAVELLER'S JOY   Common in hedgerows
    mainly in the Porlock-Minehead-Brendon Hills area
Ranunculus acris L.   MEADOW BUTTERCUP   Common throughout
R. repens L.   CREEPING BUTTERCUP   Common throughout
R. bulbosus L.   BULBOUS BUTTERCUP   Common
R. sardous Crantz   HAIRY BUTTERCUP   Rare; Somerset
R. parviflorus L.   SMALL-FLOWERED BUTTERCUP   Uncommon
R. auricomus L.   GOLDILOCKS BUTTERCUP   Uncommon; damp woods
R. sceleratus L. CELERY-LEAVED BUTTERCUP Uncommon, mainly on marshes near coast
R. flammula L. subsp. flammula LESSER SPEARWORT   Common, boggy areas
R. ficaria L. subsp. ficaria   LESSER CELANDINE   Common throughout
R. hederaceus L.   IVY-LEAVED CROWFOOT   Fairly frequent on moors
R. omiophyllus Ten.   MOORLAND CROWFOOT   The commonest moorland crowfoot
¶R. baudotii Godron   BRACKISH WATER-CROWFOOT Rare Minehead Marsh

FLOWERING PLANTS

Ranunculus aquatilis L. COMMON WATER-CROWFOOT Rare
R. peltatus Schrank POND WATER-CROWFOOT Rare
R. penicillatus(Dum.)Bab. ssp.penicillatus RIVER WATER-CROWFOOT Common in R. Barle
subsp. pseudofluitans (Syme) S.Webster STREAM WATER-CROWFOOT Local
Aquilegia vulgaris L. COLUMBINE It is doubtful whether the true wild form occurs in the Exmoor area. There are frequent garden escapes
Thalictrum flavum L. COMMON MEADOW-RUE Uncommon garden escape
A native species on Sedgemoor and in the Clyst Valley in Devon
T. minus L. LESSER MEADOW-RUE Uncommon garden escape

BERBERIDACEAE

Berberis vulgaris L. BARBERRY Rare, in hedgerows
B. glaucocarpa Stapf GREAT BARBERRY A frequent hedgerow introduction in the Porlock Vale area. Rare or absent elsewhere
B. darwinii Hook. DARWIN'S BARBERRY Bird-sown from gardens
B. stenophylla Lindley HEDGE BARBERRY Introductions may self-sow
Mahonia aquifolium (Pursh) Nutt. OREGON-GRAPE Uncommon garden escape

PAPAVERACEAE

Papaver somniferum subsp. somniferum L. OPIUM POPPY A frequent escape on wasteland
P. rhoeas L. COMMON POPPY Still frequent on arable land and waysides in the eastern part of Exmoor area
P. dubium L. subsp. dubium LONG-HEADED POPPY Rare, in waste places
subsp. lecoqii (Lamotte) Syme YELLOW-JUICED POPPY Rare
¶Meconopsis cambrica (L.) Viguier WELSH POPPY Frequent in woodlands and shady banks. An orange, as well as the usual yellow form occurs on the Brendons
Glaucium flavum Crantz YELLOW HORNED-POPPY A few places on the coast
Chelidonium majus L. GREATER CELANDINE Scattered around villages
Eschscholzia californica Cham. CALIFORNIAN POPPY Garden escape

FUMARIACEAE

Dicentra formosa (Andrews) Walp. BLEEDING-HEART Old introduction, naturalized in woodland near Simonsbath
Pseudofumaria lutea (L.) Borkh. YELLOW CORYDALIS Walls near houses; naturalized
Ceratocapnos claviculata (L.) Lidén CLIMBING CORYDALIS Frequent on forestry rides
¶Fumaria capreolata subsp. capreolata L. WHITE RAMPING-FUMITORY Common
In Minehead-Porlock area, rare elsewhere
¶F. bastardii Boreau TALL RAMPING-FUMITORY Local
Fairly frequent in Minehead-Porlock area; few other records; none from Devon
F. muralis subsp. boraei (Jordan) Pugsley COMMON RAMPING-FUMITORY Common
In hedgebanks and farmland, mainly coastal and western region; not on the moors
F. officinalis L. subsp. officinalis COMMON FUMITORY Uncommon, in arable land

PLATANACEAE

P. x hispanica Miller ex Muenchh. LONDON PLANE TREE Rare introduction. Somerset

FLOWERING PLANTS

ULMACEAE

Ulmus glabra subsp. glabra Hudson   WYCH ELM   Fairly common in old woodland

U. procera Salisb.   ENGLISH ELM   Common in hedgerows
The majestic trees which once graced such areas as the Porlock Vale and provided high nest-sites for rooks have all succombed to Dutch Elm disease since 1970. Somerset was one of the first counties in England to be struck, possibly via Bristol Docks.

CANNABACEAE

Humulus lupulus L.   HOP   Fairly common in hedgerows near villages

MORACEAE

Ficus carica L.   FIG   Rarely bird-sown from cultivated trees; Somerset

URTICACEAE

Urtica dioica L.   COMMON NETTLE   Abundant
An important food source for certain butterfly larvae.

U. urens L.   SMALL (or ANNUAL) NETTLE   Fairly frequent in the northern part of Exmoor

Parietaria judaica L.   PELLITORY-OF-THE-WALL   Frequent around villages in the northern part of Exmoor

Soleirolia soleirolii (Req.) Dandy   MIND-YOUR-OWN-BUSINESS   Introduced, now a common weed in the Minehead - Porlock areas

JUGLANDACEAE

Juglans regia L.   WALNUT   A frequent introductiion around villages

MYRICACEAE

Myrica gale L.   BOG-MYRTLE   A very small amount in one site near Wimbleball, its source unknown. Native on Sedgemoor.

FAGACEAE

Fagus sylvatica L.   BEECH   Common in hedgerows and woodlands
The traditional hedging material on Exmoor hill farms.

Nothofagus obliqua (Mirbel) Blume   ROBLE   Introduction; may self-seed

Castanea sativa Miller   SWEET CHESTNUT   Common, except on the moors

Quercus castaneifolia C.Meyer   CHESTNUT-LEAVED OAK   Uncommon introduction

Q. cerris L.   TURKEY OAK   Rather uncommon introduction

Q. ilex L.   EVERGREEN (or HOLM) OAK   Frequent in northern Exmoor, notably at Selworthy where there is a pure stand planted mid 1800's. Seeds.

Q. petraea (Mattuschka) Liebl.   SESSILE OAK   The common oak of Exmoor woodlands

Q. robur L.   PEDUNCULATE (or ENGLISH) OAK   Common
Large standard trees in field and hedgerow are usually this species.

Q. rubra L.   RED OAK   Introduction, may self-seed

BETULACEAE

Betula pendula Roth   SILVER BIRCH   Frequent but often confused with next

B. pubescens subsp. pubescens Ehrh.   DOWNY BIRCH   The common native birch on Exmoor

Alnus glutinosa (L.) Gaertner   ALDER   Common in damp places

A. incana (L.) Moench   GREY ALDER   Introduction

FLOWERING PLANTS

Carpinus betulus L. HORNBEAM Occasional in hedges, few mature trees No Devon records
Corylus avellana L. HAZEL Common except on highest moorland

PHYTOLACCACEAE

Phytolacca americana L. AMERICAN POKEWEED Very rare casual; Somerset
P. acinosa Roxb. INDIAN POKEWEED Very rare casual; Somerset

CHENOPODIACEAE

Chenopodium bonus-henricus L. GOOD-KING-HENRY No Exmoor records since 1973
C. rubrum L. RED GOOSEFOOT Scarce
C. polyspermum L. MANY-SEEDED GOOSEFOOT Fairly frequent in arable ground in Somerset Exmoor. No Devon records.
C. murale L. NETTLE-LEAVED GOOSEFOOT Rare; Somerset
C. ficifolium Smith FIG-LEAVED GOOSEFOOT Rare; Somerset
C. album L. FAT-HEN Common in arable land
Atriplex prostrata Boucher ex DC. SPEAR-LEAVED ORACHE Frequent in cultivated land
A. glabriuscula Edmondston BABINGTON'S ORACHE Rare; coastal shingle
A. patula L. COMMON ORACHE Fairly frequent in waste ground
A. portulacoides L.*(Halimione p. (L.) Aell.)* SEA-PURSLANE Very local; Porlock Weir,Som.
Beta vulgaris subsp. maritima (L.) Arcang. SEA BEET On or near the coast
  subsp. vulgaris L. Garden BEETROOT or agricultural MANGELS may occur as throw-outs
  subsp. cicla (L.) Arcang. SPINACH BEET Rare casual
Salicornia ramosissima J.Woods PURPLE (or PROCUMBENT) GLASSWORT Rare; Som.
S. pusilla x ramosissima Rare and very local in saltmarsh
S. europaea L. COMMON GLASSWORT Rare, saltmarshes, Som.
Suaeda maritima (L.) Dumort. ANNUAL SEA-BLITE Rare, saltmarshes, Somerset
Salsola kali subsp. kali L. PRICKLY SALTWORT Very rare,coastal sand, Dunster

AMARANTHACEAE

Amaranthus retroflexus L. COMMON AMARANTH A rare casual in waste places

PORTULACACEAE

Claytonia perfoliata Donn ex Willd. SPRINGBEAUTY Sandy places near coast; Somerset
C. sibirica L. PINK PURSLANE Damp woodlands/streamsides
  Mainly in southern part of Exmoor, sometimes introduced in villages
Montia fontana subsp. amporitana Sennen BLINKS Common in moorland springs & bogs
  subsp. minor Hayw. In drier sandy places

CARYOPHYLLACEAE

Arenaria serpyllifolia subsp. serpyllifolia L. THYME-LEAVED SANDWORT Uncommon
  subsp. leptoclados (Reichb.) Nyman SLENDER SANDWORT Rare
A. balearica L. MOSSY SANDWORT Rare introduction naturalised on walls; Somerset
Moehringia trinervia (L.) Clairv. THREE-NERVED SANDWORT Frequent in hedgebanks
Stellaria nemorum subsp. nemorum L. WOOD STITCHWORT Very rare, Devon

FLOWERING PLANTS

Stellaria media (L.) Villars	COMMON CHICKWEED	Very common
S. pallida (Dumort.) Crépin	LESSER CHICKWEED	Uncommon; near the coast
Stellaria neglecta Weihe	GREATER CHICKWEED	Common but not on high moor
S. holostea L.	GREATER STITCHWORT	Common
S. graminea L.	LESSER STITCHWORT	Common
S. uliginosa Murray	BOG STITCHWORT	Common in wet places
Cerastium arvense L.	FIELD MOUSE-EAR	Very rare, Minehead area
C. tomentosum L.	SNOW-IN-SUMMER	Garden escapes
C. fontanum subsp. vulgare (Hartman) Gr. & Bur.	COMMON MOUSE-EAR	Very common
C. glomeratum Thuill.	STICKY MOUSE-EAR	Very common
C. diffusum Pers.	SEA MOUSE-EAR	Local, on the coast
C. semidecandrum L.	LITTLE MOUSE-EAR	Uncommon, near the coast
Myosoton aquaticum (L.) Moench	WATER CHICKWEED	Rare
¶Moenchia erecta (L.) Gaertner,Meyer & Scherb.	UPRIGHT CHICKWEED	Very local in turf
Sagina subulata (Sw.) C.Presl	HEATH PEARLWORT	Locally common on the moors
S. procumbens L.	PROCUMBENT PEARLWORT	Very common
S. apetala Ard.	ANNUAL PEARLWORT	Fairly frequent
S. maritima G.Don	SEA PEARLWORT	A few places on the coast

(Scleranthus annuus L. ANNUAL KNAWEL Coastal fields in 1960's but no recent records)

Spergula arvensis L.	CORN SPURREY	A frequent arable weed
Spergularia rupicola Lebel ex Le Jolis	ROCK SPURREY	In a few places on coastal cliffs
S. media (L.) C.Presl	GREATER SEA SPURREY	Local on coastal mud
S. marina (L.) Griseb.	LESSER SEA SPURREY	As above but rather less
S. rubra (L.) J.S.Presl & C.Presl	SAND (or RED) SPURREY	Frequent in dry places
Lychnis coronaria (L.) Murray	ROSE CAMPION	Naturalised garden escape
L. flos-cuculi L.	RAGGED ROBIN	Local in damp fields and rushy moorland

(Agrostemma githago L. CORNCOCKLE. Although there are very old records from Combe Martin, Lynton, Parracombe, Minehead, Bossington, etc., this plant has not been seen in its traditional cornfield situation for many years. About 1993 there were attempts to reintroduce it in the Minehead/Blue Anchor areas by sowing it on road verges with a mixture of other cornfield weeds, but it is not thought to have become established.)

Silene vulgaris Garcke	BLADDER CAMPION	Rather uncommon and decreasing
S. uniflora Roth*(S.maritima)*	SEA CAMPION	Fairly common along the coast
S. latifolia Poiret subsp. alba	WHITE CAMPION	Fairly frequent on the lower ground
S. x hampeana Meusel & K.Werner	PINK CAMPION	Frequent hybrid of Red/White Campion
S. dioica (L.) Clairv.	RED CAMPION	Very common especially in hedgerows
S. gallica L.	SMALL-FLOWERED CATCHFLY	Rare in arable land
S. conica L.	SAND CATCHFLY **RDB**.	Rare. Sandy areas; Somerset
Saponaria officinalis L.	SOAPWORT	A few places generally near the coast

FLOWERING PLANTS

Dianthus barbatus L.	SWEET WILLIAM	Occasional garden escape
¶D. armeria L.	DEPTFORD PINK	Very rare. Somerset. Seen 1983 & 1988

POLYGONACEAE

Persicaria campanulata (J.D.Hook) Ronse Decraene
(Polygonum campanulatum)   LESSER KNOTWEED   Not very common as yet

P. wallichii Greut.&Burdet   HIMALAYAN KNOTWEED   Becoming increasingly common
(Polygonum polystachyum) Rampant in some areas e.g. Heddon's Mouth and near Simonsbath

P. bistorta (L.) Samp. *(Polygonum bistorta)* COMMON BISTORT   Fairly frequent

P. amplexicaulis (D.Don) Ronse Decraene *(Polygonum amplexicaule)*
                      RED BISTORT   Uncommon garden throw-out

P. amphibia (L.) Gray *(Polygonum amphibium L.)*
                      AMPHIBIOUS BISTORT   Rather uncommon

P. maculosa Gray *(Polygonum persicaria L.)*   REDSHANK   Common and widespread

P. lapathifolia (L.) Gray *(Polygonum lapathifolium L.)*
                      PALE PERSICARIA   Uncommon, in cultivated land

P. hydropiper (L.) Spach *(Polygonum hydropiper)*
                      WATER-PEPPER   Common in damp areas

Fagopyrum esculentum Moench   BUCKWHEAT   Casual in waste places or gardens

Polygonum arenastrum Boreau   EQUAL-LEAVED KNOTGRASS   Fairly common

P. aviculare L.   KNOTGRASS   Very common

Fallopia japonica (Houtt.) Ronse Decraene *(Reynoutria j.; Polygonum cuspidatum)*
                      JAPANESE KNOTWEED   Common, sometimes abundant

F. x bohemica (Chrtek & Chrtková) J.Bailey   HYBRID KNOTWEED   Rare; Somerset

F. sachalinensis (F.Schmidt ex Maxim.) Ronse Decraene *(Polygonum sachalinense; Reynoutria sachalinensis)*   GIANT KNOTWEED   Uncommon as yet, may increase

F. baldschuanica (Regel) Holub   *(Polygonum baldshuanicum; Fallopia aubertii)*
                      RUSSIAN-VINE   Uncommon escape but locally abundant

F. convolvulus (L.) Á. Löve *(Polygonum convolvulus; Reynoutria convolvulus)*
                      BLACK-BINDWEED   Frequent in arable land

Rumex acetosella subsp. acetosella L.	SHEEP'S SORREL	Very common
R. acetosa subsp. acetosa L.	COMMON SORREL	Very common
R. hydrolapathum Hudson	WATER DOCK	Rare
R. cristatus DC.	GREEK DOCK	Rare but increasing in Minehead area
R.x dimidiatus Hausskn.	(Greek x Curled Dock)	Rare, Minehead area
R.x lousleyi D.H.Kent	(Greek x Broad-leaved Dock)	Rare, Minehead area
R. crispus subsp. crispus L.	CURLED DOCK	Fairly common except on moors
R.x schulzei Hausskn.	(Curled x Clustered Dock)	Uncommon
R.x sagorskii Hausskn.	(Curled x Wood Dock)	Uncommon
R.x pseudopulcher Hausskn.	(Curled x Fiddle Dock)	Uncommon
R.x pratensis Mert.& Koch	(Curled x Broad-leaved Dock)	Uncommon
R.x heteranthos Borbás	(Curled x Marsh Dock)	Rare
R. conglomeratus Murray	CLUSTERED DOCK	Rather uncommon; surrounds moorland

FLOWERING PLANTS

Rumex sanguineus L.	WOOD DOCK	Common except on open moorland
R.x mixtus Lambert	(Wood x Fiddle Dock)	Rare
R.x dufftii Hausskn.	(Wood x Broad-leaved Dock)	Uncommon
R. pulcher L.	FIDDLE DOCK	Uncommon, mainly near the coast
R. obtusifolius L.	BROAD-LEAVED DOCK	Very common
Rumex maritimus L.	GOLDEN DOCK	Rare; Somerset

We record our thanks to Ian Green for reports of the hybrid dock species listed above.

PLUMBAGINACEAE
Armeria maritima (Miller) Willd. THRIFT   Common on coastal cliffs and shingle

CLUSIACEAE

Hypericum calycinum L.	ROSE-OF-SHARON	Fairly common garden escape
H. androsaemum L.	TUTSAN	Common garden escape
H.x inodorum Miller	TALL TUTSAN	Garden escape
H.x hircinum L.	STINKING TUTSAN	Garden escape
H. perforatum L.	PERFORATE ST. JOHN'S-WORT	Fairly common
H. tetrapterum Fries	SQUARE-STALKED ST. JOHN'S-WORT	Frequent
H. humifusum L.	TRAILING ST. JOHN'S-WORT	Frequent, dry waysides
H. pulchrum L.	SLENDER ST. JOHN'S-WORT	Common
H. hirsutum L.	HAIRY ST. JOHN'S-WORT	Rare calcicole. Somerset
H. elodes L.	MARSH ST. JOHN'S-WORT	Frequent in moorland bogs

TILIACEAE

Tilia platyphyllos Scop.	LARGE-LEAVED LIME	Introductions only. Somerset
T. x vulgaris Hayne	LIME	Introductions only, some quite old

MALVACEAE

Malva moschata L.	MUSK-MALLOW	Fairly common on non-acid soils
M. sylvestris L.	COMMON MALLOW	Common in E.of area, otherwise rare
M. neglecta Wallr.	DWARF MALLOW	Uncommon; Porlock/Minehead area
Lavatera arborea L.	TREE MALLOW	A few places on the coast
L. thuringiaca L. *(L. olbia)*	HYERES TREE-MALLOW	Garden throw-out; Somerset
Alcea rosea L.	HOLLYHOCK	Garden escape or throw-out

DROSERACEAE
Drosera rotundifolia L.   ROUND-LEAVED SUNDEW   Common in moorland bogs

VIOLACEAE
Viola odorata L.   SWEET VIOLET   Common in hedges on the lower ground
   Purple and white flowered plants occur; the white are sometimes locally abundant.

V. riviniana Reichb.	COMMON DOG-VIOLET	Common throughout
V. reichenbachiana Jordan ex Boreau	EARLY (or WOOD) DOG-VIOLET	Common, in shade
V. canina L. subsp. canina	HEATH DOG-VIOLET	Uncommon, dry heaths
V. palustris L. subsp. palustris	MARSH VIOLET	Common; moorland bogs away from coast

FLOWERING PLANTS

Viola lutea Hudson	MOUNTAIN PANSY	Rare; Somerset

Rediscovered on Exmoor in 1990 by Somerset Atlas Flora Project. (Brendon Hills)

V.x wittrockiana Gams ex Kappert	GARDEN PANSY	Garden escapes and throw-outs
V. tricolor L. subsp. tricolor	WILD PANSY	Rare; Somerset
V. arvensis Murray	FIELD PANSY	Common in arable fields in the east of area

TAMARICACEAE

Tamarix gallica L.	TAMARISK	Uncommon on Coast; Somerset

SALICACEAE

Populus alba L.	WHITE POPLAR	Rather uncommon
P.x canescens (Aiton) Smith	GREY POPLAR	Rare; Somerset
P. tremula L.	ASPEN	Rather uncommon
P. nigra L. subsp. betulifolia	BLACK POPLAR	A nationally protected tree. Local
P.x canadensis Moench	HYBRID BLACK POPLAR	Uncommon introduction
P. candicans Aiton	BALM-OF-GILEAD	Rare introduction; Somerset
Salix fragilis L.	CRACK WILLOW	Uncommon, mostly introductions
S. alba L.	WHITE WILLOW	Uncommon
S. purpurea L.	PURPLE WILLOW	Very rare, Dunster area only
S. x forbyana Smith	FINE OSIER	Rare
S. viminalis L.	OSIER	Fairly common in lowland marshes
S. x sericans Tausch ex A.Kerner	BROAD-LEAVED OSIER	. Uncommon
S. x smithiana Willd.	SILKY-LEAVED OSIER	Uncommon
S. caprea L. subsp. caprea	GOAT WILLOW	Very common
S. x reichardtii A.Kerner	GOAT X GREY WILLOW	Fairly common
S. cinerea L. subsp. oleifolia	GREY WILLOW	Very common
S. x multinervis Doell	GREY X EARED WILLOW	Uncommon
S. aurita L.	EARED WILLOW	Common on high ground
S. repens L.	CREEPING WILLOW	Uncommon or rare

BRASSICACEAE

Sisymbrium orientale L.	EASTERN ROCKET	Rare, coast near Minehead
S. officinale (L.) Scop.	HEDGE MUSTARD	Common in waste places etc.
Descurainia sophia (L.) Webb ex Prantl	FLIXWEED	Recorded mid 1980's; Somerset
Alliaria petiolata (Bieb.) Cavara & Grande	GARLIC MUSTARD	Common in hedgerows, etc
Arabidopsis thaliana (L.) Heynh.	THALE CRESS	Fairly common, waste places
Erysimum cheiranthoides L.	TREACLE MUSTARD	Rare, cultivated ground
E. cheiri (L.) Crantz. *(Cheiranthus cheiri L.)*	WALLFLOWER	Common. Old walls nr houses
Hesperis matronalis L.	DAME'S-VIOLET	Uncommon garden escape
Matthiola incana (L.) R.Br.	HOARY STOCK	Rare on sea cliffs; Somerset
Barbarea vulgaris R.Br.	WINTER-CRESS	Uncommon
B. intermedia Boreau	MEDIUM-FLOWERED WINTER-CRESS	Uncommon
B. verna (Miller) Asch.	AMERICAN WINTER-CRESS	Uncommon garden escape

FLOWERING PLANTS

Rorippa nasturtium-aquaticum (L.) Hayek	WATER-CRESS	Fairly common in streams
R. x sterilis Airy Shaw	HYBRID WATER-CRESS	Rare. Devon
R. palustris (L.) Besser	MARSH YELLOW-CRESS	Rare
R. sylvestris (L.) Besser	CREEPING YELLOW-CRESS	Rare. Somerset
Armoracia rusticana Gaertner, Meyer & Scherb.	HORSE-RADISH	Uncommon; wasteground
Cardamine trifolia L.	TREFOIL CRESS	Rare. Naturalized, Trentishoe
C. pratensis L.	CUCKOOFLOWER	Common in damp meadows & marshes
C. flexuosa With.	WAVY BITTER-CRESS	Common by streams and bogs
C. hirsuta L.	HAIRY BITTER-CRESS	Common in cultivated/rocky grnd
Arabis hirsuta (L.) Scop.	HAIRY ROCK-CRESS	Very rare. Devon
Aubrieta deltoidea (L.) DC.	AUBRETIA	Fairly frequent garden escape around villages
Lunaria annua L.	HONESTY	A long established escape in many hedgerows
Alyssum saxatile L.	GOLDEN ALISON	Uncommon garden escape
Lobularia maritima (L.) Desv.	SWEET ALISON	Garden escapes naturalized in sandy areas

Erophila verna (L.) DC.   COMMON WHITLOWGRASS Fairly common in dry, rocky areas. Somerset only. Both var. praecox & var. spathulata are thought to occur.

Cochlearia anglica L.	ENGLISH SCURVYGRASS	Uncommon or rare
C. officinalis L.	COMMON SCURVYGRASS	Uncommon; on the coast
C. danica L.	DANISH SCURVYGRASS	Our commonest scurvygrass
Capsella bursa-pastoris (L.) Medikus	SHEPHERD'S-PURSE	Common except on grassmoors

(Teesdalia nudicaulis (L.) Br. SHEPHERD'S CRESS. Was recorded 1929 on verge on Porlock Hill (N.G.Hadden). Present in fair quantity on Exmoor boundary in 1994)

Thlaspi arvense L.	FIELD PENNY-CRESS	Fairly common in east of area
Lepidium sativum L.	GARDEN CRESS	Uncommon throw-out
L. campestre (L.) R.Br.	FIELD PEPPERWORT	Rare
L. heterophyllum Benth.	SMITH'S PEPPERWORT	Rather uncommon
L. draba L. subsp. draba *(Cardaria draba (L.) Desv.* HOARY CRESS		A few places in east of area
Coronopus squamatus (Forsskål) Asch.	SWINE-CRESS	Rather uncommon, mainly in east
C. didymus (L.) Smith	LESSER SWINE-CRESS	Common on the lower ground
Diplotaxis muralis (L.) DC.	ANNUAL WALL-ROCKET or STINKWEED	Local (coast)
Brassica napus L. subsp. oleifera (DC.) Metzger OIL-SEED RAPE		Recent relics of cultivation
B. rapa L. subsp. rapa	TURNIP	Frequent relics of cultivation
B. nigra (L.) Koch	BLACK MUSTARD	Fairly frequent, mainly in the east

FLOWERING PLANTS

Sinapis arvensis L.	CHARLOCK	Common weed in agricultural & waste land
S. alba L. subsp. alba	WHITE MUSTARD	very uncommon relic of cultivation
Hirschfeldia incana (L.) Lagr.-Fossat	HOARY MUSTARD	Rare. Somerset

Cakile maritima Scop. subsp. integrifolia SEA ROCKET   One clump on coastal shingle at Minehead 1979-86. Disappeared after storm and not seen since.

Raphanus raphanistrum L. subsp. raphanistrum WILD RADISH   very uncommon

subsp. maritimus (Smith) Thell.	SEA RADISH	Only one record (1971) Somerset
R. sativus L.	GARDEN RADISH	Garden throw-outs

RESEDACEAE

Reseda luteola L.   WELD   Locally common, mainly in the east

EMPETRACEAE

Empetrum nigrum L. subsp. nigrum CROWBERRY Locally common on high damp moorland

ERICACEAE

Rhododendron ponticum L.	RHODODENDRON	Locally abundant and increasing
R. luteum Sweet	YELLOW AZALEA	Naturalized (vegetatively) in a few places in Somerset section
Gaultheria procumbens L.	CHECKERBERRY	Large patch on Brendon Hills
G. mucronata (L.f.) Hook. & Arn.	*(Pernettya mucronata)* PRICKLY HEATH	Introduced. Naturalizing
Arbutus unedo L.	STRAWBERRY-TREE	Introduced; regenerating. Som.
Calluna vulgaris (L.) Hull	HEATHER or LING	Locally abundant and dominant

About 20,000 acres of good heather moor remain on Exmoor, but this is much less than a century ago.

Erica tetralix L.	CROSS-LEAVED HEATH	Common on damp moorland
E. cinerea L.	BELL HEATHER	Forms an important constituent

of the coastal heaths and widespread on the moors but not dominant.

Vaccinium oxycoccos L.	CRANBERRY	Very local in upland bogs
V. uliginosum L.	BOG BILBERRY	Very rare

V. myrtillus L.   BILBERRY but always known as WHORTLEBERRY on Exmoor. Common Although the fruit is still common, parties of 'wort-pickers' are almost a thing of the past. They used to provide a useful source of extra pocket-money for schoolchildren.

PRIMULACEAE

Primula vulgaris Hudson	PRIMROSE	Common and locally abundant
P. x polyantha Miller	(PRIMROSE X COWSLIP)	Uncommon
P. veris L.	COWSLIP	Rare. In a few scattered calcareous areas
Cyclamen hederifolium Aiton	CYCLAMEN	Introductions which may naturalize

(Cyclamen repandum Sibth.& Smith   Is a well naturalized introduction in wood at West Porlock)

Lysimachia nemorum L.	YELLOW PIMPERNEL	Frequent in woodlands
L. nummularia L.	CREEPING-JENNY	Occasional garden escapes
L. vulgaris L.	YELLOW LOOSESTRIFE	Very rare in Exmoor area

FLOWERING PLANTS

Lysimachia punctata L.	DOTTED LOOSESTRIFE	Fairly frequent garden escape
Anagallis tenella (L.) L.	BOG PIMPERNEL	Locally common in upland bogs
A. arvensis L. subsp. arvensis	SCARLET PIMPERNEL	Common except on high ground

Blue, Pink and White varieties have all been found in Minehead area.

Glaux maritima L.	SEA-MILKWORT	Scarce, on coastal shingle
Samolus valerandi L.	BROOKWEED	Very rare, not seen recently

PITTOSPORACEAE

Pittosporum tenuifolium Gaertner   KOHUHU   Introduction; occasionally self-sown

HYDRANGEACEAE

Philadelphus coronarius L.   MOCK-ORANGE   An occasional hedgerow shrub

GROSSULARIACEAE

Escallonia macrantha Hook.& Arn.	ESCALLONIA	Occasional relics of introduction
Ribes rubrum L.	RED CURRANT	Frequent; usually bird-sown
R. nigrum L.	BLACK CURRANT	Fairly frequent, bird-sown
R. sanguineum Pursh	FLOWERING CURRANT	. Frequent garden escape
R. odoratum H.L.Wendl.	BUFFALO CURRANT	A rare casual; Somerset
R. uva-crispa L.	GOOSEBERRY	Common escape, some may be native

CRASSULACEAE

Crassula tillaea Lester-Garl.	MOSSY STONECROP	Rare and local. Somerset
C. helmsii (Kirk) Cockayne	NEW ZEALAND PYGMY-WEED	Has spread from garden ponds. Somerset
Umbilicus rupestris (Salisb.) Dandy	NAVELWORT or PENNYWORT	Common on walls Not on high, central moorland
Sempervivum tectorum L.	HOUSELEEK	Rare introduction. Somerset
Sedum telephium L. subsp. fabaria	ORPINE	Uncommon
S. spurium M.Bieb.	CAUCASIAN STONECROP	Uncommon; garden escape
S. rupestre L. *(S. reflexum L.)*	REFLEXED STONECROP	Uncommon; garden escape
¶S. forsterianum Smith	ROCK STONECROP	Native on coastal cliffs
S. acre L.	BITING STONECROP	Native in rocky areas
S. album L.	WHITE STONECROP	Fairly frequent,probably introdcd
S. anglicum Hudson	ENGLISH STONECROP	Native in rocky places
Astilbe japonica (Morren & Decne.)A.Gray	FALSE-BUCK'S-BEARD	Garden escape. Som.
Bergenia crassifolia (L.) Fritsch	ELEPHANT-EARS	Garden escape or throw-out
Saxifraga cymbalaria L.	CELANDINE SAXIFRAGE	Uncommon introduction
S.x urbium D.Webb	LONDONPRIDE	Garden escape naturalized on walls etc
S. hirsuta L.	KIDNEY SAXIFRAGE	Rare garden escape. Somerset
S. granulata L.	MEADOW SAXIFRAGE	Uncommon, damp woods
S. hypnoides L.	MOSSY SAXIFRAGE	Rare garden escape. Somerset
S. tridactylites L.	RUE-LEAVED SAXIFRAGE	Rare, Somerset
Tolmiea menziesii (Pursh) Torrey & A.Gray	PICK-A-BACK-PLANT	Garden escape. Som.

FLOWERING PLANTS

Tellima grandiflora (Pursh) Douglas ex Lindley FRINGE-CUPS   A naturalized garden escape
Chrysosplenium oppositifolium L.   OPPOSITE-LEAVED GOLDEN SAXIFRAGE   Common
C. alternifolium L.   ALTERNATE-LEAVED GOLDEN SAXIFRAGE
Much less common, mainly around the Brendon Hills area. Somerset

ROSACEAE

Spiraea salicifolia L.	BRIDEWORT	Infrequent garden escapes
Filipendula vulgaris Moench	DROPWORT	Rare, garden escape only in our area
F. ulmaria (L.) Maxim.	MEADOWSWEET	Common, damp meadows & streams
Kerria japonica (L.) DC.	KERRIA	Uncommon garden escape
Rubus tricolor Focke	CHINESE BRAMBLE	Introduction becoming naturalized
R. saxatilis L.	STONE BRAMBLE	Very rare, Devon
R. idaeus L.	RASPBERRY	Common. Some garden escapes, some native
R. phoenicolasius Maxim.	JAPANESE WINEBERRY	Rarely naturalized escape
R. fruticosus L. agg.	BRAMBLE	Abundant

There are currently 309 microspecies of bramble on the British List. Little work has been carried out regarding these on Exmoor but a few have been identified. I am indebted to Mr. L. Margetts for confirmation of most of the following. Their frequency is not known except in a few cases, and the field is wide open for further research.
R. nessensis W. Hall; R. albionis W.C.R.Watson; R. laciniatus Willd.; R. pyramidalis Kaltenb.; R. altiarcuatus Barton & Riddelsd.; R. cardiophyllus Lef.&P.J. Mueller; R. polyanthemus Lindeb.; R. prolongatus Boulay & Letendre ex Corbière; R. riddelsdellii Rilstone; R. rubritinctus Watson; R. ulmifolius Schott; R. adscitus Genev.; R. vestitus Weihe; R. dentatifolius (Briggs) Watson; R. leyanus Rogers; R. flexuosus P.J.Mueller & Lef.; R. peninsulae Rilstone; R. dasyphyllus (Rogers) E.Marshall; R. hylocharis W.C.R.Watson; R. scabripes Genev.

R. caesius L.	DEWBERRY	Fairly common
Potentilla palustris (L.) Scop.	MARSH CINQUEFOIL	Very rare. Brendon Hills, Somerset
P. anserina L.	SILVERWEED	Common, dry places
P. recta L.	SULPHUR CINQUEFOIL	Uncommon introduction. Som.
P. erecta (L.) Räusch. subsp. erecta	TORMENTIL	Very common
P. x italica Lehm.	TORMENTIL x CINQUEFOIL	Uncommon
P. anglica Laich.	TRAILING TORMENTIL	Very rare, possibly mis-identified
P. x mixta Nolte ex Reichb.	HYBRID CINQUEFOIL	Uncommon
P. reptans L.	CREEPING CINQUEFOIL	Common
P. sterilis (L.) Garcke	BARREN STRAWBERRY	Common
Fragaria vesca L.	WILD STRAWBERRY	Common
F. ananassa (Duchesne)Duchesne	GARDEN STRAWBERRY	Uncommon garden escape
Duchesnea indica (Andrews) Focke	YELLOW-FLOWERED STRAWBERRY	Rare escape.Som.
Geum rivale L.	WATER AVENS	Scarce & local. Somerset
G. x intermedium Ehrh.	HYBRID WATER AVENS	Very scarce
G. urbanum L.	WOOD AVENS	Common
Agrimonia eupatoria L.	AGRIMONY	Rather uncommon, mainly in north section

FLOWERING PLANTS

Agrimonia procera Wallr.	FRAGRANT AGRIMONY	Rare
Sanguisorba officinalis L.	GREAT BURNET	Very local (Mainly in Barle Valley)
S. minor Scop. subsp minor	SALAD BURNET	Uncommon, prefers calcareous soils
subsp. muricata (Gremli) Briq.	FODDER BURNET	Rare. Somerset
Acaena ovalifolia Ruíz Lopez & Pavón	TWO-SPINED ACAENA	Rare introduction. Somerset
Alchemilla conjuncta Bab.	SILVER LADY'S-MANTLE	Rare introduction. Somerset
A. xanthochlora Rothm.	INTERMEDIATE LADY'S-MANTLE	The commonest species of Lady's-Mantle on Exmoor. Absent from Minehead and Porlock areas.
A. filicaulis subsp. vestita (Buser) Bradshaw	LADY'S-MANTLE	Uncommon
A. mollis (Buser) Rothm.	SOFT LADY'S-MANTLE	Garden escapes
Aphanes arvensis L.	PARSLEY-PIERT	Frequent
A. inexspectata Lippert *(A. microcarpa)*	SLENDER PARSLEY-PIERT	Uncommon
Rosa multiflora Thunb.ex Murray	MANY-FLOWERED ROSE	Not seen for several years
R. arvensis Hudson	FIELD ROSE	Common but not on the highest ground
R. pimpinellifolia L.	BURNET ROSE	Only one record. Somerset
R. rugosa Thunb.ex Murray	JAPANESE ROSE	Introduction
R. x andegavensis Bast.	SHORT-STYLED FIELD ROSE x DOG-ROSE	Rare
R. canina L.	DOG-ROSE	Common except on the grass moors
R. x dumalis Bechst.	DOG-ROSE x GLAUCOUS DOG-ROSE	Rare
R. tomentosa Smith	HARSH DOWNY-ROSE	Uncommon
R. sherardii Davies	SHERARD'S DOWNY-ROSE	Fairly frequent
R. rubiginosa L.	SWEET-BRIAR	Rare
Prunus dulcis (Miller) D.Webb	ALMOND	Introduction
P. cerasifera Ehrh.	CHERRY PLUM	An introduction found in a few hedgerows
P. spinosa L.	BLACKTHORN	Common. Important nest area for birds
P. domestica L. subsp. domestica	PLUM	Introduction
subsp. insititia (L.) Bonnier & Layens	BULLACE	In a few old hedgerows
P. avium (L.) L.	WILD CHERRY	Frequent. Good specimens Brendon Hills
P. cerasus L.	DWARF CHERRY	Rare. Somerset
P. padus L.	BIRD CHERRY	Rare. Somerset
P. lusitanica L.	PORTUGAL LAUREL	Rare introduction. Somerset
P. laurocerasus L.	CHERRY LAUREL	Fairly common introduction
Chaenomeles speciosa (Sweet) Nakai	JAPANESE QUINCE	Persistent introduction. Devon
Pyrus communis L.	PEAR	Old relics of cultivation. Somerset
Malus sylvestris (L.) Miller	CRAB APPLE	Uncommon
M. domestica Borkh.	APPLE	Fairly frequent
Sorbus aucuparia L.	ROWAN	Common in moorland coombes and woods
¶S. intermedia agg.	SWEDISH WHITEBEAM	Rare
S. aria agg.	COMMON WHITEBEAM	Rare

FLOWERING PLANTS

S. latifolia agg.　　　　BROAD-LEAVED WHITEBEAM　　　　Rare
A number of rare Whitebeam trees may be found in Exmoor's coastal woods. They need expert identification, but the following have been confirmed: Sorbus anglica Hedlund; ¶S. porrigentiformis E.Warb.(endemic); ¶S. rupicola (Syme) Hedlund; S. vexans E.Warb.**RDB.**; S. subcuneata Wilm.**RDB.**; ¶S. devoniensis E.Warb.; S. 'Taxon D' found 1988 N.Devon.

Amelanchier lamarckii F.-G.Schroeder JUNEBERRY　　　　Rare introduction

Cotoneaster frigidus Wall. ex Lindley TREE COTONEASTER　A few naturalized trees. Som.

C. x watereri Exell　　　　WATERER'S COTONEASTER　　　　Garden origin

C. lacteus W.Smith　　　　LATE COTONEASTER　　　　Garden origin

C. integrifolius (Roxb.) Klotz *(C. microphyllus)*　　Garden origin, sometimes naturalized
　　　　　　　　　　　　　SMALL-LEAVED COTONEASTER

C. horizontalis Decne.　　　WALLSPRAY　　Commonly bird-sown from gardens

C. simonsii Baker　　　　HIMALAYAN COTONEASTER　　　　Introductions

C. bullatus Bois　　　　HOLLYBERRY COTONEASTER　　　　Garden origin

C. franchetii Bois　　　　FRANCHET'S COTONEASTER　　　　Garden origin

There are many other species of Cotoneaster grown in gardens which may occcasionally be found as escapes, bird-sown or throw-outs. Some may become naturalized.

Pyracantha coccinea M.Roemer　　FIRETHORN　　An uncommon bird-sown shrub

Mespilus germanica L.　　　MEDLAR　Rare. In two or three old hedgerows. Som.

Crataegus monogyna Jacq.　　　HAWTHORN　　　　　　Common
The haws form an important food-source for autumn migrant birds e.g. Redwings and Fieldfares. The shrubs and small trees also provide nest-sites.

FABACEAE

Robinia pseudoacacia L.　　　FALSE-ACACIA　　　Rare; originally introduced

Galega officinalis L.　　GOAT'S-RUE　Rare,naturalized on waste ground. Som.

Anthyllis vulneraria L. Subsp. vulneraria KIDNEY VETCH　　Scattered along the coast

Lotus glaber Miller　　　NARROW-LEAVED BIRD'S-FOOT-TREFOIL　　Rare. Devon

L. corniculatus L.　　　　COMMON BIRD'S-FOOT-TREFOIL　　　　Common

L. pedunculatus Cav. *(L. uliginosus)* GREATER BIRD'S-FOOT-TREFOIL　　Common

Ornithopus perpusillus L.　　　BIRD'S-FOOT　Fairly frequent but easily overlooked

Vicia cracca L.　　　　TUFTED VETCH　Fairly frequent off the high moors

V. sylvatica L.　　　　WOOD VETCH Local, coastal woods and Brendon Hills

V. hirsuta (L.) Gray　　　HAIRY TARE　Frequent, rough grassland and banks

V. tetrasperma (L.) Schreber　　SMOOTH TARE　Similar to above but less frequent

V. sepium L.　　　　BUSH VETCH　Common in woods and hedgerows

V. sativa L. subsp. nigra (L.) Ehrh. COMMON VETCH　Common in agricultural areas
The plant formerly known as V. angustifolia L. NARROW-LEAVED VETCH is now included in subsp. nigra. It may be found on dry grassy banks. The former fodder plant, subsp. sativa has not been recorded in recent years.

V. lathyroides L.　　　SPRING VETCH Very rare. Coast near Minehead, Som.

¶V. bithynica (L.) L.　　　　BITHYNIAN VETCH　　　　　　Very rare

FLOWERING PLANTS

Lathyrus linifolius (Reichard) Bässler var. montanus BITTER-VETCH A frequent upland sp. A form with very narrow leaves also occurs.

L. pratensis L.	MEADOW VETCHLING	Common in hedgerows etc.
L. sylvestris L.	NARROW-LEAVED EVERLASTING-PEA	Uncommon
L. latifolius L.	BROAD-LEAVED EVERLASTING PEA	Garden escape
L. nissolia L.	GRASS VETCHLING	Rare
Ononis repens L. subsp. repens	COMMON REST-HARROW	Uncommon; dry places
Melilotus altissimus Thuill.	TALL MELILOT	Rare
M. albus Medikus	WHITE MELILOT	Very rare, may no longer be here
M. officinalis (L.) Pallas	RIBBED MELILOT	Rare
Medicago lupulina L.	BLACK MEDICK	Common in north & east Exmoor
M. sativa L. subsp. sativa	LUCERNE	Uncommon relic of cultivation
M. polymorpha L. var.tuberculata	TOOTHED MEDICK	Very rare; coast near Minehead
M. arabica (L.) Hudson	SPOTTED MEDICK	Common in north & east o/w rare

¶Trifolium ornithopodioides L. *(Trigonella o.)* BIRD'S-FOOT CLOVER Locally abundant In short grassland near the coast to the north-east of area. (Somerset)

T. repens L.	WHITE CLOVER	Abundant
T. hybridum L.	ALSIKE CLOVER	Uncommon
¶T. glomeratum L.	CLUSTERED CLOVER	Rare but in good quantity at two sites in Somerset where it was rediscovered after many years, in 1993.
¶T. suffocatum L.	SUFFOCATED CLOVER	Very rare by coast. Somerset
T. fragiferum L. subsp. fragiferum	STRAWBERRY CLOVER	Very rare. Somerset
T. campestre Schreber	HOP TREFOIL	Rather uncommon
T. dubium Sibth.	LESSER TREFOIL	Very common
T. micranthum Viv.	SLENDER TREFOIL	Fairly frequent in short turf.Som.
T. pratense L.	RED CLOVER	Common
T. medium L.	ZIGZAG CLOVER	Uncommon
T. incarnatum L. subsp. incarnatum	CRIMSON CLOVER	Very rare One plant in root crop in 1991. Somerset
T. striatum L.	KNOTTED CLOVER	Uncommon
T. scabrum L.	ROUGH CLOVER	Rare, by coast. Somerset
T. arvense L.	HARE'S-FOOT CLOVER	Uncommon
T. subterraneum L.	SUBTERRANEAN CLOVER	Uncommon. Porlock-Minehead area.
Lupinus arboreus Sims	TREE LUPIN	Very rare. Near the coast
Laburnum anagyroides Medikus	LABURNUM	Self sown from planted trees

Cytisus scoparius (L.) Link subsp. scoparius BROOM Fairly common, heaths & forest rides

Genista monspessulana (L.) Johnson	MONTPELLIER BROOM	Garden escape. Somerset
G. anglica L.	PETTY WHIN	Very rare. Somerset
Ulex europaeus L.	GORSE or FURZE	Very common, bushy shrub
U. gallii Planchon	WESTERN GORSE	Very common, low growing shrub

FLOWERING PLANTS

ELAEAGNACEAE
Hippophae rhamnoides L.   SEA-BUCKTHORN   Planted on coast near Minehead
HALORAGACEAE
Myriophyllum alterniflorum DC. ALTERNATE WATER-MILFOIL Common in upland streams
GUNNERACEAE
Gunnera tinctoria (Molina) Mirbel   GIANT RHUBARB Introduced. Some may be self-sown
LYTHRACEAE
Lythrum salicaria L.   PURPLE LOOSESTRIFE   Uncommon
L. portula (L.) D.Webb   WATER-PURSLANE   Fairly common in damp areas
THYMELAEACEAE
Daphne laureola L.   SPURGE-LAUREL   Rare. Somerset
ONAGRACEAE
Epilobium hirsutum L.   GREAT WILLOWHERB   Common by lowland waters
E. parviflorum Schreber   HOARY WILLOWHERB   Frequent. Shady places
E. montanum L.   BROAD-LEAVED WILLOWHERB   Common
E. lanceolatum Sebast. & Mauri   SPEAR-LEAVED WILLOWHERB Frequent, waste places
E. tetragonum L.   SQUARE-STALKED WILLOWHERB   Frequent
E. obscurum Schreber   SHORT-FRUITED WILLOWHERB   Frequent
E. roseum Schreber   PALE WILLOWHERB   Rare
E. ciliatum Raf.   AMERICAN WILLOWHERB   Frequent
E. palustre L.   MARSH WILLOWHERB   Common in acid boggy areas
E. brunnescens (Cockayne) Raven & Engelhorn   Can be found along many Exmoor waters
NEW ZEALAND WILLOWHERB   particularly Hoaroak
Chamerion angustifolium (L.) Holub ROSEBAY WILLOWHERB   Very common
A notable feature along roadsides on the Brendon Hills and elsewhere.
Oenothera glazioviana Micheli ex Martius *(Oe. erythrosepala)*
LARGE-FLOWERED EVENING-PRIMROSE Uncommon
Oe. stricta Ledeb. ex Link   FRAGRANT EVENING-PRIMROSE   Rare
Minehead-Dunster Beach area
Fuchsia magellanica Lam.   FUCHSIA   Introduction, sometimes naturalized
Circaea lutetiana L.   ENCHANTER'S-NIGHTSHADE   Common in woods
CORNACEAE
Cornus sanguinea L.   DOGWOOD   Fairly common in hedgerows
C. sericea L.   RED-OSIER DOGWOOD   Rare. Introduction
VISCACEAE
Viscum album L.   MISTLETOE   Only found within 10 miles of Minehead
Has been noted on the following host trees: Apple, Crab Apple, Ornamental Willow,
Lime, Hawthorn, False Acacia and Lilac. Only survived 3 years on the last-named.
CELASTRACEAE
Euonymus europaeus L.   SPINDLE   Fairly common in north and east of area

FLOWERING PLANTS

AQUIFOLIACEAE
Ilex aquifolium L.　　　　　　HOLLY　　　　Common except on the grass moors
BUXACEAE
Buxus sempervirens L.　　　　BOX　　　　Naturalized in some hedgerows
EUPHORBIACEAE
Mercurialis perennis L.　　　　DOG'S MERCURY　Common in woods and hedgerows
M. annua L.　　　　　　　　ANNUAL MERCURY　　Weed of cultivated ground
　　　　　　　　　　　　　　　Common in Somerset area, not Devon Exmoor
Euphorbia hyberna L.　　　　IRISH SPURGE **RDB**.　　Rare. Woodlands. Devon
E. helioscopia L.　　　　　　SUN SPURGE　Fairly frequent in cultivated land
E. lathyris L.　　　　　　　　CAPER SPURGE　Fairly frequent in waste places
E. exigua L.　　　　　　　　DWARF SPURGE　　Rare. Arable land. Somerset
E. peplus L.　　　　　　　　PETTY SPURGE　　　　Common garden weed
E. amygdaloides L.　　　　　WOOD SPURGE　　Rare. Woods and sea cliffs
(There are records of ¶E. paralias L. SEA SPURGE from Minehead area up to 1953.)
RHAMNACEAE
Frangula alnus Miller　　　　ALDER BUCKTHORN　　　　　　　　Very rare
  There is at least one old tree in woodland near Dulverton, Somerset.
VITACEAE
Parthenocissus quinquefolia (L.) Planchon VIRGINIA-CREEPER Introduced.Sometimes natlzd
LINACEAE
Linum bienne Miller　　　　　PALE FLAX　　　An uncommon calcicole. Somerset
L. usitatissimum L.　　FLAX　　Has recently become a frequent crop and escapes occur
L. catharticum L.　　　　　　FAIRY FLAX　　　　Frequent in dry sandy soils
POLYGALACEAE
Polygala vulgaris L. subsp. vulgaris COMMON MILKWORT An rather uncommon calcicole
P. serpyllifolia Hose　　　　　HEATH MILKWORT　　Common on acid moorland
HIPPOCASTANACEAE
Aesculus hippocastanum L　　HORSE-CHESTNUT Many old introductions which seed
A. carnea Zeyher　　　　　　RED HORSE-CHESTNUT　　　Recent introductions
ACERACEAE
Acer platanoides L.　　　　　NORWAY MAPLE　Recent introductiions now seeding
A. campestre L.　　　　　　　FIELD MAPLE Native. Occurs mainly in east of area
A. pseudoplatanus L.　　　　SYCAMORE　　　Introduction. Becoming 'abundant
OXALIDACEAE
Oxalis corniculata L.　　　　PROCUMBENT YELLOW-SORREL　　Garden escape
O. stricta L.　　　　　　　　UPRIGHT YELLOW-SORREL　　Rare garden escape
O. articulata Savigny　　　　PINK-SORREL　　　　　　　　Garden escape
O. acetosella L.　　　　　　WOOD-SORREL Native. Very common in woods etc.
  Frequently found with varying shades of pink flowers.

97

FLOWERING PLANTS

Oxalis latifolia Kunth	GARDEN PINK-SORREL	Uncommon but pernicious weed
O. incarnata L.	PALE PINK-SORREL	Garden escape

GERANIACEAE

Geranium endressii Gay	FRENCH CRANE'S-BILL	Garden escape
G. x oxonianum Yeo	DRUCE'S CRANE'S-BILL	Uncommon garden escape
G. versicolor L.	PENCILLED CRANE'S-BILL	Very local
G. rotundifolium L.	ROUND-LEAVED CRANE'S-BILL	Rare. Somerset
G. pratense L.	MEADOW CRANE'S-BILL	Probably garden escape only
G. sanguineum L.	BLOODY CRANE'S-BILL	Garden escape
G. columbinum L.	LONG-STALKED CRANE'S-BILL	Rather uncommon
G. dissectum L.	CUT-LEAVED CRANE'S-BILL	Common
G. x magnificum N.Hylander	PURPLE CRANE'S-BILL	Uncommon garden escape
G. pyrenaicum Burman f.	HEDGEROW CRANE'S-BILL	Frequent but local
G. pusillum L.	SMALL-FLOWERED CRANE'S-BILL	Rare
G. molle L.	DOVE'S-FOOT CRANE'S-BILL	Common off the moors
G. macrorrhizum L.	ROCK CRANE'S-BILL	Garden escape
G. lucidum L.	SHINING CRANE'S-BILL	Locally common
G. robertianum L.	HERB-ROBERT	Very common

subsp. maritimum (Bab.) H.G.Baker occurs on coastal shingle.

G. phaeum L.	DUSKY CRANE'S-BILL	Garden escape
¶Erodium maritimum (L.) L'Hér.	SEA STORK'S-BILL	Scarce. Near the coast
¶E. moschatum (L.) L'Hér.	MUSK STORK'S-BILL	Very local. Nr the coast. Som.
E. cicutarium (L.) L'Hér.	COMMON STORK'S-BILL	Uncommon and local

BALSAMINACEAE

Impatiens glandulifera Royle	INDIAN BALSAM	Fairly common

ARALIACEAE

Hedera helix L. subsp. helix	COMMON IVY	Very common

Provides food and shelter for birds and does not often harm trees.

subsp. hibernica (Kirchner) D.McClint. Reports probably refer to H. 'Hibernica', an escape from cultivation.

APIACEAE

Hydrocotyle vulgaris L.	MARSH PENNYWORT	Common in Exmoor bogs
Sanicula europaea L.	SANICLE	Common in Exmoor woodlands
Chaerophyllum temulum L.	ROUGH CHERVIL	Common in hedgerows
Anthriscus sylvestris (L.) Hoffm.	COW PARSLEY	Very common, sometimes abundant
A. caucalis M.Bieb.	BUR PARSLEY	Rare. Somerset
¶Scandix pecten-veneris L.	SHEPHERD'S-NEEDLE	Very rare. Somerset

This formerly common cornfield weed occured recently in 2 places after soil disturbance.

Myrrhis odorata (L.) Scop.	SWEET CICELY	Rare. (Somerset) Long established
Smyrnium olusatrum L.	ALEXANDERS	Common in hedgerows near the coast

FLOWERING PLANTS

Conopodium majus (Gouan) Loret	PIGNUT	Common in woods and short moorland grass
Pimpinella major (L.) Hudson	GREATER BURNET-SAXIFRAGE	Very rare. Devon
P. saxifraga L.	BURNET-SAXIFRAGE	Frequent in dry grassland
Aegopodium podagraria L.	GROUND-ELDER	A common, troublesome weed
Berula erecta (Hudson) Cov.	LESSER WATER-PARSNIP	Very rare. Somerset
Crithmum maritimum L.	ROCK SAMPHIRE	On sea-cliffs or shingle
Oenanthe fistulosa L.	TUBULAR WATER-DROPWORT	Very rare. Somerset
O. pimpinelloides L.	CORKY-FRUITED WATER-DROPWORT	Very rare
O. crocata L.	HEMLOCK WATER-DROPWORT	Common by water

Aethusa cynapium L. subsp. cynapium FOOL'S PARSLEY Common in arable and waste land
    subsp. agrestis (Wallr.) Dostál   Less common in arable land

Foeniculum vulgare Miller	FENNEL	Frequent near the coast
Silaum silaus (L.) Schinz & Thell.	PEPPER SAXIFRAGE	Very rare. Somerset
Conium maculatum L.	HEMLOCK	Frequent, waste ground

Bupleurum subovatum Link ex Sprengel FALSE THOROW-WAX Uncommon bird-seed alien

Apium graveolens L.	WILD CELERY	Uncommon, usually near the coast
A. nodiflorum (L.) Lagasca	FOOL'S WATER-CRESS	Common by streams
Petroselinum segetum (L.) Koch	CORN PARSLEY **RDB.**	Rare
Sison amomum L.	STONE PARSLEY	Uncommon
Ammi majus L.	BULLWORT	Occasionally casual in gardens
Angelica sylvestris L.	WILD ANGELICA	Common by streams and rivers
A. archangelica L.	GARDEN ANGELICA	One record, Minehead 1995
Pastinaca sativa L. var. hortensis	GARDEN PARSNIP	Rare throw-out
var. sylvestris	WILD PARSNIP	Rare, roadsides. Somerset
Heracleum sphondylium L. subsp. sphondylium HOGWEED		Very common
H. mantegazzianum Sommier & Levier GIANT HOGWEED		Rare. Somerset
Torilis japonica (Houtt.) DC.	UPRIGHT HEDGE-PARSLEY	Frequent, hedgerows etc
T. nodosa (L.) Gaertner	KNOTTED HEDGE-PARSLEY	Uncommon
Daucus carota L.	WILD CARROT	Rather uncommon, dry grassland

GENTIANACEAE

Centaurium erythraea Rafn   COMMON CENTAURY   Rather uncommon
    (C. pulchellum (Sw.) Druce LESSER CENTAURY. Recent records unconfirmed. Recorded Ley Hill c1930 Norman Hadden)

Blackstonia perfoliata (L.) Hudson   YELLOW-WORT   Rare
    (Gentianella campestris (L.) Boerner FIELD GENTIAN. Recorded between Oare and Porlock by Norman Hadden in 1940s but no recent records despite searches made.)

APOCYNACEAE

Vinca minor L.	LESSER PERIWINKLE	Naturalized in many hedgerows
V. difformis Pourret	INTERMEDIATE PERIWINKLE	Rare garden escape

FLOWERING PLANTS

Vinca major L. GREATER PERIWINKLE Frequent garden escape

SOLANACEAE

Nicandra physalodes (L.) Gaertner APPLE-OF-PERU Rare alien
Lycium barbarum L. DUKE OF ARGYLL'S TEAPLANT Local on coast
Hyoscyamus niger L. HENBANE Rare and local
Lycopersicon esculentum Miller TOMATO Occasional garden throw-out etc.
Solanum nigrum L. subsp. nigrum BLACK NIGHTSHADE Frequent in Somerset section
S. physalifolium Rusby GREEN NIGHTSHADE Rare. Minehead
S. dulcamara L. BITTERSWEET Fairly common
S. tuberosum L. POTATO Garden throw-outs
S. laciniatum Aiton KANGAROO APPLE Rare garden escape
Datura stramonium L. THORN-APPLE Rare, poisonous, agricultural weed

CONVOLVULACEAE

Convolvulus arvensis L. FIELD BINDWEED Common below 1000 ft contour
Calystegia sepium (L.) R.Br. HEDGE BINDWEED Common in lowland hedgerows
C. x lucana (Ten.) Don HYBRID BINDWEED Rare. Somerset
C. silvatica (Kit.) Griseb. LARGE BINDWEED Fairly common; lowland hedges

CUSCUTACEAE

Cuscuta epithymum (L.) L. LESSER DODDER Frequent on coastal heaths
This tiny parasite may be found on Gorse, Whortleberry, Wood Sage and Heathers.

MENYANTHACEAE

Menyanthes trifoliata L. BOGBEAN Local in upland bogs, occasionally abundant
Nymphoides peltata Kuntze FRINGED WATER-LILY Introduction
There was a 1986 report from Dunster Hawn but it has not persisted there.

POLEMONIACEAE

Polemonium caeruleum L. JACOB'S LADDER Rare garden escape

HYDROPHYLLACEAE

Phacelia tanacetifolia Benth. PHACELIA Garden escape

BORAGINACEAE

(Lithospermum arvense L. FIELD GROMWELL. Recorded as an occasional weed in Porlock area in 1960s - N.G.Hadden)

Echium vulgare L. VIPER'S-BUGLOSS Local on the coast
Pulmonaria officinalis L. LUNGWORT Garden escapes sometimes naturalized
Symphytum officinale L. COMMON COMFREY Rather local in distribution
S. x uplandicum Nyman RUSSIAN COMFREY Uncommon
S. 'Hidcote Blue' HIDCOTE COMFREY Garden escape or throw-out
S. grandiflorum DC. CREEPING COMFREY Naturalized garden escape. Som.
S. orientale L. WHITE (or SOFT) COMFREY Rare and local
Brunnera macrophylla (Adams) I.M.Johnston GREAT FORGET-ME-NOT Garden escape
Anchusa arvensis (L.) M.Bieb. *(Lycopsis arvensis)* BUGLOSS Rare and local. Somerset

FLOWERING PLANTS

Pentaglottis sempervirens (L.) Tausch ex L.Bailey   GREEN ALKANET
      Common in hedgerows and waste ground below 1000 ft contour
Borago officinalis L.   BORAGE   Garden escape
Trachystemon orientalis (L.) Don ABRAHAM-ISAAC-JACOB   Rare garden escape. Som.
Myosotis scorpioides L.   WATER FORGET-ME-NOT   Fairly frequent
                     on the banks of the larger waters below 1000 ft.
M. secunda A.Murray   CREEPING FORGET-ME-NOT   Common
   The commonest forget-me-not on Exmoor. In most upland bogs and streams.
M. laxa Lehm. subsp. caespitosa   TUFTED FORGET-ME-NOT   Scarce
M. sylvatica Hoffm.   WOOD FORGET-ME-NOT   Garden escapes only
M. arvensis (L.) Hill   FIELD FORGET-ME-NOT   Common in arable land
M. ramosissima Rochel   EARLY FORGET-ME-NOT   Rare
M. discolor Pers.   CHANGING FORGET-ME-NOT   Fairly common
Cynoglossum officinale L.   HOUND'S-TONGUE   Sandy plances. Rare. Somerset

VERBENACEAE
Verbena officinalis L.   VERVAIN   Rather rare; mainly near the coast. Som.

LAMIACEAE
Stachys officinalis (L.) Trev.St.Léon BETONY   Fairly common in grassy places
S. sylvatica L.   HEDGE WOUNDWORT Common except on grass moor
S. x ambigua Smith   HYBRID WOUNDWORT   Uncommon
S. palustris L.   MARSH WOUNDWORT   Frequent in damp places
S. arvensis (L.) L.   FIELD WOUNDWORT Uncommon, arable land. Som.
Ballota nigra L. subsp.foetida BLACK HOREHOUND   Local. Mainly Minehead area
(Leonurus cardiaca L. MOTHERWORT. Hancock's *History of Minehead* (1900) states
'Plentiful on Woodcombe slopes' and it occurred as a garden escape at Bossington from
1913-1930 but not seen since. *The Somerset Flora* Roe, 1981.)
Lamiastrum galeobdolon (L.) Ehrend. & Polatschek subsp. montanum (Pers.) E.& P.
                    YELLOW ARCHANGEL   Common in wood and hedges
   Subsp. argentatum (Smejkal) Stace   Frequent garden escape which naturalizes quickly
Lamium album L.   WHITE DEAD-NETTLE   Frequent; hedgerows
L. maculatum (L.) L.   SPOTTED DEAD-NETTLE   Uncommon garden escape
L. purpureum L.   RED DEAD-NETTLE   Common in cultivated ground
L. hybridum Villars   CUT-LEAVED DEAD-NETTLE Rare; cultivated ground
L. amplexicaule L.   HENBIT DEAD-NETTLE   Uncommon. Somerset
Galeopsis tetrahit L.   COMMON HEMP-NETTLE   Common
G. bifida Boemn.   BIFID HEMP-NETTLE   Distribution uncertain
Phlomis fruticosa L.   JERUSALEM SAGE   Rare garden escape. Somerset
¶Melittis melissophyllum L.   BASTARD BALM   Rare, woods and wood borders
¶Marrubium vulgare L.   WHITE HOREHOUND   Very rare, possibly now gone
Scutellaria galericulata L.   SKULLCAP   Very local, by River Barle. Somerset
S. minor Hudson   LESSER SKULLCAP   Frequent on wet moorland

FLOWERING PLANTS

Teucrium scorodonia L.	WOOD SAGE	Common
Ajuga reptans L.	BUGLE	Common in damp woods and meadows
Nepeta x faassenii Bergmans ex Stearn	GARDEN CAT-MINT	Rare garden escape. Som.
Glechoma hederacea L.	GROUND-IVY	Common apart from the grass moors
Prunella vulgaris L.	SELFHEAL	Very common everywhere
Melissa officinalis L.	BALM	Uncommon garden escape. Somerset
Clinopodium ascendens (Jordan) Samp. *(Calamintha ascendens)*	COMMON CALAMINT	Frequent in the Minehead to Porlock area
C. vulgare L.	WILD BASIL	Rather uncommon. Somerset
Origanum vulgare L.	WILD MARJORAM	Uncommon; some reports may be escapes from cultivation
Thymus pulegioides L.	LARGE THYME	Rare
T. polytrichus A.Kerner ex Borbás subsp. britannicus (Ronn.) Kerguélen *(T.praecox)*	WILD THYME	Frequent; lt soils particularly nr coast
Lycopus europaeus L.	GIPSYWORT	Rather uncommon; marshland
Mentha arvensis L.	CORN MINT	Uncommon. Fields and arable land
M. x verticillata L.	WHORLED MINT	Fairly common
M. aquatica L.	WATER MINT	Very common
M. x piperita L.	PEPPERMINT	Rather uncommon
var. dumetorum	HAIRY PEPPERMINT	Very rare. Somerset
M. spicata L.	SPEARMINT	Garden escapes
M. x villosa Hudson	APPLE-MINT	Uncommon
M. suaveolens Ehrh.	ROUND-LEAVED MINT	Uncommon
M. pulegium L.	PENNYROYAL	Appeared as a garden weed in Porlock
M. requienii Benth.	CORSICAN MINT	Naturalized in gardens. Somerset
Rosmarinus officinalis L.	ROSEMARY	Occasionally self-sown from gardens
Salvia verbenaca L. *(S.horminoides)*	WILD CLARY	Rare in dry sandy places

CALLITRICHACEAE

Callitriche stagnalis Scop.	COMMON WATER-STARWORT	Common on wet mud
C. platycarpa Kütz.	VARIOUS-LEAVED WATER-STARWORT	In streams
C. obtusangula Le Gall	BLUNT-FRUITED WATER-STARWORT	In streams
C. hamulata Kütz. ex Koch	INTERMEDIATE WATER-STARWORT	Ponds & ditches

Distribution and status of the latter three Water-starworts on Exmoor is uncertain.

PLANTAGINACEAE

Plantago coronopus L.	BUCK'S-HORN PLANTAIN	Common near the coast
P. maritima L.	SEA PLANTAIN	Local in coastal mud or salt-marshes
P. major L. subsp. major	GREATER PLANTAIN	Very common everywhere
P. media L.	HOARY PLANTAIN	Uncommon and very local
P. lanceolata L.	RIBWORT PLANTAIN	Very common everywhere
Littorella uniflora (L.) Asch.	SHOREWEED	Local at edges of larger rivers & lakes

FLOWERING PLANTS

BUDDLEJACEAE
Buddleja davidii Franchet　　BUTTERFLY-BUSH　　Commonly naturalized escape

OLEACEAE
Forsythia x intermedia hort.ex Zabel　FORSYTHIA　　Occasionally naturalized in hedgerows
Fraxinus excelsior L.　　ASH　　A common tree in hedgerow and woodland
Many fine specimens exist, often to be found near farmsteads.
Syringa vulgaris L.　　LILAC　　Persistent escape in some hedges near houses
Ligustrum vulgare L.　　WILD PRIVET　　Frequent in hedges and near the coast
L. ovalifolium Hassk.　　GARDEN PRIVET　　Presistent garden escape in hedges

SCROPHULARIACEAE
Verbascum blattaria L.　　MOTH MULLEIN　　Very rare casual. Devon
¶V. virgatum Stokes　　TWIGGY MULLEIN　　Rare casual
V. phlomoides L.　　ORANGE MULLEIN　　Rare casual
V. thapsus L.　　GREAT MULLEIN　　The commonest species; persistent
V. nigrum L.　　DARK MULLEIN　　Rare casual
¶V. lychnitis L. forma lutea　　YELLOW-FLOWERED WHITE MULLEIN　　Very local
The British species is normally var. alba and the Yellow-flowered form grows only on National Trust land near Bossington. It thus calls for definite conservation policies.
Scrophularia nodosa L.　　COMMON FIGWORT　　Common in dry situations
S. auriculata L.　　WATER FIGWORT　　Less common; damp places
Mimulus moschatus Douglas ex Lindley　MUSK　　Very rare
M. guttatus Fischer ex DC.　　MONKEYFLOWER　　Rather uncommon
M. x robertsii Silverside　　HYBRID MONKEYFLOWER　　Fairly common
M. luteus L.　　BLOOD-DROP-EMLETS　　Rather uncommon
Antirrhinum majus L.　　SNAPDRAGON Fairly common on old walls & buildings
Chaenorhinum minus (L.) Lange　　SMALL TOADFLAX　　Very rare (W.Som.Railway)
Misopates orontium (L.) Raf.　　WEASEL'S-SNOUT　　Rare arable weed, Porlock Vale
Asarina procumbens Miller　　PROCUMBENT SNAPDRAGON　　A rare introduction
There have been two reports, one in Porlock area 1985 and one from Minehead 1994.
Cymbalaria muralis Gaertner,Meyer & Scherb. subsp. muralis.　　Common on old walls
　　IVY-LEAVED TOADFLAX　　around villages
Kickxia elatine (L.) Dumort.　　SHARP-LEAVED FLUELLEN　　Uncommon. Somerset
K. spuria (L.) Dumort.　　ROUND-LEAVED FLUELLEN　　Rare. Somerset
Linaria vulgaris Miller　　COMMON TOADFLAX　　Fairly common; not on moors
This plant seems to have declined slightly, possibly due to hedge-trimming.
L. purpurea (L.) Miller　　PURPLE TOADFLAX　　Common near dwellings
L. repens (L.) Miller　　PALE TOADFLAX　　Rare
Digitalis purpurea L.　　FOXGLOVE　　Common, sometimes abundant
Veronica serpyllifolia L. subsp. serpyllifolia THYME-LEAVED SPEEDWELL　Very common
V. officinalis L.　　HEATH SPEEDWELL　　Common on acid moorland
V. chamaedrys L.　　GERMANDER SPEEDWELL　　Very common

FLOWERING PLANTS

V. montana L.	WOOD SPEEDWELL	Common in woodland
V. scutellata L.	MARSH SPEEDWELL	Frequent in moorland bogs
V. beccabunga L.	BROOKLIME	Common in the lower streams
V. catenata Pennell	PINK WATER-SPEEDWELL	Formerly on Minehead Marsh but not seen there since 1970s
V. arvensis L.	WALL SPEEDWELL	Common
V. agrestis L.	GREEN FIELD-SPEEDWELL	Uncommon; arable land
V. polita Fries	GREY FIELD-SPEEDWELL	Fairly frequent
V. persica Poiret	COMMON FIELD-SPEEDWELL	Common
V. filiformis Smith	SLENDER SPEEDWELL	Common in lawns and verges
V. hederifolia L. subsp. hederifolia	IVY-LEAVED SPEEDWELL	Common on lower ground
subsp. lucorum (Klett & Richter) Hartl		Less common than the type
V. longifolia L.	GARDEN SPEEDWELL	Rare garden escape
Hebe salicifolia (G.Forster) Pennell	KOROMIKO	Garden escape
H. barkeri (Cockayne) Wall	BARKER'S HEBE	Garden escape
¶Sibthorpia europaea L.	CORNISH MONEYWORT	Increasing; on streambanks

Melampyrum pratense L. subsp. pratense COW-WHEAT   Common in woods and heathland Hemiparasitic on whortleberry. Foodplant of the rare Heath Fritillary butterfly.

Euphrasia. There are 82 species, sub-species and hybrid EYEBRIGHTS currently on the British List. These are a difficult group needing expert identification but the following have been confirmed in the Exmoor area; their status however has not been investigated.

Euphrasia anglica Pugsley

E. nemorosa (Pers.) Wallr.

E. confusa Pugsley

E. micrantha Reichb.   (There may be others)

Odontites vernus (Bellardi) Dumort. subsp. serotinus	RED BARTSIA	Fairly frequent
Rhinanthus minor L. subsp. minor	YELLOW-RATTLE	Fairly common on grassy banks and verges, mainly in south and west of area
Pedicularis palustris L.	MARSH LOUSEWORT or RED-RATTLE	Fairly frequent in moorland bogs
P. sylvatica L. subsp. sylvatica	LOUSEWORT	Common on damp moorland

OROBANCHACEAE

Lathraea squamaria L.	TOOTHWORT	A rare parasite on hazel
L. clandestina L.	PURPLE TOOTHWORT	A very rare parasite on willow near Porlock but not seen recently. Introduction.
Present for a number of years		
¶Orobanche rapum-genistae Thuill.	GREATER BROOMRAPE	Rare on gorse. Somerset
O. alba Steph. ex Willd. var rubra	THYME BROOMRAPE	On garden thyme; Som. 1978
¶O. hederae Duby	IVY BROOMRAPE	Uncommon, on ivy
O. minor Smith	COMMON BROOMRAPE	Uncommon, various hosts

LENTIBULARIACEAE

Pinguicula lusitanica L.	PALE BUTTERWORT	Uncommon in upland bogs

FLOWERING PLANTS

A survey *The Conservation status of P. lusitanica on Exmoor* undertaken by Matthew Jones in 1991 looked at all the known sites and concluded that poaching by cattle and drainage were causing reduction of the plant on Exmoor.

P. grandiflora Lam.	LARGE-FLOWERED BUTTERWORT	One site on Exmoor. Som.

CAMPANULACEAE

Campanula patula L.	SPREADING BELLFLOWER	Garden escape
C. persicifolia L.	PEACH-LEAVED BELLFLOWER	Garden escape
C. medium L.	CANTERBURY-BELLS	Garden escape
C. portenschlagiana Schultes	ADRIA BELLFLOWER	Common near dwellings
C. poscharskyana Degen	TRAILING BELLFLOWER	Common near dwellings
C. latifolia L.	GIANT BELLFLOWER	Established on Brendon Hills
C. trachelium L.	NETTLE-LEAVED BELLFLOWER	Very rare
C. rotundifolia L.	HAREBELL	Very rare
Wahlenbergia hederacea (L.) Reichb.	IVY-LEAVED BELLFLOWER	Common on the moors
Jasione montana L.	SHEEP'S-BIT	Common on dry moorland, walls etc.
Lobelia erinus L.	GARDEN LOBELIA	Garden escapes

RUBIACEAE •

Sherardia arvensis L.	FIELD MADDER	Arable fields. Common in north & e.
Galium odoratum (L.) Scop.	WOODRUFF	Frequent in woodlands
G. uliginosum L.	FEN BEDSTRAW	Uncommon. Mainly on grass moors
G. palustre L. agg. subsp. palustre	MARSH BEDSTRAW	Very common on damp moorland
subsp. elongatum (C.Presl) Arcang.	Comparative status of subspp. not known.	
G. verum L.	LADY'S BEDSTRAW	Rather uncommon & decreasing
G. mollugo L. subsp. mollugo	HEDGE BEDSTRAW	Common in lower lying hedgerows
G. saxatile L.	HEATH BEDSTRAW	Very common
G. aparine L.	CLEAVERS	Very common in hedgerows & fields
Cruciata laevipes Opiz	CROSSWORT	Uncommon or rare
Rubia peregrina L.	WILD MADDER	Frequent along coast

CAPRIFOLIACEAE

Sambucus nigra L.	ELDER	Very common in hedges, woods etc.
S. ebulus L.	DWARF ELDER or DANEWORT	Very rare
Viburnum opulus L.	GUELDER-ROSE	Uncommon, in hedges
V. lantana L.	WAYFARING TREE	Rare, non tolerant of acid soils
V. tinus L.	LAURUSTINUS	Naturalized in a few places
Symphoricarpos albus (L.) S.F.Blake	SNOWBERRY	Naturalized in many places
Leycesteria formosa Wallich	HIMALAYAN HONEYSUCKLE	Ntrlizd., coastal woods
Lonicera pileata Oliver	BOX-LEAVED HONEYSUCKLE	Introduced
L. nitida E.Wilson	WILSON'S HONEYSUCKLE	Relics of cultivation

FLOWERING PLANTS

Lonicera xylosteum L.	FLY HONEYSUCKLE	Bird-sown from gardens
L. japonica Thunb.ex Murray	JAPANESE HONEYSUCKLE	Garden escape
L. periclymenum L.	HONEYSUCKLE	Very common in woods & hedges

ADOXACEAE

Adoxa moschatellina L.　MOSCHATEL　Fairly common in woods & hedgebanks

VALERIANACEAE

Valerianella locusta (L.) Laterr.	COMMON CORNSALAD	Uncommon
¶V. carinata Lois.	KEELED-FRUITED CORNSALAD	More common than above species, on walls and waste ground
¶V. dentata (L.) Pollich	NARROW-FRUITED CORNSALAD	Very rare. Som.
Valeriana officinalis L.	COMMON VALERIAN	Common by waters and damp meadows except around Minehead
V. pyrenaica L.	PYRENEAN VALERIAN	Local, around Dulverton
V. dioica L.	MARSH VALERIAN	Scarce; damp meadows
Centranthus ruber (L.) DC.	RED VALERIAN	Common on walls near dwellings

DIPSACACEAE

Dipsacus fullonum L.	WILD TEASEL	Frequent on waste ground
D. pilosus L.	SMALL TEASEL	Very rare. Somerset
Knautia arvensis (L.) Coulter	FIELD SCABIOUS	Frequent on dry banks
Succisa pratensis Moench	DEVIL'S-BIT SCABIOUS	Frequent; damp moorland, river banks, also on coastal cliffs

ASTERACEAE *(COMPOSITAE)*

Carlina vulgaris L.	CARLINE THISTLE	Uncommon; near the coast
Arctium lappa L.	GREATER BURDOCK	Very rare. Devon
A. minus (Hill) Bernh. subsp. pubens (Bab.) P.Fourn. and subsp. minus	LESSER BURDOCK	Common except on grass moors both occur, but distribution not known.
Carduus tenuiflorus Curtis	SLENDER THISTLE	Rare, on the coast
C. crispus L. subsp. multiflorus	WELTED THISTLE	Uncommon
C. nutans L.	MUSK or NODDING THISTLE	Locally common
Cirsium eriophorum (L.) Scop.	WOOLLY THISTLE	A spectacular, rare, thistle
C. vulgare (Savi) Ten.	SPEAR THISTLE	Very common
C. dissectum (L.) Hill	MEADOW THISTLE	Very rare. A non prickly thistle
C. x forsteri (Smith) Loudon	MEADOW X MARSH THISTLE	Rare, Exmoor border
C. acaule (L.) Scop.	DWARF THISTLE	Very rare
C. palustre (L.) Scop.	MARSH THISTLE	Very common on damp ground
C. arvense (L.) Scop.	CREEPING THISTLE	Abundant. Attracts butterflies
Onopordum acanthium L.	COTTON THISTLE	Rare garden escape
Silybum marianum (L.) Gaertner	MILK THISTLE	Rare
Serratula tinctoria L.	SAW-WORT	Very rare in our area

FLOWERING PLANTS

Centaurea scabiosa L.	GREATER KNAPWEED	Very rare
C. montana L.	PERENNIAL CORNFLOWER	Garden throw-outs
C. cyanus L.	CORNFLOWER	Garden escapes - none seen in cornfields for many years
C. solstitialis L.	YELLOW STAR-THISTLE	Very rare casual
C. nigra L.	COMMON KNAPWEED	Common

Formerly split into two subspp. nigra and nemoralis, both of which occur.

Cichorium intybus L.	CHICORY	Uncommon escapes from cultivation
Lapsana communis L. subsp. communis	NIPPLEWORT	Very common
Hypochaeris radicata L.	CAT'S-EAR	Abundant
H. glabra L.	SMOOTH CAR'S-EAR	Very rare, near Minehead, Som.
Leontodon autumnalis L.	AUTUMN HAWKBIT	Very common
L. hispidus L.	ROUGH HAWKBIT	Fairly common
L. saxatilis Lam.	LESSER HAWKBIT	Common
Picris echioides L.	BRISTLY OXTONGUE	Locally common, not on moors
P. hieracioides L.	HAWKWEED OXTONGUE	Uncommon
Tragopogon pratensis L. subsp. minor	GOAT'S-BEARD	Local, mainly around Minehead
T. porrifolius L.	SALSIFY	Rare casual, possibly bird-seed alien. Som.
Sonchus arvensis L.	PERENNIAL SOW-THISTLE	Fairly common
S. oleraceus L.	SMOOTH SOW-THISTLE	Very common
S. asper (L.) Hill	PRICKLY SOW-THISTLE	Very common
Lactuca serriola L.	PRICKLY LETTUCE	Local, spreading from Minehead
L. virosa L.	GREAT LETTUCE	Only at Minehead, may spread
L. tatarica (L.) C.Meyer	BLUE LETTUCE	Formerly in Minehead, last seen 1988
Cicerbita macrophylla (Willd.) Wallr.	BLUE SOW-THISTLE	Naturalized, Rockford, Devon
Mycelis muralis (L.) Dumort.	WALL LETTUCE	Fairly common to north & east
Taraxacum Wigg.	DANDELIONS	

There are currently 226 microspecies of Dandelion on the British List but little work has been done on them on Exmoor as they need expert identification. Visiting botanists have confirmed the following:
  T. oxoniense Dahlst.; T. praestans Lindb.; T. faeroense (Dahlst.) Dahlst.; T. bracteatum Dahlst.; T. nordstedtii Dahlst.; T. dahlstedtii Lindb.f.; T. obliquilobum Dahlst.

Crepis capillaris (L.) Wallr.	SMOOTH HAWK'S-BEARD	Common
C. vesicaria L. subsp. taraxacifolia	BEAKED HAWK'S-BEARD	Common

Pilosella peleteriana (Mérat) F.Schultz & Schultz-Bip. *(Hieracium peleterianum Mérat)*
    SHAGGY MOUSE-EAR HAWKWEED   Rare

P. officinarum F.Schultz & Schultz-Bip. *(Hieracium pilosella L.)*
    MOUSE-EAR HAWKWEED   Common, dry grassy banks

P. praealta (Villars ex Gochnat) F.Schultz & Schultz-Bip. *(Hieracium praealtum Vill.ex Goch.)* TALL MOUSE-EAR HAWKWEED   Garden weed in Minehead 1979-84

P. aurantiaca (L.) F.Schultz & Schultz-Bip. subsp. carpathicola (Naeg.& Peter) Soják *(Hieracium brunneocroceum Pugsley)* FOX-AND-CUBS   Naturalized garden escape

FLOWERING PLANTS

HIERACIUM L. (HAWKWEEDS) As with dandelions and brambles there are many microspecies (about 250) of Hieracium on the British List, which need specialist identification. We have been able to get some of these confirmed as follows:
- Sect. Sabauda (Fries) F. Williams: H. sabaudum L.
- Sect. Umbellata F. Williams: H. umbellatum L. subsp. umbellatum;
  - subsp. bichlorophyllum (Druce & Zahn) Sell & C.West
- Sect. Tridentata (Fries) F.Williams: H. trichocaulon (Dahlst.) Johansson
- Sect. Vulgata (Fries) F.Williams: H. lepidulum Stenstroem;
  - H. subamplifolium (Zahn) Roffey
  - H. cheriense Jordan ex Boreau;
  - H. acuminatum Jordan;
  - H. diaphanum Fries;
  - H. maculatum Smith;
  - H. grandidens Dahlst.
- Sect. Oreadea Zahn: H. pseudoleyi (Zahn) Roffey;
  - H. eustomon (E.F.Linton) Roffey

Filago vulgaris Lam.	COMMON CUDWEED	Rare, dry gravelly places
Anaphalis margaritacea (L.) Benth.	PEARLY EVERLASTING	Garden throw-out
Gnaphalium uliginosum L.	MARSH or WAYSIDE CUDWEED	Common on tracks

(G. sylvaticum L. WOOD CUDWEED. Probably now extinct on Exmoor. Recorded near Roadwater 1927 and 'in hilly pastures' by Norman Haddon. Has decreased elsewhere.)

Inula helenium L.	ELECAMPANE	Garden escapes
I. conyzae (Griess.) Meikle	PLOUGHMAN'S SPIKENARD	Uncommon; nr coast
Pulicaria dysenterica (L.) Bernh.	COMMON FLEABANE	Fairly frequent
Solidago virgaurea L.	GOLDENROD	Common in woods, hedges & cliffs
S. canadensis L.	CANADIAN GOLDENROD	Garden escape
S. gigantea Aiton	EARLY GOLDENROD	Garden escape
Aster x salignus Willd.	COMMON MICHAELMAS DAISY	Garden escape
A. tripolium L.	SEA ASTER	Local in brackish mud. Somerset
Erigeron glaucus Ker Gawler	BEACH ASTER or SEASIDE DAISY	Garden escape
E. karvinskianus DC.	MEXICAN FLEABANE	Well established near dwellings
Conyza canadensis (L.) Cronq.	CANADIAN FLEABANE	Rare on waste ground. Som.
C. sumatrensis (Retz.) E.Walker	GUERNSEY FLEABANE	First recorded at Minehead 1994, may increase as it has elsewhere in England
Bellis perennis L.	DAISY	Very common throughout
Tanacetum parthenium (L.) Schultz-Bip.	FEVERFEW	Common around villages
T. vulgare L.	TANSY	Uncommon, some are garden escapes
Seriphidium maritimum (L.) Polj. (*Artemisia maritima*)	SEA WORMWOOD	Recorded from Porlock Weir but not seen recently
Artemisia vulgaris L.	MUGWORT	Common on rough ground
A. absinthium L.	WORMWOOD	Uncommon and decreasing
A. biennis Willd.	SLENDER MUGWORT	Birdseed alien. Som.
Achillea ptarmica L.	SNEEZEWORT	Rare in damp grassland
A. millefolium L.	YARROW	Very common

FLOWERING PLANTS

Chamaemelum nobile (L.) All.	CHAMOMILE	Rare, in short turfy grass
Anthemis cotula L.	STINKING CHAMOMILE	Uncommon, arable land. Som.
Chrysanthemum segetum L.	CORN MARIGOLD	Rare, local; occas. abundant
Leucanthemum vulgare Lam.	OXEYE DAISY	Fairly common in old grassland
L.x superbum (Bergmans ex J.Ingram) Kent	SHASTA DAISY	Estab. escape from gardens
Matricaria recutita L.	SCENTED MAYWEED	Fairly common
M. discoidea DC.(M.matricarioides)	PINEAPPLE-WEED	Very common, tracks & gateways
Tripleurospermum maritimum (L.) Koch	SEA MAYWEED	Frequent near the coast
T. inodorum (L.) Schultz-Bip.	SCENTLESS MAYWEED	Common inland
Senecio cineraria DC.	SILVER RAGWORT	Naturalized on sea cliffs
S. x albescens Burb. & Colgan		Rare
S. jacobaea L.	COMMON RAGWORT	Common
S. aquaticus Hill	MARSH RAGWORT	Frequent, streams and river banks
S. erucifolius L.	HOARY RAGWORT	Rare
S. squalidus L.	OXFORD RAGWORT	Frequent around habitations
S. vulgaris L.	GROUNDSEL	Common in cultivated land
S. sylvaticus L.	HEATH GROUNDSEL	Fairly common on dry heaths
S. viscosus L.	STICKY GROUNDSEL	Uncommon
Brachyglottis 'Sunshine'	SHRUB RAGWORT	Garden throw-outs
Doronicum pardalianches L.	LEOPARD'S-BANE	Occasionally well naturalized
D.x excelsum (N.E.Br.)Stace	HARPER CREWE'S LEOPARD'S-BANE	Garden escape
D. plantagineum L.	PLANTAIN-LEAVED LEOPARD'S-BANE	Garden escape
Tussilago farfara L.	COLTSFOOT	Frequent, bare ground and waysides
Petasites hybridus (L.) Gaertner, Meyer & Scherb.	BUTTERBUR	Frequent, river banks
P. japonicus (Siebold & Zucc.) Maxim.	GIANT or CREAMY BUTTERBUR	Rare. Somerset
P. fragrans (Villars) C.Presl	WINTER HELIOTROPE	Common on hedgebanks

Increasing at an alarming rate and becoming a severe threat to native hedgerow flora.

Calendula officinalis L.	POT MARIGOLD	Garden escapes
Helianthus annuus L.	SUNFLOWER	Casual
Galinsoga quadriradiata Ruíz Lopez & Pavón (G. ciliata)	SHAGGY SOLDIER	Rare garden weed. Somerset
Bidens tripartita L.	TRIFID BUR-MARIGOLD	Rare. Marshes; ditches.Som.
Eupatorium cannabinum L.	HEMP AGRIMONY	Common in damp places

FLOWERING PLANTS
Class: LILIIDAE (MONOCOTYLEDONS)

ALISMATACEAE
Alisma plantago-aquatica L.　　　　WATER-PLANTAIN　Uncommon in slow-moving water
HYDROCHARITACEAE
Elodea canadensis Michaux　　　　CANADIAN WATERWEED　　　　　　Uncommon
E. nuttallii (Planchon) H.St.John　　NUTTALL'S WATERWEED　　　　　　Uncommon
　This plant is generally on the increase in slow-moving waters. No Devon records yet.
Lagarosiphon major (Ridley) Moss　　CURLY WATERWEED　　Rare introduction. Som.
APONOGETONACEAE
Aponogeton distachyos L.f.　　　　CAPE PONDWEED　　　Rare introduction. Som.
JUNCAGINACEAE
Triglochin palustre L.　　　　　　MARSH ARROWGRASS　　Rare. Wet grass moorland
T. maritimum L.　　　　　　　　SEA ARROWGRASS　　　Rare. Saltmarsh. Som.
POTAMOGETONACEAE
Potamogeton natans L.　　　　　　BROAD-LEAVED PONDWEED　Rare; ponds & rivers
P. polygonifolius Pourret　　　　　BOG PONDWEED　Common; moorland streams & bogs
P. pusillus L.　　　　　　　　　LESSER PONDWEED　　　　Very rare; R. Avill 1976
P. berchtoldii Fieber　　　　　　SMALL PONDWEED　　Uncommon; rivers & streams
P. crispus L.　　　　　　　　　CURLED PONDWEED　　Rare; ditches and marshes
P. pectinatus L.　　　　　　　　FENNEL PONDWEED　　　Very rare; ponds. Som.
　(**RUPPIACEAE**. Ruppia maritima L. BEAKED TASSELWEED. Recorded on Porlock
Marsh by Norman Haddon, also formerly on Minehead Marsh, but no current records)
ZANNICHELLIACEAE
Zannichellia palustris L.　　　　　HORNED PONDWEED　　　　　　Rare .Somerset
ARACEAE
Lysichiton americanus Hultén & H.St.John AMERICAN SKUNK-CABBAGE　　Becoming
　　　　　　　　　　　　　　　naturalized along one or two streams. Somerset
Arum maculatum L.　　　　　　　LORDS-AND-LADIES　　Very common below 1000 ft.
A. maculatum x A. italicum　　　A very rare hybrid recorded from Somerset Exmoor
A. italicum Miller subsp. italicum　ITALIAN LORDS-AND-LADIES Natd gardn throw-out
¶ subsp. neglectum (F.Towns.)Prime　Very rare, shingle at edge of field. Somerset
LEMNACEAE
Spirodela polyrhiza (L.) Schleiden *(Lemna polyrhiza)*
　　　　　　　　　　　　　　　GREATER DUCKWEED　　　Rare. Minehead marshes
Lemna gibba L.　　　　　　　　FAT DUCKWEED　　Very rare. Minehead & Porlock
L. minor L.　　　　　　　　　COMMON DUCKWEED　　　　　　　　　　Common
L. trisulca L.　　　　　　　　IVY-LEAVED DUCKWEED　　Rare. Minehead marshes
L. minuta Kunth　　　　　　　LEAST DUCKWEED　1st record Minehead marsh 1994

FLOWERING PLANTS

JUNCACEAE

Juncus squarrosus L.	HEATH RUSH	Common on the moors
J. tenuis Willd.	SLENDER RUSH	Uncommon; damp waysides & tracks
J. compressus Jacq.	ROUND-FRUITED RUSH	Very rare. Devon
J. gerardii Lois.	SALTMARSH RUSH	Very local near the coast
J. foliosus Desf.	LEAFY TOADRUSH	Fairly common on higher ground
J. bufonius L.	TOAD-RUSH	Very common in boggy land
J. subnodulosus Schrank	BLUNT-FLOWERED RUSH	Very local; Devon
J. articulatus L.	JOINTED RUSH	Common on the moor
J. x surrejanus Druce ex Stace &Lam.	JOINTED x SHARP-FLOWERED RUSH	Frequent
J. acutiflorus Ehrh. ex Hoffm.	SHARP-FLOWERED RUSH	Common on the moor
J. bulbosus L.	BULBOUS RUSH	Common
J. inflexus L.	HARD RUSH	Uncommon except in Minehead marsh
J. effusus L.	SOFT RUSH	Very common

Inflorescence is often compact (var. subglomeratus DC.) and resembling the next sp.

J. conglomeratus L.	COMPACT RUSH	Common on the higher moorland
Luzula forsteri (Smith) DC.	SOUTHERN WOODRUSH	Scarce

One site in Devon Exmoor plus a few locations on the Brendon Hills

L. pilosa (L.) Willd.	HAIRY WOODRUSH	Common; woods & shady banks
L. sylvatica (Hudson) Gaudin	GREAT WOODRUSH	Common in woods
L. luzuloides (Lam.) Dandy & Wilm.	WHITE WOODRUSH	Garden escape, may ntlze. Som.
L. campestris (L.) DC.	FIELD WOODRUSH	Common in short old grassland
L. multiflora (Ehrh.) Lej.	HEATH WOODRUSH	Frequent on the moors

CYPERACEAE

Eriophorum angustifolium Honck.	COMMON COTTONGRASS	Common; boggy moorland
E. vaginatum L.	HARE'S-TAIL COTTONGRASS	Common, as above
Trichophorum cespitosum (L.) Hartman	DEERGRASS	Common on the higher western moors
Eleocharis palustris (L.) Roemer & Schultes subsp. palustris	COMMON SPIKE-RUSH	Wet moorland and marshes
E. multicaulis (Smith) Desv.	MANY-STALKED SPIKE-RUSH	Uncommon
E. quinqueflora (F.Hartmann) O.Schwarz	FEW-FLOWERED SPIKE-RUSH	Very rare. Som.
Bolboschoenus maritimus (L.) Palla *(Scirpus m.)*	SEA CLUB-RUSH	Very local near the coast. Som.
Scirpus sylvaticus L.	WOOD CLUB-RUSH	Borders southern Exmoor
Schoenoplectus lacustris (L.) Palla *(Scirpus l.)*	COMMON CLUB-RUSH	Doubtful record
S. tabernaemontani (Gmelin) Palla	GREY CLUB-RUSH	Minehead & Porlock Marshes
Isolepis setacea (L.) R.Br.	BRISTLE CLUB-RUSH	Frequent; easily overlooked
I. cernua (Vahl) Roemer & Schultes	SLENDER CLUB-RUSH	Very rare. Som.
Eleogiton fluitans (L.) Link	FLOATING CLUB-RUSH	Scarce but increasing. Som.

FLOWERING PLANTS

Cyperus eragrostis Lam.	PALE GALINGALE	Casual alien. Som.
Rhynchospora alba (L.) M.Vahl	WHITE BEAK-SEDGE	Very rare. Devon
Carex paniculata L.	GREATER TUSSOCK-SEDGE	Frequent; wet moorland
C. otrubae Podp.	FALSE FOX-SEDGE	Local. Marshes
C. spicata Hudson	SPIKED SEDGE	Rare
C. muricata subsp. lamprocarpa Celak.	PRICKLY SEDGE	Uncommon
C. divulsa Stokes subsp. divulsa	GREY SEDGE	Frequent in northern part of Exmoor
C. arenaria L.	SAND SEDGE	Very local. Somerset
C. disticha Hudson	BROWN SEDGE	Rare, ponds on Brendon Hills. Som.
C. remota L.	REMOTE SEDGE	Common; woods surrounding moor
C. ovalis Gooden.	OVAL SEDGE	Common on the moors
C. echinata Murray	STAR SEDGE	Common on damp moorland
C. hirta L.	HAIRY SEDGE	Fairly frequent, river valleys
C. acutiformis Ehrh.	LESSER POND SEDGE	Unconfirmed records only
C. rostrata Stokes	BOTTLE SEDGE	Frequent on the moors
C. pendula Hudson	PENDULOUS SEDGE	Increasing in shady places
C. sylvatica Hudson	WOOD-SEDGE	Rather uncommon; woodlands
C. flacca Schreber	GLAUCOUS SEDGE	Uncommon; non acid soils
C. panicea L.	CARNATION SEDGE	Very common; wet moorland
C. laevigata Smith	SMOOTH-STALKED SEDGE	Fairly common
C. binervis Smith	GREEN-RIBBED SEDGE	Common on moorland
C. extensa Gooden.	LONG-BRACTED SEDGE	Rare. Devon
C. hostiana DC.	TAWNY SEDGE	Frequent on damp moorland
C. x fulva Gooden.	TAWNY x COMMON YELLOW SEDGE	Uncommon
C. viridula Michaux subsp. oedocarpa (Andersson) B.Schmid *(C. demissa Hornem.)*	COMMON YELLOW SEDGE	Common on moorland
subsp. viridula *(C. serotina Mérat)*	SMALL-FRUITED YELLOW SEDGE	Rare. Devon
C. pallescens L.	PALE SEDGE	Uncommon
C. caryophyllea Latour.	SPRING SEDGE	Fairly common in short turf
C. pilulifera L.	PILL SEDGE	Fairly common in moorland areas
C. nigra (L.) Reichard	COMMON SEDGE	Common in upland areas
C. pulicaris L.	FLEA SEDGE	Fairly common in upland areas

FLOWERING PLANTS
GRASSES

POACEAE *(GRAMINEAE)*

Pleioblastus pygmaeus (Miq.) Nakai	DWARF BAMBOO	Introduction
Sasa palmata (Burb.) Camus	BROAD-LEAVED BAMBOO	Introduction
Pseudosasa japonica (Siebold & Zucc. ex Steudel) Makino ex Nakai		
	ARROW BAMBOO	Introduction
Nardus stricta L.	MAT-GRASS	Common on damp moorland
Milium effusum L.	WOOD MILLET	Frequent in shady woodland
Festuca pratensis Hudson	MEADOW FESCUE	Frequent in southern half of area
F. arundinacea Schreber	TALL FESCUE	Fairly frequent
F. gigantea (L.) Villars	GIANT FESCUE	Fairly frequent in shady woodland
F. rubra L. subsp. rubra	RED FESCUE	Very common

A very variable species divided into seven subspecies. Also recorded is:

subsp. juncea (Hackel) K.Richter		Local
F. ovina L. subsp ovina	SHEEP'S FESCUE	Very common
subsp. hirtula (Hackel ex Travis) M.Wilk. *(F. tenuifolia Sibth.)*		Scarce
X F. loliaceum (Hudson) P.Fourn.	HYBRID FESCUE	Fairly frequent
Lolium perenne L.	PERENNIAL RYE-GRASS	Very common
L. multiflorum Lam.	ITALIAN RYE-GRASS	Introduced. Often on verges
Vulpia fasciculata (Forsskål) Fritsch	DUNE FESCUE	Very rare and local. Somerset
V. bromoides (L.) Gray	SQUIRREL-TAIL FESCUE	Frequent. Dry places
V. myuros (L.) C.Gmelin	RAT'S-TAIL FESCUE	Uncommon. Somerset
V. ciliata Dumort. subsp. ambigua	BEARDED FESCUE	Very rare. 1 report only. Som.
Cynosurus cristatus L.	CRESTED DOG'S-TAIL	Very common throughout
Puccinellia maritima (Hudson) Parl.	COMMON SALT-MARSH GRASS	Very local. Som.
P. distans (Jacq.) Parl.	REFLEXED SALT-MARSH GRASS	Very local. Som.
Briza media L.	QUAKING GRASS	Local. Somerset
B. maxima L.	GREATER QUAKING GRASS	Introduced. Somerset
Poa annua L.	ANNUAL MEADOW-GRASS	Very common everywhere
P. trivialis L.	ROUGH MEADOW-GRASS	Very common throughout
P. humilis Ehrh. ex Hoffm. *(P. subcaerulea Smith)*		
	SPREADING MEADOW-GRASS	Frequent, walls etc.
P. pratensis L.	SMOOTH MEADOW-GRASS	Common
P. angustifolia L.	NARROW-LEAVED MEADOW-GRASS	Rare. Som.
P. compressa L.	FLATTENED MEADOW-GRASS	Uncommon;dry places
P. nemoralis L.	WOOD MEADOW-GRASS	Frequent in woodlands
¶P. bulbosa L.	BULBOUS MEADOW-GRASS	Rare; near coast. Som.
Dactylis glomerata L.	COCK'S-FOOT	Very common

FLOWERING PLANTS

Catapodium rigidum (L.) C.E.Hubb. *(Desmazeria rigida (L.) Tutin)*		
	FERN-GRASS	Dry places, mostly near the coast
Catapodium marinum (L.) C.E. Hubb.	SEA FERN-GRASS	Local; on the coast. Somerset
Parapholis strigosa (Dumort.) C.E.Hubb.	HARD-GRASS	Rare and local. Coastal marsh
¶P. incurva (L.) C.E.Hubb.	CURVED HARD-GRASS	Very rare in coastal marsh
Glyceria maxima (Hartman) O.Holmb.	REED SWEET-GRASS	Rare; rivers & ponds. Som.
G. fluitans (L.) R.Br.	FLOATING SWEET-GRASS	Common; streams & marsh
G. declinata Bréb.	SMALL SWEET-GRASS	Fairly common, wet places
G. notata Chevall. *(G. plicata (Fries) Fries)*	PLICATE SWEET-GRASS	Rather uncommon
Melica uniflora Retz.	WOOD MELICK	Frequent in woods & shady banks
Helictotrichon pubescens (Hudson) Pilger	DOWNY OAT-GRASS	Scarce
Arrhenatherum elatius (L.) P.Beauv. ex J.S. Presl & C.Presl		
	FALSE OAT-GRASS	Very common throughout
Avena fatua L.	WILD OAT	Arable weed
A. sativa L	OAT	Escapes from cultivation
Trisetum flavescens (L.) P.Beauv.	YELLOW OAT-GRASS	Frequent in east o/w scarce
Deschampsia cespitosa (L.) P.Beauv.	TUFTED HAIR-GRASS	Common on damp moorland
D. flexuosa (L.) Trin.	WAVY HAIR-GRASS	Common
		A typical moorland grass on Exmoor
Holcus lanatus L.	YORKSHIRE FOG	Common in a variety of habitats
H. mollis L.	CREEPING SOFT-GRASS	Common; woods & hedges
Aira caryophyllea L.	SILVER HAIR-GRASS	Common except s.west Exmoor
A. praecox L.	EARLY HAIR-GRASS	Common on dry slopes
Anthoxanthum odoratum L.	SWEET VERNAL GRASS	Very common throughout
Phalaris arundinacea L.	REED CANARY-GRASS	Frequent by larger waterways
P. aquatica L.	BULBOUS CANARY-GRASS	Rare casual
P. canariensis L.	CANARY-GRASS	Bird-seed alien. No Devon reports
Agrostis capillaris L. *(A.tenuis Sib.)*	COMMON BENT	Very common
A. stolonifera L.	CREEPING BENT	Very common
A. curtisii Kerguélen *(A. setacea Curtis)*		Common on coastal heaths where it mingles
	BRISTLE BENT	with the heather. Turns pale gold
A. canina L.	VELVET BENT	Common on moorland
A. vinealis Schreber	BROWN BENT	Common on dry moorland
Calamagrostis epigejos (L.) Roth	WOOD SMALL-REED	Rare. Somerset
Ammophila arenaria (L.) Link	MARRAM	Rare. Minehead golf links
Lagurus ovatus L.	HARE'S-TAIL	Very local in sandy places. Somerset

This has become established on the coast between Minehead and Dunster since 1990.

Polypogon viridis (Gouan) Breistr. *(Agrostis semiverticillata (Forsskål) C.Chr.)*
WATER-BENT   Pavement edges & roadsides
First noted in Minehead in 1989 since when it has increased and spread. Suspect introduced with tomato boxes.

FLOWERING PLANTS

Alopecurus pratensis L.	MEADOW FOXTAIL	Common except on high moorland
A. x brachystylus Peterm.	MEADOW x MARSH FOXTAIL	Uncommon
A. geniculatus L.	MARSH FOXTAIL	Common in damp grassland
A. x plettkei Mattf.	MARSH x BULBOUS FOXTAIL	Rare
¶A. bulbosus Gouan	BULBOUS FOXTAIL	Rare. Coastal marsh. Som.
A. myosuroides Hudson	BLACK-GRASS	Rather uncommon
Phleum pratense L.	TIMOTHY	Common
P. bertolonii DC.	SMALLER CATSTAIL	Uncommon; in grassland
P. arenarium L.	SAND CAT'S-TAIL	Rare, coast near Minehead
Bromus commutatus Schrader	MEADOW BROME	Uncommon
B. racemosus L.	SMOOTH BROME	Rare. Devon
B. hordeaceus L. subsp. hordeaceus	SOFT BROME	Common; fields and verges

Bromopsis ramosa (Hudson) Holub *(Bromus ramosus)*
HAIRY BROME   Fairly common in woodlands

¶Anisantha diandra (Roth) Tutin ex Tzvelev *(Bromus diandrus)*
GREAT BROME   Very uncommon. Som.

A. rigida (Roth) N.Hylander *(Bromus rigidus)*
RIPGUT BROME   Rare and very local. Som.

A. sterilis (L.) Nevski *(Bromus sterilis)*   Very common but not on
BARREN BROME   central moorland

Ceratochloa cathartica (Vahl) Herter *(Bromus willdenowii Kunth)*
RESCUE BROME   Rare. Somerset

Brachypodium sylvaticum (Hudson) P.Beauv.   Common in woods and hedges
WOOD FALSE BROME   below 1000 ft.

Elymus caninus (L.) L.	BEARDED COUCH	Rare

Elytrigia repens (L.) Desv. ex Nevski subsp. repens *(Agropyron repens)*
COMMON COUCH   Common weed in cultivated land

E. atherica (Link) Kerguélen ex Carreras Martinez *(Elymus pycnanthus (Godron) Meld.)*
SEA COUCH   Local. On the coast

E. juncea (L.) Nevski subsp. boreoatlantica (Simonet & Guin.) N.Hylander *(Elymus farctus)*
SAND COUCH   Very local; coast near Minehead. Som.

Leymus arenarius (L.) Hochst.	LYME GRASS	Rare; coast near Minehead. Som.
Hordeum distichon L.	TWO-ROWED BARLEY	Agricultural escapes
H. murinum L. subsp murinum	WALL BARLEY	Locally common. Not on the moors
H. secalinum Schreber	MEADOW BARLEY	Local. Low lying meadows
Triticum aestivum L.	BREAD WHEAT	Agricultural escapes
Danthonia decumbens (L.) DC.	HEATH GRASS	Common on the moors

Cortaderia selloana (Schultes & Schultes f.) Asch. & Graebner
PAMPAS GRASS   Garden throw-outs

Molinia caerulea (L.) Moench subsp. caerulea PURPLE MOOR-GRASS   Common
   Forms dominant patches often covering several acres on damp moorland. The leaves
   give a seasonal colour change to the moors - blue-green in summer turning to deep
   gold in winter breaking up and blowing about in the wind when they are known as

FLOWERING PLANTS

'flying bent'. Traditional management is by swaling.

Phragmites australis (Cav.) Trin. ex Steudel *(Phragmites communis Trin.)*
COMMON REED   Very local/see over...
There is a good reed bed at Porlock Marsh which is occasionally harvested for thatching material on the Porlock Manor Estate. Smaller beds exist on Minehead/Dunster Marshes; all are important nest sites for birds such as reed and sedge warblers.

Cynodon dactylon (L.) Pers.   BERMUDA-GRASS   Very rare
Found near Minehead Golf Club in 1974. Later covered with tarmac for car park. Reappeared at edge of tarmac 1989 but under constant threat. **RDB**.

Spartina x townsendii Groves & J.Groves
TOWNSEND'S CORD-GRASS   Rare
Our only records are in coastal mud, Porlock Weir

Echinochloa crusgalli (L.) P.Beauv.   COCKSPUR   Birdseed alien
Setaria viridis (L.) P.Beauv.   GREEN BRISTLE-GRASS   Birdseed alien

(The following grasses have also been found as casuals, all probably from bird seed: Panicum miliaceum L. COMMON MILLET; Setaria verticillata (L.) P.Beauv. ROUGH BRISTLE-GRASS; Setaria pumila (Poiret) Roemer & Schultes YELLOW BRISTLE-GRASS.)

BUR-REEDS & BULRUSHES

SPARGANIACEAE

Sparganium erectum L. subsp. neglectum (Beeby) K.Richter
BRANCHED BUR-REED   Fairly frequent ponds/ditches
S. emersum Rehmann   UNBRANCHED BUR-REED   Very rare. Som.
S. natans L.   LEAST BUR-REED   Very rare indeed. Som.

TYPHACEAE

Typha latifolia L.   BULRUSH   Fairly frequent in ponds & ditches

------

LILIACEAE

Narthecium ossifragum (L.) Hudson BOG ASPHODEL   Frequent on wet moorland
Sometimes dominant over large areas of an acre or more
Hemerocallis fulva (L.) L.   ORANGE DAY-LILY   Garden throw-outs
H. lilioasphodelus L.   YELLOW DAY-LILY   Garden throw-outs
Tulipa gesneriana L.   GARDEN TULIP   Garden throw-outs
Fritillaria meleagris L.   FRITILLARY   Introduced. Naturalized in grassland
Lilium pyrenaicum Gouan   PYRENEAN LILY   Rare. Long naturalized in Devon
Convallaria majalis L.   LILY-OF-THE-VALLEY Rare. Occasionally naturalized
Polygonatum multiflorum (L.) All. SOLOMON'S-SEAL   Garden escape
P. x hybridum Bruegger   GARDEN SOLOMON'S-SEAL   Garden escape

FLOWERING PLANTS

Polygonatum odoratum (Miller) Druce ANGULAR SOLOMON'S-SEAL Rare garden escape
(Maianthemum kamtishatis MAY LILY is well naturalized in wood at West Porlock Somerset)

Ornithogalum angustifolium Boreau STAR-OF-BETHLEHEM *(O. umbellatum auct., non L.)*
Introduced or garden escapes but sometimes persistent

Scilla bifolia L.	ALPINE SQUILL	Garden escape
S. lilio-hyacinthus L.	PYRENEAN SQUILL	Garden escape
S. peruviana L.	AUTUMN SQUILL	Garden escape

Hyacinthoides non-scripta (L.) Chouard ex Rothm. *(Endymion non-scriptus (L.) Garcke*
BLUEBELL   Common
Frequent in woodlands, particularly on Brendon Hills. Often on hillsides under bracken.

H. non-scripta x H. hispanica	HYBRID BLUEBELL	The common garden escape
H. hispanica (Miller) Rothm.	SPANISH BLUEBELL	Uncommon garden escape
Chionodoxa forbesii Baker	GLORY-OF-THE-SNOW	Garden throw-out
Muscari armeniacum Leichtlin ex Baker	GARDEN GRAPE-HYACINTH	Garden throw-out
Allium schoenoprasum L.	CHIVES	Garden throw-out
A. roseum L.	ROSY GARLIC	Uncommon garden escape

A. triquetrum L.   THREE-CORNERED LEEK   Originally introduced,
now a troublesome weed in northern (coastal) area of Exmoor

A. ursinum L.   RAMSONS   Abundant in some woods and hedgerows
A. carinatum L.   KEELED GARLIC   Very rare. Somerset
A. ampeloprasum L. var. babingtonii *(A. babingtonii Borrer)* **RDB.**
BABINGTON'S LEEK Rare. Porlock Marsh since C1916

A. vineale L.   WILD ONION   Grassy verges. Frequent in east
Usually var. compactum.

Nectaroscordum siculum (Ucria) Lindley HONEY GARLIC Introduction; natd Horner estuary
Leucojum aestivum L. subsp. pulchellum SUMMER SNOWFLAKE   Garden throw-out

Galanthus nivalis L.   SNOWDROP   Many garden escapes and introductions
Possibly native in the well-known 'Snowdrop Valley' near Timberscombe and in a few nearby areas. Volume of visitors in Spring are causing some decline by trampling.

G. nivalis x G. plicatus		Introduction
G. caucasicus (Baker) Grossh.	CAUCASIAN SNOWDROP	Introduction
Narcissus tazetta L.	BUNCH-FLOWERED DAFFODIL	Garden throw-out
N. poeticus L.	PHEASANT'S-EYE DAFFODIL	Garden throw-out

N. pseudonarcissus L. subsp. pseudonarcissus
                           WILD DAFFODIL   In old meadows and orchards
   subsp. major (Curtis) Baker GARDEN DAFFODIL   Introductions, escapes, etc

Asparagus officinalis L. subsp officinalis GARDEN ASPARAGUS Uncommon escape. Som.
Ruscus aculeatus L.   BUTCHER'S-BROOM   Garden escapes but naturalized
in at least one hedgerow for 80 or more years. Somerset

FLOWERING PLANTS

IRIDACEAE

Sisyrinchium bermudiana L.	BLUE-EYED-GRASS	No current receords but noted in 1959 and 1989 by roadside, Dunkery Beacon!
S. striatum Smith	PALE YELLOW-EYED-GRASS	Garden escape. Som.
Iris germanica L.	BEARDED IRIS	Garden throw-outs
Iris pseudacorus L.	YELLOW IRIS	Fairly common; streams, meadows, etc.
I. foetidissima L.	STINKING IRIS	Frequent on hedgebanks where soil is not acid. Mainly near the coast
Crocus tommasinianus Herbert	EARLY CROCUS	Garden escapes
Gladiolus communis subsp. byzantinus (Miller) A.P.Ham. EASTERN GLADIOLUS		Garden escapes Hedgerows, etc. Som.
Crocosmia paniculata (Klatt) Goldblatt	AUNT ELIZA	Garden escape
C. x crocosmiiflora (Lemoine) N.E.Br. MONTBRETIA		Frequent. Garden origin Well naturalized along R.Barle

AGAVACEAE

Cordyline australis (G.Forster) Endl. CABBAGE PALM   A self-sown plant flowered in a Minehead garden in 1995!

DIOSCOREACEAE

Tamus communis L.   BLACK BRYONY   Common below 1000 ft contour

ORCHIDACEAE

Epipactis helleborine (L.) Crantz   BROAD-LEAVED HELLEBORINE   Scarce. Somerset

Neottia nidus-avis (L.) Rich.   BIRD'S-NEST ORCHID   Saprophytic on beech litter in a few Somerset woodlands

Listera ovata (L.) R.Br.   COMMON TWAYBLADE   Uncommon, calcareous soil

L. cordata (L.) R.Br.   LESSER TWAYBLADE   Rare and local
This small orchid, which grows beneath heather, is one of the gems of the Exmoor flora. There were two current records until 1994 when it was found in four new locations in the Dunkery area. It is a shy flowerer and difficult to spot being only a few inches high.

Spiranthes spiralis (L.) Chevall.   AUTUMN LADY'S-TRESSES   Very local
Occurs in short grass in an area between Porlock S.E. to the Brendons, Somerset. In favourable years can be abundant over small areas - one ENHS member had over 200 on garden lawn.

Platanthera chlorantha (Custer) Reich. GREATER BUTTERFLY ORCHID   V. rare, Barle valley

Anacamptis pyramidalis (L.) Rich   PYRAMIDAL ORCHID   One report from Brendon Hills

(Gymnadenia conopsea (L.) R.Br. FRAGRANT ORCHID. A few old records only)

Dactylorhiza fuchsii (Druce) Soó   COMMON SPOTTED-ORCHID   Uncommon
Not common on Exmoor as prefers more basic soil but it occurs in scattered locations.

D. x grandis (Druce) P.Hunt   COMMON SPOTTED x MARSH ORCHID   Very rare

D. maculata (L.) Soó subsp. ericetorum HEATH SPOTTED ORCHID   Common on acid moors

D. x hallii (Druce) Soó   HEATH SPOTTED x MARSH ORCHID   Rare

D. praetermissa (Druce) Soó   SOUTHERN MARSH ORCHID   Uncommon

Orchis mascula (L.) L.   EARLY PURPLE ORCHID   Common in woods, hedgebanks and grass verges

FLOWERING PLANTS

O. morio L. GREEN-WINGED ORCHID Very rare
(O. apifera Hudson BEE ORCHID. Recorded Porlock Marsh 1920s; Brendon Hills 1973)

References:
Clapham, Tutin & Moore, *Flora of the British Isles* (Cambridge University Press, 1987)
J.G. Dony, S.L. Jury & F.H. Perring *English Names of Wild Flowers* (B.S.B.I. 1986)
C.J. Giddens, *Flowers of Exmoor* (Alcombe Books, Minehead 1979)
"   *Atlas to the Flowers of Exmoor* (Alcombe Books, Minehead 1984)
P.Green, I.Green & G.Crouch *The Somerset Atlas Flora* (In preparation)
Ivemey-Cook, *Atlas of the Devon Flora* (Devonshire Association, Exeter 1984)
D.H. Kent, *List of Vascular Plants of the British Isles* (B.S.B.I. 1992)
R.G.B. Roe *The Flora of Somerset* (S.A.N.H.S. Taunton, 1981)
Clive Stace *New Flora of the British Isles* (Cambridge University Press, 1991)

THE FAUNA

INVERTEBRATES ALONG THE COAST

The Exmoor coast-line is about 30 miles in length and includes stretches of steep cliffs, some of the highest in the country, sometimes sheer and often very friable and subject to landslips and in places wooded down to the tide-line. There are short stretches of sandy beach, some patches of clay or mud, and rock strewn beaches inhospitable to sailor or swimmer but providing rock-pools and habitats ideal for maritime life. In places the numerous moorland waters spill out to meet the sea and here the brackish water provides habitat for mussel beds and the green Enteromorpha seaweeds on which many of the creatures feed.

There is great variation in tides on this stretch of coast. At Minehead Harbour, on spring tides, the water can rise and fall by 9.1m (30ft) and recede nearly a mile to low-water mark on the ebb. Neap tides, however, only rise and fall about 6m (20 ft) and the low-water mark at such times is not far from the beach-head. Thus it is on the spring tides that things normally covered by water can be examined, including the submarine forests off Minehead and Porlock Weir. Some of the rocky promontories are never uncovered, there is just a rise and fall of the water. There is still the lingering threat of pollution on our beaches and it is necessary to guard against this at all times. A study of the maritime creatures may help in this respect.

Since 1974 the Exmoor Natural History Society has been observing life on Exmoor's coast; our chief Maritime Recorder has been H.E. 'Fred' Porter who has been assisted by John Hill and David Hawkes. In the early days they were guided by Dr. J.H. Crothers and found his courses from the Nettlecombe Field Centre invaluable. We are greatly indebted to Dr. Crothers for his guidance.

Phylum: PROTOZOA

Class: SARCODINEA

Order: FORAMINIFERIDA

HYPERAMMINIDAE

Haliphysema tumanowiczi Bowerbank   on Sea-mats (Bryozoa)   Locally common

Class: CILIATEA

Order: HETEROTRICHIDA

FOLLICULINIDAE

Folliculina ampulla (Müller)   Scarce

Phylum: PORIFERA (SPONGES)

Class: CALCAREA

HOMOCOELIDAE
Leucosolenia coriacea (Montagu)   under rocks   Local
SYCETTIDAE
Sycon ciliatum (Fabricius)   stony beaches   Frequent
GRANTIIDAE
Grantia compressa (Fabricius) PURSE SPONGE   rocks   Frequent
Leuconia nivea (Grant)   Scarce

Class: DEMOSPONGIARIA

Order: TETRACTINOMORPHA

OSCARELLIDAE
Oscarella lobularis (Schmidt)   stones, rocks & seaweeds   Frequent
CLAVULIDAE
Cliona celata Grant   BORING SPONGE   rocks & shells   Scarce
Suberites carnosus (Johnston)   shells   Scarce
AXINELLIDAE
Hymeniacidon perleve (Montagu)   encrustation on rocks   Local

Order: CERATINOMORPHA

SPONGIIDAE
Drysidea fragilis (Montagu)   beneath rocks   Locally frequent
HAPLOSCLERIDAE
Haliclona oculata (Pallas)   rocks   Common
DESMACIDONIDAE
Raspailia hispida (Montagu)   rocks   Scarce
Hialchondria panicea (Pallas) BREADCRUMB SPONGE   rocks & shells   Locally common

COASTAL INVERTEBRATES

Phylum: COLENTERATA

Class: HYDROZOA (HYDROIDS or SEA-FIRS)

Order: ANTHOMEDUSAE

TUBULARIIDAE

Tubularia indivisa (L.)	ORGAN PIPES	rock pools	Frequent

Order: LEPTOMEDUSAE

CAMPANULARIIDAE

Sertularella polyzonias (L.)		rocks	Frequent
S. fusiformis Hincks		rocks	Rare
S. cupressina (L.)	WHITE WEED	rocks & shells	Frequent

PLUMULARIIDAE

Kirchenpaueria pinnata (L.)	rocks	Frequent
Ventromma halecioides (Alder)	rocks	Local
Plumularia setacea (Ellis & Solander)	rocks	Uncommon

Order: SIPHONOPHORA

PHYSALIIDAE

Physalia physalis (L.)	PORTUGUESE MAN-O'-WAR	Very rare
	One stranded Minehead Beach, 1976	

Class: SCYPHOMEDUSAE (JELLY-FISH)

Order: SEMAEOSTOMAE

PELAGIIDAE

Chrysaora hysoscella (L.)	COMPASS JELLYFISH	Occasionally stranded on beaches

AURELIIDAE

Aurelia aurita (L.)	COMMON JELLYFISH	Common, occasionally abundant

Order: RHIZOSTOMAE

RHIZOSTOMIDAE

Rhizostoma octopus (L.)	OCTOPUS JELLYFISH	Frequent
	Large shoal off High Veer Point, summer 1987	

COASTAL INVERTEBRATES

Class: ANTHOZOA (SEA ANEMONES & CORALS)

Order: ACTINIARIA

ACTINIIDAE

Actinia equina (L.)	BEADLET ANEMONE	Rocks and rock-pools, common
Anemonia sulcata (Pennant)	SNAKELOCKS ANEMONE	Fairly common on rocks
Tealia felina (L.)	DAHLIA ANEMONE	Rocky crevices; locally common

SAGARTIIDAE

Sagartia troglodytes (Price)　　　　　　　　　　Rocks in sandy places; very rare

Phylum: CTENOPHORA

Class: NUDA (SEA GOOSEBERRIES)

Beroe cucumis Fabricius　　　　Uncommon in open water or stranded on beaches

Phylum: PLATYHELMINTHES

Class: TURBELLARIA (FLATWORMS)

Order: TRICLADIDA

PROCERODIDAE

Procerodes ulvae (Oersted)　Usually under stones where freshwater streams run on beach
　　　　　　　　　　　　　　　　　　　　　　　　　　　　　Locally common

Order: POLYCLADIDA

LEPTOPLANIDAE

Leptoplana tremellaris (Müller)　　Under stones　　　　　　　　　　　Local

Phylum: NEMERTINI

Class: ANOPLA (RIBBON WORMS)

Order: PALAEONEMERTINI

TUBULANIDAE

Tubulanus annulatus (Montagu)　　　　under stones　　　　　　　Very rare

Order: HETERONEMERTINI

LINEIDAE

Lineus longissimus (Gunnerus) BOOTLACE WORM　　　　Under stones; rare

Lineus ruber (Müller) RED RIBBON WORM

Bootlace worms can reach a length of 5m (15 ft) or more

Under stones; common

Class: ENOPLA (RIBBON WORMS)

Order: HOPLONEMERTINI

EMPLECTONEMATIDAE

Emplectonema neesi (Oersted)	sandy shores	Frequent

PROSORHOCMIDAE

Oerstedia dorsalis (Abildgaard)	under seaweeds	Uncommon

AMPHIPORIDAE

Amphiporus lactifloreus (Johnston)	under stones on lower shore	Uncommon

Phylum: ANNELIDA

Class: ARCHIANNELIDA (SEGMENTED/BRISTLE WORMS)

DINOPHILIDAE

Dinophilus sp.	amongst seaweeds	Frequent

Class: POLYCHAETA (BRISTLE WORMS)

POLYNOIDAE (SCALE WORMS)

Lepidonotus clava (Montagu)	under rocks and pebbles	Rare
L. squamatus (L.)	under rocks	Common
Harmothoë impar (Johnston)	under rocks	Locally common
H. extenuata (Grube)	under rocks	Locally common
Polynoë scolopendrina Savigny	rock crevices	Rare

SIGALIONIDAE

Sthenelais boa (Johnston)	under rocks	Uncommon

PHYLLODOCIDAE (PADDLE WORMS)

Eteone longa (Fabricius)	in sand	Locally common
E. flava (Fabricius)	usually in sand	Locally common
Pirakia punctifera (Grube)		Rare
Phyllodoce laminosa Savigny	under stones & in crevices	Uncommon
Anaitides maculata (L.)	under rocks	Uncommon

HESIONIDAE

Kefersteinia cirrata (Keferstein)	among shells & stones	Rare

COASTAL INVERTEBRATES

SYLLIDAE

Odontosyllis ctenostoma Claparède	among stones	Rare
Typosyllis armillaris (Müller)	rock crevices	Uncommon

NEREIDAE

Neanthes diversicolor (O.F.Müller) RAG WORM	in sand or mud	Frequent
N. virens (Sars) KING RAG WORM	in sand and shallow water	Frequent
N. irrorata (Malmgren)		Rare
Nereis pelagica L.	under stones etc.	Common
Platynereis dumerilii (Aud. & Milne-Edwards)		Uncommon

NEPHTHYIDAE (CATWORMS)

Nephthys hombergi Savigny	sand or mud	Uncommon
N. cirrosa Ehlers	sand	Locally common

GLYCERIDAE

Glycera convoluta Keferstein	sand	Rare

GONIADIDAE

Goniada emerita Aud. & Milne-Edwards	rocks	Rare

EUNICIDAE

Lysidice ninetta Aud. & Milne-Edwards	rocky shores	Rare
Marphysa sanguinea (Montagu)	rock crevices	Uncommon

LUMBRINERIDAE

Lumbrineris latreilli Aud. & Milne-Edwards	under stones	Rare

ARABELLIDAE

Arabella iricolor (Montagu)		Rare

ORBINIIDAE

Scoloplos armiger (O.F.Müller)	sand or mud	Uncommon

PARAONIDAE

Paraonis fulgens (Levinson)	burrows in sand	Local

SPIONIDAE

Nerine bonnieri Mesnil	sand	Rare
N. cirratulus (Delle Chiaje)	on seabed in sand or mud	Uncommon
Scolelepis ciliatus (Keferstein)	in sand	Uncommon
Spio filicornis (Müller)	in sand	Locally common
Pygospio elegans Claparède	sand and mud	Frequent

CIRRATULIDAE (THREAD WORMS)

Cirratulus cirratus (Müller)	under rocks and stones	Frequent
Tharyx marioni (Saint-Joseph)	sand and mud	Rare

FLABELLIGERIDAE

Pherusa plumosa (Müller)	among rocks	Rare

COASTAL INVERTEBRATES

OPHELIIDAE

Travisia forbesii Johnston	sandy beach	Rare

ARENICOLIDAE

Arenicola marina (L.)   LUGWORM   sandy beaches   Locally abundant
Much dug for by fishermen for bait

SABELLARIIDAE (HONEYCOMBE WORMS)

Sabellaria alveolata (L.)   sand and shingle on lower shore   Common
Builds protective tubes from sand grains which may form reefs as occurs at Minehead

S. spinulosa Leuckart   Uncommon

AMPHARETIDAE

Melinna cristata (Sars)   sand   Rare

TEREBELLIDAE (Tube dwelling polychaetes; the tubes covered with mud, sand, etc.)

Neoamphitrite figulus (Dalyell)   amongst Laminaria   Locally abundant
Amphitrite affinis Malmgren   Rare
Eupolymnia nebulosa (Montagu)   stony beach   Rare
Amphitritides gracilis (Grube)   stony beaches   Common
Lanice conchilega (Pallas)   SAND MASON   upright tubes of sand   Locally common
Nicolea venustula (Montagu)   Common
Thelepus setosus (Quatrefages)   Common in Porlock Bay

SABELLIDAE (FAN WORMS)

Pseudopotamilla reniformis (Müller)   stony beaches   Common

SERPULIDAE - Tubes closed by a characteristic 'stopper' or operculum.

Apomatus similis Marion & Bobretzky   on stones   Uncommon
Pomatoceros triqueter (L.)   on rocks   Common
Filograna implexa Berkeley   on pebbles and shells   Common
Protula tubularia (Montagu)   on rocks, stones, shells   Fairly common
Dexiospira pagenstecheri (Quatrefages)   Uncommon
Spirorbis borealis Daudin *(Laeospira tridentatus (Levinsen)*
   on seaweeds, shells & rocks   Common
Laeospira rupestris (Gee & Knight-Jones)   Rare
L. corallinae (de Silva & Knight-Jones)   on Corallina   Very local

Class: **MYZOSTOMARIA**

Myzostoma cirriferum Leuckart   Rare

Class: **OLIGOCHAETA**

Oligocladus sanguinolentus Quatrefages   FLATWORM
   under stones & seaweed   Common

COASTAL INVERTEBRATES

Phylum: NEMATODA (ROUND WORMS)

Tylenchus fucicola on brown seaweeds Frequent

Phylum: SIPUNCULA

(Cylindrical worms with anterior mouths)
Golfingia elongata (Keferstein) burrows in mud/clay Frequent
G. vulgaris (Blainville) Uncommon

Phylum: ARTHROPODA Sub-Phylum: CRUSTACEA

Class: COPEPODA

Order: EUCOPEPODA

LERNAEIDAE
Lernaeocera lusci (Basset-Smith) Parasite on fish

Class: CIRRIPEDIA (BARNACLES)

Order: THORACICA

LEPADIDAE
Lepas anatifera (L.) GOOSE BARNACLE Frequently washed ashore on marine debris
VERRUCIDAE
Verruca stroemia (Müller) BARNACLE under rocks Common
CHTHAMALIDAE
Chthamalus stellatus (Poli) on rocks Uncommon
C. montagui Southward on rocks Common
BALANIDAE - ACORN BARNACLES
Balanus balanus (L.) on rocks Frequent
B. crenatus Bruguiére underwater rocks Very common
B. perforatus Bruguiére on rocks Locally common
B. balanoides (L.) rocks, etc. Common
Elminius modestus Darwin on rocks Common
 This Australian barnacle was first noted near Southampton in 1940s and has since spread around our shores.

COASTAL INVERTEBRATES
Class: MALACOSTRACA (SLATERS, SHRIMPS, CRABS etc.)

Order: CUMACEA

BODOTRIIDAE

Cumopsis goodsiri (Van Beneden)	sandy beaches	Common

DIASTYLIDAE

Diastylis rathkei (Krøyer)	muddy beaches	Rare

Order: TANAIDACEA

TANAIDAE

Tanaissus lilljeborgi (Stebbing)	Among stones, seaweed, etc.	locally common

Order: ISOPODA

ANTHURIDAE

Cyathura carinata (Krøyer)	stony beaches	Uncommon

LIMNORIIDAE

Limnoria lignorum (Rathke)	GRIBBLE	bores into wood	Uncommon

CIROLANIDAE

Eurydice affinis Hansen	upper shore	Very rare

SPHAEROMATIDAE

Sphaeroma rugicauda Leach	saltmarshes	Very local
Dynamene bidentata (Adams)	amongst seaweeds	Locally common

IDOTEIDAE

Idotea baltica (Pallas)	amongst seaweeds	Uncommon
I. chelipes (Pallas)	brackish water	Rare
I. granulosa Rathke	amongst seaweeds	Uncommon
I. linearis (L.)	amongst rocks	Uncommon

JANIRIDAE

Janira maculosa Leach	under rocks	Frequent
J. albifrons Leach	under stones	Frequent

MUNNIDAE

Munna minuta Hansen	amongst seaweeds	Uncommon

LIGIIDAE

Ligia oceanica (L.)	SEA SLATER	rocks	Common

COASTAL INVERTEBRATES

Order: AMPHIPODA (SANDHOPPERS etc.)

HAUSTORIIDAE

Bathyporeia pelagica (Bate)	in sand	Locally common
B. pilosa Lindström	in sand	Locally common
Haustorius arenarius (Slabber)	in sand	Local
Urothoë brevicornis Bate	in sand	Locally abundant

CALLIOPIDAE

Apherusa bispinosa Bate		Very rare
Calliopus crenulatus Chevreux & Fage	rockpools	Uncommon

GAMMARIDAE

Gammarellus angulosus (Rathke)	rockpools	Local
G. homari (Fabricius)	rockpools	Local
Maera othonis (Milne-Edwards)		Rare
Gammarus locusta (L.)	under rocks	Rare
(Other Gammarus spp see Freshwater section)		
Marinogammarus marinus (Leach)		Uncommon
M. stoerensis (Reid)		Uncommon

DEXAMINIDAE

Dexamine spinosa (Montagu)		Rare

TALITRIDAE

Talitrus saltator (Montagu)	SANDHOPPER	decaying seaweeds	Common

AMPHITHOIDAE

Amphithoë rubricata (Montagu)	amongst seaweeds	Common

COROPHIIDAE

Corophium volutator (Pallas)	coastal mud	Locally common

An important food-source for wading birds on Porlock Marsh.

PODOCERIDAE

Dulichia porrecta (Bate)	rock pools	Rare

HYPERIIDAE

Hyperia galba (Montagu)	Occasionally found inside stranded jellyfish

CAPRELLIDAE

Caprella spp.	GHOST (or SKELETON) SHRIMPS	Common

Order: MYSIDACEA

MYSIDAE

Siriella armata (Milne-Edwards)	OPOSSUM SHRIMPS	rock pools	Rare
Praunus inermis (Rathke)		rock pools & shallow water	Uncommon

COASTAL INVERTEBRATES

Mesopodopsis slabberi (Van Beneden)	rock pools	Common
Neomysis integer (Leach)		Common

Order: DECAPODA (PRAWNS, CRABS, etc.)

PALAEMONIDAE

Palaemon elegans Rathke	PRAWN	shallow water	Rare
P. serratus (Pennant)	COMMON PRAWN	shallow water/rock pools	Fairly common
P. varians (Leach)	DITCH PRAWN	brackish water	Locally common

ALPHEIDAE

Athanas nitescens (Montagu)	rock pools and seaweeds	Locally frequent
Alpheus macrocheles (Hailstone)		Very rare

HIPPOLYTIDAE

Eualus pusiolus (Krøyer)	rock pools	Common
Hippolyte varians Leach CHAMELEON PRAWN	rock pools and seaweeds	Common
Thoralus cranchi (Leach)	rock pools	Common

PROCESSIDAE

Processa edulis (Risso)	under rocks	Rare

PANDALIDAE

Pandalus montagui Leach AESOP PRAWN	rock pools	Locally common

CRANGONIDAE

Crangon crangon (L.) COMMON SHRIMP	shallow water	Common
Philocheras fasciatus (Risso) BANDED SHRIMP	shallow water	Locally common

NEPHROPSIDAE

Homarus gammarus (L.) LOBSTER	deep pools in rock fissures	Fairly common

AXIIDAE

Axius stirhynchus Leach		Local
Palinurus vulgaris (Latreille) CRAWFISH	pools and rock crevices	Fairly common

GALATHEIDAE - SQUAT LOBSTERS

Galathea nexa Embleton	under rocks	Uncommon
G. squamifera Leach	under rocks	Uncommon
G. strigosa (L.)	under rocks	Uncommon

PORCELLANIDAE

Porcellana longicornis (L.) LONG-CLAWED PORCELAIN CRAB		Locally abundant
	under stones and in *Laminaria* holdfasts	
P. platycheles (Pennant) BROAD-CLAWED PORCELAIN CRAB		Occasional
	under stones among mud and gravel	

PAGURIDAE - HERMIT CRABS

Eupagurus bernhardus (L.)	in old gastropod shells	Very common

Eupagurus cuanensis (Thompson)		Infrequent
Anapagurus hyndmanni (Bell)	in gastropod shells	Fairly common

LEUCOSIIDAE

Ebalia tuberosa (Pennant)	gravelly shores	Uncommon

MAIIDAE - SPIDER CRABS

Maia squinado (Herbst) SPINY SPIDER CRAB	among rocks on lower shore	Uncommon
Eurynome aspera (Pennant)	among rocks	Rare
Inachus leptochirus (L.)	among rocks	Rare
Macropodia rostrata (L.) SPIDER CRAB	among rocks	Rare

PORTUNIDAE - SWIMMING CRABS

Portumnus latipes (Pennant)	sandy shores	Fairly common
Carcinus maenus (L.) COMMON SHORE CRAB	sandy and rocky shores	Very common
Macropipus puber (L.) VELVET SWIMMING CRAB	among rocks	Fairly common

CANCRIDAE

Cancer pagurus L. EDIBLE CRAB	Small specimens are not uncommon in rock pools; larger ones occur in deeper water

XANTHIDAE

Xantho pilipes Milne-Edwards		Local
Pilumnus hirtellus (L.) HAIRY CRAB	rock pools	Frequent

Class: PYCNOGONIDA (SEA-SPIDERS)

PYCNOGONIDAE

Pycnogonum littorale (Ström)	under rocks	Uncommon

NYMPHONIDAE

Nymphon gracile Leach	rock pools & shallow water	Rare
N. rubrum Hodge	rock pools	Rare

AMMOTHEIDAE

Acheilia echinata (Hodge)	among rocks or seaweed	Uncommon

Sub-Phylum: INSECTA

Please see appropriate Orders for details of maritime insects.

COASTAL INVERTEBRATES

Phylum: MOLLUSCA

Class: POLYPLACOPHORA (CHITONS)

Order: PALAEOLORICATA

CRYPTOPLACIDAE

Acanthochitona crinita (Pennant)	rock pools	Local

LEPIDOCHITONIDAE

Lepidochitona cinerea (L.)	under stones	Common

LEPIDOPLEURIDAE

Lepidopleurus asellus (Gmelin) COAT-OF-MAIL	under stones	Uncommon
Tonicella marmorea (Fabricius)	under stones	Rare
T. rubra (L.)	under stones	Uncommon

Class: GASTROPODA (SEA SLUGS & SNAILS)

Order: ARCHAEOGASTROPODA

FISSURELLIDAE

Emarginula reticulata Sowerby SLIT LIMPET	on rocks	Common
Diodora apertura (Montagu) KEY-HOLE LIMPET	on rocks	Uncommon

PATELLIDAE

Patella vulgata L. COMMON LIMPET	on rocks	Abundant
P. depressa Pennant BLACK-FOOTED LIMPET	on rocks	Local
Patella aspera Lamarck CHINA LIMPET	on rocks	Uncommon
Patella pellucida (L.) BLUE-RAYED LIMPET	on *Laminaria*	Locally common

ACMAEIDAE

Acmaea virginea (Müller) WHITE TORTOISESHELL LIMPET	on seaweeds	Rare

TROCHIDAE - TOP-SHELLS

Calliostoma zizyphinum (L.) PAINTED TOP-SHELL	rocks and stones	Common
Monodonta lineata (da Costa) THICK TOP-SHELL	on rocks	Very common
Gibbula cineraria (L.) GREY TOP-SHELL	among stones & seaweed	Common
G. umbilicalis (da Costa) PURPLE TOP-SHELL	on rocks	Common

TURBINIDAE

Tricolia pullus (L.) PHEASANT SHELL	rock pools	Common

COASTAL INVERTEBRATES

Order: MESOGASTROPODA

LITTORINIDAE - CHINK SHELLS AND WINKLES

Lacuna crassior (Montagu)		rock pools	Uncommon
L. pallidula (da Costa)		on seaweeds	Uncommon
L. parva (da Costa)		rock pools	Frequent
L. vincta (Montagu)	BANDED CHINK SHELL	on seaweeds	Uncommon
Littorina littoralis (L.)	FLAT PERIWINKLE	on seaweeds	Common
L. littorea (L.)	EDIBLE WINKLE	on rocks	Locally common
L. neritoides (L.)	SMALL WINKLE	crevices on upper shore	Locally common
L. saxatilis (Olivi) s.l.	ROUGH WINKLE	on rocks and stones	Very common

RISSOIDAE - TALL SPIRE SHELLS

Cingula semicostata (Montagu)	lower shore	Uncommon
C. semistriata (Montagu)	lower shore	Common
Alvania crassa (Kanmacher)	rocks	Uncommon
Rissoa parva (da Costa)	stones in shallow water	Locally common

BARLEEIIDAE

Barleeia unifasciata (Montagu)	on sea-weeds	Uncommon

TRIPHORIDAE

Triphora perversa (L.)	lower littoral zone	Rare

TORNIDAE

Tornus subcarinatus (Montagu)	Uncommon

CALYPTRAEIDAE

Crepidula fornicata (L.)	SLIPPER LIMPET	Shells have been found occasionally

CYPRAEIDAE

Trivia monacha (da Costa)	COWRIE	A number of empty shells found Lynmouth 1980
T. arctica (Montagu)		laminaria zone in deeper water — Rare

Order: STENOGLOSSA

MURICIDAE

Nucella lapillus (L.)	DOG WHELK	sand, gravel and rocks	Very common
Ocenebra aciculata (Lamarck)			Rare
O. erinacea (L.)	STING WINKLE	sand, gravel and rocks	Common

BUCCINIDAE

Buccinum undatum L.	COMMON WHELK	shallow water	Common
	Egg cases are frequently washed ashore at Minehead		

NASSARIIDAE

Nassarius incrassatus (Strom)	THICK-LIPPED DOG-WHELK	Frequent under stones

Nassarius reticulatus (L.)	NETTED DOG-WHELK		
		under stones	Uncommon

Order: PYRAMIDELLOMORPHA

PYRAMIDELLIDAE

Odostomia lukisi Jeffreys	TALL SPIRED SHELL		Rare
O. plicata (Montagu)			Uncommon

Order: APLYSIOMORPHA

APLYSIIDAE

Aplysia punctata Cuvier	SEA HARE	Among seaweed. Common on N.Devon coast

Order: PLEUROBRANCHOMORPHA

PLEUROBRANCHIDAE

Berthella plumula (Montagu)	under rocks at low-water mark	Rare

Order: SACOGLOSSA

ELYSIIDAE

Elysia viridis (Montagu)	SEA SLUG	among algae	Rare

Order: NUDIBRANCHIA (SEA SLUGS)

GONIODORIDIDAE

Goniodoris nodosa (Montagu)	between tide-marks	Common

ONCHIDORIDIDAE

Adalaria proxima (Alder & Hancock)	between tide-marks	Uncommon
Acanthodoris pilosa (Müller) - various colour forms occur		Common
Onchidoris bilamellata (Müller)	between tide-marks	Common

POLYCERIDAE

Polycera nothus (Johnston)	on seaweed in shallow water	Rare
Thecacera pennigera (Montagu)		Rare
Limacia clavigera (Müller)	shallow water	Rare

ARCHIDORIDIDAE

Archidoris pseudoargus (Rapp) SEA LEMON	among rocks in deeper water	Uncommon

COASTAL INVERTEBRATES

KENTRODORIDIDAE

Jorunna tomentosa (Cuvier)	among rocks	Rare

CORYPHELLIDAE

Coryphella pedata (Montagu)		Locally frequent
C. pellucida (Alder & Hancock)	among rocks	Rare

EUBRANCHIDAE

Eubranchus tricolor Forbes	among rocks	Rare

Class: BIVALVIA (MUSSELS, COCKLES, OYSTERS)

Order: NUCULOIDA

NUCULIDAE

Nucula turgida Leckenby & Marshall	NUT SHELL	in sand	Fairly common
N. nucleus (L.)	COMMON NUT SHELL		Of doubtful occurrence

Order: DYSODONTA

MYTILIDAE

Modiolus barbatus (L.)	BEARDED HORSE MUSSEL	rocks	Rare
Musculus discors L.	GREEN CRENELLA	under rocks and seaweeds	Frequent
Mytilus edulis (L.)	COMMON MUSSEL	on rocks, often forming beds	Common

Order: OSTREIFORMES

OSTREIDAE

Ostrea edulis L.	FLAT OYSTER	Some remains of old oyster beds occur

Order: PSEUDOLAMELLIBRANCHIA

ANOMIIDAE

Anomia ephippium L.	SADDLE OYSTER	rocks	Locally common

PECTINIDAE

Chlamys distorta (da Costa)	HUNCHBACK SCALLOP	Low water mark	Rare
C. varia (L.)	VARIEGATED SCALLOP	Rocky coasts	Uncommon

Order: EULAMELLIBRANCHIA

ERYCINIDAE

Lasaea rubra (Montagu)	A minute bivalve which may be found in maritime lichens

Kellia suborbicularis (Montagu)　　In fine sand under stones　　　　Locally common

CARDIIDAE

Cerastoderma edule (L.)　　COMMON COCKLE　burrows in sand below LWM　Common

VENERIDAE

Venerupis sp. (? saxatilis (Fleuriau)) PULLET　burrows in sand on lower shore Uncommon

SCROBICULARIIDAE

Abra tenuis (Montagu)　　　　An unconfirmed record from gravel, Minehead, 1972
Scrobicularia plana (da Costa) PEPPERY FURROW burrows in mud/sand　　Fairly common

TELLINIDAE

Macoma balthica (L.)　　BALTIC TELLIN　burrows in mud/sand　　Fairly common
Tellina tenuis (da Costa)　THIN TELLIN　burrows in sand　　　Fairly common

SOLENIDAE

Ensis siliqua (L.)　　POD RAZOR　burrows in sand on lower shore　　Rare

HIATELLIDAE

Hiatella arctica (L.)　　WRINKLED ROCK BORER　　　Fairly common
　　　　　　　　　　　Attached by byssus to rocks or shells

PHOLADIDAE

Barnea candida L.　　WHITE PIDDOCK　in clay　　　Locally common
Pholas dactylus L.　　COMMON PIDDOCK　bores into soft rock, wood　　Local
Sphenia binghami Turton　　　　　　　　　　　　　　Common

TEREDINIDAE

Teredo nivalis L.　　SHIP WORM　bores into submerged wood
　　　　Locally common and occasionally washed ashore in driftwood

Class: CEPHALOPODA

Order: DECAPODA

SEPIIDAE

Sepia officinalis (L.)　　COMMON CUTTLEFISH　　Sandy bays and estuaries
　　　　　　Skeletons or 'bone' frequently found on strandline

SEPIOLIDAE

Sepiola atlantica (d'Orbigny)　LITTLE CUTTLE　shallow water　　Rare

LOLIGINIDAE

Loligo forbesi Steenstrup　　COMMON SQUID　　Egg capsules may be found in shallow
　　　　　　　　　　　　water, but adults seldom approach the shore

Order: OCTOPODA

OCTOPODIDAE

Octopus vulgaris Lamarck　　COMMON OCTOPUS　　One stranded Minehead 1986

COASTAL INVERTEBRATES

Phylum: BRYOZOA

Class: STENOLAEMATA (SEA MATS)

Order: CYCLOSTOMATA

CRISIIDAE - mat-forming colonies on seaweeds, shells, rocks, etc.

Crisidia cornuta (L.)	Rare; in small colonies
C. eburnea (L.)	Common
C. aculeata Hassall	Fairly common
C. denticulata (Lamarck)	Rare
TUBULIPORIDAE	
Tubulipora lobifera Hastings	Common
T. liliacea (Pallas)	Uncommon(?)
DIASTOPORIDAE	
Berenicea patina (Lamarck)	Locally common
B. sarniensis (Norman)	Locally common
LICHENOPORIDAE	
Disporella hispica (Fleming)	Common

Class: GYMNOLAEMATA (SEA MATS)

Order: CHEILOSTOMATA

AETIDAE		
Aeta anguina (L.)		Rare
SCRUPARIIDAE		
Scruparia ambigua (d'Orbigny)		Rare
MEMBRANIPORIDAE		
Membranipora membranacea (L.)	SEA-MAT	Locally common
Electra pilosa (L.)	HAIRY SEA-MAT	Common
E. monostachys (Busk)		Uncommon
Callopora lineata (L.)		Fairly common
C. dumerilii (Audouin)		Uncommon
C. aurita (Hincks)		Common
FLUSTRIDAE		
Flustra foliacea (L.)	HORNWRACK	Locally common

SCRUPOCELLARIIDAE
Scrupocellaria scrupea Busk	Rare
S. scruposa (L.)	Uncommon
S. reptans (L.)	Rare

BICELLARIELLIDAE
Bicellariella ciliata (L.)	Common

BUGULIDAE
Bugula fulva Ryland	Frequent
B. turbinata Alder	Frequent

HIPPOTHOIDAE
Hippothoa distans MacGillivray	Common
Chorizopora brogniarti (Audouin)	Rare

ESCHARELLIDAE
Escharella immersa (Fleming)	Common
E. ventricosa (Hassall)	Uncommon
E. variolosa (Johnston)	Uncommon

SCHIZOPORELLIDAE
Schizomavella linearis (Hassall)	Common
Escharina spinifera (Johnston)	Common

HIPPOPORINIDAE
Cryptosula pallasiana (Moll)	Common

MICROPORELLIDAE
Microporella ciliata (Pallas)	Rare

SMITTINIDAE
Smittoidea reticulata (MacGillivray)	Uncommon

EXOCHELLIDAE
Escharoides coccineus (Abildgaard)	Rare

CELLEPORIDAE
Celleporaria pumicosa (Pallas)	Uncommon
Celliporina hassalii (Johnston)	Uncommon

Order: **CTENOSTOMATA**

ALCYONIDIIDAE
Alcyonidium gelatinosum (L.)	Attached to rocks & seaweeds	Frequent
A. polyoum (Hassall)		Frequent
A. hirsutum (Fleming)	On seaweeds	Frequent

FLUSTRELLIDAE
Flustrellidra hispida (Fabricius)   On Fucus   Common
VESICULARIIDAE
Amathia lendigera (L.)   Uncommon
WALKERIIDAE
Walkeria uva (L.)   Frequent

Phylum: ECHINODERMATA

Class: CRINOIDEA (FEATHER STARS (10 arms))

ANTEDONIDAE
Antedon bifida (Pennant)   FEATHER STAR   Rock pools & crevices   Rare

Class: ASTEROIDEA (STAR FISHES)

Order: SPINULOSA

SOLASTERIDAE
Crossaster papposus (L.)   SUN STAR   sand and stones   Uncommon
ECHINASTERIDAE
Henricia oculata Pennant   sand and gravel   Fairly common

Order: FORCIPULATA

ASTERIIDAE
Asterias rubens L.   COMMON STARFISH   rocks and stones   Locally common

Class: OPHIUROIDEA – BRITTLE STARS

Order: OPHIURAE

OPHIOTRICHIDAE
Ophiothrix fragilis (Abildgaard) BRITTLE STAR under stones, seaweeds, etc.   Frequent
OPHIOCOMIDAE
Ophiocomina nigra (Abildgaard)   rocks, seaweeds, sand   Rare
AMPHIURIDAE
Amphipholis squamata (Delle Chiaje)   under rocks, seaweeds   Rare

Class: ECHINOIDEA (SEA URCHINS)

Order: DIADEMATOIDEA

ECHINIDAE

Psammechinus miliaris Müller	GREEN SEA URCHIN	among rocks	Uncommon
Echinus esculentus L.	COMMON SEA URCHIN	among rocks and seaweed	Local

Class: HOLOTHUROIDEA (SEA CUCUMBERS)

Order: DENDROCHIROTA

CUCUMARIIDAE

Cucumaria saxicola Brady & Robertson	SEA GHERKIN	among stones	Local
C. lactea (Forbes & Goodsir)	WHITE SEA CUCUMBER	on stony bottoms	Rare

Phylum: CHORDATA

Class: ASCIDIACEA (SEA SQUIRTS)

Order: ENTEROGONA

ASCIDIIDAE

Ascidia mentula (Müller)	In shallow water	Very rare
A. conchilega (Müller)	In shallow water	Common

Order: PLEUROGONA

STYELIDAE

Polycarpa pomaria (Savigny)	Rare
Botrylloides leachi (Savigny)	Rare

PYURIDAE

Pyura tessellata (Forbes)	Frequent

References:

Barret & Younge *Pocket Guide to the Sea Shore* (1973) Collins.

Boyden, Crothers, Little & Mettam *Intertidal Invertebrata Fauna of the Severn Estuary* Field Studies Council (1977)

Eales, N.B. *Littoral Fauna of Great Britain* Cambridge University Press (1952)

FRESHWATER LIFE

The waters of Exmoor are extensive. Springs in higher ground give rise to narrow and fast flowing streams which eventually become rivers of which the Exe, Barle and Lyn are the most well known. In the past some of the waters may well have been diverted for agricultural purposes. In recent years water authorities have likewise altered water courses for the construction of reservoirs.

Systematic studies have been carried out by the Freshwater Biological Association. M. R. Newton, Senior Biologist, South West Water Authority and Dr. G.P. Green, Senior Biologist, Wessex Water Authority kindly made their records available to the Exmoor Natural History Society for the first edition of the *Flora & Fauna*. Other data have been received from the West Somerset School, Nettlecombe Field Centre and members of the Society. Local ponds and rhines have been used for this field work.

Certain phyla such as ROTIFERA et al are still seriously under-represented and because microscope facilities have not always been available to us some species have been designated to Family status only. Levels of abundance relate to the records collated and should be regarded with caution especially with respect to life in lentic waters. Here, sampling has been carried out on a local scale and not on a tetrad basis covering the entire National Park.

Many of the obvious members of the aquatic communities are in fact the aquatic larvae of members of the class Insecta and in the case of the Hemiptera (Bugs) and the Coleoptera (Beetles) have been included in the appropriate sections of this work to avoid duplication. Odonata (Dragon/Damselflies) also have their own section in the Check-list.

Classification follows Maitland, Dr.A.S. *A Coded Checklist of Animals occurring in Fresh Water in the British Isles* (1977) Institute of Terrestrial Ecology, Edinburgh.

Olive Russell, B.Sc., M.I. Biol.
Recorder, Freshwater Invertebrates, E.N.H.S.

Phylum: COELENTERATA

Class: HYDROZOA (POLYPS)

Order: HYDROIDA

HYDRIDAE

Hydra oligactis (Pallas)		Occasional
Chlorohydra viridissima (Pallas)	GREEN HYDRA	Occasional

Phylum: PLATYHELMINTHES

Class: TURBELLARIA (FLAT WORMS)

Order: TRICLADIDA

PLANARIIDAE

Polycelis nigra (Müller)	Occasional
Polycelis tenuis (Ijima)	Rare
P. felina (Dalyell)	Abundant
Dugesia lugubris (Schmidt)	Rare
Phagocata vitta (Duges)	Occasional

DENDROCOELIDAE

Dendrocoelum lacteum (Müller)	Occasional

Phylum: NEMATOMORPHA

Class: GORDIOIDEA (THREAD WORMS)

CHORDODIDAE

Gordius villoti Rosa	Status uncertain

Phylum: ROTIFERA

Class: BDELLOIDEA

PHILODINIDAE

Rotaria rotatoria (Pallas)	Status uncertain

Class: MONOGONONTA (WHEEL ANIMALCULES)

TRICHOCERIDAE

Trichocerca porcellus (Gosse) An unconfirmed record from Winn Brook	'Amongst algae'

CONOCHILIDAE

Conochilus hippocrepis (Schrank)	Status uncertain

COLLOTHECIDAE

Collotheca campanulata (Dobie)	Status uncertain

FRESHWATER INVERTEBRATES

Phylum: MOLLUSCA

Class: GASTROPODA (SNAILS)

Order: MESOGASTROPODA

VALVATIDAE
Valvata sp.   Rare
HYDROBIIDAE
Hydrobia ulvae (Pennant)   Local
Potamopyrgus jenkinsi (Smith)   JENKINS' SPIRE SHELL   Common
Bithynia tentaculata (L.)   Rare

Order: BASOMMATOPHORA

LYMNAEIDAE
Lymnaea stagnalis (L.)   GREAT POND SNAIL   Occasional
L. peregra (Müller)   WANDERING SNAIL   Common
PHYSIDAE
Physa fontinalis (L.)   BLADDER SNAIL   Rare
PLANORBIDAE
Planorbis planorbis (L.)   SMALL RAMSHORN SNAIL   Under stones in slow-moving water
P. albus Müller   RAMSHORN SNAIL   Rare
P. contortus (L.)   Rare
ANCYLIDAE
Ancylus fluviatilis Müller   RIVER LIMPET   Common

Class: BIVALVIA

Order: HETERODONTA

SPHAERIIDAE
Sphaerium corneum (L.)   PEA MUSSEL   Uncommon
Pisidium personatum Malm   PEA COCKLE   Rare
P. subtruncatum Malm   Rare
P. nitidum Jenyns   Rare

FRESHWATER INVERTEBRATES

Phylum: ANNELIDA

Class: OLIGOCHAETA (TRUE WORMS)

Order: PLESIOPORA PLESIOTHECATA

NAIDIDAE

Chaetogaster diaphanus (Gruithuisen)	Rare
Ophidonais serpentina (Müller)	Rare
Nais alpina Sperber	Rare
N. elingius Müller	Rare
N. pardalis	Rare
Stylaria lacustris (L.)	Occasional

TUBIFICIDAE

Tubifex tubifex (Müller)	BLOOD WORMS	Occasional
T. ignotus (Stolc)		Rare
T. costatus Claparède		In brackish mud
Psammoryctes barbata (Grube)		Occasional
Limnodrilus hoffmeisteri Claparède		Common
Peloscolex ferox (Eisen)		Rare
Rhyacodrilus coccineus (Vejdovsky)		Occasional
Aulodrilus pluriseta Piquet		Occasional

Order: PLESIOPORA PROSOTHECATA

ENCHYTRAEIDAE	POT WORM FAMILY	In rivers and ponds
HAPLOTAXIDAE		
Haplotaxis gordioides (Hartmann)		Rare

LUMBRICULIDAE – Members of this family of worms are abundant in the River Exe but in most cases have not been classified down to species.

Lumbriculus variegatus (Müller)		Fairly common
Stylodrilus heringianus Claparède		Common
LUMBRICIDAE		
Eiseniella tatraedra (Savigny)	SQUARE-TAILED WORM	Common

Order: POLYCHAETA

NEREIDAE (BRISTLE WORMS)

Nereis succinea Leach	In brackish mud

FRESHWATER INVERTEBRATES

Class: HIRUDINEA (LEECHES)
Order: RHYNCHOBDELLAE

PISCICOLIDAE

Piscicola geometra (L.)	FISH LEECH	Uncommon

GLOSSIPHONIIDAE

Theromyzon tessulatum (Müller)	Rare
Glossiphonia heteroclita (L.)	Rare
G. complanata (L.)	Occasional
Helobdella stagnalis (L.)	Rare

Order: GNATHOBDELLAE
HIRUDIDAE

Haemopsis sanguisuga (L.)	HORSE LEECH	Uncommon

Order: PHARYNGOBDELLAE
ERPOBDELLIDAE

Erpobdella octoculata (L.)	Occasional

Phylum: ARTHROPODA
Sub-phylum: CHELICERATA
Class: ARACHNIDA (SPIDERS & MITES)
Sub-class: ACARI

Order: HYDRACARINA (WATER MITES)

HYDRYPHANTIDAE

Protzia eximia (Protz)	Fairly frequent

HYDRODROMIDAE

Hydrodroma despicuens (Müller)	Rare

SPERCHONIDAE - In fast-running streams

Sperchon brevirostris Koenike	Rare
S. clupeifer Piersig	Occasional
S. glandulosus Koenike	Occasional
S. hibernicus Halbert	Rare
S. papillosus Thor	Occasional
S. setiger Thor	Occasional

FRESHWATER INVERTEBRATES

LEBERTIIDAE – mostly in running water

Lebertia castalia Viets	Status not known
L. maglioi Thor	Status not known
L. rufipes Koenike	Status not known
Pilolebertia porosa Thor	Status not known

TORRENTICOLIDAE – usually in running water

Torrenticola anomala (Koch)	Status not known
T. brevirostris (Halbert)	Status not known
T. elliptica Maglio	Status not known
Monatractides madritensis (Viets)	Status not known

HYGROBATIDAE – in fast streams or cold springs

Hygrobates calliger Piersig	Rare
H. fluviatilis (Ström)	Occasional
H. longipalpis (Hermann)	Rare
H. nigromaculatus Lebert	Rare
Atractides nodipalpis (Thor)	Common
A. tener (Thor)	Uncommon
Octomegapus octoporus Piersig	Uncommon

(Order: ARANEAE Water Spider included in separate section on Arachnida)

Phylum: CRUSTACEA

Class: BRANCHIOPODA

Order: CLADOCERA (WATER FLEAS)

DAPHNIIDAE

Daphnia hyalina Leydig	In still water and ponds	Occasional
Simocephalus vetulus (Müller)	In various wet locations	Common

Class: COPEPODA

Order: CYCLOPOIDEA (COPEPODS)

CYCLOPOIDAE

Cyclops spp. There are many species of the well-known CYCLOPS which occur in most areas of standing water.

FRESHWATER INVERTEBRATES

Class: BRANCHIURA
(PARASITIC FISH LICE)

ARGULIDAE

Argulus foliaceus (L.) These lice attach themselves to freshwater fish.   Common

Class: MALACOSTRACA
Order: ISOPODA

ASELLIDAE - Woodlouse-like crustaceans

Asellus aquaticus (L.)   WATER SLATER   Common

A. meridianus Racovitza   Occasional

Order: AMPHIPODA

COROPHIIDAE

Corophium volutator (Pallas)   In brackish mud
  These shrimp-like creatures are an important source of food for wading birds on Porlock Marsh.

GAMMARIDAE - FRESHWATER SHRIMPS

Gammarus deubeni Lilljeborg   Occasional in brackish water

G. pulex (L.)   Abundant in running waters

G. zaddachi Sexton   Occasional

Niphargus aquilex Schiodte A rare species of eyeless shrimp which dwells under gravel etc.

Phylum: INSECTA

(Order: COLLEMBOLA (SPRING-TAILS) - see separate section)

Class: PTERYGOTA, sub-class: EXOPTERYGOTA

Order: EPHEMEROPTERA (MAYFLIES)

The mayflies are an interesting group of insects, the adults being rarely found far from water and the nymphs always aquatic. They are unique in that the sub-imago undergoes a further moult, often within minutes of emerging from the water. Many hundreds of the sub-imago usually emerge together; these are known as 'duns' by fishermen and their emergence referred to as the 'hatch.' Adults are known as 'spinners'. Despite their English name, mayflies of one form or another can be found throughout much of the year. The scientific name of the Order refers to the short life of the winged imago which does not feed and seldom lives more than a couple of days. The nymphs have 3 tails; adults 2 or 3.
The English names given are Fishermen's names for the Duns.

FRESHWATER INVERTEBRATES

BAETIDAE

Baetis scambus Eaton	SMALL DARK OLIVE	Common
Baetis vernus Curtis	MEDIUM OLIVE	Common
B. buceratus Eaton		Rare
B. rhodani (Pictet)	LARGE DARK OLIVE	Abundant
B. muticus (L.)	IRON BLUE	Occasional
B. niger (L.)		Rare
Centroptilum luteolum (Müller)	SMALL SPURWING or PALE WATERY	Rare
Cloeon dipterum (L.)	POND OLIVE	Occasional

HEPTAGENIIDAE

Rhithrogena semicolorata (Curtis)	OLIVE UPRIGHT	Abundant
Heptagenia sulphurea (Müller)	YELLOW MAY DUN	Rare
H. lateralis (Curtis)	DUSKY YELLOWSTREAK or DARK DUN	Rare
Ecdyonurus venosus (Fabricius)	LATE MARCH BROWN	Common
E. torrentis Kimmins	LARGE BROOK DUN	Fairly common
E. dispar (Curtis)	AUTUMN DUN or AUGUST DUN	Fairly common

LEPTOPHLEBIIDAE

Paraleptophlebia submarginata (Stephens)	TURKEY BROWN	Occasional
Habrophlebia fusca (Curtis)	DITCH DUN	Fairly common

EPHEMERELLIDAE

Ephemerella ignita (Poda)	BLUE WINGED OLIVE	Common

EPHEMERIDAE

Ephemera vulgata L.	DRAKE MACKEREL	Occasional
E. danica Müller	MAYFLY or GREEN DRAKE	Occasional

CAENIDAE

Caenis macrura Stephens	ANGLER'S CURSE	Rare
C. moesta Bengtsson *(syn. C. luctuosa)*	ANGLER'S CURSE	Occasional
C. rivulorum Eaton	ANGLER'S CURSE	Fairly common

SIPHLONURIDAE

Isonychia ignota (Walker)	SUMMER DUN	Occasional

Order: PLECOPTERA (STONEFLIES)

Stonefly nymphs are distinguished from mayflies by the presence of only two tails. They are typical of fast-running stony, upland streans and are sometimes referred to as 'creepers.' The adults are poor fliers and spend most of their short lives (1-3 weeks) amongst waterside vegetation.

TAENIOPTERYGIDAE   STONEFLIES

Taeniopteryx nebulosa (L.)	Uncommon in slow-flowing water
Brachyptera risi (Morton)	Common in upland streams

FRESHWATER INVERTEBRATES

NEMOURIDAE

Protonemura praecox (Morton)	Uncommon
P. meyeri (Pictet)	Common
Amphinemura sulcicollis (Stephens)	Abundant
Nemoura cinerea (Retzius)	Uncommon

LEUCTRIDAE — NEEDLE or WILLOW FLIES

Leuctra geniculata (Stephens)	Fairly common
L. inermis Kempny	Common
L. hippopus (Kempny)	Fairly common
L. nigra (Olivier)	Uncommon
L. fusca (L.)	Common

PERLODIDAE — LARGE STONEFLIES

Perlodes microcephala (Pictet)		Fairly common
Isoperla grammatica (Poda)	(adults known as YELLOW SALLIES)	Abundant

PERLIDAE

Dinocras cephalotes (Curtis)	Common in fast running upland waters
Perla bipunctata Pictet	Fairly common in fast running upland waters
P. carlukiana Klap.	Horner Water 1952 SANHS

CHLOROPERLIDAE

Chloroperla torrentium (Pictet)	(adults known as SMALL YELLOW SALLIES)	Abundant
C. tripunctata (Scopoli)		Common

(Orders: ODONATA (DRAGONFLIES), HEMIPTERA (BUGS), COLEOPTERA (BEETLES), MEGALOPTERA (ALDERFLIES), and NEUROPTERA (SPONGEFLIES & LACEWINGS)
- please see separate sections)

Order: TRICHOPTERA (CADDIS FLIES)

RHYACOPHILIDAE - larval cases constructed of silk & small stones, attached to a rock.

Rhyacophila dorsalis (Curtis)	Abundant
R. obliterata McLachlan	Rare
R. munda McLachlan	Fairly common
Glossosoma conformis Neboiss	Occasional
G. boltoni Curtis	Occasional
Agapetus fuscipes Curtis	Common
A. ochripes Curtis	*see below
A. delicatulus McLachlan	*see below

PHILOPOTAMIDAE - larvae construct tubular nets, closed at one end.

Philopotamus montanus (Donovan)	Fairly common

FRESHWATER INVERTEBRATES

Wormaldia occipitalis (Pictet)	*see below
W. subnigra McLachlan	Rare

POLYCENTROPIDAE – larvae in tubular nets camouflaged with debris

Plectrocnemia conspersa (Curtis)	Rare
P. geniculata McLachlan	Rare
Polycentropus flavomaculatus (Pictet)	Fairly common
P. kingii McLachlan	Fairly common

PSYCHOMYIIDAE – larvae in tubes of silk, attached to stones, camouflaged with debris.

Ecnomus tenellus (Rambur)	*see below
Psychomyia pusilla (Fabricius)	Occasional

HYDROPSYCHIDAE – larvae build trumpet shaped nets amongst plants and stones.

Hydropsyche pellucidula (Curtis)	Common/abundant
H. contubernalis McLachlan	Rare
H. instabilis (Curtis)	Occasional
H. siltalai Dohler	Abundant
Cheumatopsyche lepida (Pictet)	Rare

HYDROPTILIDAE – young larvae free-living until fifth instar when they construct cases made from secreted material, sometimes covered with sand.

Hydroptila spp.	Rare
Ithytrichia spp.	Rare
Oxyethira spp.	Rare

PHRYGANEIDAE – the largest of the caddis flies. Larval cases, up to 9mm made from cut pieces of vegetation.

Phryganea grandis L.	*see below

LIMNEPHILIDAE – cases in a variety of designs according to genera.

Drusus annulatus Stephens	Common
Ecclisopteryx guttulata (Pictet)	Occasional
Limnephilus rhombicus (L.)	Rare
L. flavicornis (Fabricius)	Found in brackish ditch, status not known
L. marmoratus Curtis	*see below
L. stigma Curtis	Found in brackish ditch, status not known
L. lanatus Curtis	*see below
L. affinis Curtis	*see below
L. centralis Curtis	*see below
L. sparsus Curtis	*see below
L. auricula Curtis	*see below
L. vittatus (Fabricius)	Found in brackish ditch, status not known
Glyphotaelius pellucidus (Retzius)	*see below
Anabolia nervosa Curtis	Rare
Potamophylax latipennis (Curtis)	*see below

FRESHWATER INVERTEBRATES

Potamophylax cingulatus (Stephens)	Rare
Halesus radiatus (Curtis)	*see below
H. digitatus (Schrank)	*see below
Stenophylax permistus McLachlan	*see below
S. vibex (Curtis)	*see below
S. sequax (McLachlan)	*see below
Chaetopteryx villosa (Fabricius)	*see below

MOLANNIDAE - a distinctive case made of sand grains.

Molanna angustata Curtis	Occasional

ODONTOCERIDAE - cases made of coarse sand grains slightly tapered and curved.

Odontocerum albicorne (Scopoli)	Fairly common

LEPTOCERIDAE - cases typically slender, usually curved, of various materials.

Arthripsodes cinereus (Curtis)	Rare
A. albifrons (L.)	Occasional
A. commutatus (Rostock)	Rare
Mystacides nigra (L.)	*see below
M. azurea (L.)	Rare
Setodes argentipunctellus McLachlan	Rare

GOERIDAE - a characteristic tube-case of coarse sand and pebbles.

Goera pilosa (Fabricius)	*see below
Silo pallipes (Fabricius)	Common

LEPIDOSTOMATIDAE - case usually of cut vegetation, square in section.

Crunoecia irrorata (Curtis)	Rare
Lepidostoma hirtum (Fabricius)	Common
Lasciocephala basalis (Kolenati)	Rare

BRACHYCENTRIDAE - case cylindrical, slightly tapering, made of translucent material.

Brachycentrus subnubilus Curtis	Rare

SERICOSTOMATIDAE - smooth case cylindrical, curved, tapering made of sand grains.

Sericostoma personatum (Spence)	Abundant

* Denotes species taken in light-trap at Nettlecombe and thus no information on status.

For other freshwater creatures, please see appropriate sections.

References:

A good, general work is:

Fitter, R. & Manuel, R. *A Field Guide to the Freshwater Life of Britain & North-west Europe* Collins (1986)

Phylum: MOLLUSCA – TERRESTRIAL (SNAILS and SLUGS)

Class: GASTROPODA

Edmund J. Houghton, Ph.C. was E.N.H.S. Recorder of Terrestrial Mollusca until his death in 1995 just as this edition of the *Flora and Fauna* was in preparation. The list which follows is, therefore a reprint of the list in the First Edition for which Mr Houghton wrote in his preface:

"The late Norman Hadden writing in 1923 says in his *Additions to the Mollusca of Somerset:* 'West Somerset cannot by any means be called a rich collecting ground for mollusca, as the soil is markedly deficient in lime, and large areas are covered with heather, whortleberry and similar calcifuge plants.' This type of ecology and the common abhorrence of 'slugs and snails' makes the number of recorders small compared with those of more popular phyla. May this short catalogue serve to encourage others to make good the deficiencies."

Sub-Class: PULMONATA

Order: BASOMMATOPHORA

ELLOBIIDAE (HOLLOW-SHELLED SNAILS)

Carychium minimum Müller	Marshes, damp woodland	Local
C. tridentatum (Risso)	Woods, damp grassland	Local

SUCCINEIDAE (AMBER SNAILS)

Succinea putris (L.)	Pond margins	Local
Oxyloma pfeifferi (Rossmässler)	Marshland	Uncommon

(O. sarsi (Esmark) Marshland species recorded by Norman Hadden but no recent records)

PYRAMIDULIDAE (ROCK SNAILS)

(Pyramidula rupestris (Draparnaud) A lichen feeder recorded by Norman Hadden; no recent records)

VERTIGINIDAE (WHORL SNAILS)

Vertigo pusilla Müller	Leaf litter, old walls, dry banks	Local

PUPILLIDAE (CHRYSALIS SNAILS)

Pupilla muscorum (L.)	Coastal turf, stone walls, scree	Local
Lauria cylindracea (da Costa)	Woods, dry grassland, stone walls	Fairly frequent

VALLONIIDAE (GRASS SNAILS)

Vallonia costata (Müller)	Coastal turf, stone walls, leaf litter	Occasional

(V. excentrica (Sterki) Recorded in dry situations by Norman Hadden; no recent records)

(Acanthinula aculeata (Müller) Recorded from woods and hedgerows by Norman Hadden; no recent records)

SNAILS & SLUGS

ENIDAE (BULINS)
(Ena obscura (Müller) Recorded from woods, etc. by Norman Hadden; no recent records.)

ENDODONTIDAE (DISCUS SNAILS)

Punctum pygmaeum (Draparnaud)	Coastal woods	Locally frequent
Discus rotundatus (Müller)	Deciduous woodland, gardens	Frequent

ARIONIDAE (ROUND-BACK SLUGS)

Arion ater (L.) GREAT BLACK SLUG	Widespread	Common
A. subfuscus (Draparnaud)	Widespread	Common
A. fasciatus (Nilsson)	Gardens	Local
A. hortensis Férussac	Cultivated land	Common
A. intermedius Normand	Woods, hedgerows, gardens	Local

VITRINIDAE (GLASS SNAILS)

Vitrina pellucida (Müller)	Varied terrestrial habitats	Local

ZONITIDAE

Vitrea crystallina (Müller)	Damp places	Uncommon
Nesovitrea hammonis (Ström)	Woods, marshes, grassland	Common
Aegopinella pura (Alder)	Deciduous leaf litter	Local
Oxychilus alliarius (Miller)	GARLIC GLASS SNAIL	Local
	Tolerant of acidic sites in woods and grass moorland	
Zonitoides excavatus (Alder)	Damp acidic sites in woods and marsh	Local
Z. nitidus (Müller)	Littoral zones of rivers and ponds	Local

MILACIDAE

Milax gagates (Draparnaud)	Fields	Local
M. sowerbyi (Férussac)	Gardens	Local

LIMACIDAE (KEELBACK SLUGS)

Limax maximus L. GREAT GREY SLUG	Woodlands	Fairly common
(L. cinereoniger Wolf A woodland species recorded by Norman Hadden, no recent records)		
L. flavus L.	Gardens	Widespread
L. marginatus Müller	Woodlands and stony substrates	Local
Deroceras laeve (Müller)	Very damp sites	Local
D. reticulatum (Müller) NETTED SLUG	Gardens, cultivated land	Common

EUCONULIDAE

Euconulus fulvus (Müller)	Damp woods, grass moorland & marshes	Frequent

FERUSSACIIDAE (SPIRE SNAILS)

Cecilioides acicula (Müller)	Subterranean; usually calcareous soils	Local

CLAUSILIIDAE (DOOR SNAILS)

Cochlodina laminata (Montagu)	Woodland	Uncommon
Clausilia bidentata (Ström)	TWO-TOOTHED DOOR SNAIL	
	Damp places, rocks, woodland, etc.	Locally common

SNAILS & SLUGS

Balea perversa (L.)	Amongst moss and lichen	Uncommon

TESTACELLIDAE

Testacella maugei Férussac	Manured gardens	Uncommon

HELICIDAE (TYPICAL SNAILS)

Candidula intersecta (Poiret)	Coastal	Local
Cernuella virgata (da Costa)	Coastal	Local
Ashfordia granulata (Alder)	Amongst herbs in deciduous woodlands	Frequent
Zenobiella subrufescens (Miller)	Damp deciduous woodland	Local
Trichia hispida (L.)	Damp deciduous woodland	Local
T. striolata (Pfeiffer)	STRAWBERRY SNAIL Gardens and damp, shady sites	Locally common
Arianta arbustorum (L.)	Damp fields, woods, hedgerows	Scarce
Helicigona lapicida (L.)	FLAT WALL SNAIL Rocky and stony substrates	Rare
Cepaea nemoralis (L.)	GROVE SNAIL woods, hedges, fields,etc. Various colour forms - much favoured by thrushes.	Common
C. hortensis (Müller)	WHITE LIPPED SNAIL Woods, hedges, fields, etc.	Common
Helix aspersa Müller	GARDEN SNAIL a garden pest, also in woods, hedgerows, etc.	Very common

References:
Kerney, M.P. and Cameron, R.A.D. *A Field Guide to the Land Snails of Britain and Northwest Europe.* Collins (1979).

Hadden, N. *Mollusca of Somerset.* Journal of Conchology Vol.17, No.3 (1923).

Class: OLIGOCHAETA (EARTHWORMS)
(See also Freshwater Section)

Order: HAPLOTAXIDA

LUMBRICIDAE

Allolobophora chlorotica (Savigny)	GREEN WORM	Damp pastures and woodlands
Aporrectodea caliginosa (Savigny)	GREY WORM	Cultivated soil, gardens & stream banks
A. longa (Ude)	LONG WORM	Deciduous woodlands, meadows, and gardens
A. rosea (Savigny)	ROSE WORM	Fields, gardens, pastures, woods & marshes
Dendrobaena octaedra (Savigny)		In moss, beneath stones, deciduous & coniferous woods
D. pygmaea (Savigny)		Mossy banks of woodland streams. Rare
Dendrodrilus rubidus (Savigny)	TREE WORM	Deciduous woodlands: beneath bark, stumps, under stones and in moss
Eisenia fetida (Savigny)	BRANDLING WORM	Humus-rich loam, clay, manure and compost heaps
E. veneta (Rosa)	VENETIAN WORM	Deciduous woodland, leaf litter
Lumbricus castaneus (Savigny)	CHESTNUT WORM	Beneath deciduous leaf litter
L. festivus (Savigny)	RUBESCENT WORM	Meadows, river banks, dung
L. rubellus Hoffmeister	MARSH WORM	Variable soils
L. terrestris L.	COMMON EARTHWORM	Fields, gardens, woods
Octolasion cyaneum (Savigny)	BLUE-GREY WORM	Damp, deciduous leaf litter
O. tyrtaeum tyrtaeum (Savigny)	WHITE WORM	Woodland, gardens and pasture

Reference:
Sims, R.W. & Gerard, B.M. *Synopses of the British Fauna No.31: Earthworms* (1985). Linnean Society.

Class: CRUSTACEA

Order: ISOPODA (WOODLICE & allies)

A woodlouse (lucky-pig, granferjig, cheese bug) is a familiar sight, but only since the launch of the Isopod Survey Scheme in 1968 has recording been carried out throughout the British Isles. Of the 37 species on the British list, the nine so far recorded on Exmoor are mainly the more common woodlice.

Thelma M. Cheek
Recorder of Isopoda, E.N.H.S.

Sub-Order: ONISCIDEA Section: DIPLOCHETA

Section: SYNOCHETA

Superfamily: TRICHONISCOIDEA
TRICHONISCIDAE

Trichoniscus pusillus Brandt	On open ground	Common

Section: CRINOCHETA

Superfamily: ONISCOIDEA
ONISCIDAE

Oniscus asellus L.	Found in all areas	Common
PHILOSCIIDAE		
Philoscia muscorum (Scopoli)	Grassland	Common
PLATYARTHRIDAE		
Platyarthrus hoffmannseggi Brandt	Associates with yellow ants	Uncommon
Superfamily: PORCELLIONOIDEA		
ARMADILLIDIIDAE		
Armadillidium depressum Brandt	In and near buildings	Common
A. nasatum Budde-Lund		Uncommon
A. vulgare (Latreille)	PILL BUG	Common
PORCELLIONIDAE		
Porcellio scaber Latreille	In a variety of habitats	Common
P. spinicornis Say		Common

Reference:

Hopkin, S. *A Key to the Woodlice of Britain and Ireland* (1991) Field Studies Council.

Class: MYRIAPODA
Order: CHILOPODA — CENTIPEDES

HIMANTARIIDAE

Haplophilus subterraneus (Shaw)	Oak woodland; gardens
Geophilus carophagus (Leach)	Oak woodland

Order: SCOLOPENDROMORPHA

CRYPTOPSIDAE

Cryptops hortensis (Leach)	Gardens

Order: LITHOBIOMORPHA (STONE DWELLERS)

LITHOBIIDAE

Lithobius forficatus (L.)	Gardens
L. variegatus (Leach)	Oak woodlands
L. melanops (Newport)	Beneath bark of decaying wood
L. crassipes (Koch)	Oak leaf litter

Order: DIPLOPODA — MILLIPEDES

POLYXENIDAE

Polyxenus lagurus (L.)		Beneath lichens on trees and bark; leaf litter

GLOMERIDAE

Glomeris marginata (Vill.)		On woodland leaf litter

POLYDESMIDAE

Brachydesmus superbus (Latzel)		Fields
Polydesmus angustus (Latzel)		Gardens; oak woodland

STRONGYLOSOMIDAE

Oxidus gracilis (Koch)		Greenhouses

CRASPEDOSOMIDAE

Polymicrodon polydesmoides (Leach)		Beech leaf litter

BLANIULIDAE

Blaniulus guttulatus (Bosc)	SPOTTED SNAKE MILLIPEDE	Compost heaps
Proteroiulus fuscus (Am Steim)		Oak woodland leaf litter and compost heaps

IULIDAE

Tachypodoiulus niger (Leach)	BLACK MILLIPEDE	Oak woodland leaf litter
Cylindroiulus punctatus (Leach)		Oak woodland, beneath bark of rotting wood

Class: INSECTA (INSECTS)

Sub-class: APTERYGOTA (WINGLESS INSECTS)

Order: THYSANURA (BRISTLETAILS)

MACHILIDAE
Petrobius brevistylus Carpenter　　　　ROCKHOPPER　　　　Common on the coast

LEPISMATIDAE
Lepisma saccharina　　　　　　　　　SILVERFISH　　　　　Common in buildings
Thermobia domestica　　　　　　　　FIREBRAT　　　　　　Less common in buildings

Order: DIPLURA
(TWO-TAILED BRISTLETAILS)

CAMPODEIDAE
Campodea sp.　　　　　　　　　　　　　　　　　Common in compost heaps, etc.

Order: PROTURA (PROTURANS)

These microscopic insects lacking eyes and antennae occur under stones, bark and in soil.

Order: COLLEMBOLA (SPRING-TAILS)

PODURIDAE
Podura aquatica L.　　　　　　　　　　　　　　　Common on surface water

HYPOGASTRURIDAE
Anurida tullbergi Schott　Has been found grazing on the film of bacteria and algae on coast at low tide

A. maritima Laboulbène　　　　　　　　　　　　　Common on the coast

Order: ODONATA
(DRAGONFLIES)

The following list is compiled from data collated by the Exmoor Natural History Society (1977 - 95) together with additional records from John C. Keylock and Christian White. Christian has also produced some distribution maps for Exmoor Odonata which were published in the *Exmoor Naturalist* No. 21, Spring 1995.

Classification is adapted mainly from Davis (1981) *Synopsis of World Genera*.

Roger Butcher

Sub-Order: ZYGOPTERA – DAMSELFLIES

CALOPTERYGIDAE

Calopteryx virgo (L.)	BEAUTIFUL DEMOISELLE	Common
C. splendens (Harris)	BANDED DEMOISELLE	Fairly common

LESTIDAE - Sub-family: LESTINAE

Lestes sponsa (Hansemann)	EMERALD DAMSELFLY	Scarce

COENAGRIONIDAE - Sub-family: COENAGRIONINAE

Pyrrhosoma nymphula (Sulzer)	LARGE RED DAMSELFLY	Common
Coenagrion puella (L.)	AZURE DAMSELFLY	Fairly common
C. pulchellum (Vander Linden)	VARIABLE DAMSELFLY	Rare

    Sub-family: ISCHNURINAE

Enallagma cyathigerum (Charpentier)	COMMON BLUE DAMSELFLY	Common
Ischnura elegans (Vander Linden)	BLUE-TAILED DAMSELFLY	Locally frequent

Sub-order: ANISOPTERA – TRUE DRAGONFLIES

AESHNIDAE Sub-family: AESHNINAE

Aeshna juncea (L.)	COMMON HAWKER	Fairly common
A. mixta Latreille	MIGRANT HAWKER	Scarce
A. cyanea (Müller)	SOUTHERN HAWKER	Locally frequent
A. grandis (L.)	BROWN HAWKER	Rare
Anax imperator Leach	EMPEROR DRAGONFLY	Locally frequent

    Sub-family: BRACHYTRONINAE

Brachytron pratense (Müller)	HAIRY DRAGONFLY	Rare

CORDULEGASTERIDAE

Cordulegaster boltoni (Donovan)	GOLDEN-RINGED DRAGONFLY	Common

DRAGONFLIES

LIBELLULIDAE Sub-family: LIBELLULINAE

Libellula quadrimaculata L.	FOUR-SPOTTED CHASER	Scarce
L. depressa L.	BROAD-BODIED CHASER	Fairly common
Orthetrum cancellatum (L.)	BLACK-TAILED SKIMMER	Rare
O. coerulescens (Fabricius)	KEELED SKIMMER	Locally frequent

Sub-family: SYMPETRINAE

Sympetrum striolatum (Charpentier)	COMMON DARTER	Common
S. fonscolombei (Sélys)	RED-VEINED DARTER	Rare vagrant
		Last recorded on Exmoor 1941
S. danae (Sulzer)	BLACK DARTER	Locally frequent

Reference:

Askew, R.R. *The Dragonflies of Europe* (1988) Harley Books, Colchester.

Super-order: **ORTHOPTERA**

Order: **SALTATORIA**

Sub-order: **ENSIFERA**
(CRICKETS and BUSH-CRICKETS)

In the first edition of *The Flora and Fauna* the late T.J. 'Bill' Richards wrote:

"To a trained ear, Bush-crickets and Grasshoppers can be identified by their 'song' and this method has led me in the past to many of the finds on the following list."

As a result of Bill's work, these invertebrates are fairly well recorded on Exmoor. Of the 30 species on the British List 15 have been found. We are also most grateful to Robert Cropper of Burnham-on-Sea for checking the list and offering further comments.

TETTIGONIIDAE - BUSH-CRICKETS. Sub-family: **PHANEROPTERINAE**

Leptophyes punctatissima (Bosc)	SPECKLED BUSH-CRICKET	Occasional

Sub-family: **MECONEMATINAE**

Meconema thalassinum (DeGeer)   OAK BUSH-CRICKET   Common
Deciduous trees and shrubs

Sub-family: **CONOCEPHALINAE**

Conocephalus dorsalis (Latreille)   SHORT-WINGED CONEHEAD   Rare

Sub-family: **TETTIGONIINAE**

Tettigonia viridissima L.   GREAT GREEN BUSH-CRICKET
Locally common

Sub-family: **DECTICINAE**

Pholidoptera griseoaptera (DeGeer)   DARK BUSH-CRICKET   Occasional & local

RHAPHIDOPHORIDAE - WINGLESS CAMEL-CRICKETS

Tachycines asynamorus Adelung   GREENHOUSE CAMEL-CRICKET
Occasionally imported with plants; one, 1985, in a greenhouse

Sub-order: **CAELIFERA**
(GROUND-HOPPERS and GRASSHOPPERS)

TETRIGIDAE - GROUND-HOPPERS

Tetrix subulata (L.)   SLENDER GROUND-HOPPER   Uncommon
T. undulata (Sowerby)   COMMON GROUND-HOPPER   Locally abundant

ACRIDIDAE - GRASSHOPPERS   Sub-family: **LOCUSTINAE**

Stethophyma grossum (L.)   **RDB2.**   LARGE MARSH GRASSHOPPER   Rare;
on damp heathland

Sub-family: GOMPHOCERINAE

Omocestus viridulus (L.)	COMMON GREEN GRASSHOPPER	Common
O. rufipes (Zetterstedt)	WOODLAND GRASSHOPPER	Rare
Myrmeleotettix maculatus (Thunberg)	MOTTLED GRASSHOPPER	Abundant in heathland
Chorthippus brunneus (Thunberg)	FIELD GRASSHOPPER	Common on coast and some inland sites, scarce on high ground
Chorthippus albomarginatus (DeGeer)	LESSER MARSH GRASSHOPPER	Rare
Chorthippus parallelus (Zetterstedt)	MEADOW GRASSHOPPER	Very common

References:

Brown, V.K. *Grasshoppers*. Naturalists' Handbook 2 (1983) Cambridge University Press.

Haes, E.C.M. *Provisional Atlas of the Insects of the British Isles*, 6, Orthoptera BRC. NERC.

Ragge, D.R. *Grasshoppers, Crickets and Cockroaches of the British Isles*, (1965) Warne.

Bellman, Heiko *A Field Guide to the Grasshoppers and Crickets of Britain and Northern Europe* (1988) Collins.

Order: BLATTODEA – COCKROACHES

BLATTIDAE

Blatta orientalis L.	COMMON COCKROACH	Rubbish dumps

Order: DERMAPTERA – EARWIGS

Four species of Earwigs occur in Britain but only one is recorded on Exmoor. JAH

FORFICULIDAE

Forficula auricularia L.	COMMON EARWIG	Very common

Order: PSOCOPTERA (PSOCIDS) BOOKLICE AND BARKLICE

The Psocoptera are commonly known as Booklice and Barklice and are small algae and fungi feeding insects. New (1974) lists some 90 species but only 50 are widespread out of doors, the rest being imported on timber, plants and stored products. The group is very under recorded and the following list is the result of three days collecting in the autumn of 1987. Nomenclature follows New (1974). *Psocoptera* Handbooks Ident. British Insects I 7 RESL.

John A. Hollier

TROGIIDAE

Trogium pulsatorium (L.)	BOOK LOUSE	In old libraries and books

LEPIDOPSOCIDAE

Pteroxanium kelloggi (Ribaga)		Litter dwelling

LICE

PSOCIDAE
Metylophorus nebulosus (Stephens) — On bark, widespread
Psococerastis gibbosa (Sulzer) — On foliage, local

PHILOTARSIDAE
Philotarsus picicornis (Fab.) — On foliage, common

ELIPSOCIDAE
Elipsocus hyalinus (Stephens) — On foliage, common
E. westwoodi McLachan — On foliage, common

PERIPSOCIDAE
Peripsocus phaeopterus (Stephens) — On bark, widespread

ECTOPSOCIDAE
Ectopsocus briggsi McLachan — On foliage, common

STENOPSOCIDAE
Graphopsocus cruciatus (L.) — On foliage, common
Stenopsocus immaculatus (Stephens) — On foliage, common

CAECILIIDAE
Caecilius burmeisteri Brauer — Conifers, common
C. flavidus (Stephens) — On foliage, common
C. fuscopterus (Latreille) — On foliage, common
Enderleinella obsoleta (Stephens) — Conifers, occasional

Order: MALLOPHAGA (BITING LICE)

TRICHODECTIDAE
Trichodectes melis — Commonly found on badgers, also strays on foxes

There are many other species of biting-lice found mainly on birds but they need specialist identification.

Order: ANOPLURA (SUCKING LICE)

Various species may occur on cattle, pigs, dogs and humans.

Order: HEMIPTERA (BUGS)

The hemiptera, or true bugs, are a large and varied order of insects which all have sucking mouthparts. Most are herbivores, although some of the heteroptera are predatory, or omnivorous. Few records have been added since the last edition, and the aphids in particular are very poorly known.

There are no comprehensive works on the hemiptera. Southwood and Leston (1959) is the last account of the heteroptera, and now out of print. Nomenclature here follows Dolling (1984) as updated by the heteroptera recording scheme. The leafhoppers and psyllids are covered by the Royal Entomological Society *Handbook* series, and nomenclature here follows LeQuesne & Payne (1981) and Hodkinson & White (1979). The rest of the nomenclature follows Kloet & Hincks (1964).

The status of this group is reviewed by Kirby (1992), the recomendations of which are accepted. The Exmoor list does not have many unusual species, perhaps an indication of under-recording. There are too few records to make meaningful comments about the abundance of the species in the national park, although there are a few comparative studies (Hollier 1989).

I am grateful to Bill Dolling (Natural History Museum) and Mike Wilson (National Museum of Wales) for help with identifications, and to Walter LeQuesne for help and advice. I also thank Keith Alexander (National Trust), Bernard Nau, Peter Kirby and the above for records to supplement those of the members.

John A. Hollier
Recorder of Hemiptera, E.N.H.S.

Sub-order: HETEROPTERA

SHIELDBUGS

ACANTHOSOMATIDAE

Acanthosoma haemorrhoidale (L.)		Hawthorn (Crataegus)
Elasmostethus interstinctus (L.)		Birch (Betula)
E. tristriatus (Fabricius)		Juniper (naturalised on garden cypress)
Elasmucha grisea (L.)		Birch (Betula)

CYDNIDAE

Legnotus limbosus (Geoffroy)		Herbs
Sehirus bicolor (L.)		Labiates
S. biguttatus (L.)	Notable.	Cow-wheat (Malampyrum)

PENTATOMIDAE

Podops inuncta (Fabricius)	Grasses
Aelia acuminata (L.)	Grasses
Palomena prasina (L.)	Trees and shrubs
Dolycoris baccarum (L.)	Deciduous trees
Piezodorus lituratus (Fabricius)	Gorse (Ulex)
Pentatoma rufipes (L.)	Deciduous trees
Picromerus bidens (L.)	Predatory in grasslands

BUGS

Troilus luridus (Fabricius)	Predatory in trees
Zicrona caerulea (L.)	Predatory in grassland

SQUASHBUGS

COREIDAE

Syromastus rhombeus (L.) *(Verlusia rhombea)*	Sandy places
Enoplops scapha (Fabricius)	Grassland herbs
Coreus marginatus (L.)	Docks (Rumex)
Coriomerus denticulatus (Scopoli)	Grassland herbs

ALYDIDAE

Alydus calcaratus (L.)	Heathland herbs

RHOPALIDAE

Corizus hyoscyami (L.)	Restharrow (Ononis)
Rhopalus subrufus (Gmelin)	Grassland herbs
Myrmus miriformis (Fallén)	Grasses

GROUNDBUGS

LYGAEIDAE

Heterogaster urticae (Fabricius)		Nettle (Urtica)
Chilacis typhae (Perris)		GreatReedmace (Typha)
Nysius ericae (Schilling)		Grassland herbs
Kliedocerys resedae (Panzer)		Birch (Betula)
K. trunculatus (Walker)		Heaths
Rhyparochromus pini (L.)	Notable.	Heaths
Megalonotus dilatatus (Herrich-Schäffer)	Notable.	Heaths
Trapezonotus dispar Stål		Heath and grasslands
Macrodema micropterum (Curtis)		Heaths
Stygnocoris fuligineus (Geoffroy)		Grasslands
S. sabulosus (Fallén)		Grasslands
S. rusticus (Fallén)		Grasslands
Ischnocoris angustulatus (Boheman)		Heaths
Drymus brunneus (Sahlberg)		Grasslands
D. ryei Douglas & Scott		Grasslands
D. sylvaticus (Fabricius)		Grasslands
Scolopstethus affinis (Schilling)		Nettles (Urtica)
S. decoratus (Hahn)		Heather (Calluna)
S. thomsoni Reuter		Nettles (Urtica)
Gastrodes grossipes (DeGeer)		Pine (Pinus)

STILTBUGS

BERYTINIDAE

Cymus claviculus (Fallén)	Grassland herbs

BUGS

Cymus melanocephalus Fieber	Rushes
Berytinus montivagus (Meyer)	Legumes
Metatropis rufescens (Herrich-Schäffer)	Enchanter's Nightshade (Circaea)

LACEBUGS
TINGIDAE

Campylosteira verna (Fallén)	Moss
Acalypta brunnea (Germar)	Moss
Dictyonota strichnocera Fieber	Gorse (Ulex)
Tingis ampliata (Herrich-Schäffer)	Thistles
T. cardui (L.)	Thistles
Physatocheila dumetorum (Herrich-Schäffer)	Ivy (Hedera)

ASSASSIN BUGS
REDUVIIDAE

Empicoris vagabundus (L.)	Predator on trees and shrubs
Coranus subapterus (DeGeer)	Predator in heaths

DAMSEL BUGS
NABIDAE

Nabis ferus (L.)	Predator in grasslands
N. ericetorum Scholtz	Predator in grasslands
N. rugosus (L.)	Predator in grasslands
Anaptus major (Costa)	Predator in grasslands
Aptus mirmicoides (Costa)	Predator in grasslands
Nabicula flavomarginatus (Scholtz)	Predator in grasslands
N. limbatus (Dahlbom)	Predator in grasslands

FLOWER BUGS
CIMICIDAE

Temnostethus gracilis (Horvath)	Predator on trees
T. pusillus (Herrich-Schäffer)	Predator on trees
Anthocoris confusus Reuter	Predator on trees and shrubs
A. nemoralis (Fabricius)	Predator on trees and shrubs
A. nemorum (L.)	Ubiquitous predator
A. simulans Reuter	Predator on Ash (Fraxinus) or Elm (Ulmus)
Tetraphleps bicuspis (Herrich-Schäffer)	Predator on conifers
Orius majusculus (Reuter)	Predator on trees, shrubs and herbs
O. niger (Wolff)	Predator on trees, shrubs and herbs
Xylocoris cursitans (Fallén)	Predator on logs and stumps
Cardiastethus fasciiventris (Garbiglietti)	Predator on trees
Xylocoridea brevipennis Reuter	Notable. Predator on Apple and Thorn

BUGS

MICROPHYSIDAE

Loricula elegantula (Barensprung)	Predator on trees
Loricula pselaphiformis Curtis	Predator on trees

PLANT BUGS

MIRIDAE

Monalocoris filicis (L.)	Ferns
Bryocoris pteridis (Fallén)	Ferns
Deraeocoris lutescens (Schilling)	Deciduous trees
D. ruber (L.)	Grassland herbs
Lopus decolor (Fallén)	Grassland herbs
Megalocoleus molliculus (Fallén)	Yarrow (Achillea)
Amblytylus nasutus (Kirschbaum)	Grassland herbs
Macrotylus paykulli (Fallén)	Restharrow (Ononis)
Harpocera thoracica (Fallén)	Oak (Quercus)
Phylus coryli (L.)	Hazel (Corylus)
P. melanocephalus (L.)	Oak (Quercus)
P. palliceps (Fieber)	Oak (Quercus)
Psallus ambiguus (Fallén)	Deciduous trees
P. perrisi (Mulsant & Rey)	Oak (Quercus)
P. wagneri Ossiannilsson	Oak (Quercus)
P. scholtzi Fieber	Alder (Alnus)
P. falleni Reuter	Birch (Betula)
P. lepidus (Fieber)	Ash (Fraxinus)
P. haematodes (Gmelin)	Willow (Salix)
P. flavellus Stichel	Ash (Fraxinus)
P. diminutus (Kirschbaum)	Oak (Quercus) and Poplar (Populus)
P. varians (Herrich-Schäffer)	Oak (Quercus)
Compsidolon salicellus (Herrich-Schäffer)	Hazel (Corylus) and Sallow (Salix)
Atractotomus magnicornis (Fallén)	Spruce (Picea)
Plagiognathus arbustorum (Fabricius)	Highly polyphagous in grasslands
P. chrysanthemi (Wolff)	Highly polyphagous in grasslands
Sthenarus rotermundi (Scholtz)	White Poplar (Populus alba)
Asciodema obsoletum (Fieber)	Gorse (Ulex)
Neodicyphus rhododendroni (Dolling)	Rhododendron
Dicyphus constrictus (Boheman)	Polyphagus on herbs
D. epilobii Reuter	Hairy Willowherb (Epilobium hirsutum)
D. errans (Wolff)	Polyphagous on herbs
D. stachydis Reuter	Hedge Woundwort (Stachys sylvatica)

BUGS

Dicyphus pallicornis (Meyer-Dur)	Foxglove (Digitalis)
D. globulifer (Fallén)	Campions (Silene)
Campyloneura virgula (Herrich-Schäffer)	Predator on deciduous trees
Philophorus perplexus Douglas & Scott	Predator on deciduous trees
Orthocephalus saltator (Hahn)	Composites
Malacocoris chlorizans (Panzer)	Hazel (Corylus) and Apple (Malus)
Cyllecoris histrionicus (L.)	Oak (Quercus)
Dryophilocoris flavoquadrimaculatus (DeGeer)	Oak (Quercus)
Heterotoma merioptera (Scopoli)	Grassland herbs
Blepharidopterus angulatus (Fallén)	Deciduous trees
Orthotylus tenellus (Fallén)	Deciduous trees
O. marginalis Reuter	Deciduous trees
O. ochrotrichus Fieber	Deciduous trees and herbs
O. prasinus (Fallén)	Deciduous trees
O. ericetorum (Fallén)	Heath
O. virescens (Douglas & Scott)	Broom (Cytisus)
Mecomma ambulans (Fallén)	Woodland herbs
Pithanus maerkeli (Herrich-Schäffer)	Predator in grasslands
Lygus rugulipennis Poppius	Polyphagous on herbs
Liocoris tripustulatus (Fabricius)	Nettles (Urtica)
Orthops cervinus (Herrich-Schäffer)	Lime (Tilia)
O. campestris (L.)	Umbellifers
O. kalmi (L.)	Umbellifers
Lygocoris pabulinus (L.)	Deciduous trees and herbs
L. contaminatus (Fallén)	Birch (Betula)
L. viridis (Fallén)	Lime (Tilia)
L. lucorum (Meyer-Dur)	Polyphagous on herbs
Calocoris quadripunctatus (Villers)	Oak (Quercus)
C. stysi Wagner	Woodland herbs
C. norvegicus (Gmelin)	Grassland herbs
Adelphocoris lineolatus (Goeze)	Grassland herbs
Megacoelum infusum (Herrich-Schäffer)	Oak (Quercus)
Stenotus binotatus (Fabricius)	Grasses
Phytocoris dimidatus Kirschbaum	Oak (Quercus) and Plum (Prunus)
P. longipennis Flor	Deciduous trees
P. tiliae (Fabricius)	Oak (Quercus)
P. varipes Boheman	Grassland and dune herbs
Capsus ater (L.)	Grassland herbs
Pantilius tunicatus (Fabricius)	Alder (Alnus)

BUGS

Acertropis gimmerthali (Flor)	Grasses
Stenodema calcaratum (Fallén)	Grasses
S. holsatum (Fabricius)	Grasses
S. laevigatum (L.)	Grasses
Notostira elongata (Geoffroy)	Grasses
Trigonotylus ruficornis (Geoffroy)	Grasses
Leptopterna dolabrata (L.)	Grasses
L. ferrugata (Fallén)	Grasses

FRESHWATER SHORE BUGS

SALDIDAE

Saldula c-album (Fieber)	Predators near water
S. saltatoria (L.)	Predators near water

WATER MEASURERS

HYDROMETRIDAE

Hydrometra stagnorum (L.)	Predator on water surface

WATER CRICKETS

VELIIDAE

Velia caprai Tamanini	Predator on water surface
V. saulii Tamanini	Predator on water surface

POND SKATERS

GERRIDAE

Gerris lacustris (L.)	Predator on water surface
Aquarius najas (DeGeer)	Predator on water surface, mainly on rivers
Limnoporus rufoscutellatus Latreille	Predator on water surface

WATER SCORPION

NEPIDAE

Nepa cinerea L.	Predator in ponds or slow moving water

SAUCER BUG

NAUCORIDAE

Ilyocoris cimicoides (L.)	Predator in ponds, or slow moving water

WATER BOATMEN

NOTONECTIDAE

Notonecta glauca L.	Predator in ponds, or slow moving water

CORIXIDAE

Corixa punctata (Illinger)	Omnivores in ponds, or slow moving water

Sub-order: HOMOPTERA
Section: AUCHENORRYNCHA

CERCOPIDAE — FROG HOPPERS

Aphrophora alni (Fallén)	Deciduous trees

BUGS

Philaenus spumaris (L.)	Highly polyphagous
Neophilaenus exclamationis (Thunberg)	Grasses and herbs
N. lineatus (L.)	Grasses and herbs
Cercopis vulnerata Illiger	Woodland

TREE HOPPERS
MEMBRACIDAE

Centrotus cornutus (L.)	Deciduous trees

LEAFHOPPERS
CICADELLIDAE

Ulopa reticulata (Fabricius)	Heathers (Calluna & Erica)
Megaphthalmus scabripennis Edwards	Grasses
M. scanicus (Fallén)	Grasses
Cicadella viridis (L.)	Grasses and rushes
Evacanthus interruptus (L.)	Grasses
Idiocerus confusus Flor	Sallows (Salix)
I. distinguendus Kirschbaum	White Poplar (Populus alba)
I. fulgidus (Fabricius)	Black Poplar (Populus nigra)
I. lituratus (Fallén)	Sallows (Salix)
I. similis Kirschbaum	Sallows (Salix)
I. vitreus (Fabricius)	Poplars (Populus)
Iassus lanio (L.)	Oak (Quercus)
Oncopsis alni (Schrank)	Alder (Alnus)
O. avellanae Edwards	Hazel (Corylus)
O. flavicollis (L.)	Birch (Betula)
O. subangulata (J.Sahlberg)	Birch (Betula)
O. tristris (Zetterstedt)	Birch (Betula)
Macropsis scutellata (Boheman)	Nettle (Urtica)
Agallia consobrina Curtis	Grasses
Eupelix cuspidata (Fabricius)	Grasses
Aphrodes albifrons (L.)	Grasses
A. makarovi Zachvatkin *(A. bicinctus (Schrank))*	Grasses
Deltocephalus pulicaris (Fallén)	Grasses
Arocephalus punctum (Flor)	Grasses
Adarrus oscellaris (Fallén)	Grasses
Jassargus distinguendus (Flor)	Grasses
J. flori (Fieber)	Grasses
Diplocolenus abdominalis (Fabricius)	Grasses
Arthaldeus pascuellus (Fallén)	Grasses

Arthaldeus striifrons (Kirschbaum)	Grasses
Psammotettix confinis (Dahlbom)	Grasses
P. nodosus (Ribaut)	Grasses
P. putoni (Then)	Grasses
Sardius argus (Marshall)	Grasses
Allygus mixtus (Fabricius)	Deciduous trees
A. modestus Scott	Deciduous trees
Conosanus obsoletus (Kirschbaum)	Grasses
Euscelis incisus (Kirschbaum)	Grasses
E. lineolatus (Brulle)	Grasses
Streptanus aemulans (Kirschbaum)	Grasses
S. marginatus (Kirschbaum)	Grasses
Mocydia crocea (Herrich-Schäffer)	Grasses
Mocydiopsis attenuata (Germar)	Grasses
M. parvicauda Ribaut	Grasses
Thamnotettix confinis (Zetterstedt)	Grasses
Pseudotettix subfuscus (Fallén)	Deciduous trees
Lamprotettix nitidulus (Fabricius)	Grasses
Cicadula aurantipes (Edwards)	Grasses and sedges
C. persimilis (Edwards)	Grasses and sedges
Elymana sulphurella (Zetterstedt)	Grasses
Macrosteles laevis (Ribaut)	Grasses and herbs
M. sexnotatus (Fallén)	Grasses and herbs
M. viridigriseus (Edwards)	Grasses
Balclutha punctata (Fabricius)	Grasses, herbs and shrubs
Alebra albostriella (Fallén)	Oak (Quercus)
A. wahlbergi (Boheman)	Oak (Quercus) and Elm (Ulmus)
Notus flavipennis (Zetterstedt)	Grasses
Forcipata forcipata (Flor)	Grasses and sedges
Dikraneura variata Hardy	Grasses and sedges
Elemyanoviana mollicula (Boheman)	Grasses and herbs
Empoasca vitis (Goethe)	Highly polyphagous
Kybos betulicola (Wagner)	Birch (Betula)
K. populi (Edwards)	Poplar (Populus)
K. smaragdula (Fallén)	Sallow (Salix)
Eurhadina concinna (Germar)	Oak (Quercus)
E. pulchella (Fallén)	Oak (Quercus)
Eupteryx atropunctata (Goeze)	Grassland herbs
E. aurata (L.)	Grassland herbs

BUGS

Eupteryx cyclops Matsumura	Grassland herbs
E. filicium (Newman)	Ferns
E. florida Ribaut	Grassland herbs
E. melissae Curtis	Labiates
E. notata Curtis	Labiates
E. stachyderum (Hardy)	Labiates
E. thoulessi Edwards	Labiates
E. urticae (Fabricius)	Labiates
Aguriahana stellulata (Burmeister)	Deciduous trees
Ribautiana cruciata (Ribaut)	Deciduous trees
R. debilis (Douglas)	Deciduous trees
R. scalaris (Ribaut)	Oak (Quercus)
R. tenerrima (Herrich-Schäffer)	Deciduous trees
R. ulmi (L.)	Elm (Ulmus)
Eupterocyba jucunda (Herrich-Schäffer)	Alder (Alnus)
Linnavuoriana decempunctata (Fallén)	Birch (Betula)
L. sexmaculata (Hardy)	Sallow (Salix)
Typhlocyba quercus (Fabricius)	Oak (Quercus) and Beech (Fagus)
Lindbergina aurovittata (Douglas)	Deciduous trees
Fagocyba carri Edwards	Oak (Quercus)
F. cruenta (Herrich-Schäffer)	Oak (Quercus)
Edwardsiana avellanae (Edwards)	Hazel (Corylus)
E. bergmanni (Tullgren)	Birch (Betula) and Alder (Alnus)
E. crategi (Douglas)	Deciduous trees
E. frustrator (Edwards)	Deciduous trees
E. geometrica (Schrank)	Alder (Alnus)
E. hippocastani (Edwards)	Deciduous trees
E. plebeja (Edwards)	Oak (Quercus)
E. rosae (L.)	Rose (Rosa)
Alnetoidia alneti (Dahlbom)	Deciduous trees
Zyginidia scutellaris (Herrich-Schäffer)	Grasses
Hauptidia maroccana (Melichar)	Foxglove (Digitalis)
Zygina angusta Lethierry	Deciduous trees
Z. flammigera (Geoffroy)	Deciduous trees

PLANT HOPPERS

CIXIIDAE

Oliarus leporinus (L.)	Notable.	Grasses and herbs
Tachycixius pilosus (Olivier)		Grasses and herbs
Cixius cunicularis (L.)		Grasses and herbs

BUGS

Cixius nervosus (L.)		Grasses and herbs

DELPHACIDAE

Asiraca clavicornis (Fabricius)	Notable.	Grasses
Kelisia sabulicola Wagner		Dune grasses
Stenocranus minutus (Fabricius)		Grasses
Chloriana unicolor (Herrich-Schäffer)		Reeds
Conomelus anceps (Germar)		Rushes
Ditropis pteridis (Spinola)		Ferns
Stiroma affinis Fieber		Grasses
Criomorphus albomarginatus Curtis		Grasses
Dicranotropis hamata (Boheman)		Grasses
Muellerianella fairmairei (Perris)		Grasses
Hyledelphax elegantulus (Boheman)		Grasses
Javesella discolor (Boheman)		Grasses
J. dubia (Kirschbaum)		Grasses
J. forcipata (Boheman)		Grasses
J. obscurella (Boheman)		Grasses
J. pellucida (Fabricius)		Grasses
Xanthodelphax stramineus (Stål)		Grasses

ISSIDAE

Issus coleoptratus (Fabricius)	Deciduous trees

Section: STERNORRHYNCHA
PLANT LICE

PSYLLIDAE

Psyllopsis fraxini (L.)	Galls on Ash (Fraxinus)
Psylla alni (L.)	Alder (Alnus)
P. brunneipennis Edwards	Willows (Salix)
P. buxi (L.)	Galls on Box (Buxus)
P. mali Schmidtberger	Apple (Malus)
P. melanoneura Förster	Hawthorn (Crataegus)
P. peregrina Förster	Hawthorn (Crataegus)

TRIOZIDAE

Trioza alacris Flor	Gall on Bay (Laurus)
T. centranthi (Vallot)	Gall on Red Valerian (Centranthus)
T. remota Förster	Gall on Oak (Quercus)
T. urticae (L.)	Nettle (Urtica)

WHITEFLIES

ALEYRODIDAE

Aleyrodes proletella (L.)	CABBAGE WHITEFLY	Locally common on Brassicas

BUGS

Trialeurodes vaporariorum (Westwood) GREENHOUSE WHITEFLY — In greenhouses

APHIDS

LACHNIDAE

Neotrama caudata (Del Geurcio)	Lettuce roots

CALLAPHIDIDAE

Myzocallis castanicola (Baker)	Sweet Chestnut (Castanea sativa)
M. coryli (Goeze)	Hazel (Corylus)
Tuberculoides annulatus (Hartig)	
Phyllaphis fagi (L.)	Beech (Fagus)
Euceraphis punctipennis (Zetterstedt)	Birch (Betula)

APHIDIDAE

Aphis fabae Scopoli	Highly polyphagous
Dysaphis sorbi (Kaltenbach)	Galls on Rowan (Sorbus aucuparia)
Hayhurstia atriplicis (L.)	Galls on Chenopodiaceae (Goosefoot family)
Myzus persicae (Sulzer)	Highly polyphagous
Cryptomyzus ribis (L.)	Galls on Currant (Ribes)

PEMPHIGIDAE

Eriosoma lanigerum (Hausmann)	Galls on Apple (Malus)
Schizoneura ulmi (L.)	Galls on Elm (Ulmus)
Tetraneura ulmi (L.)	Galls on Elm (Ulmus)
Thecabius affinis (Kaltenbach)	Galls on Poplar (Populus)
Prociphilus fraxini (Geoffroy)	Galls on Ash (Fraxinus)
Pemphigus bursarius (L.)	Galls on Poplar (Populus)
P. spirothecae Passerini	Galls on Poplar
P. lysimachiae (Borner)	Galls on Poplar (Populus)

ADELGIDAE

Adelges abietis (L.)	Galls on spruce (Picea)

References:
Dolling, W.R. *Comments on the terrestrial heteroptera recording card, cross index from Southwood and Leston.* (1984) Heteroptera Recording Scheme,
Hodkinson, I.D. & White, I.M. Psylloidea *Handbooks for the Identification of British Insects* 2: 5(a) (1979)
Hollier, J.A. *Grassland Hemiptera from Exmoor.* (1989) Somerset Archaeological and Natural History Society 132:335-340
Kirby, P. *A review of the scarce and threatened Hemiptera of Great Britain.* J.N.C.C. (1992)
Kloet & Hincks (1964) Checklist of British Insects *Handbooks for the Identification of British Insects* 11: 1
LeQuesne, W.J. & Payne, K.R. (1981) Cicadellidae (Typhlocybinae) with a checklist of the British Auchenorrhyncha *Handbooks for the Identification of British Insects* 2:2(c)
Southwood, T.R.E & Leston, D. (1959) *Land and Water Bugs of the British Isles.* Warne.

Order: THYSANOPTERA – THRIPS

There are many species of these tiny insects, usually common on flowers, sometimes swarming in thousands during humid weather giving rise to the common name 'Thunderflies'. The species require specialist identification.

LACEWINGS

The lacewings are a small group of nocturnal, and largely arboreal, insects. The adults and larvae are carnivorous, and many are important as predators of aphids. The larvae of *Sialis* are aquatic and those of *Osmylus* are semi-aquatic. There has been a lot of work on the taxonomy of this group over the last ten years, and four orders are now recognised. Nomenclature here follows Plant (1994), although identification still relies on Fraser (1959) or Killington (1936-7). The review of the conservation status of this group by Kirby (1991) has been superseded by Plant (1994), whose recommendations are followed here. Although there are twice as many species recorded here than there were in the first edition, the group is still under-recorded. I am grateful to Colin Plant for confirming some of my identifications.

John A. Hollier

Order: RAPHIDIOPTERA (SNAKE FLIES)

RAPHIDIIDAE

Atlantoraphidia maculicollis (Stephens)	Locally abundant, associated with pines or larches

Order: MEGALOPTERA (ALDER FLIES)

SIALIDAE

Sialis lutaria (L.)	Found near slow moving or still water
S. fuliginosa Pictet	Found near clear streams
S. nigripes Pictet	Local (Old records only)

Order: NEUROPTERA (LACEWINGS)

CONIOPTERYGIDAE

Coniopteryx tineiformis Curtis	Common on deciduous trees
Conwenzia sp.	Deciduous trees, common

OSMYLIDAE

Osmylus fulvicephalus (Scopoli)	Found in deciduous woodland near streams

HEMEROBIIDAE

Micromus variegatus (Fabricius)	Eurytopic, widespread and common
M. paganus (L.)	Common in many habitats amongst low-growing vegetation
Hemerobius humulinus L.	Common in deciduous trees
H. simulans Walker	Associated with larch or spruce
H. stigma Stephens	Associated with pine

LACEWINGS

Hemerobius atrifrons McLachan	Local, apparently confined to larch
H. micans Olivier	Common on oaks
H. lutescens Fabricius	Common on deciduous trees
H. marginatus Stephens	Chiefly on birch
Wesmaelius betulinus (Ström)	Eurytopic, widespread and common
W. subnebulosus (Stephens)	Ubiquitous
Symperobius pellucidus (Walker)	Local, in canopy of trees
S. fuscescens (Wallengren)	Local, in canopy of pines

CHRYSOPIDAE

Chrysopa perla (L.)	Common in scrub
Chrysoperla carnea (Stephens)	Ubiquitous
Chrysopidia ciliata (Wesmael)	Common in deciduous trees
Cunctochrysa albolineata (Killington)	Common in deciduous trees
Mallada flavifrons (Brauer)	Mixed woodland or heath
Nineta flava (Scopoli)	Common on deciduous trees
N. vittata (Wesmael)	Common on deciduous trees

Order: MECOPTERA (SCORPION FLIES)

PANORPIDAE

Panorpa communis L.	Common in woods and hedgerows

References:

Fraser, F.C. Mecoptera, Megaloptera and Neuroptera. *Handbooks Ident. British Insects* 1 (12 & 13) RESL (1959)

Killington, F.J. *A Monograph of the British Neuroptera* 2 vols. Ray Society, (1936 & 1937)

Kirby, P. *A Review of the scarcer Neuroptera of Great Britain*. NCC, Peterborough (1991)

Plant, C.W. *Provisional Atlas of the Lacewings and Allied Insedts (Neuroptera, Megaloptera, Raphidioptera and Mecoptera) of Britain and Ireland.* ITE, Monks Wood (1994).

Order: LEPIDOPTERA
(BUTTERFLIES & MOTHS)

Exmoor National Park is situated within the areas of TWO Watsonian vice-counties, namely 4 (North Devon) and 5 (South Somerset) and the appropriate vice-county number is given before the status column in the Check-list which follows. Authors' names have been given in full with the exception of the following where suitable appreviations have been used:

Herrich-Schäffer	H.-S.	Humphreys & Westwood	H.& W.
Bechstein & Scharfenburg	B.& S.	Lienig & Zeller	L.& Z.
Denis & Schiffermüller	D.& S.	Fischer von Röslerstamm	F.v R.
Linnaeus	L.		

Status on Exmoor has been given when known and food-plants/food material have been included for the micro-moths.

The classification adopted is that given in Bradley & Fletcher *Recorder's Log-book of British Butterflies and Moths* (1979) but incorporating a number of inevitable name changes and minor classification changes, especially in the case of the Pyralidae and where a family has been reduced to sub-family level or a sub-family elevated to full family status. Where changes in binomials have taken place, the B.& F. names are given in brackets below the name in current use.

The Recorder wishes to acknowledge the assistance of the following: The late Duke of Newcastle, Edward Pelham-Clinton, for much valuable help prior to his untimely death in 1988 and for supplying many records from North Devon and the Porlock area; Mr Brian Baker, of Reading, who compiled an excellent list while operating a moth-trap in Porlock in 1985 and for his continuing support and help with both light-trapping and genitalia determinations; the late Dr H.M. Chappell for many records over a long period at Minehead and Selworthy, his records being published in *Proceedings* Somerset Archaeological & Natural History Society from which they were abstracted; Mr Robert Heckford for a number of records of micro-moths, particularly from the North Devon area. Records have also been supplied by Mr Paul Harding of the Biological Records Centre and Mr Adrian Riley of Rothamsted; a small number have been taken from Turner *Lepidoptera of Somerset* (1955).

In view of the virtual absence of calcareous soils, sand-dune complexes and extensive marshes, it is to be expected that many species, common in such habitats, would be absent and thus the substantial number discovered to date must represent a high level of recording coverage.

While it is true that the majority of the so-called macro-moths may be readily obtained by the use of a mercury-vapour light trap, this is not so in the case of many of their smaller brethren which tend to wander much less, often remaining in the vicinity of their food-plants and can only be located by diligent field-work combined with a sound knowledge of field botany and of the life-cycles of the moths themselves. Even so, many micros are seldom seen in the adult state and recourse must be had to breeding the imagines from larvae collected in the field. Butterflies are the group most reported by the general membership of the Society and the rare Heath Fritillary *Mellicta athalia* (Rottemburg) was first discovered breeding on Exmoor in 1982. Thus the importance of field-work cannot be too strongly emphasised.

John Robbins,
Recorder of Lepidoptera,
Exmoor Natural History Society.

MOTHS

Sub-order: ZEUGLOPTERA

MICROPTERIGIDAE   V.C.

Micropterix tunbergella (Fabricius)	on Crataegus flowers	4,5	Fairly common
M. aureatella (Scopoli)	on flowers of Carex spp.	4,5	Fairly common
M. aruncella (Scopoli)	on Crataegus flowers	4,5	Very common
M. calthella (L.)	on various flowers	5	Uncommon

Sub-order: DACNONYPHA

ERIOCRANIIDAE

Eriocrania subpurpurella (Haworth)	on Quercus spp.	4,5	Very common
E. sparrmannella (Bosc)	on Betula spp.	5	Fairly common
E. salopiella (Stainton)	on Betula spp.	5	Fairly common
E. haworthi Bradley	on Betula spp.	5	Common
E. sangii (Wood)	on Betula spp.	5	Common
E. semipurpurella (Stephens)	on Betula spp.	5	Fairly common

Sub-order: EXOPORIA

HEPIALIDAE

Hepialus humuli (L.)	GHOST MOTH	4,5	Uncommon
H. sylvina (L.)	ORANGE SWIFT	4,5	Uncommon
H. hecta (L.)	GOLD SWIFT	4,5	Uncommon
H. lupulinus (L.)	COMMON SWIFT	4,5	Common
H. fusconebulosa (DeGeer)	MAP-WINGED SWIFT	5	Occasional

Sub-order: MONOTRYSIA

NEPTICULIDAE

Bohemannia pulverosella (Stainton) *(Ectoedemia pulverosella Stt.)*	on Malus cultivars	4,5	Common
Etainia decentella (Herrich-Schäffer)	on wing of samara of Acer pseudoplatanus	5	
Ectoedemia spinosella De Joannis	on Prunus spinosa	5	Very local
E. angulifasciella (Stainton)	on Rosa spp.	4,5	Common
E. atricollis (Stainton)	on Malus & Crataegus	4,5	Common
E. occultella (L.)*(argentipedella Zeller)*	on Betula spp.	4,5	Common

MOTHS

Ectoedemia minimella (Zetterstedt) *(mediofasciella Haworth)* on Betula spp.		4,5	Rare
E. albifasciella (Heinemann)	on Quercus spp.	4,5	Very common
E. subbimaculella (Haworth)	on Quercus spp.	5	Local
E. heringi (Toll)	on Quercus spp.	5	Very local
Fomoria septembrella (Stainton)	on Hypericum spp.	4,5	Fairly common
Stigmella aurella (Fabricius)	on Rubus spp.	4,5	Abundant
S. fragariella (Heyden)	on Rubus spp., Fragaria & Agrimonia	5	Uncommon
S. dulcella (Heinemann)	on Fragaria vesca	4,5	Very common
S. splendidissimella (Herrich-Schäffer)	on Rubus spp.	4,5	Very common
S. marginicolella (Stainton)	on Ulmus spp.	5	Very common
S. continuella (Stainton)	on Betula spp.	5	Uncommon
S. speciosa (Frey)	on Acer pseudoplatanus	4,5	Fairly common
S. sorbi (Stainton)	on Sorbus aucuparia	5	Uncommon
S. plagiocolella (Stainton)	on Prunus spinosa	4,5	Very common
S. salicis (Stainton)	on Salix spp.	4,5	Very common
S. obliquella (Heinemann)	on smooth-leaved Salix	5	Fairly common
S. myrtillella (Stainton)	on Vaccinium myrtillus	4,5	Uncommon
S. trimaculella (Haworth)	on Populus spp.	5	Fairly common
S. floslactella (Haworth)	on Corylus avellana	4,5	Abundant
S. tityrella (Stainton)	on Fagus sylvatica	4,5	Very common
S. incognitella (Herrich-Schäffer) *(pomella Vaughan)* on Malus		5	Local
S. perpygmaeella (Doubleday)	on Crataegus	4,5	Common
S. ulmivora (Fologne)	on Ulmus spp.	5	Uncommon
S. hemargyrella (Kollar)	on Fagus	4,5	Very common
S. paradoxa (Frey)	on Crataegus	5	
A single mine of this scarce species from Woodcock Gardens, 1994.			
S. atricapitella (Haworth)	on Quercus spp.	4,5	Common
S. ruficapitella (Haworth)	on Quercus spp	4,5	Very common
S. suberivora (Stainton)	on Quercus ilex	5	Fairly common
S. roborella (Johansson)	on Quercus petraea	5	
S. svenssoni (Johansson)	on Quercus petraea	4,5	
S. minusculella (Herrich-Schäffer)	on Pyrus cultivar	5	Very rare
S. anomalella (Goeze)	on Rosa spp.	4,5	Common
S. centifoliella (Zeller)	on Rosa spp.	5	Very local
S. viscerella (Stainton)	on Ulmus spp.	5	Fairly common
S. malella (Stainton)	on Malus	5	Uncommon
S. hybnerella (Hübner)	on Crataegus	4,5	Very common
S. oxyacanthella (Stainton)	on Crataegus, Malus, Sorbus	5	Fairly common
S. nylandriella (Tengstrom)	on Sorbus aucuparia	4,5	Very common

MOTHS

Stigmella magdalenae (Klimesch)	on Sorbus aucuparia	4,5	Very common
S. crataegella (Klimesch)	on Crataegus	4,5	Very common
S. prunetorum (Stainton)	on Prunus spinosa	5	Very local
S. betulicola (Stainton)	on Betula seedlings	5	Local
S. microtheriella (Stainton)	on Corylus & Carpinus	4,5	Abundant
S. luteella (Stainton)	on Betula spp.	4,5	Fairly common
S. sakhalinella Puplesis *(distinguenda Heinemann)*	on Betula spp.	5	
S. glutinosae (Stainton)	on Alnus glutinosa & cordata	5	Fairly common
S. alnetella (Stainton)	on Alnus glutinosa & cordata	4,5	Very common
S. lapponica (Wocke)	on Betula spp.	4,5	Very common
S. confusella (Wood)	on Betula spp.	4,5	Very common
Enteucha acetosae (Stainton) *(S. acetosae Stainton)*	on Rumex acetosa	4	

The first record for Somerset, Devon or Cornwall, 1990

TISCHERIIDAE

Tischeria ekebladella (Bjerkander)	on Quercus spp. & Castanea	4,5	Fairly common
T. dodonea Stainton	on Quercus spp. & Castanea	5	Single record only
T. marginea (Haworth)	on Rubus spp.	4,5	Common

INCURVARIIDAE   sub-family Incurvariinae

Phylloporia bistrigella (Haworth)	on Betula spp.		4,5	Uncommon
Incurvaria pectinea (Haworth)	on Betula spp. & Corylus		5	Fairly common
I. masculella (D. & S.)	on Crataegus		5	Common
I. oehlmanniella (Hübner) *(Lampronia oe. Hübner)*	on Vaccinium myrtillus		5	Uncommon
I. praelatella (D. & S.) *(Lampronia prae. D.& S.)*	on Fragaria vesca		4,5	Rare

sub-family: Prodoxinae

Lampronia rubiella (Bjerkander)	on Rubus idaeus	5	Very local
L. fuscatella (Tengstrom)	in galls on Betula twigs	5	

sub-family: Nematopogoninae

Nematopogon swammerdamella (L.)	in open woodland	4,5	Common
N. schwarziellus (Zeller)	in woodland	4,5	Common
N. metaxella (Hübner)	on dead leaves and on growing plants	5	

sub-family: Adelinae

Nemophora degeerella (L.)	in woodland	4,5	Fairly common
Adela reaumurella (L.)	in swarms around bushes	4,5	Very common
A. croesella (Scopoli)	probably on Ligustrum	5	Single record only
A. rufimitrella (Scopoli)	on Alliaria petiolata	5	Uncommon
A. fibulella (D. & S.)	on Veronica chamaedrys	5	

MOTHS

HELIOZELIDAE

Heliozela sericiella (Haworth)	beneath bark of Quercus	4,5	Uncommon
H. resplendella (Stainton)	on Alnus glutinosa	4,5	Uncommon
H. hammoniella Sorhagen	on Betula spp.	4,5	Rare
Antispila metallella (D.& S.) *(A.pfeifferella Hübner)* on Swida sanguinea		5	Very rare
A. petryi Martini	on Swida sanguinea	5	Very common

Sub-order: DITRYSIA

COSSIDAE sub-family: **Zeuzerinae**

Zeuzera pyrina (L.)	LEOPARD MOTH	4,5	Rare

sub-family: **Cossinae**

Cossus cossus (L.)	GOAT MOTH	4,5	Rare

ZYGAENIDAE sub-family: **Procridinae**

Adscita statices (L.)	THE FORESTER	4	
	A single (unconfirmed) record from N.Devon Exmoor		

sub-family: **Zygaeninae**

Zygaena filipendulae (L.)	SIX-SPOT BURNET	4,5	Fairly common
Z. trifolii (Esper)	FIVE-SPOT BURNET	4,5	

PSYCHIDAE

This family is poorly represented on Exmoor. Its members are often referred to as **BAGWORMS** from the elaborate cases constructed by the larvae. Only two British species have winged females capable of flight; the others are apterous and some even lack both legs and antennae.

sub-family: **Taleporiinae**

Narycia monilifera (Geoffroy)	on lichens on fences & tree-trunks	5	Fairly common
Diplodoma herminata (Geoffroy)	on decaying leaves & fungi	5	
Taleporia tubulosa (Retzius)	on decaying leaves & lichens	5	

sub-family: **Psychinae**

Luffia ferchaultella (Stephens)	on lichens on trees, rocks & fences	5	
Psyche casta (Pallas)	on grasses, lichens, etc.	4,5	Fairly common

TINEIDAE

A family with a fair proportion of pest species with which many of the public must be familiar, although the advent of synthetic fibres has meant that those species which were very common in the past are now declining in numbers and some have become quite rare. Many species are found in bird nests and such bizarre materials as horns and hooves, owl pellets and dead animals. The two species of Psychoides are exceptional in that they feed on green plants.

sub-family: **Teichobiinae**

Psychoides verhuella Bruand	on various ferns	4,5	Fairly common

MOTHS

Psychoides filicivora (Meyrick)	on various ferns	4,5	Very common

sub-family: **Meessiinae**

Infurcitinea argentimaculella (Stainton) on Lepraria & other lichens		5	Single record only

sub-family: **Nemapogoninae**

Nemapogon cloacella (Haworth) CORK MOTH	on bracket fungi	5	Fairly common
N. clematella (Fabricius)	in dead wood or fungi	5	Uncommon
Triaxomera parasitella (Hübner)	in dead wood or fungi	5	Rare

sub-family: **Tineinae**

Monopis laevigella (D.& S.) *(M.rusticella Hübner)*	in bird nests, etc.	4,5	Common
M. weaverella (Scott)	in bird nests or carcases	5	Fairly common
M. obviella (D.& S.) *(M.ferruginella Hübner)* in bird nests or animal refuse		5	F. common
M. crocicapitella (Clemens)	in bird nests, etc.	5	Single record only
Tineola bisselliella (Hümmel)	in houses	5	
Niditinea fuscella (L.) *(N. fuscipunctella Haworth)* in bird nests		5	
Tinea columbariella Wocke	in bird nests, etc.	5	
T. pellionella (L.)	in bird nests and in houses	5	Single record only
T. pallescentella Stainton	in a variety of animal refuse	4	Single record only
T. semifulvella Haworth	in bird nests, etc.	5	Very common
T. trinotella Thunberg	in bird nests	5	Common

OCHSENHEIMERIIDAE

Ochsenheimeria mediopectinellus (Haworth) on various grasses		4	Local
O. urella Fischer von Röslerstamm on various grasses		4,5	Local
O. vacculella F.von R. on various grasses		5	Single record only

LYONETIIDAE sub-family: **Cemiostominae**

Leucoptera laburnella (Stainton)	on Laburnum	5	Locally common
L. malifoliella (Costa)	on Crataegus	5	Locally common

sub-family: **Lyonetiinae**

Lyonetia clerkella (L.) on various shrubby Rosaceae & on Betula spp.   4,5   Very common
Although often abundant in the lowlands, it seems singularly rare on the higher ground.

sub-family: **Bedelliinae**

Bedellia somnulentella (Zeller)   on Convolvulus & Calystegia   4,5
Does not occur every year but when it does it is often very common

BUCCULATRICIDAE –formerly included with the Lyonetiidae; now enjoys full family status

Bucculatrix maritima Stainton	on Aster tripolium	5	
B. albedinella Zeller	on Ulmus spp.	5	Fairly common
B. cidarella Zeller	on Alnus glutinosa	5	
B. ulmella Zeller	on Quercus spp.	4,5	
B. bechsteinella (B.& S.) *(crataegi Zeller)*	on Crataegus	5	
B. demaryella (Duponchel)	on Betula & Corylus	4,5	

MOTHS

GRACILLARIIDAE sub-family: Gracillariinae

The larvae leave their leaf-mines in the later instars and feed externally.

Caloptilia elongella (L.)	on Alnus glutinosa	5	Fairly common
C. betulicola (Hering)	on Betula spp.	4,5	Common
C. alchimiella (Scopoli)	on Quercus spp.	4,5	Fairly common
C. robustella Jäckh	on Quercus spp.	5	Uncommon
C. stigmatella (Fabricius)	on Populus or Salix spp.	4,5	Very common
C. semifascia (Haworth)	on Acer campestre	5	Common
C. leucapennella (Stephens)	on Quercus ilex	5	Single record only
C. syringella (Fabricius)	on Fraxinus, Ligustrum & Syringa	4,5	Common
Aspilapteryx tringipennella (Zeller)	on Plantago lanceolata	5	Common
Parornix betulae (Stainton)	on Betula seedlings	5	Fairly common
P. anglicella (Stainton)	on Crataegus	4,5	Abundant
P. devoniella (Stainton)	on Corylus	4,5	Abundant
P. scoticella (Stainton)	on Sorbus aucuparia	4	
P. finitimella (Zeller)	on Prunus spp.	4,5	Uncommon
P. torquillella (Zeller)	on Prunus spinosa	5	Very common
Callisto denticulella (Thunberg)	on Malus, inc. cultivars	5	Fairly common
Acrocercops brongniardella (Fabricius)	on Quercus spp., inc. Q. ilex	5	Common

sub-family: Lithocolletinae

The larvae complete their life-cycles without leaving the mines. Thirty-six species are found on Exmoor, of the fifty-five on the British List.

Phyllonorycter harrisella (L.)	on Quercus spp.	4,5	Common
P. heegeriella (Zeller)	on Quercus spp.	4,5	Fairly common
P. quercifoliella (Zeller)	on Quercus spp.	4,5	Abundant
P. messaniella (Zeller)	chiefly on Quercus ilex	4,5	Abundant
P. oxyacanthae (Frey)	on Crataegus	4,5	Abundant
P. sorbi (Frey)	on Sorbus aucuparia	4,5	Abundant
P. blancardella (Fabricius)	on Malus, inc. cultivars	5	Common
P. cydoniella (D.& S.)	on Cydonia, Malus & Pyrus	5	Rare
P. spinicolella (Zeller) *(pomonella Zeller)*	on Prunus spp.	4,5	Very common
P. cerasicolella (H.-S.)	on Prunus cerasus & avium	5	Rare
P. corylifoliella (Hübner)	on Crataegus & Sorbus	4,5	Common
P. viminiella (Sircom)	on Salix spp.	4,5	Abundant

Although the textbooks give the food-plant as smooth-leaved Salix species, this is not the case on Exmoor where this moth has been bred, on numerous occasions, from the rough-leaved sallows as well as the smooth-leaved osiers.

P. salicicolella (Sircom)	on Salix spp.	5	Common
P. dubitella (H.-S.)	on Salix caprea	5	Local

MOTHS

Phyllonorycter hilarella (Zetterstedt) on Salix spp., esp. caprea		4,5	Local
P. cavella (Zeller) on Betula spp.		5	Rare
P. ulicicolella (Stainton)	on Ulex	5	Single record only
P. maestingella (Müller)	on Fagus	4,5	Abundant

This species even occurs in Beech hedges on high moorland.

P. coryli (Nicelli)	on Corylus	4,5	Abundant
P. quinnata (Geoffroy)	on Carpinus betulus	5	Rare
P. rajella (L.)	on Alnus glutinosa, etc.	4,5	Abundant
P. anderidae (Fletcher)	on Betula seedlings	4,5	Local
P. quinqueguttella (Stainton)	on Salix repens	5	Very local
P. nigrescentella (Logan	on Vicia sepium	5	Local
P. lautella (Zeller)	on Quercus, esp. seedlings	4,5	Uncommon
P. schreberella (Fabricius)	on Ulmus spp.	5	Very common
P. ulmifoliella (Hübner)	on Betula spp.	4,5	Abundant
P. emberizaepenella (Bouché)	on Lonicera, Symphoricarpos & Leycesteria	4,5	Local
P. tristrigella (Haworth)	on Ulmus spp., esp. glabra	4,5	Fairly common
P. stettinensis (Nicelli)	on Alnus glutinosa	5	Fairly common
P. froelichiella (Zeller)	on Alnus glutinosa	5	Uncommon
P. nicellii (Stainton)	on Corylus	4,5	Common
P. kleemannella (Fabricius)	on Alnus glutinosa	4,5	Common
P. trifasciella (Haworth)	on Lonicera & Leycesteria	4,5	Common
P. acerifoliella (Zeller)	on Acer campestre	5	Common
P. platanoidella (De Joannis)	on Acer platanoides	4	Very rare
P. geniculella (Ragonot)	on Acer pseudoplatanus	4,5	Fairly common

sub-family: Phyllocnistinae

Phyllocnistis unipunctella (Stephens) on Populus	5	Fairly common

SESIIDAE

This family, the **CLEARWING MOTHS**, is poorly represented on Exmoor, but this is to be expected from their known distribution.

sub-family: Sesiinae

Sesia bembeciformis (Hübner)	in trunks of Salix caprea	5	Single record only

sub-family: Paranthreninae

Synanthedon tipuliformis (Clerck)	in the wood of Ribes spp.	5	Single record only
Bembecia muscaeformis (Esper)	in cushions of Armeria maritima	4	Single record only

CHOREUTIDAE

Anthophila fabriciana (L.)	on Urtica dioica	4,5	Abundant

This moth occurs wherever nettles are to be found and must be one of the most abundant of British lepidoptera.

GLYPHIPTERIGIDAE

Glyphipterix simpliciella (Stephens)	on Dactylis	4,5	Common

MOTHS

Glyphipterix fuscoviridella (Haworth)	on Luzula campestris	5	Fairly common
G. thrasonella (Scopoli)	on Juncus spp.	5	Abundant

YPONOMEUTIDAE   sub-family: Argyresthiinae

Argyresthia laevigatella H.-S.	on Larix spp.	5	Uncommon
A. brockeella (Hübner)	on Betula & Alnus	4,5	Very common
A. goedartella (L.)	on Betula & Alnus	4,5	Abundant
A. sorbiella (Treitschke)	on Sorbus aucuparia	4	No recent record
A. curvella (L.) *(arcella Fabricius)*	on Malus, inc. cultivars	5	Fairly common
A. retinella Zeller	on Betula spp.	4,5	Very common
A. glaucinella Zeller	in bark of Quercus spp.	5	Uncommon
A. spinosella (Stainton) *(mendica Haworth)* on Prunus spinosa		5	Common
A. conjugella Zeller	on Sorbus aucuparia	4,5	Very common
A. semifusca (Haworth)	on Crataegus or Sorbus	4,5	Fairly common
A. pruniella (Clerck)	on Prunus cerasus	5	Single record only
A. bonnetella (L.) *(curvella L.)*	on Crataegus	5	Very common
A. albistria (Haworth)	on Prunus spinosa	4,5	Very common
A. semitestacella (Curtis)	on Fagus	5	Fairly common

sub-family: Yponomeutinae

Yponomeuta evonymella (L.)   (on Prunus padus)   5
In view of the virtual absence of the food-plant, it is fairly certain that those moths recorded in the south of England are migrants. This hypothesis is borne out by the often very large numbers seen in moth-traps and the fact that it does not appear every year.

Y. padella (L.)	on Prunus spinosa	5	Uncommon
Y. malinellus Zeller	on Malus	4,5	Fairly common
Y. cagnagella (Hübner)	on Euonymus europaeus	5	Fairly common
Y. plumbella (D.& S.)	on Euonymus europaeus	5	Fairly common
Zelleria hepariella Stainton	on Fraxinus	5	Uncommon
Pseudoswammerdamia combinella (Hübner) on Prunus spinosa		5	Very common
Swammerdamia caesiella (Hübner)	on Betula spp.	5	Uncommon
S. pyrella (Villers)	on Crataegus & Malus	5	Uncommon
Paraswammerdamia albicapitella (Scharfenburg) on Prunus spinosa		5	Rare
P. lutarea (Haworth)	on Crataegus or Sorbus	5	Uncommon
Cedestis subfasciella (Stephens)	on Pinus spp.	5	Single record only
Roeslerstammia erxlebella (Fabricius)	on Betula & Tilia	5	Occasional
Prays fraxinella (Bjerkander) ASH BUD MOTH	on Fraxinus	5	Common
Scythropia crataegella (L.)	on Crataegus & Cotoneaster	5	Fairly common

sub-family: Plutellinae

Ypsolopha mucronella (Scopoli)	on Euonymus europaeus	5	Fairly common
Y. nemorella (L.)	on Lonicera	5	Uncommon

MOTHS

Ypsolopha dentella (Fabricius)	on Lonicera	4,5	Common
Y. scabrella (L.)	on Crataegus or Malus	5	Fairly common
Y. alpella (D.& S.) on Quercus spp.		5	Rare
Y. sylvella (L.)	on Quercus spp.	5	Rare
Y. parenthesella (L.)	on Quercus & Betula	4,5	Fairly common
Y. ustella (Clerck)	on Quercus spp.	4,5	Very common
Y. sequella (Clerck)	on Acer campestre	5	Fairly common
Y. vittella (L.)	on Ulmus or Fagus	5	Single record only
Plutella xylostella (L.) DIAMOND-BACK MOTH on Cruciferae		4,5	Abundant

sub-family: Orthotaeliinae

Orthotaelia sparganella (Thunberg)	on Sparganium, etc.	5	Single record only No recent record

sub-family: Acrolepiinae

Digitivalva pulicariae (Klimesch)	on Pulicaria dysenterica	4,5	Fairly common

EPERMENIIDAE

Epermenia chaerophyllella (Goeze)	on Heracleum, etc.	5	Fairly common

SCHRECKENSTEINIIDAE

Schreckensteinia festaliella (Hübner)	on Rubus fruticosus agg.	4,5	Uncommon

COLEOPHORIDAE

Metriotes lutarea (Haworth)	on Stellaria holostea	5	Local

Coleophora - The larvae of these moths construct portable cases, either of portions of the food-plant or of silk which they manufacture at all or some stages in their development. Feeding takes place from within the case, the larva eating the parenchyma as far as it can reach. This results in small blotches with a central hole but containing no frass. The case may be enlarged or replaced as the larva grows. The angle made between the plane of the mouth-opening and the axis of the case is of value in the determination of the species. Most species mine leaves but some are seed-feeders.

Coleophora lutipennella (Zeller)	on Quercus spp.	5	Fairly common
C. gryphipennella (Hübner)	on Rosa spp.	4,5	Common
C. flavipennella (Duponchel)	on Quercus spp.	5	Uncommon
C. serratella (L.)	on Alnus, Betula, Ulmus, etc.	4,5	Very common
Often a pest of Elm hedges.			
C. prunifoliae Doets	on Prunus spinosa	5	Very local
C. spinella (Schrank) (cerasivorella Packard) on Crataegus, Malus & Prunus		5	Very common
C. lusciniaepennella (Treitschke) (viminetella Zeller) on Salix spp.		4,5	Rare
C. violacea (Ström)	on Prunus spinosa	5	
C. juncicolella Stainton	on Calluna or Erica	4,5	Common
C. trifolii (Curtis)	on Melilotus or Trifolium spp.	5	Single record only
C. frischella (L.)	on Trifolium repens	5	
C. mayrella (Hübner)	on Trifolium repens	5	Uncommon
C. deauratella L.& Z.	on Trifolium pratense	5	Single record only
C. lithargyrinella Zeller	on Stellaria holostea	4,5	Local

MOTHS

Coleophora solitariella Zeller	on Stellaria holostea	5	Rare
C. laricella (Hübner)	on Larix spp.	5	Fairly common
C. ibipennella Zeller *(ardeaepennella Scott)* on Quercus spp.		5	Single record only
C. pyrrhulipennella Zeller	on Calluna or Erica	4,5	Uncommon
C. albicosta (Haworth)	on Ulex	5	Very common
C. discordella Zeller	on Lotus corniculatus	4,5	Uncommon
C. striatipennella (Nylander)	on Stellaria graminea	5	Uncommon
C. follicularis (Vallot) *(troglodytella Duponchel)* on Pulicaria dysenterica		5 Uncommon	
C. peribenanderi (Toll)	on Cirsium arvense	5	Uncommon
C. argentula (Stephens)	on Achillea millefolium	5	Single record only
C. obscenella H.-S. *(virgaureae Stainton)* on Solidago virgaurea		4	Single record only
C. atriplicis Meyrick	on Halimione	5	Very local
C. otidipennella (Hübner) *(murinipennella Duponchel)*		5	
	on Luzula campestris or multiflora		Single record only
C. sylvaticella Wood	on Luzula sylvatica	4	
C. glaucicolella Wood	on Juncus gerardii	5	Local
C. alticolella Zeller	on Juncus spp.	5	Very common
C. adjunctella Hodgkinson	on Juncus gerardii	5	Local
C. salicorniae Wocke	on Salicornia spp.	5	Very local

ELACHISTIDAE
With the exception of Perittia, the larvae mine the leaves of Gramineae, Cyperaceae or Juncaceae.

Perittia obscurepunctella (Stainton)	on Lonicera. No recent record.	4	single record only
Elachista regificella Sircom	on Luzula spp.	4,5	Uncommon
E. atricomella Stainton	on Dactylis	4,5	Fairly common
E. albifrontella (Hübner)	on Dactylis & Holcus	4,5	Fairly common
E. apicipunctella Stainton	on various Gramineae	5	Single record only
E. canapennella (Hübner) *(pulchella Haworth)* on Arrhenatherum or Holcus		4,5	Common
E. rufocinerea (Haworth)	on Arrhenatherum or Holcus	5	Common
E. argentella (Clerck)	on various Gramineae	4,5	Common
E. subocellea (Stephens)	on Brachypodium sylvaticum	5	Single record only
E. megerlella (Hübner)	on Brachypodium sylvaticum	4,5	Uncommon
E. unifasciella (Haworth)	on Dactylis glomerata	5	Single record only
E. gangabella Zeller	on Brachypodium sylvaticum	4	Single record only
Biselachista trapeziella (Stainton)	on Luzula sylvatica & pilosa	4,5	Uncommon

OECOPHORIDAE
Apart from the usual plant feeders, this family contains a number of species that feed on dead wood or decaying leaves and includes the two abundant House-moths Hofmannophila and Endrosis.

MOTHS

sub-family: Oecophorinae

Schiffermuelleria grandis (Desvignes) in dead wood   5   Very local
A nationally rare species, but very common in the vicinity of Porlock. in 1994 the species was bred from samples of dead wood collected near the village, no less than five adults being reared.

Species	Habitat		Status
S. subaquilea (Stainton)	on moorland	4	Single record only
Batia lunaris (Haworth)	under dead bark	5	Fairly common
B. lambdella (Donovan)	in dead wood, esp. Ulex	5	Common
B. unitella (Hübner)	under decaying bark	5	Fairly common
Borkhausenia fuscescens (Haworth)	on decaying leaves	5	Common
Telechrysis tripuncta (Haworth)	probably in dead wood	5	Rare
Hofmannophila pseudospretella (Stainton) in animal or vegetable debris; often in houses		5	Abundant
Endrosis sarcitrella (L.) in bird nests &on varied animal or vegetable debris		5	Abundant
Esperia sulphurella (Fabricius)	in dead wood in hedges	4,5	Very common
Alabonia geoffrella (L.)	in decayed wood	5	Fairly common
Carcina quercana (Fabricius)	on Quercus spp. & other trees	4,5	Common
Pseudatemelia josephinae (Toll)	on decaying leaves	5	Uncommon
P. flavifrontella (D.& S.)	on decaying leaves	5	Rare
P. subochreella (Doubleday)	on decaying leaves, etc.	5	Fairly common

sub-family: Chimbachinae

Diurnea fagella (D.& S.)   on Quercus spp., Fagus, etc.   5   Common
The larva appears to have a catholic taste in its choice of food-plant since it has also been bred by the Recorder from Rubus and Carpinus.

D. phryganella (Hübner)   on Quercus spp. & Vaccinium   5   Single record only
As the flight period is late October to November, the moth may well have been missed thus accounting for the single record.

sub-family: Depressariinae

Species	Host		Status
Semioscopis avellanella (Hübner)	on Betula spp.	5	Single record only
Depressaria daucella (D.& S.)	on Oenanthe crocata	5	Uncommon
D. pastinacella (Duponchel)	on Heracleum sphondylium	4,5	Very common
D. badiella (Hübner)	on Hypochaeris, Sonchus, etc.	4	Single record only
D. pulcherrimella Stainton	on Conopodium	5	Single record only
D. aegopodiella (Hübner)*(albipunctella Hübner)*on several Umbelliferae		5	Fairly common
D. chaerophylli Zeller	on Chaerophyllum	5	Uncommon
Agonopterix heracliana (L.)	on several Umbelliferae	5	Abundant
A. ciliella (Stainton) on Heracleum & Angelica		5	No recent record
A. subpropinquella (Stainton)	on Cirsium, Carduus, etc.,	5	Fairly common
A. alstromeriana (Clerck)	on Conium maculatum	5	Single record only
A. propinquella (Treitschke)	on Carduus	5	Uncommon
A. arenella (D.& S.)	on Centaurea, Arctium, etc.	4,5	Very common
A. ocellana (Fabricius)	on Salix spp.	5	Fairly common

MOTHS

Agonopterix assimilella (Treitschke)	on Sarothamnus	4,5	Rare
A. scopariella (Heinemann)	on Sarothamnus	4	Single record only
A. ulicetella (Stainton)	on Ulex	4,5	Fairly common
A. nervosa (Haworth)	on Ulex or Sarothamnus	4,5	Common
A. carduella (Hübner)	on Carduus, Cirsium, Arctium 4		No recent record
Agonopterix conterminella (Zeller)	on Salix spp.	5	Local
A. angelicella (Hübner)	on Angelica or Heracleum	5	Occasional

sub-family: Ethmiinae

Ethmia dodecea (Haworth)	on Lithospermum	5	Single record only

The single example taken at light in 1994 would appear to be a wanderer since the food-plant is a calcicole and not present in the vicinity.

sub-family: Stathmopodinae

Stathmopoda pedella (L.)	in fruits of Alnus glutinosa	5	No recent record

GELECHIIDAE

A large family (over 160 species on the British list) of which many are rather small and drab and of secretive habits. The most noticeable features are the presence of long, recurved labial palps and the emarginate termen of the hind-wing (the classical 'pointing finger'), although not all of them possess the latter feature. Published material on the family is scattered throughout the entomological journals and thus rather difficult of access and so they are not the easiest group to study and it is fairly certain that they are under-recorded on Exmoor. A select group of British lepidopterists is currently working on the family but unfortunately the results will not be available until 1997 at the earliest.

sub-family: Aristoteliinae

Paltodora cytisella (Curtis)	on Pteridium aquilinum	5	Common
Eulamprotes atrella (D.& S.)	on Hypericum perforatum	5	Fairly common
E. unicolorella (Duponchel)	among Lotus corniculatus	4	
Argolamprotes micella (D.& S.)	on Rubus spp.	4,5	Rare
Monochroa tenebrella (Hübner)	on Rumex acetosella	5	Fairly common
M. palustrella (Douglas)	on Rumex crispus	5	Single record only
Chrysoesthia sexguttella (Thunberg)	on Chenopodium & Atriplex	5	Single record only
Aristotelia ericinella (Zeller)	on Calluna	5	Uncommon

sub-family: Gelechiinae

Recurvaria leucatella (Clerck)	on Crataegus or Malus	5	
Exoteleia dodecella (L.)	on Pinus sylvestris	4	Single record only
Athrips mouffetella (L.)	on Lonicera	5	Single record only
Xenolechia aethiops (H.& W.)	on Erica spp.	5	Single record only
Teleiodes vulgella (Hübner)	on Crataegus or Prunus spinosa 5		Single record only
T. decorella (Haworth)	on Quercus spp.	5	Fairly common
T. proximella (Hübner)	on Betula or Alnus	5	Single record only
T. fugitivella (Zeller)	on Ulmus spp.	5	Single record only
Teleiopsis diffinis (Haworth)	on Rumex acetosella	5	Fairly common
Bryotropha affinis (Haworth)	on mosses	5	Common

MOTHS

Bryotropha similis (Stainton)	on mosses	5	Single record only
B. senectella (Zeller)	on mosses	5	Common
B. terrella (D.& S.)	on various Gramineae	5	Common
B. domestica (Haworth)	on mosses	5	Uncommon
Mirificarma mulinella (Zeller)	on Ulex	4,5	Very common
Aroga velocella (Zeller)	on Rumex acetosella	5	Single record only
Neofaculta ericetella (Geyer)	on Calluna	4,5	Abundant
Platyedra subcinerea (Haworth)	on Malva sylvestris.	5	Single record only No recent record
Scrobipalpa samadensis (Pfaffenzeller)	on Plantago coronopus	5	Single record only
S. ocellatella (Boyd)	on Beta	5	Single record only
S. nitentella (Fuchs)	on Chenopodium or Suaeda	5	Single record only
S. costella (H. & W.)	on Solanum dulcamara	4,5	Fairly common
S. acuminatella (Sircom)	on Cirsium, Carduus, etc.	5	Single record only
Caryocolum blandella (Douglas)	on Stellaria holostea	5	Common
C. tricolorella (Haworth)	on Stellaria holostea	5	Common

sub-family: **Anacampsinae**

Sophronia semicostella (Hübner)	on Anthoxanthum odoratum	5	Single record only
Aproaerema anthyllidella (Hübner)	on Trifolium spp., etc.	5	Single record only
Anacampsis populella (Clerck)	on Populus & Salix spp.	5	Uncommon

sub-family: **Chelariinae**

Anarsia spartiella (Schrank)	on Ulex	5	Fairly common
Hypatima rhomboidella (L.)	on Betula & Corylus	5	Common

sub-family: **Dichomerinae**

Brachmia blandella (Fabricius)	on Ulex	5	Fairly common

sub-family: **Symmocinae**

Oegoconia quadripuncta (Haworth)	on decaying vegetation	5	Single record only

BLASTOBASIDAE

Blastobasis lignea Walsingham	in fresh & decaying leaves & in various conifers, etc.	4,5	Very common

MOMPHIDAE
With a sole exception, the larvae of Momphidae feed on members of the family Onagraceae, either Circaea or Epilobium spp.

sub-family: **Batrachedrinae**

Batrachedra praeangusta (Haworth)	on Populus or Salix spp.	5	Uncommon

sub-family: **Momphinae**

Mompha langiella Hübner	on Circaea or Epilobium spp.	4,5	Very common
M. terminella (H.& W.)	on Circaea lutetiana	4,5	Local
M. raschkiella (Zeller)	on Epilobium angustifolium	4,5	Common
M. conturbatella (Hübner)	on Epilobium angustifolium	4	Single record only

MOTHS

Mompha lacteella (Stephens)	on Epilobium hirsutum	4,5	Uncommon
M. propinquella (Stainton)	on Epilobium spp.	5	Uncommon
M. subbistrigella (Haworth)	on Epilobium montanum	5	Fairly common
M. epilobiella (D. & S.)	on Epilobium hirsutum	4,5	Common

COSMOPTERIGIDAE - Formerly included with the Momphidae but now enjoys full family status

sub-family: Cosmopteriginae

Cosmopterix orichalcea Stainton	on various grasses	5	Rare
Limnaecia phragmitella Stainton	on Typha latifolia	5	No recent record

sub-family: Blastodacninae

Blastodacna hellerella (Duponchel)	in berries of Crataegus	5	Common
B. atra (Haworth)	on Malus	5	Uncommon

SCYTHRIDIDAE

Scythris grandipennis (Haworth)	on Ulex	5	Single record only

TORTRICIDAE   sub-family: **Cochylinae**

With very few exceptions, the larvae feed under cover in the roots, rootstocks, stems and seed-heads.

Phtheochroa inopiana (Haworth) *(Hysterosia inopiana Haworth)*	on Pulicaria dysenterica	5	Uncommon
Phalonidia affinitana (Douglas)	on Aster tripolium	5	Local
P. gilvicomana (Zeller)	on Mycelis or Lapsana	4	No recent record
Cochylimorpha straminea (Haworth)	on Centaurea nigra	5	No recent record
Agapeta hamana (L.)	on Carduus spp.	4,5	Abundant
A. zoegana (L.)	on Centaurea nigra	4	Single record only
Aethes cnicana (Westwood)	on flowers of Cirsium	4,5	
A. rubigana (Treitschke)	on Arctium lappa	4,5	Common
Eupoecilia angustana (Hübner)	on various herbaceous plants	5	Common
Cochylis dubitana (Hübner)	on Senecio jacobaea, Crepis, etc.	5	Fairly common
C. atricapitana (Stephens)	on Senecio jacobea	5	Fairly common
C. nana (Haworth)	on Betula catkins	5	Uncommon

sub-family: Tortricinae

A large group with much variation in size, some being quite large. In general, the larvae spin leaves together with silk to make a protective chamber in which to feed. Many species are polyphagous in that they will often accept a wide variety of food-plant. Quite a few are pest species, examples being the Pea moth, the Codling moth and the Oak-leaf roller.

Pandemis corylana (Fabricius)	CHEQUERED FRUIT TORTRIX on Corylus, Quercus, etc.	4,5	Abundant
P. cerasana (Hübner)	BARRED FRUIT-TREE TORTRIX on various fruit-trees, etc.	4,5	Abundant
P. heparana (D.& S.)	DARK FRUIT-TREE TORTRIX on various trees and shrubs	4,5	Very common

MOTHS

Archips podana (Scopoli)	LARGE FRUIT-TREE TORTRIX on various trees and shrubs	4,5	Abundant
A. xylosteana (L.)	VARIEGATED GOLDEN TORTRIX on various trees and shrubs	5	Very common
A. rosana (L.) ROSE TORTRIX	on various fruit and other trees	5	Rare
Argyrotaenia ljungiana (Thunberg) *(pulchellana Haworth)* on Erica, Calluna, Vaccinium, etc.		5	Single record only
Choristoneura hebenstreitella (Müller) on Quercus spp., etc.		5	Rare
Cacoecimorpha pronubana (Hübner) CARNATION TORTRIX on many plants		5	Common
Syndemis musculana (Hübner)	on Betula or Quercus	4,5	Very common
Ptycholomoides aeriferanus (H.-S.)	on Larix	5	Uncommon
Aphelia viburnana (D.& S.)	BILBERRY TORTRIX on Vaccinium & Erica	4,5	Common
A. paleana (Hübner)	TIMOTHY TORTRIX on various grasses,etc.	4,5	Uncommon
A. unitana (Hübner)	on Heracleum, Rubus, etc.	4	Rare
Clepsis senecionana	on Vaccinium	4,5	Uncommon
C. spectrana (Treitschke)	CYCLAMEN TORTRIX on Epilobium, Filipendula, etc.	5	Rare
C. consimilana (Hübner)	on Ligustrum, etc.	4,5	Very common

Epiphyas postvittana (Walker) LIGHT BROWN APPLE MOTH various shrubs 5 V.common
Since its introduction to Cornwall in 1936, this Australian species has spread considerably in the south of Britain.

Ptycholoma lecheana (L.)	on various trees and shrubs	4,5	Rare
Lozotaeniodes formosanus (Geyer)	on Pinus sylvestris	5	Common

First recorded from Surrey in 1945, this strikingly beautiful pine-feeder has spread rapidly and is rather common in the Porlock area.

Lozotaenia forsterana (Fabricius)	on Hedera, Lonicera, etc.	5	Very common
Epagoge grotiana (Fabricius)	on Quercus, Crataegus or Rubus	4,5	Fairly common
Capua vulgana (Frölich)	on Carpinus	4,5	Fairly common
Philedone gerningana (D.& S.)	on Vaccinium, Potentilla, etc.	5	Rare

A typically northern species which just reaches Exmoor.

Ditula angustiorana (Haworth)	on many trees and shrubs	5	Common
Pseudargyrotoza conwagana (Fabricius) on Fraxinus		4,5	Very common
Sparganothis pilleriana (D.& S.)	on many herbaceous plants	5	Rare
Eulia ministrana (L.)	on Betula spp.	5	Single record only

Bred on one occasion from a larva on Betula.

Cnephasia longana (Haworth)	on wide range of herbaceous spp.	5	No recent record
C. stephensiana (Doubleday)	GREY TORTRIX on herbaceous plants	5	Fairly common
C. asseclana (D.& S.)*(interjectana Haworth)* FLAX TORTRIX on herbaceous plants		4,5	Common
C. incertana (Treitschke) LIGHT GREY TORTRIX on herbaceous plants		4,5	Common
Tortricodes alternella (D.& S.)	on Quercus, Betula, etc.	5	Fairly common
Eana osseana (Scolpoli)	polyphagous on herbaceous plants	5	Single record only
E. incanana (Stephens)	on Hyacinthoides non-scripta	5	

MOTHS

Aleimma loeflingiana (L.)	on Quercus or Acer spp.	4,5	Very common
Tortrix viridana (L.) GREEN OAK TORTRIX	on Quercus spp.	4,5	Abundant
Acleris bergmanniana (L.) *(Croesia b. L.)*	on Rosa spp.	4,5	Fairly common
A. forsskaleana (L.) *(Croesia f. L.)*	on Acer campestre	4,5	Very common
A. holmiana (L.) *(Croesia h. L.)*	on Prunus, Malus, etc.	5	Rare
A. laterana (Fabricius)	on various shrubs	4,5	Very common
A. caledoniana (Stephens)	on Vaccinium	5	Single record only
A. sparsana (D. & S.)	on Fagus or Acer pseudoplatanus	5	Common
A. rhombana (D.& S.) RHOMBOID TORTRIX	on many shrubs	4,5	Very common
A. aspersana (Hübner)	on Potentilla or Fragaria	5	Fairly common
A. ferrugana (D.& S.)	on Quercus spp.	5	Fairly common
A. notana (Donovan)	on Betula spp.	5	Common
A. variegana (D.& S.) GARDEN ROSE TORTRIX	on Rosa spp., etc.	5	Common
A. boscana (Fabricius)	on Ulmus spp.	5	Fairly common
A. hastiana (L.)	on Salix spp.	5	Single record only
A. cristana (D. & S)	on Prunus, Crataegus, etc.	4,5	Rare
A. hyemana (Haworth)	on Calluna or Erica	5	Fairly common
A. literana (L.)	on Quercus spp.	5	Rare
A. emargana (Fabricius)	on Salix, Populus, etc.	4,5	Uncommon

sub-family: Chlidanotinae

Olindia schumacherana (Fabricius)	on Ranunculus ficaria, etc.	4,5	Fairly common

sub-family: Olethreutinae

A very large sub-family whose members may, in general, be separated from the Tortricinae by the presence of a number of costal strigulae and, in a number of examples, an ocellus. This is a circular marking in the tornal area of the wing containing several fine lines and often outlined by metallic scales.

Celypha striana (D.& S.)	on Taraxacum	5	Common
Olethreutes rivulana (Scopoli)	on Filipendula, etc.	5	Single record only
O. lacunana (D. & S.)	on various plants	4,5	Abundant
O. bifasciana (Haworth)	on Pinus spp.	5	Fairly common
O. arcuella (Clerck)	on decaying leaves on the ground	5	Rare

A singularly beautiful species which is nationally rather rare.

Hedya pruniana (Hübner) PLUM TORTRIX	on Prunus spinosa	5	Very common
H. dimidioalba (Retzius) *(H. nubiferana Haworth)* MARBLED ORCHARD TORTRIX			
	on Crataegus, Prunus, etc.	4,5	Abundant
H. ochroleucana (Frölich)	on Rosa or Malus	5	Fairly common
H. salicella (L.)	on Salix or Populus	5	No recent record
Orthotaenia undulana (D.& S.)	on Lonicera, Betula, etc.	4,5	Very common
Apotomis turbidana (Hübner)	on Betula spp.	5	Fairly common
A. betuletana (Haworth)	on Betula spp.	4,5	Very common

MOTHS

Apotomis sauciana sauciana (Frölich) - The southern sub-species. on Vaccinium 5   Rare

Endothenia gentianaeana (Hübner)   on Dipsacus fullonum   5   Local
An attractive moth, the larvae of which feed inside the flower-heads. Bred by the
Recorder, on two occasions, from seed-heads collected on the Porlock shingle beach.

E. ericetana (H.& W.)	on Stachys spp.	5	Single record only
E. quadrimaculana (Haworth)	on Stachys palustris	5	Very local
Lobesia abscisana (Doubleday)	on Cirsium arvense	5	Single record only
L. littoralis (H. & W.)	on Armeria maritima	5	Single record only

Bactra furfurana (Haworth)   on Eleocharis palustris   5   Very local
Common in one small area of Porlock marsh.

B. lancealana (Hübner)	on Juncus spp.	4,5	Abundant
B. robustana (Christoph)	on Scirpus maritimus	5	Very local
Eudemis profundana (D.& S.)	on Quercus spp.	4,5	Very common
Ancylis subarcuana (Douglas)	on Salix repens	5	Very local
A. mitterbacheriana (D.& S.)	on Quercus or Fagus	5	Single record only
A. myrtillana (Treitschke)	on Vaccinium	4,5	Fairly common
Epinotia subocellana (Donovan)	on rough-leaved Salix spp.	5	Single record only
E. bilunana (Haworth)	on Betula spp.	5	Common
E. ramella (L.)	on Betula spp.	4,5	Very common

The form costana is almost as common as the type.

E. immundana (F. v R.)	on Alnus or Betula	4,5	Very common
E. tetraquetrana (Haworth)	on Alnus or Betula	4,5	Uncommon
E. nisella (Clerck)	on Salix spp.	5	Fairly common
E. tenerana (D.& S.) NUT BUD MOTH	on Corylus	5	Very common
E. tedella (Clerck)	on Picea abies, etc.	5	Common
E. nanana (Treitschke)	on Picea spp.	5	Rare
E. cruciana (L.) WILLOW TORTRIX	on Salix spp.	4,5	Uncommon
E. abbreviana (Fabricius)	on Ulmus	4,5	Very common
E. sordidana (Hübner)	on Alnus glutinosa	5	Rare
E. brunnichana (L.)	on Betula, Corylus or Salix	5	Common
E. solandriana (L.)	on Betula, Corylus or Salix	4,5	Very common
Crocidosema plebejana Zeller	on Lavatera arborea	5	Single record only

Rhopobota naevana (Hübner) HOLLY TORTRIX on Ilex   4,5   Common
A heathland race, common on Exmoor, which feeds on Bilberry has been regarded by
some authorities as a separate species under the name of R. geminana Barrett.

Zeiraphera ratzeburgiana (Ratzeburg)	on Picea abies	5	Fairly common
Z. isertana (Fabricius)	on Quercus spp.	4,5	Very common
Z. diniana (Guenée)	on Larix and Pinus	4,5	Rare
Gypsonoma aceriana (Duponchel)	on Populus	5	Single record only
G. dealbana (Frölich)	on Crataegus, etc.	4,5	Common

MOTHS

Epiblema cynosbatella (L.)	on Rosa spp.	5	Very common
E. uddmanniana (L.)	on Rubus spp.	4,5	Very common
E. trimaculana (Haworth)	on Crataegus	5	Uncommon
E. rosaecolana (Doubleday)	on Rosa spp.	4,5	Common
E. roborana (D. & S.)	on Rosa spp.	5	Very common
E. incarnatana (Hübner)	on Rosa spp.	5	Uncommon
E. foenella (L.)	on Artemisia vulgaris	5	Rare
E. scutulana (D.& S.)	on Cirsium vulgare	5	Fairly common
Epiblema sticticana (Fabricius)	on Tussilago	5	Fairly common
Eucosma tripoliana (Barrett)	on Aster tripolium	5	Single record only
E. campoliliana (D.& S.)	on Senecio jacobaea	5	Common
E. cana (Haworth)	on Cirsium or Carduus	4,5	Very common
Spilonota ocellana (D.& S.) BUD MOTH	on Rosaceous shrubs	4,5	Very common
Clavigesta purdeyi (Durrant)	on Pinus spp.	5	Uncommon
Rhyacionia buoliana (D.& S.) PINE SHOOT MOTH	on Pinus spp.	5	Single record only
R. pinicolana (Doubleday)	on Pinus sylvestris	5	Single record only
R. pinivorana (L.& Z.) SPOTTED SHOOT MOTH	on Pinus sylvestris	4,5	Uncommon
Enarmonia formosana (Scopoli) CHERRY BARK MOTH	on Malus or Prunus spp. 5		Single record only
Lathronympha strigana (Fabricius)	on Hypericum perforatum	5	Rare
Collicularia microgrammana (Guenée)	on Ononis repens	5	Single record only
Strophedra weirana (Douglas)	on Fagus	5	Fairly common
Pammene albuginana (Guenée)	on Quercus spp.	4	Single record only
P. aurantiana (Staudinger)	on Acer pseudoplatanus	5	Fairly common

First recorded for Britain in 1943 and has now spread widely in the south.

P. regiana (Zeller)	on Acer spp., in the seeds	5	Rare
P. fasciana (L.)	on Quercus or Castanea	5	Fairly common
P. germmana (Hübner)	possibly in fruits of Prunus domestica or in shoots of Quercus 5		Single record only
P. rhediella (Clerck) FRUITLET MINING TORTRIX	on Crataegus	5	Fairly common
Cydia funebrana (Treitschke) PLUM FRUIT MOTH		5	Single record only
C. jungiella (Clerck)	on Vicia spp.	5	Uncommon
C. succedana (D.& S.)	on Ulex & Lotus spp.	4,5	Abundant
C. nigricana (Fabricius) PEA MOTH		5	Uncommon

on wild and cultivated species of Vicia and Pisum sativum

C. splendana (Hübner)	on Quercus spp. or Castanea	4,5	Common
C. pomonella (L.) CODLING MOTH	on Malus fruits	5	Very common
C. aurana (Fabricius)	on Heracleum	5	Uncommon

An unmistakable moth usually seen on the flowers of the food-plant.

Dichrorampha petiverella (L.)	on Achillea millefolium	5	Common

MOTHS

Dichrorampha flavidorsana Knaggs	on Tanacetum vulgare.	\multicolumn{2}{l}{Sits by day on the flowers.}

Dichrorampha flavidorsana Knaggs   on Tanacetum vulgare. Sits by day on the flowers.
                                                                5   Local

Species	Host	Code	Status
Dichrorampha flavidorsana Knaggs	on Tanacetum vulgare. Sits by day on the flowers.	5	Local
D. plumbagana (Treitschke)	on Achillea millefolium	5	Single record only
D. simpliciana (Haworth)	on Artemisia vulgaris	5	Occasional
D. gueneeana Obraztsov	on Achillea or Tanacetum	5	Single record only

ALUCITIDAE

Alucita hexadactyla (L.) TWENTY-PLUME MOTH on Lonicera 4,5   Very common
    The only British moth of this family. Easily recognised by the division of each wing into six separate lobes.

PYRALIDAE

    A large family containing a number of migrants and adventive species. There are eleven sub-families in Britain, showing a wide range in form and size, many being larger than some of the so-called macro-lepidoptera. Some are pest species of stored products and are thus of economic importance.

sub-family: Crambinae

Includes the abundant Grass-moths of the genera Crambus and Agriphila.

Species	Host	Code	Status
Chilo phragmitella (Hübner)	on Phragmites	5	Single record only
Chrysoteuchia culmella (L.)	on various Gramineae	4,5	Abundant
Crambus pascuella (L.)	on Gramineae, esp. Poa spp.	5	Common
C. pratella (L.)	on various Gramineae	5	Single record only
C. lathoniellus (Zincken) *(nemorella Hübner)*	various Gramineae	4,5	Abundant
C. perlella (Scopoli)	on various Gramineae	4,5	Abundant

The form warringtonellus Stainton is very common.

Species	Host	Code	Status
Agriphila selasella (Hübner)	on various Gramineae	5	Uncommon
A. straminella (D. & S.)	on Festuca ovina, etc.	4,5	Abundant

The most common of the Exmoor species.

Species	Host	Code	Status
A. tristella (D. & S.)	on various Gramineae	4,5	Abundant
A. inquinatella (D. & S.)	on various Gramineae	5	Very common
A. latistria (Haworth)	on Gramineae, esp. Bromus spp.	5	Rare
A. geniculea (Haworth)	on various Gramineae	4,5	Very common
Catoptria pinella (L.)	on various Gramineae or Carex	4,5	Very common
C. margaritella (D. & S.)	on mosses	5	Occasional
C. falsella (D. & S.)	on mosses	5	Rare
Pediasia contaminella (Hübner)	on Festuca ovina	5	Single record only
P. aridella (Thunberg)	on Puccinellia, etc.	5	Single record only
Platytes cerussella (D. & S.)	on various Gramineae	5	Local

Abundant in a limited area of the Porlock shingle beach.

sub-family: Scopariinae

Species	Host	Code	Status
Scoparia subfusca Haworth	on Tussilago or Picris	5	Rare
S. ambigualis (Treitschke)	possibly on mosses	4,5	Abundant
S. ancipitella (La Harpe) *(ulmella Knaggs)*	possibly on lichens on trees	5	Single record only
Dipleurina lacustrata (Panzer) *(Eudonia crataegella Hübner)*		4,5	Abundant

MOTHS

	on mosses on tree-trunks		
Eudonia truncicolella (Stainton)	on mosses growing on the ground	4,5	Very common
E. angustea (Curtis)	on mosses on walls	4,5	Very common
E. mercurella (L.)	on mosses	4,5	Very common

sub-family: Nymphulinae

These are known as 'china-marks' from the wing pattern of dark lines on a white background. The larvae are completely aquatic and the adults mainly nocturnal, often visiting light-traps some distance from the nearest water.

Elophila nymphaeata (L.) *(Nymphula nymphaeata L.)* BROWN CHINA-MARK
    on Potamogeton or Sparganium   5   Uncommon

Cataclysta lemnata (L.) SMALL CHINA-MARK on Lemna spp.   5   Single record only

sub-family: Acentropinae

Acentria ephemerella (D.& S.) *(Acentria nivea Olivier)* WATER VENEER
    on submerged aquatic vegetation   5   Common

On hot summer nights, large swarms of this species may visit a light-trap, often far from water and usually accompanied by numbers of Corixid bugs. The females are dimorphic, one form being wingless and completely aquatic, mating with the males at the surface of the water.

sub-family: Evergestinae

Evergestis forficalis (L.) GARDEN PEBBLE on various Cruciferae   5   Very common
E. pallidata (Hufnagel)   on Barbarea and other spp. of Cruciferae   5   Rare

sub-family: Pyraustinae

Medium-sized to very large moths, often brightly coloured. The sub-family includes a number of migrant species.

Pyrausta aurata (Scopoli)	on Nepeta, Mentha, Calamintha	5	Local
P. purpuralis (L.)	on Mentha arvensis or Thymus	5	Uncommon
P. cespitalis (D.& S.)	on Plantago spp.	4,5	Fairly common
P. cingulata (L.)	on Thymus drucei or Salvia	5	Very rare
Uresiphita polygonalis (D.& S)	(on Sarothamnus or Genista)	5	Very rare immigrant
Ostrinia nubilalis (Hübner) EUROPEAN CORN-BORER on Artemisia vulgaris		5	Rare
Eurrhypara hortulata (L.) SMALL MAGPIE on Urtica dioica		4,5	Very common
Perinephela lancealis (D.& S.)	on Eupatorium, etc.	4,5	Common
Phlyctaenia coronata (Hufnagel) *(Eurrhypara coronata Hufnagel)* on Sambucus nigra		4,5	Fairly common
P. stachydalis (Germar) *(Anania stachydalis Germar)*		5	
	on Stachys sylvatica or S. palustris.		Single record only
Mutuuraia terrealis (Treitschke) *(Eurrhypara terrealis Treitschke)* on Solidago virgaurea		4,5	Rare
Ebulea crocealis (Hübner)	on Pulicaria or Inula	5	Rare
Udea lutealis (Hübner) *(U. elutalis D.& S.)* on various herbaceous spp.		4,5	Very common
U. prunalis (D.& S.)	on various Labiatae	4,5	Abundant
U. olivalis (D.& S.)	on various Labiatae	4,5	Abundant
U. ferrugalis (Hübner)	on various herbaceous spp.	4,5	Common immigrant
Mecyna asinalis (Hübner)	on Rubia peregrina	4,5	Local

MOTHS

The food-plant is chiefly coastal and also local. Colonies in the Porlock area show abundant signs of the larval 'window-feeding'.

Nomophila noctuella (D.& S.)	on Trifolium, etc.	4,5	Common immigrant
Dolicharthria punctalis (D.& S.)	on Lotus corniculatus	5	Very local
Diasemia reticularis (L.)	(on Picris spp. ?)	5	Very rare immigrant
Diasemiopsis ramburialis (Duponchel)		5	Very rare immigrant
Pleuroptya ruralis (Scopoli)	on Urtica dioica	4,5	Abundant
Palpita unionalis (Hübner) SCARCE OLIVE-TREE PEARL		5	Rare immigrant

Recorded twice only, in 1973 and 1994.

sub-family: Pyralinae

Hypsopygia costalis (Fabricius) GOLD TRIANGLE on grass & clover hay.		4,5	Abundant
Synaphe punctalis (Fabricius)	on Hypnum cupressiforme	5	Single record only
Orthopygia glaucinalis (L.)	on dead & decaying vegetable matter	5	Fairly common
Pyralis farinalis (L.) MEAL MOTH	in stored cereals	5	

Can be common in grainstores, barns and flour mills but seldom seen at large. A single example taken at light in 1987.

Endotricha flammealis (D.& S.)	on Lotus uliginosus	5	Uncommon

sub-family: Galleriinae

The larvae feed in the nests of Hymenoptera (Bees & Wasps).

Achroia grisella (Fabricius) LESSER WAX MOTH in bee hives		5	Rare

Taken on three occasions between 1991 and 1994, but stated to come rarely to light so may well be more common.

Aphomia sociella (L.)   BEE MOTH   in nests of wasps and Bumble-bees. Very common Comes readily to light.

sub-family: Phycitinae

A large sub-family of mainly medium-sized moths. The males of some species have thickened bases to the antennae and are often referred to as 'knot-horns'.

Anerastia lotella (Hübner)	on various Gramineae	5	Single record only
Cryptoblabes bistriga (Haworth)	on Alnus or Quercus spp.	5	Rare
Metriostola betulae (Goeze)	on Betula spp.	5	Rare
Pyla fusca (Haworth)	on Erica or Vaccinium	5	Common

May also breed on heathers in gardens.

Phycita roborella (D. & S.)	on Quercus spp. or Malus	4,5	Very common
Pempelia palumbella (D.& S.)(Oncocera palumbella D.&S.)on Erica, Calluna, etc.		5	Common
P. formosa (Haworth)(Oncocera formosa Haworth) on Ulmus spp.		5	Single record only
Hypochalcia ahenella (D.& S.)	on Helianthemum?	5	Single record only

This species probably utilises other food-plants.

Dioryctria abietella (D.& S.)	on Pinus sylvestris	5	Fairly common

Taken as large specimens which are thought to be of immigrant origin.

D. mutatella Fuchs	on Pinus sylvestris	5	Single record only
Pempeliella diluta (Haworth) (Pempelia dilutella Hübner) on Thymus drucei		5	Single record
Acrobasis repandana (Fabricius)	on Quercus spp.	5	Uncommon
A. consociella (Hubner)	on Quercus spp.	5	Uncommon
Numonia suavella (Zincken) (Eurhodope suavella Zincken) on Prunus or Crataegus		5	Rare
N. advenella (Zincken)	on Crataegus and Sorbus	5	Fairly common

Bred from spinnings on Sorbus aucuparia in 1993.

MOTHS

N. marmorea (Haworth)	on Prunus, Crataegus or Sorbus	5	Single record only
Euzophera cinerosella (Zeller)	on Artemisia absinthium	5	Single record only
E. pinguis (Haworth)	on Fraxinus	5	Common

The larvae feed under the living bark. The chosen tree is eventually killed causing the colony to move to a fresh tree.

Myelois cribrella (Hübner)	on various thistles, esp. Cirsium vulgare	5	Common

On 20 June, 1994, no less than 14 freshly emerged specimens were counted on a single plant of Cirsium vulgare.

Assara terebrella (Zincken)	on Picea abies	5	Single record only
Ancylosis oblitella (Zeller)	on Chenopodiaceae in salt-marshes	5	Single record only
Homoeosoma nebulella (D.& S.)	on Cirsium vulgare or Senecio jacobaea	5	Rare
Homoeosoma sinuella (Fabricius)	on Plantago spp.	5	Local

Present in good numbers on the Porlock shingle beach.

Phycitodes binaevella (Hübner)	on Cirsium vulgare	5	Fairly common
P. saxicola (Vaughan)	on Senecio, Tanacetum, etc.	5	Very rare
P. maritima (Tengstrom)*(P.carlinella Heinemann)*	on Senecio, Tanacetum, Achillea	5	Rare
Ephestia elutella (Hübner) CACAO MOTH	on stored foodstuffs	5	Single record only
E. parasitella Staudinger	on dry vegetable refuse	5	Common

Unlike other Ephestia spp., it is not a pest of warehouses and is found only out of doors.

E. kuehniella Zeller	In flour mills. No recent record.	5	Single record only

PTEROPHORIDAE   sub-family: Platyptiliinae

Marasmarcha lunaedactyla (Haworth)	on Ononis repens	5	Very local

Bred on two occasions from larvae taken on a small patch of the food-plant on Bossington shingle beach. Also taken at light in Porlock and Minehead.

Amblyptilia acanthadactyla (Hübner)	on Stachys sylvatica, etc.	5	Rare
A. punctidactyla (Haworth)	on several herbaceous spp.	5	Very common
Platyptilia calodactyla (D. & S.)	on Solidago virgaurea	4,5	Rare
P. gonodactyla (D.&mS.)	on Tussilago farfara	5	Single record only
P. pallidactyla (Haworth)	on Achillea	5	Common
Stenoptilia zophodactylus (Duponchel)	on Centaurium	5	Single record only
S. pterodactyla (L.)	on Veronica chamaedrys	5	Fairly common

sub-family: Pterophorinae

Pterophorus pentadactyla (L.)	on Convolvulus or Calystegia	5	Very common
Leioptilus osteodactylus (Zeller)	on Solidago or Senecio	4	Single record only
L. tephradactyla (Hübner)	on Solidago virgaurea	4	Rare
Emmelina monodactyla (L.)	on Convolvulus or Calystegia	5	Very common

The members of this family are collectively known as 'Plume-moths' from the fact of having the forewing divided into two lobes and the hindwing into three. They are slender and have very long legs and are rather unmothlike in appearance.

BUTTERFLIES

HESPERIIDAE
This family are known as the Skippers from their darting flight. The fore- and hindwings are held in different planes when at rest, giving them a very distinctive appearance. They are the most moth-like of the butterflies.

sub-family: **Hesperiinae**

Thymelicus sylvestris (Poda)	SMALL SKIPPER	4,5	Common
T. lineola (Ochsenheimer) ESSEX SKIPPER			Recorded from a single site in VC 5, 1992
Ochlodes venata (Bremer & Grey)	LARGE SKIPPER	4,5	Very common

sub-family: **Pyrginae**

Erynnis tages (L.)	DINGY SKIPPER	4,5	Uncommon
Pyrgus malvae (L.)	GRIZZLED SKIPPER	4,5	Rare

PIERIDAE
The Whites and Sulphurs which include the notorious 'Cabbage Whites' so detested by gardeners (with good reason) although Pieris napi feeds only on wild members of the cabbage family.

sub-family: **Dismorphiinae**

Leptidea sinapis (L.)   WOOD WHITE   4,5
Although there are a number of records up to 1982, the Recorder has been unable to confirm its continued presence on Exmoor.

sub-family: **Coliadinae**

Colias hyale (L.)   PALE CLOUDED YELLOW   5   Single record only
C. croceus (Geoffroy)   CLOUDED YELLOW   4,5   Common
This well-known migrant appears in most years but in some it can be encountered in prodigious numbers.

Gonepteryx rhamni (L.)   BRIMSTONE   4,5   Fairly common
Present almost every year but as wandering males in early and late summer.

sub-family: **Pierinae**

Pieris brassicae (L.)   LARGE WHITE   4,5   Abundant
Local populations reinforced by immigration.

P. rapae (L.)   SMALL WHITE   4,5   Abundant
Local populations reinforced by immigration.

P. napi (L.)   GREEN-VEINED WHITE   4,5   Very common

Anthocharis cardamines (L.)   ORANGE-TIP   4,5   Very common
The orange-tipped males are familiar to everyone but the white females are often mistaken for one of the Whites.

LYCAENIDAE   sub-family: **Theclinae**

Callophrys rubi (L.)   GREEN HAIRSTREAK   4,5   Very common
Found wherever gorse is plentiful. The well camouflaged eggs are laid singly near the tips of tender young shoots.

BUTTERFLIES

Thecla betulae (L.) BROWN HAIRSTREAK 5 Very rare
A single record only but the species is easily missed and likely to be noticed only when the females are egg-laying. Best located by searching for the conspicuous eggs on the bare twigs of old blackthorn during the winter months.

Quercusia quercus (L.) PURPLE HAIRSTREAK 4,5 Common
Plentiful in all the oakwoods but tends to remain high up and thus not often noticed.

Satyrium w-album (Knoch) *(Strymonidia w-album Knoch)* WHITE-LETTER HAIRSTREAK
Last seen in the Porlock area in 1985. 5 Rare

sub-family: Lycaeninae

Lycaena phlaeas (L.) SMALL COPPER 4,5 Common

sub-family: Polyommatinae

Plebejus argus (L.) SILVER-STUDDED BLUE 4
An unconfirmed record of larvae from Holdstone Down.

Aricia agestis (D.& S.) BROWN ARGUS 5 Very rare
May no longer be present

Polyommatus icarus (Rottemberg) COMMON BLUE 4,5 Very common

Celastrina argiolus (L.) HOLLY BLUE 4,5 Common
A remarkable instance of two broods feeding on different food-plants; the spring brood on holly and the summer brood on ivy.

Hamearis lucina (L.) DUKE OF BURGUNDY FRITILLARY 5
An early record from Timberscombe, presumably on primrose which is sometimes used as a food-plant. It is doubtful if it still occurs on Exmoor.

Ladoga camilla (L.) WHITE ADMIRAL 4,5
Last recorded in 1982. Its continued presence is very doubtful.

sub-family: Limenitinae

Vanessa atalanta (L.) RED ADMIRAL 4,5 Fairly common
Numbers vary from year to year, but mostly fairly common.

Cynthia cardui (L.) PAINTED LADY 4,5 Immigrant
Numbers vary greatly from year to year.

Aglais urticae (L.) SMALL TORTOISESHELL 4,5 Abundant

Nymphalis polychloros (L.) LARGE TORTOISESHELL 4,5 Very rare
Two early records which could refer to immigrants. It is now a nationally rare species.

Inachis io (L.) PEACOCK 4,5 Very common

Polygonia c-album (L.) COMMA 4,5 Common
This once uncommon species has made a remarkable comeback.

sub-family: Argynninae

Boloria selene (D.& S.) SMALL PEARL-BORDERED FRITILLARY 4,5 Common
Very common in the Lyn and Barle valleys.

B. euphrosyne (L.) PEARL-BORDERED FRITILLARY 4,5 Rare
A woodland species which has seriously declined nationally.

Argynnis adippe (D.& S.) HIGH BROWN FRITILLARY 4,5 Uncommon

A. aglaja (L.) DARK GREEN FRITILLARY 4,5 Common

A. paphia (L.) SILVER-WASHED FRITILLARY 4,5 Common
Horner Wood is undoubtedly the best place to see this magnificent butterfly.

BUTTERFLIES

sub-family: Melitaeinae

Eurodryas aurinia (Rottemberg)   MARSH FRITILLARY   4,5   Uncommon
Present at several sites but in rather low density.

Mellicta athalia (Rottemberg)   HEATH FRITILLARY   4,5   Common
Exmoor's most famous butterfly, with over 20 colonies which are regularly monitored by members of the Society. A national rarity.

sub-family: Satyrinae

Pararge aegeria (L.)	SPECKLED WOOD	4,5	Abundant
Lasiommata megera (L.)	THE WALL	4,5	Common
Melanargia galathea (L.)	MARBLED WHITE	5	Local
Hipparchia semele (L.)	GRAYLING	4,5	Common
Pyronia tithonus (L.)	GATEKEEPER	4,5	Abundant
Maniola jurtina (L.)	MEADOW BROWN	4,5	Abundant
Coenonympha pamphilus (L.)	SMALL HEATH	4,5	Very common

Abundant on areas of high moorland.

Aphantopus hyperantus (L.)   RINGLET   4,5   Common

sub-family: Danainae

Danaus plexippus (L.)   MONARCH   5   Rare immigrant
A North American species which occasionally wanders to Britain.

MACRO-MOTHS

LASIOCAMPIDAE

Trichiura crataegi (L.)	PALE EGGAR	4,5	Very rare
Malacosoma neustria (L.)	THE LACKEY	4,5	Rare
Lasiocampa trifolii (D.& S.)	GRASS EGGAR	4	

A single (unconfirmed) record from N. Devon.

L. quercus (L.)	OAK EGGAR	4,5	Fairly common
L. quercus callunae Palmer	NORTHERN OAK EGGAR	4,5	Common
Eriogaster lanestris (L.)	SMALL EGGAR	5	

There are two Exmoor records given on the distribution map in MBGBI (Heath & Emmet, 1991) Vol.7 pt.2, but it has not been possible to trace their source. A species which has undergone a serious decline in recent years but still present in Somerset.

Poecilocampa populi (L.)   DECEMBER MOTH   4,5   Common

Macrothylacia rubi (L.)   FOX MOTH   4,5   Very common
Larvae are often encountered on Exmoor tracks in spring, en route to a suitable pupation site.

Euthrix potatoria (L.) *(Philudoria potatoria L.)* THE DRINKER   4,5   Common
Larvae can be very common in damp, low-lying areas of the moor.

Phyllodesma ilicifolia (L.)   SMALL LAPPET   4,5
The occurrence of this extremely rare species rests on two (unconfirmed) records of larvae, one from Lynton in 1864 and the other from Porlock in 1938. It was last taken in Britain in 1965 at Weston-Super-Mare.

Gastropacha quercifolia (L.)   THE LAPPET   4,5   Rare

MOTHS

SATURNIIDAE sub-family: Saturniinae

Pavonia pavonia (L.)	THE EMPEROR MOTH	4,5	Fairly common

Males may be seen dashing over the heather moors in sunshine. The females fly at night, sometimes coming to light.

DREPANIDAE

Falcaria lacertinaria (L.)	SCALLOPED HOOK-TIP	4,5	Common
Drepana binaria (Hufnagel)	OAK HOOK-TIP	5	Common
D. cultraria (Fabricius)	BARRED HOOK-TIP	5	Uncommon
D. falcataria (L.)	PEBBLE HOOK-TIP	4,5	Common
Cilix glaucata (Scopoli)	CHINESE CHARACTER	4,5	Common

THYATIRIDAE

Thyatira batis (L.)	PEACH BLOSSOM	4,5	Common
Habrosyne pyritoides (Hufnagel)	BUFF ARCHES	4,5	Very common
Tethea ocularis (L.)	FIGURE OF EIGHTY	5	Uncommon
Tetheella fluctuosa (Hübner)	SATIN LUTESTRING	5	Very rare

Assumed to be a wanderer, as the nearest colony is in S. Wales. The moth was taken at light in 1994 at Porlock.

Ochropacha duplaris (L.)	COMMON LUTESTRING	5	Common
Cymatophorima diluta (D.& S.)	OAK LUTESTRING	4,5	Common
Achlya flavicornis (L.)	YELLOW-HORNED	4,5	Common
Polyploca ridens (Fabricius)	FROSTED GREEN	4,5	Fairly common

GEOMETRIDAE sub-family: Archiearinae

Archiearis parthenias (L.)	ORANGE UNDERWING	5	Rare

Flies in sunshine, mostly high up, at the edges of birchwoods and can easily be missed.

sub-family: Oenochrominae

Alsophila aescularia (D.& S.)	MARCH MOTH	4,5	Very common

sub-family: Geometrinae

Pseudoterpna pruinata (Hufnagel)	GRASS EMERALD	4,5	Common
Geometra papilionaria (L.)	LARGE EMERALD	4,5	Common
Comibaena bajularia (D.& S.)	BLOTCHED EMERALD	4,5	Fairly common
Hemithea aestivaria (Hübner)	COMMON EMERALD	4,5	Very common
Hemistola chrysoprasaria (Esper)	SMALL EMERALD	5	Uncommon
Jodis lactearia (L.)	LITTLE EMERALD	4,5	Uncommon

sub-family: Sterrhinae

In general, rather small insects of slender build and often attractively coloured. They are referred to as 'Waves'.

Cyclophora annulata (Schulze)	THE MOCHA	5	Very rare

A beautiful moth, recorded on only two occasions in 1963 and 1994.

C. porata (L.)	FALSE MOCHA	4,5	Last recorded 1971
C. punctaria (L.)	MAIDEN'S BLUSH	5	Fairly common
C. linearia (Hübner)	CLAY TRIPLE LINES	5	Uncommon

MOTHS

Timandra griseata (Petersen)	BLOOD-VEIN	5	Common
Scopula marginepunctata (Goeze)	MULLEIN WAVE	4,5	Local
S. imitaria (Hübner)	SMALL BLOOD-VEIN	5	Fairly common
S. immutata (L.)	LESSER CREAM WAVE	5	Single record only
S. floslactata (Haworth)	CREAM WAVE	5	Very common
S. ternata (Schrank)	SMOKY WAVE	4,5	Common

A northern species generally rare in the south-west and only common on Exmoor.

Idaea sylvestraria (Hübner)	DOTTED BORDER WAVE	5	Rare
I. biselata (Hufnagel)	SMALL FAN-FOOTED WAVE	4,5	Very common
I. fuscovenosa (Goeze)	DWARF CREAM WAVE	5	Common
I. seriata (Schrank)	SMALL DUSTY WAVE	5	Fairly common
I. dimidiata (Hufnagel)	SINGLE-DOTTED WAVE	4,5	Common
I. subsericeata (Haworth)	SATIN WAVE	5	Fairly common
I. trigeminata (Haworth)	TREBLE BROWN-SPOT	5	Very common
I. emarginata (L.)	SMALL SCALLOP	5	Very rare
I. aversata (L.)	RIBAND WAVE	4,5	Abundant
I. straminata (Borkhausen)	PLAIN WAVE	5	Common
Rhodometra sacraria (L.)	THE VESTAL	5	Rare immigrant

sub-family: Larentiinae

A very large group with 116 species recorded for Exmoor.

Orthonama vittata (Borkhausen)	OBLIQUE CARPET	5	Very rare
O. obstipata (Fabricius)	THE GEM	4,5	Rare immigrant
Xanthorhoe designata (Hufnagel)	FLAME CARPET	4,5	Common
X. spadicearia (D.& S.)	RED TWIN-SPOT CARPET	4,5	Abundant
X. ferrugata (Clerck)	DARK-BARRED TWIN-SPOT CARPET	4,5	Common
X. montanata (D.& S.)	SILVER-GROUND CARPET	4,5	Very common
X. fluctuata (L.)	GARDEN CARPET	4,5	Very common
Scotopteryx chenopodiata (L.)	SHADED BROAD-BAR	5	Fairly common
S. mucronata (Scopoli)	LEAD BELLE	4,5	Common
S. luridata (Hufnagel	JULY BELLE	4,5	Very common
Catarhoe rubidata (D.& S.)	RUDDY CARPET	5	Very rare
Epirrhoe tristata (L.)	SMALL ARGENT & SABLE	5	Very rare
E. alternata (Müller)	COMMON CARPET	4,5	Very common
E. rivata (Hübner)	WOOD CARPET	5	Rare
E. galiata (D.& S.)	GALIUM CARPET	4,5	Uncommon
Camptogramma bilineata (L.)	YELLOW SHELL	4,5	Common
Entephria caesiata (D.& S.)	GREY MOUNTAIN CARPET	5	Very rare

A north-western species in Britain, occurring as far south as S. Wales, with occasional stragglers found on the coastal regions of Exmoor.

Larentia clavaria (Haworth)	THE MALLOW	5	Rare

MOTHS

Anticlea badiata (D.& S.)	SHOULDER-STRIPE	4,5	Abundant
A. derivata (D.& S.)	THE STREAMER	4,5	Common
Mesoleuca albicillata (L.)	BEAUTIFUL CARPET	4,5	Uncommon
Lampropteryx suffumata (D.& S.)	WATER CARPET	4,5	Common
L. otregiata (Metcalfe)	DEVON CARPET	4,5	Very local
Cosmorhoe ocellata (L.)	PURPLE-BAR	4,5	Common
Nebula salicata (Hübner) *(Coenotephria salicata Hübner)*	STRIPED TWIN-SPOT CARPET	4,5	Very rare
Eulithis prunata (L.)	THE PHOENIX	4,5	Fairly common
E. testata (L.)	THE CHEVRON	4,5	Fairly common
E. populata (L.)	NORTHERN SPINACH	4,5	Very common
E. mellinata (Fabricius)	THE SPINACH	4,5	Very common
E. pyraliata (D.& S.)	BARRED STRAW	4,5	Common
Ecliptopera silaceata (D.& S.)	SMALL PHOENIX	4,5	Common
Chloroclysta siterata (Hufnagel)	RED-GREEN CARPET	5	Common
C. miata (L.)	AUTUMN GREEN CARPET	5	Rare
C. citrata (L.)	DARK MARBLED CARPET	4,5	Fairly common
C. truncata (Hufnagel)	COMMON MARBLED CARPET	4,5	Abundant
Cidaria fulvata (Forster)	BARRED YELLOW	5	Common
Plemyria rubiginata (D.& S.)	BLUE-BORDERED CARPET	5	Single record only
Thera firmata (Hübner)	PINE CARPET	5	Common
T. obeliscata (Hübner)	GREY PINE CARPET	4,5	Common
T. britannica (Turner)*(T. variata D.& S.)*	SPRUCE CARPET	5	Abundant
Electrophaes corylata (Thunberg)	BROKEN-BARRED CARPET	4,5	Fairly common
Colostygia olivata (D.& S.)	BEECH-GREEN CARPET	4,5	Rare
C. multistrigaria (Haworth)	MOTTLED GREY	5	Fairly common
C. pectinataria (Knoch)	GREEN CARPET	4,5	Very common
Hydriomena furcata (Thunberg) A very variable species.	JULY HIGHFLYER	4,5	Very common
H. impluviata (D.& S.)	MAY HIGHFLYER	5	Rare
H. ruberata (Freyer)	RUDDY HIGHFLYER	5	Rare
Horisme vitalbata (D.& S.)	SMALL WAVED UMBER	5	Rare
H. tersata (D.& S.)	THE FERN	5	Uncommon
Melanthia procellata (D.& S.)	PRETTY CHALK CARPET	5	Uncommon
Rheumaptera hastata (L.)	ARGENT & SABLE	5	Single record only
R. undulata (L.) Perhaps the most strikingly marked of the carpets.	SCALLOP SHELL	5	Uncommon
Triphosa dubitata (L.)	THE TISSUE	5	Rare

Hibernates in caves or outbuildings, often in large numbers. A wanderer on Exmoor owing to the absence of the food-plant.

MOTHS

Euphyia biangulata (Haworth)	CLOAKED CARPET	5	Very local

Appears to be confined to the Porlock area, where it is common.

E. unangulata (Haworth)	SHARP-ANGLED CARPET	5	Very rare
Epirrita dilutata (D.& S.)	NOVEMBER MOTH	4,5	Very common
E. christyi (Allen)	PALE NOVEMBER MOTH	4,5	Rare
E. autumnata (Borkhausen)	AUTUMNAL MOTH	5	Very common
Operophtera brumata (L.)	WINTER MOTH	4,5	Abundant

Visits lighted windows during mild weather throughout the winter, often in large numbers

O. fagata (Scharfenberg)	NORTHERN WINTER MOTH	5	Rare
Perizoma affinitata (Stephens)	THE RIVULET	4,5	Fairly common
P. alchemillata (L.)	SMALL RIVULET	4,5	Fairly common
P. bifaciata (Haworth)	BARRED RIVULET	5	Very local
P. albulata (D.& S.)	GRASS RIVULET	5	Rare
P. flavofasciata (Thunberg)	SANDY CARPET	4,5	Common
P. didymata (L.)	TWIN-SPOT CARPET	4,5	Fairly common on moorland

Eupithecia spp. - These are the Pugs, a group which seems to present the most difficulties to beginners, although fresh well-marked specimens can be fairly readily identified. In the case of worn examples, genitalia examination becomes the only reliable means.

Eupithecia tenuiata (Hübner)	SLENDER PUG	5	Uncommon
E. inturbata (Hübner)	MAPLE PUG	5	Very rare
E. haworthiata Doubleday	HAWORTH'S PUG	5	Uncommon
E. plumbeolata (Haworth)	LEAD-COLOURED PUG	4,5	Uncommon
E. linariata (D.& S.)	TOADFLAX PUG	4,5	Fairly common
E. pulchellata Stephens	FOXGLOVE PUG	4,5	Common
E. exiguata (Hübner)	MOTTLED PUG	5	Uncommon
E. pygmaeata (Hübner)	MARSH PUG	5	Single record only No recent record
E. venosata (Fabricius)	NETTED PUG	4,5	Rare
E. centaureata (D.& S.)	LIME-SPECK PUG	4,5	Occasional
E. intricata (Zetterstedt)	FREYER'S PUG	5	Single record only
E. satyrata (Hübner)	SATYR PUG	5	Single record only No recent record
E. absinthiata (Clerck)	WORMWOOD PUG	4,5	Common
E. goossensiata Mabille	LING PUG	5	Single record only No recent record
E. assimilata Doubleday	CURRANT PUG	5	Single record only
E. expallidata Doubleday	BLEACHED PUG	5	Rare
E. vulgata (Haworth)	COMMON PUG	4,5	Very common
E. tripunctaria H.-S.	WHITE-SPOTTED PUG	4,5	Fairly common
E. denotata (Hübner) ssp. jasioneata Crewe	JASIONE PUG	4	Single record only No recent record

MOTHS

Eupithecia subfuscata (Haworth)	GREY PUG	4,5	Common
E. icterata (Villers)	TAWNY-SPECKLED PUG	4,5	Common
E. succenturiata (L.)	BORDERED PUG	5	Uncommon
E. simpliciata (Haworth)	PLAIN PUG	5	Rare
E. distinctaria H.-S.	THYME PUG	4,5	Very rare No recent record
E. indigata (Hübner)	OCHREOUS PUG	5	Uncommon
E. nanata (Hübner)	NARROW-WINGED PUG	4,5	Common
E. virgaureata Doubleday	GOLDEN-ROD PUG	4,5	Rare
E. abbreviata Stephens	BRINDLED PUG	4,5	Common
E. dodoneata Guenée	OAK-TREE PUG	4,5	Fairly common
E. phoeniceata (Rambur)	CYPRESS PUG	5	Fairly common

The first British specimen was recorded from Cornwall in 1959. Has since spread along the coast and to some inland areas.

E. lariciata (Freyer)	LARCH PUG	5	Local
E. tantillaria Boisduval	DWARF PUG	5	Occasional
Chloroclystis v-ata (Haworth)	THE V-PUG	4,5	Fairly common
C. rectangulata (L.)	GREEN PUG	4,5	Fairly common
C. debiliata (Hübner)	BILBERRY PUG	5	

Recorded on five occasions but not since 1989

Gymnoscelis rufifasciata (Haworth)	DOUBLE-STRIPED PUG	4,5	Abundant
Chesias legatella (D.& S.)	THE STREAK	5	Very rare
C. rufata (Fabricius)	BROOM-TIP	5	Single record only
Aplocera plagiata (L.)	TREBLE-BAR	4,5	Occasional
Odezia atrata (L.)	CHIMNEY SWEEPER	4,5	Local
Discoloxia blomeri (Curtis)	BLOMER'S RIVULET	5	Very rare
Venusia cambrica Curtis	WELSH WAVE	4,5	Rare

A northern moorland species whose range extends to S.W. England.

Euchoeca nebulata (Scopoli)	DINGY SHELL	5	Uncommon
Asthena albulata (Hufnagel)	SMALL WHITE WAVE	5	Occasional
Hydrelia flammeolaria (Hufnagel)	SMALL YELLOW WAVE	5	Common
H. sylvata (D.& S.)	WAVED CARPET	4,5	Very rare
Lobophora halterata (Hufnagel)	THE SERAPHIM	5	Uncommon
Trichopteryx carpinata (Borkhausen)	EARLY TOOTH-STRIPED	4,5	Common
Pterapherapteryx sexalata (Retzius)	SMALL SERAPHIM	4,5	Uncommon
Acasis viretata (Hübner)	YELLOW-BARRED BRINDLE	4,5	Occasional

sub-family: Ennominae

Abraxas grossulariata (L.)	THE MAGPIE	4,5	Common
A. sylvata (Scopoli)	CLOUDED MAGPIE	4,5	Rare
Lomaspilis marginata (L.)	CLOUDED BORDER	4,5	Very common

MOTHS

Species	Common name	Area	Status
Ligdia adustata (D.& S.)	SCORCHED CARPET	4,5	Very common
Semiothisa wauaria (L.)	THE V-MOTH	5	Very rare
S. notata (L.)	PEACOCK MOTH	4,5	Uncommon
S. alternaria (Hübner)	SHARP-ANGLED PEACOCK	4,5	Fairly common
S. liturata (Clerck)	TAWNY-BARRED ANGLE	4,5	Common
S. clathrata (L.)	LATTICED HEATH	5	Very rare
Cepphis advenaria (Hübner)	LITTLE THORN	5	Very rare
Petrophora chlorosata (Scopoli)	BROWN SILVER-LINE	4,5	Abundant

Abundant in areas of dense Bracken.

Species	Common name	Area	Status
Plagodis pulveraria (L.)	BARRED UMBER	5	Common
P. dolabraria (L.)	SCORCHED WING	4,5	Common
Pachycnemia hippocastanaria (Hübner)	HORSE-CHESTNUT	4,5	Common
Opisthograptis luteolata (L.)	BRIMSTONE MOTH	4,5	Abundant
Epione repandaria (Hufnagel)	BORDERED BEAUTY	5	Rare
Pseudopanthera macularia (L.)	SPECKLED YELLOW	4,5	Very common

This common species flies in sunshine and is not seen at light.

Species	Common name	Area	Status
Apeira syringaria (L.)	LILAC BEAUTY	5	Uncommon
Ennomos quercinaria (Hufnagel)	AUGUST THORN	4,5	Fairly common
E. alniaria (L.)	CANARY-SHOULDERED THORN	4,5	Very common
E. fuscantaria (Haworth)	DUSKY THORN	4,5	Fairly common
E. erosaria (D.& S.)	SEPTEMBER THORN	4,5	Fairly common
Selenia dentaria (Fabricius)	EARLY THORN	4,5	Very common
S. lunularia (Hübner)	LUNAR THORN	4,5	Fairly common
S. tetralunaria (Hufnagel)	PURPLE THORN	4,5	Fairly common
Odontopera bidentata (Clerck)	SCALLOPED HAZEL	4,5	Common
Crocallis elinguaria (L.)	SCALLOPED OAK	4,5	Common
Ourapteryx sambucaria (L.)	SWALLOW-TAILED MOTH	4,5	Common
Colotois pennaria (L.)	FEATHERED THORN	4,5	Very common
Angerona prunaria (L.)	ORANGE MOTH	5	Single record only
Apocheima hispidaria (D.& S.)	SMALL BRINDLED BEAUTY	5	Single record only
A. pilosaria (D.& S.)	PALE BRINDLED BEAUTY	5	Fairly common
Lycia hirtaria (Clerck)	BRINDLED BEAUTY	4,5	Uncommon
Biston strataria (Hufnagel)	OAK BEAUTY	5	Common
B. betularia (L.)	PEPPERED MOTH	4,5	Common

Famous for the melanic forms produced in industrial areas. The very black form (carbonaria Jordan) occasionally turns up, as well as the partially melanic form insularia.

Species	Common name	Area	Status
Agriopis leucophaearia (D.& S.)	SPRING USHER	4,5	Fairly common
A. aurantiaria (Hübner)	SCARCE UMBER	4,5	Uncommon
A. marginaria (Fabricius)	DOTTED BORDER	4,5	Common
Erannis defoliaria (Clerck)	MOTTLED UMBER	4,5	Very common

MOTHS

Menophra abruptaria (Thunberg)	WAVED UMBER	5	Fairly common
Peribatodes rhomboidaria (D.& S.)	WILLOW BEAUTY	4,5	Very common
Deileptenia ribeata (Clerck)	SATIN BEAUTY	5	Rare
Alcis repandata (L.)	MOTTLED BEAUTY	4,5	Abundant
A. jubata (Thunberg)	DOTTED CARPET	4,5	Very local
Cleorodes lichenaria (Hufnagel)	BRUSSELS LACE	4,5	Local
Ectropis bistortata (Goeze)	THE ENGRAILED	4,5	Uncommon
E. crepuscularia (D.& S.)	SMALL ENGRAILED	4,5	Uncommon
Paradarisa consonaria (Hübner) *(Ectropis consonaria Hübner)* SQUARE SPOT		4,5	Rare
P. extersaria (Hübner)		5	Rare
Aethalura punctulata (D.& S.)	GREY BIRCH	5	Single record only
Ematurga atomaria (L.)	COMMON HEATH	4,5	Very common
Bupalus piniaria (L.)	BORDERED WHITE	5	Fairly common
Cabera pusaria (L.)	COMMON WHITE WAVE	4,5	Very common
C. exanthemata (Scopoli)	COMMON WAVE	4,5	Very common
Lomographa bimaculata (Fabricius)	WHITE PINION-SPOTTED	5	Uncommon
L. temerata (D. & S.)	CLOUDED SILVER	4,5	Fairly common
Theria primaria (Haworth)	EARLY MOTH	4,5	Occasional
Campaea margaritata (L.)	LIGHT EMERALD	4,5	Very common
Hylaea fasciaria (L.)	BARRED RED	4,5	Common
Gnophos obscuratus (D. & S.)	THE ANNULET	4,5	Occasional
Aspitates ochrearia (Rossi)	YELLOW BELLE	5	Rare
Dyscia fagaria (Thunberg)	GREY SCALLOPED BAR	5	Single record only
Perconia strigillaria (Hübner)	GRASS WAVE	4,5	Uncommon

SPHINGIDAE sub-family: **Sphinginae**

Agrius convolvuli (L.)	CONVOLVULUS HAWK-MOTH	5	Rare immigrant
Acherontia atropos (L.)	DEATH'S-HEAD HAWK-MOTH	4,5	Rare immigrant
Sphinx ligustri L.	PRIVET HAWK-MOTH	4,5	Fairly common
Hyloicus pinastri (L.)	PINE HAWK-MOTH	5	Single record only
Mimas tiliae (L.)	LIME HAWK-MOTH	4,5	Uncommon
Smerinthus ocellata (L.)	EYED HAWK-MOTH	4,5	Fairly common
Laothoe populi (L.)	POPLAR HAWK-MOTH	4,5	Very common

sub-family: **Macroglossinae**

Hemaris tityus (L.)	NARROW-BORDERED BEE HAWK-MOTH	5	Very rare
Macroglossum stellatarum (L.)	HUMMING-BIRD HAWK-MOTH	4,5	common immigrant

This attractrive immigrant turns up in most years and is sometimes fairly common. It is fond of feeding on the flowers of Red Valerian.

Hyles lineata (Fabricius)	STRIPED HAWK-MOTH	5	Very rare immigrant Single record only

MOTHS

Deilephila elpenor (L.)	ELEPHANT HAWK-MOTH	4,5	Very common
D. porcellus (L.)	SMALL ELEPHANT HAWK-MOTH	4,5	Fairly common

NOTODONTIDAE
The Prominents, so-called from the presence of a thoracic hump. The adults are seldom seen by day but come readily to light, especially the males.

Phalera bucephala (L.)	BUFF-TIP	4,5	Very common
Cerura vinula (L.)	PUSS MOTH	4,5	Fairly common
Furcula bicuspis (Borkhausen)	ALDER KITTEN	5	Very rare
F. furcula (Clerck)	SALLOW KITTEN	4,5	Uncommon
F. bifida (Brahm)	POPLAR KITTEN	4,5	Very rare
Stauropus fagi (L.)	LOBSTER MOTH	4,5	Fairly common

The vernacular name alludes to the appearance of the curious larva.

Notodonta dromedarius (L.)	IRON PROMINENT	4,5	Common
Eligmodonta ziczac (L.)	PEBBLE PROMINENT	4,5	Common
Peridea anceps (Goeze)	GREAT PROMINENT	4,5	Common
Pheosia gnoma (Fabricius)	LESSER SWALLOW PROMINENT	4,5	Very common
P. tremula (Clerck)	SWALLOW PROMINENT	4,5	Common
Ptilodon capucina (L.)	COXCOMB PROMINENT	4,5	Fairly common
Ptilodontella cucullina (D. & S.)	MAPLE PROMINENT	5	Rare
Pterostoma palpina (Clerck)	PALE PROMINENT	4,5	Common
Drymonia dodonaea (D. & S.)	MARBLED BROWN	4,5	Common
D. ruficornis (Hufnagel)	LUNAR MARBLED BROWN	4,5	Common
Clostera curtula (L.)	CHOCOLATE-TIP	5	Rare
Diloba caeruleocephala (L.)	FIGURE OF EIGHT	5	Very local

LYMANTRIIDAE

Orgyia antiqua (L.)	VAPOURER	4,5	Uncommon

The males fly in sunshine but the females are wingless.

Calliteara pudibunda (L.)	PALE TUSSOCK	4,5	Common
Euproctis similis (Fuessly)	YELLOW-TAIL	5	Fairly common
Lymantria monacha (L.)	BLACK ARCHES	4,5	Common

ARCTIIDAE   sub-family: **Lithosiinae**
Small to medium sized moths with narrow elongate forewings. The larvae feed on lichens and algae. The moths are collectively known as Footmen.

Miltochrista miniata (Forster)	ROSY FOOTMAN	4,5	Very common
Nudaria mundana (L.)	MUSLIN FOOTMAN	4,5	Fairly common
Atolmis rubricollis (L.)	RED-NECKED FOOTMAN	4,5	Rare
Cybosia mesomella (L.)	FOUR-DOTTED FOOTMAN	5	Fairly common
Eilema sororcula (Hufnagel)	ORANGE FOOTMAN	5	Rare
E. griseola (Hübner)	DINGY FOOTMAN	4,5	Fairly common
E. caniola (Hübner)	HOARY FOOTMAN	4,5	Fairly common
E. complana (L.)	SCARCE FOOTMAN	4,5	Fairly common

MOTHS

Eilema deplana (Esper)	BUFF FOOTMAN	4,5	Fairly common
E. lurideola (Zincken)	COMMON FOOTMAN	4,5	Abundant
Lithosia quadra (L.)	FOUR-SPOTTED FOOTMAN	5	Occasional

sub-family: Arctiinae

Utetheisa pulchella (L.)	CRIMSON-SPECKLED	5	Very rare immigrant
Parasemia plantaginis (L.)	WOOD TIGER	4,5	Very local
Arctia caja (L.)	GARDEN TIGER	4,5	Common
A. villica (L.)	CREAM-SPOT TIGER	4,5	Fairly common
Diacrisia sannio (L.)	CLOUDED BUFF	4,5	Fairly common

Males may readily be disturbed during the day from heather moorland; the females are less often seen.

Spilosoma lubricipeda (L.)	WHITE ERMINE	4,5	Very common
S. lutea (Hufnagel)	BUFF ERMINE	4,5	Very common
S. urticae (Esper)	WATER ERMINE	5	Single record only
Diaphora mendica (Clerck)	MUSLIN MOTH	4,5	Common

The white females fly by day and look very different from the brown males.

Phragmatobia fuliginosa (L.)	RUBY TIGER	4,5	Fairly common
Tyria jacobaeae (L.)	THE CINNABAR	4,5	Common

NOLIDAE – A small family of small moths, characterised by small protruding tufts of dark scales on the forewings.

Nola cucullatella (L.)	SHORT-CLOAKED MOTH	5	Rare
N. confusalis (H.-S.)	LEAST BLACK ARCHES	5	Common

NOCTUIDAE – The largest family of macro-lepidoptera in the British Isles with over 400 species in 14 sub-families, all with representatives on Exmoor.

sub-family: Noctuinae

Euxoa obelisca (D. & S.)	SQUARE-SPOT DART	4,5	Rare
E. tritici (L.)	WHITE-LINE DART	5	Uncommon
E. nigricans (L.)	GARDEN DART	4,5	Uncommon
Agrostis cinerea (D. & S.)	LIGHT FEATHERED RUSTIC	5	Rare
A. vestigialis (Hufnagel)	ARCHER'S DART	5	Very rare
A. segetum (D. & S.)	TURNIP MOTH	4,5	Common
A. clavis (Hufnagel)	HEART & CLUB	5	Uncommon
A. exclamationis (L.)	HEART & DART	4,5	Abundant
A. trux (Hübner) ssp. lunigera Stephens	CRESCENT DART	4,5	Fairly common
Agrotis ipsilon (Hufnagel)	DARK SWORD-GRASS	4,5	Common immigrant
A. puta (Hübner)	SHUTTLE-SHAPED DART	4,5	Common
Axylia putris (L.)	THE FLAME	4,5	Common
Actebia praecox (L.) *(Ochropleura praecox L.)*	PORTLAND MOTH	5	Single record only
Ochropleura plecta (L.)	FLAME-SHOULDER	4,5	Very common
Eugnorisma depuncta (L.)	PLAIN CLAY	5	Rare

MOTHS

Standfussiana lucernea (L.)	NORTHERN RUSTIC	4	Single record only
A northern species which just reaches the Exmoor coast.			
Noctua pronuba (L.)	LARGE YELLOW UNDERWING	4,5	Abundant
N. comes Hübner)	LESSER YELLOW UNDERWING	4,5	Very common
N. fimbriata (Schreber)	BROAD-BORDERED YELLOW UNDERWING	4,5	Common
N. janthe Borkhausen *(N. janthina D.& S.)*	LESSER BROAD-BORDERED YELLOW UNDERWING	4,5	Very common
N. interjecta Hübner	LEAST YELLOW UNDERWING	4,5	Fairly common
Spaelotis ravida (D. & S.)	STOUT DART	5	Single record only
Graphiphora augur (Fabricius)	DOUBLE DART	5	Very rare
Paradiarsia glareosa (Esper)	AUTUMNAL RUSTIC	4,5	Fairly common
Lycophotia porphyrea (D. & S.)	TRUE-LOVERS KNOT	4,5	Very common
Peridroma saucia (Hübner)	PEARLY UNDERWING	4,5	Fairly common immigrant
Diarsia mendica (Fabricius)	INGRAILED CLAY	4,5	Very common
D. dahlii (Hübner)	BARRED CHESTNUT	4,5	Rare
D. brunnea (D. & S.)	PURPLE CLAY	4,5	Common
D. rubi (Vieweg)	SMALL SQUARE-SPOT	4,5	Very common
Xestia c-nigrum (L.)	SETACEOUS HEBREW CHARACTER	4,5	Very common
X. ditrapezium (D. & S.)	TRIPLE-SPOTTED CLAY	4,5	Common
X. triangulum (Hufnagel)	DOUBLE SQUARE-SPOT	4,5	Very common
X. baja (D. & S.)	DOTTED CLAY	4,5	Common
X. rhomboidea (Esper)	SQUARE-SPOTTED CLAY	5	Single record only
Xestia castanea (Esper)	NEGLECTED RUSTIC	4,5	Uncommon
X. sexstrigata (Haworth)	SIX-STRIPED RUSTIC	4,5	Common
X. xanthographa (D. & S.)	SQUARE-SPOT RUSTIC	4,5	Very common
X. agathina (Duponchel)	HEATH RUSTIC	4,5	Uncommon
Naenia typica (L.)	THE GOTHIC	4,5	Rare
Anaplectoides prasina (D. & S.)	GREEN ARCHES	4,5	Common
Cerastis rubricosa (D. & S.)	RED CHESTNUT	4,5	Common
C. leucographa (D. & S.)	WHITE-MARKED	5	Single record only

sub-family: Hadeninae

Anarta myrtilli (L.)	BEAUTIFUL YELLOW UNDERWING	4,5	Common
Frequently encountered flying rapidly over heather moorland.			
Discestra trifolii (Hufnagel)	THE NUTMEG	5	Uncommon
Hada nana (Hufnagel)	THE SHEARS	4,5	Common
Polia nebulosa (Hufnagel)	GREY ARCHES	4,5	Common
Sideridis albicolon (Hübner)	WHITE COLON	5	Single record only
Mamestra brassicae (L.)	CABBAGE MOTH	4,5	Common
Melanchra persicariae (L.)	DOT MOTH	4,5	Very common
Lacanobia w-latinum (Hufnagel)	LIGHT BROCADE	5	Fairly common

MOTHS

Laconobia thalassina (Hufnagel)	PALE-SHOULDERED BROCADE	4,5	Common
L. suasa (D. & S.)	DOG'S TOOTH	5	Fairly common
L. oleracea (L.)	BRIGHT-LINE BROWN-EYE	4,5	Common
Papestra biren (Goeze)	GLAUCOUS SHEARS	5	Very rare
Ceramica pisi (L.)	BROOM MOTH	4,5	Very common
Hecatera bicolorata (Hufnagel)	BROAD-BARRED WHITE	5	Uncommon
Hadena rivularis (Fabricius)	THE CAMPION	4,5	Fairly common
H. perplexa (D. & S.)	TAWNY SHEARS	5	Uncommon
H. luteago (D. & S.)	BARRETT'S MARBLED CORONET	5	Single record only
H. confusa (Hufnagel)	MARBLED CORONET	4,5	Rare
H. bicruris (Hufnagel)	THE LYCHNIS	4,5	Common
Cerapteryx graminis (L.)	ANTLER MOTH	4,5	Fairly common

Numbers vary considerably from year to year. Can be a pest of upland pasture.

Tholera cespitis (D. & S.)	HEDGE RUSTIC	4,5	Uncommon
T. decimalis (Poda)	FEATHERED GOTHIC	4,5	Occasional
Panolis flammea (D. & S.)	PINE BEAUTY	5	Rare
Egira conspicillaris (L.)	SILVER CLOUD	5	Single record only
Orthosia cruda (D. & S.)	SMALL QUAKER	4,5	Abundant
O. miniosa (D. & S.)	BLOSSOM UNDERWING	4,5	Very rare
O. opima (Hübner)	NORTHERN DRAB	5	Single record only
O. gracilis (D. & S.)	POWDERED QUAKER	4,5	Common
O. cerasi (Fabricius) *(O.stabilis D.& S.)*	COMMON QUAKER		Very common
O. incerta (Hufnagel)	CLOUDED DRAB	4,5	Common
O. munda (D. & S.)	TWIN-SPOTTED QUAKER	4,5	Common
O. gothica (L.)	HEBREW CHARACTER	4,5	Very common
Mythimna turca (L.)	DOUBLE-LINE	4,5	Rare
M. conigera (D. & S.)	BROWN-LINE BRIGHT-EYE	5	Rare
M. ferrago (Fabricius)	THE CLAY	4,5	Common
M. vitellina (Hübner)	THE DELICATE	5	Uncommon immigrant
M. pudorina (D. & S.)	STRIPED WAINSCOT	5	Rare
M. straminea (Treitschke)	SOUTHERN WAINSCOT	5	Uncommon
M. impura (Hübner)	SMOKY WAINSCOT	4,5	Very common
M. pallens (L.)	COMMON WAINSCOT	4,5	Very common
M. litoralis (Curtis)	SHORE WAINSCOT	5	Single record only
M. unipuncta (Haworth)	WHITE-SPECK	5	Rare immigrant
M. comma (L.)	SHOULDER-STRIPED WAINSCOT	5	Fairly common
M. putrescens (Hübner)	DEVONSHIRE WAINSCOT	4,5	Rare

sub-family: Cuculliinae

Cucullia absinthii (L.)	THE WORMWOOD	5	Very rare

MOTHS

Cucullia chamomillae (D. & S.)	CHAMOMILE SHARK	5	Rare
C. umbratica (L.)	THE SHARK	4,5	Common
C. verbasci (L.)	THE MULLEIN	5	Uncommon
Brachylomia viminalis (Fabricius)	MINOR SHOULDER-KNOT	5	Uncommon
Brachionycha sphinx (Hufnagel)	THE SPRAWLER	5	Very local
Dasypolia templi (Thunberg)	BRINDLED OCHRE	5	Very rare
Aporophyla nigra (Haworth)	BLACK RUSTIC	4,5	Common
Lithophane semibrunnea (Haworth)	TAWNY PINION	5	Rare
L. hepatica (Clerck) *(L. socia Hufnagel)*	PALE PINION	4,5	Occasional
L. ornitopus (Hufnagel)	GREY SHOULDER-kNOT	4,5	Occasional
L. leautieri (Boisduval) ssp. hesperica Boursin	BLAIR'S SHOULDER-KNOT	5	Fairly common

First recorded in 1951 on the Isle of Wight, this moth has gradually increased its range

Xylena vetusta (Hübner)	RED SWORD-GRASS	4,5	Rare
Xylocampa areola (Esper)	EARLY GREY	4,5	Common
Allophyes oxyacanthae (L.)	GREEN-BRINDLED CRESCENT	4,5	Common
Dichonia aprilina (L.)	MERVEILLE DU JOUR	4,5	Uncommon
Dryobotodes eremita (Fabricius)	BRINDLED GREEN	5	Fairly common
Mniotype adusta (Esper) *(Blepharita adusta Esper)*	DARK BROCADE	5	Single record only
Polymixis flavicincta (D. & S.)	LARGE RANUNCULUS	4,5	Uncommon
Eumichtis lichenea (Hübner)	FEATHERED RANUNCULUS	5	Fairly common
Eupsilia transversa (Hufnagel)	THE SATELLITE	4,5	Common
Conistra vaccinii (L.)	THE CHESTNUT	4,5	Very common
C. ligula (Esper)	DARK CHESTNUT	4,5	Uncommon
C. rubiginea (D. & S.)	DOTTED CHESTNUT	5	Very rare

Not recorded in the County until recent years. The first Exmoor records were of two post-hibernation examples at Porlock in 1993.

Agrochola circellaris (Hufnagel)	THE BRICK	4,5	Fairly common
A. lota (Clerck)	RED-LINE QUAKER	4,5	Common
A. macilenta (Hübner)	YELLOW-LINE QUAKER	4,5	Very common
A. helvola (L.)	FLOUNCED CHESTNUT	4,5	Fairly common
A. litura (L.)	BROWN-SPOT PINION	5	Occasional
A. lychnidis (D. & S.)	BEADED CHESTNUT	5	Very common
Atethmia centrago (Haworth)	CENTRE-BARRED SALLOW	4,5	Fairly common
Omphaloscelis lunosa (Haworth)	LUNAR UNDERWING	5	Very common
Xanthia citrago (L.)	ORANGE SALLOW	5	Very rare
X. aurago (D. & S.)	BARRED SALLOW	5	Uncommon
X. togata (Esper)	PINK-BARRED SALLOW	4,5	Rare
X. icteritia (Hufnagel)	THE SALLOW	4,5	Uncommon
X. gilvago (D. & S.)	DUSKY-LEMON SALLOW	5	Very rare

MOTHS

sub-family: Acronictinae

Acronicta megacephala (D. & S.)	POPLAR GREY	4,5	Uncommon
A. leporina (L.)	THE MILLER	4,5	Uncommon
A. alni (L.)	ALDER MOTH	4,5	Fairly common
A. tridens (D. & S.)	DARK DAGGER	4,5	Rare
A. psi (L.)	GREY DAGGER	4,5	Common
A. rumicis (L.)	KNOT-GRASS	4,5	Very common
Craniophora ligustri (D. & S.)	THE CORONET	4,5	Fairly common
Cryphia domestica (Hufnagel)	MARBLED BEAUTY	5	Common
C. muralis muralis (Forster)	MARBLED GREEN	5	Rare

sub-family: Amphipyrinae

Amphipyra pyramidea (L.)	COPPER UNDERWING	4,5	Fairly common
A. berbera Rungs ssp. svenssoni Fletcher	SVENSSON'S COPPER UNDERWING	4,5	Occasional
A. tragopoginis (Clerck)	MOUSE MOTH	4,5	Occasional
Mormo maura (L.)	OLD LADY	4,5	Uncommon

Since this striking moth seldom comes to light, it is likely to be under-recorded.

Rusina ferruginea (Esper)	BROWN RUSTIC	4,5	Common
Thalpophila matura (Hufnagel)	STRAW UNDERWING	5	Single record only
Euplexia lucipara (L.)	SMALL ANGLE-SHADES	4,5	Common
Phlogophora meticulosa (L.)	ANGLE SHADES	4,5	Very common
Ipimorpha retusa (L.)	DOUBLE KIDNEY	4,5	Rare
Ipimorpha subtusa (D. & S.)	THE OLIVE	5	Uncommon
Enargia paleacea (Esper)	ANGLE-STRIPED SALLOW	5	Very rare immigrant
Parastichtis suspecta (Hübner)	THE SUSPECTED	5	Single record only
P. ypsillon (D. & S.) *(Enargia ypsillon D.& S)* DINGY SHEARS		5	Very rare
Cosmia affinis (L)	LESSER-SPOTTED PINION	4,5	Occasional
C. diffinis (L.)	WHITE-SPOTTED PINION	5	Single record only
C. trapezina (L.)	THE DUN-BAR	4,5	Very common
C. pyralina (D. & S.)	LUNAR-SPOTTED PINION	5	Rare
Apamea monoglypha (Hufnagel)	DARK ARCHES	4,5	Abundant
A. lithoxylaea (D. & S.)	LIGHT ARCHES	4,5	Fairly common
A. oblonga (Haworth)	CRESCENT-STRIPED	5	Single record only No recent record
A. crenata (Hufnagel)	CLOUDED-BORDERED BRINDLE	4,5	Common
A. epomidion (Haworth)	CLOUDED BRINDLE	4,5	Fairly common
A. remissa (Hübner)	DUSKY BROCADE	4,5	Occasional
A. unanimis (Hübner)	SMALL CLOUDED BRINDLE	5	Single record only
A. anceps (D. & S.)	LARGE NUTMEG	5	Very local
A. sordens (Hufnagel)	RUSTIC SHOULDER-KNOT	5	Rare

MOTHS

Apamea scolopacina (Esper)	SLENDER BRINDLE	4,5	Fairly common
A. ophiogramma (Esper)	DOUBLE LOBED	4,5	Rare
Oligia strigilis (L.)	MARBLED MINOR	5	Fairly common
O. versicolor (Borkhausen)	RUFOUS MINOR	4,5	Common
O. latruncula (D. & S.)	TAWNY MARBLED MINOR	5	Common
O. fasciuncula (Haworth)	MIDDLE-BARRED MINOR	4,5	Common
Mesoligia furuncula (D. & S.)	CLOAKED MINOR	4,5	Common
M. literosa (Haworth)	ROSY MINOR	4,5	Fairly common
Mesapamea secalis (L.)	COMMON RUSTIC	4,5	Very common
M. didyma (Esper) *(secalella Remm)*	LESSER COMMON RUSTIC	5	
Photedes minima (Haworth	SMALL DOTTED BUFF	4,5	Uncommon
P. pygmina (Haworth)	SMALL WAINSCOT	4,5	Fairly common
Eremobia ochroleuca (D. & S.)	DUSKY SALLOW	5	Rare
Luperina testacea (D. & S.)	FLOUNCED RUSTIC	4,5	Very common
Amphipoea lucens (Freyer	LARGE EAR	5	Uncommon

A moorland species of western and northern Britain.

A. fucosa (Freyer) ssp. paludis Tutt	SALTERN EAR	5	Fairly common
A. oculea (L.)	EAR MOTH	4,5	Fairly common
Hydraecia micacea (Esper)	ROSY RUSTIC	4,5	Common
Gortyna flavago (D. & S.)	FROSTED ORANGE	4,5	Common
Celaena haworthii (Curtis)	HAWORTH'S MINOR	5	Single record only No recent record
C. leucostigma (Hübner)	THE CRESCENT	5	Rare
Nonagria typhae (Thunberg)	BULRUSH WAINSCOT	5	Rare
Archanara geminipuncta (Haworth)	TWIN-SPOTTED WAINSCOT	5	Very local
Rhizedra lutosa (Hübner)	LARGE WAINSCOT	5	Rare
Coenobia rufa (Haworth)	SMALL RUFOUS	4,5	Very rare
Charanycha trigrammica (Hufnagel)	TREBLE-LINES	4,5	Common
Hoplodrina alsines (Brahm)	THE UNCERTAIN	4,5	Common
H. blanda (D. & S.)	THE RUSTIC	4,5	Common
H. ambigua (D. & S.)	VINE'S RUSTIC	5	Common
Spodoptera exigua (Hübner)	SMALL MOTTLED WILLOW	5	Rare immigrant
Caradrina morpheus (Hufnagel)	MOTTLED RUSTIC	4,5	Common
C. clavipalpis (Scopoli)	PALE MOTTLED WILLOW	5	Common
Chilodes maritimus (Tauscher)	SILKY WAINSCOT	5	Single record only

A local species of reed-beds, recorded from Porlock Weir.

Stilbia anomala (Haworth)	THE ANOMALOUS	4,5	Fairly common
Panemeria tenebrata (Scopoli)	SMALL YELLOW UNDERWING	5	Single record only

Found by the Recorder near Porlock in 1988 and still the only Exmoor record for this delightful little moth.

MOTHS

sub-family: Heliothinae

Pyrrhia umbra (Hufnagel)	BORDERED SALLOW	4,5	Rare
Heliothis armigera (Hübner)	SCARCE BORDERED STRAW	5	Rare immigrant
H. viriplaca (Hufnagel)	MARBLED CLOVER	5	Single record only No recent record
H. peltigera (D. & S.)	BORDERED STRAW	4,5	Uncommon immigrant

sub-family: Acontiinae

Eublemma ostrina (Hübner)	PURPLE MARBLED	5	Very rare immigrant
E. parva (Hübner)	SMALL MARBLED	5	Very rare immigrant
Protodeltote pygarga (Hufnagel) *(Lithacodia pygarga Hufnagel)* MARBLED WHITE SPOT		5	Very local
Deltote uncula (Clerck) *(Eustrotia uncula Clerck)* SILVER HOOK		5	Single record only

sub-family: Chloephorinae

Bena prasinana (L.)	SCARCE SILVER-LINES	4,5	Rare
Pseudoips fagana (Fabricius)	GREEN SILVER-LINES	4,5	Fairly common

sub-family: Sarrothripinae

Nycteola revayana (Scopoli)	OAK NYCTEOLINE	5	Rare

sub-family: Pantheinae

Colocasia coryli (L.)	NUT-TREE TUSSOCK	4,5	Fairly common

sub-family: Plusiinae

Chrysodeixis chalcites (Esper)	GOLDEN TWIN-SPOT	5	Very rare immigrant
Trichoplusia ni (Hübner)	THE NI MOTH	5	Very rare immigrant
Diachrysia chrysitis (L.)	BURNISHED BRASS	4,5	Common
Polychrysia moneta (Fabricius)	GOLDEN PLUSIA	5	Single record only
Plusia festucae (L.)	GOLD-SPOT	4,5	Uncommon
Autographa gamma (L.)	SILVER Y	4,5	Abundant immigrant

Perhaps the best-known of all the immigrants since it flies as often by day as by night.

A. pulchrina (Haworth)	BEAUTIFUL GOLDEN Y	4,5	Common
A. jota (L.)	PLAIN GOLDEN Y	4,5	Fairly common
A. bractea (D. & S.)	GOLD SPANGLE	4	Single record only No recent record
Abrostola trigemina (Werneburg)	DARK SPECTACLE	4,5	Rare
A. triplasia (L.)	THE SPECTACLE	4,5	Very common

sub-family: Catocalinae

Catocala nupta (L.)	RED UNDERWING	5	Rare
Callistege mi (Clerck)	MOTHER SHIPTON	5	Rare

sub-family: Ophiderinae

Lygephila pastinum (Treitschke)	THE BLACKNECK	5	Single record only
L. craccae (D. & S.)	SCARCE BLACKNECK	4,5	Very local

The food-plant, Wood Vetch, is also very local on Exmoor.

MOTHS

Scoliopteryx libatrix (L.)   THE HERALD   4,5   Fairly common
Adults may be found hibernating, sometimes in numbers, in old sheds, barns & outhouses.

Phytometra viridaria (Clerck)   SMALL PURPLE-BARRED   5   Occasional
A heath and moorland species which feeds on Milkwort.

Laspeyria flexula (D. & S.)   BEAUTIFUL HOOK-TIP   5   Very local

Rivula sericealis (Scopoli)   STRAW-DOT   4,5   Fairly common

sub-family: Hypeninae

Hypena crassalis (Fabricius)   BEAUTIFUL SNOUT   4,5   Fairly common
Although rather local in Britain as a whole, it is rather common on the Exmoor moorland since the larva feeds on Bilberry. Both males and females come to light.

H. proboscidalis (L.)   THE SNOUT   4,5   Very common
Being double-brooded, this very common moth may be seen throughout the summer until October. The vernacular name derives from the prominent labial palps.

H. rostralis (L.)   BUTTONED SNOUT   5   Rare

Schrankia taenialis (Hübner)   WHITE-LINE SNOUT   5   Single record only

S. costaestrigalis (Stephens)   PINION-STREAKED SNOUT   4,5   Occasional

Herminia tarsipennalis (Treitschke)   THE FAN-FOOT   4,5   Common

H. grisealis (D. & S.) *(H. nemoralis Fabricius)* SMALL FAN-FOOT   4,5   Very common

(Total: 1202)

References:
Bradley, J.D. & Fletcher, D.S. *A Recorder's Log-book of British Butterflies and Moths* Curwen Books (1979)
Emmet, A.M. *A Field Guide to the smaller British Lepidoptera*. British Entomology & Natural History Society (1988)
Howarth, T.G. *Colour Identification Guide to Butterflies of the British Isles*. Viking Books (1984)
Skinner, B. *Colour Identification Guide to Moths of the British Isles*. Viking Books. (1984)
Robbins, J. *The Moths & Butterflies of Exmoor National Park*. Exmoor Natural History Society, (Minehead 1990)

Order: DIPTERA (TRUE FLIES)

The list of flies in the first edition of the *Flora & Fauna of Exmoor* (1988) was compiled by Anita and John Hollier in a rather short period of time but it formed an excellent basis for the current list. It is still necessary to note that this very large group (around 6000 species on the British List) is very much under-recorded on Exmoor but it is a rather specialised field and our Society currently lacks an experienced and knowledgeable recorder of Diptera.

My own special interest is in the leaf-mining fauna and as such I have been able to add in excess of 120 species from this large group.

Alan Stubbs carried out an excellent survey of Horner Wood in 1993, on behalf of the National Trust, which added considerably to our records. The Mycetophilidae (Fungus Gnats) were well represented, the identifications being carried out by Peter Chandler of the B.E.N.H.S. (He is the Curator of that Society).

In 1995, an attempt was made to boost our recording level and I personally collected well over 100 specimens of Diptera. Peter Chandler very kindly came to my rescue by agreeing to identify my specimens (which had been carefully set and staged to make his task easier!) and this resulted in a further 58 new records. The List which follows has now grown to 634 species from the original total of 202 but there is much more recording to be done on Exmoor.

The classification and sequence follows Kloet and Hincks (1976) with, inevitably, a few recently adopted name changes and additions and the occasional elevation of some sub-families to full family status (e.g. Limoniidae and Keroplatidae).

John Robbins

See also Appendix I on page 120.

Sub-Order: NEMATOCERA (THREAD-HORNS)

TRICHOCERIDAE - WINTER GNATS

Trichocera hiemalis (DeGeer)	in woodland	Common

TIPULIDAE - CRANE-FLIES Sub-family: TIPULINAE

Dolichopeza albipes (Stroem)	wet rock seepages	Local
Tipula unca Wiedemann		Common
T. hortorum L.	fields, meadows and gardens	Common
T. scripta Meigen		Common
T. fascipennis Meigen		Common
T. selene Meigen	breeds in dead wood on wet soil	Rare
T. montium Egger	river banks, ponds and water meadows	
T. pruinosa Wiedemann	muddy marshes	Local
T. oleracea L.		Very common
T. paludosa Meigen	damp sites	
T. fulvipennis DeGeer	moorland fringes	Common
T. maxima Poda	damp sites in woodland	Local

LIMONIIDAE - CRANE-FLIES

Limonia macrostigma (Schummel)		Common

FLIES

Limonia nubeculosa Meigen		Common
L. phragmitidis (Schulz) *(L. tripunctata (Fabricius))*		Common
L. dumetorum Meigen		Common
L. aquosa (Verrall)	shaded wet rocks	Rare
L. autumnalis (Staeger)		Common
L. didyma Meigen	by streams	Local
L. fusca (Meigen)	by streams	Local
L. affinis (Schummel)	by streams	Fairly common
L. duplicata (Doane)		Common
Pedicia rivosa (L.)	damp sites	
P. littoralis (Meigen)	by streams	Local
P. straminea (Meigen)	seepages	Local
P. occulata (Meigen)	open seepages	Local
P. immaculata (Meigen)		Common
P. claripennis (Verrall)	open seepages	Local
Dicranota bimaculata (Schummel)	damp sites	
D. pavida (Haliday)	damp sites	Common
Paradelphomyia senilis (Haliday)		Common
Epiphragma ocellaris (L.)	dead wood	Local
Austrolimnophila ochracea (Meigen)		Common
Pseudolimnophila lucorum (Meigen)		Common
P. sepium (Verrall)		Common
Limnophila maculata (Meigen)		Common
L. mundata (Loew)	aquatic larvae	Rare
L. submarmorata (Verrall)	aquatic larvae in mud	Locally common
L. ferruginea (Meigen)	damp sites	
L. aperta Verrall		Local
L. fulvonervosa (Schummel)		Common
L. punctata (Schrank)	damp sites	
L. nemoralis (Meigen)		
L. separata (Walker)		Common
Pilaria batava (Edwards)	seepages, usually rather basic	Local
P. discicollis (Meigen)		Common
P. fuscipennis (Meigen)	seepages	Rare
Neolimnomyia filata (Walker) *(Pilaria filata (Walker))*		Common
Gonomyia abscondita Lackschewitz		Common
Lipsothrix nervosa Edwards	seepages in woods	Local
L. remota (Walker)		Common
Erioptera divisa (Walker)	grassy seepages	Local

FLIES

Erioptera fuscipennis Meigen		Common
E. lutea Meigen f. taeniota		Common
E. trivialis Meigen		Common
E. maculata Meigen		Common
E. occoecata (Edwards)		Common
Ormosia nodulosa (Macquart)	dead wood by streams	Common
Scleroprocta pentagonalis (Loew)	dead wood by streams	Very rare
S. sororcula (Zetterstedt)	dead wood by streams	Rare
Tasiocera fuscescens (Lackschewitz)		Common
T. murina (Meigen)		Common
Molophilus appendiculatus (Staeger)		Common
M. bifidus Goetghebuer		Common
M. medius de Meijere		Common
M. occultus de Meijere	wet ground	Local
M. ochraceus (Meigen)		Common
M. serpentiger Edwards		Common

PSYCHODIDAE - OWL MIDGES Sub-family: PSYCHODINAE

Pericoma canescens (Meigen)	varied damp sites	
P. fallax Eaton	varied damp sites	
P. fuliginosa (Meigen)	in light trap	
P. neglecta Eaton	varied damp sites	
P. nubila (Meigen)	varied damp sites	
Mormia caliginosa (Eaton)	varied damp sites	
Psychoda alternata Say	varied damp sites	

PTYCHOPTERIDAE

Ptychoptera albimana (Fabricius)		Common
P. lacustris Meigen	by streams	Local

DIXIDAE - MENISCUS MIDGES

Dixa puberula Loew	near water	Common
D. submaculata Edwards	seepages	Locally common

CHAOBORIDAE - PHANTOM MIDGES

Chaoborus crystallinus (DeGeer)	larvae in ponds	

CULICIDAE - MOSQUITOES Sub-family: ANOPHELINAE

Anopheles spp.

Sub-family: CULICINAE

Aedes rusticus (Rossi)	woodland	
Culiseta annulata (Schrank)	lentic water	
Culex pipiens L.	lentic water	

FLIES

THAUMALEIDAE

Thaumalea testacea Ruthé — shaded wet rocks

CERATOPOGONIDAE – BITING MIDGES Sub-family: **FORCIPOMYIINAE**

Forcipomyia bipunctata (L.)

Sub-family: CERATOPOGONINAE

Culicoides obsoletus (Meigen)

CHIRONOMIDAE – NON-BITING MIDGES Sub-family: **TANYPODINAE**

Tanypus sp.	damp sites
Apsectrotanypus trifascipennis (Zetterstedt)	lotic water
Macropelopia sp.	lotic water
Thienemannimyia sp.	lotic water
Zavrelimyia sp.	lotic water

Sub-family: DIAMESINAE

Diamesa sp.	
Potthastia gaedii (Meigen)	lotic water
P. longimana Kieffer	lotic water

Sub-family: ORTHOCLADIINAE

Brillia longifurca Kieffer	lotic water
B. modesta (Meigen)	lotic water
Cardiocladius sp.	lotic water
Eukiefferiella sp.	lotic water
Eurycnemus crassipes (Panzer)	lotic water
Heterotrissocladius sp.	lotic water
Prodiamesa olivacea (Meigen)	lotic water
Psectrocladius sp.	lotic water
Rheocricotopus sp.	lotic water
Synorthocladius semivirens (Kieffer)	lotic water
Corynoneura sp.	lotic water
Epoicocladius flavens (Malloch)	lotic water
Metriocnemus sp.	lotic water
Parametriocnemus stylatus (Kieffer)	lotic water
Thienemanniella sp.	lotic water

Sub-family: CHIRONOMINAE

Chironomus plumosus (L.)	larvae aquatic; adults crepuscular
Demicryptochironomus vulneratus (Zetterstedt)	lotic water
Microtendipes sp.	lotic water
Pentapedilum sp.	lotic water
Stempellinella sp.	lotic water

FLIES

SIMULIIDAE - BLACK FLIES

Simulium angustitarse (Lundström)	lotic water
S. aureum Fries	lotic water
Simulium brevicaule Dorier & Grenier	lotic water
S. vernum Macquart	lotic water
S. equinum (L.)	lotic water
S. ornatum Meigen	lotic water
S. argyreatum Meigen	lotic water
S. reptans (L.)	lotic water
S. rheophilum (Knoz)	lotic water

ANISOPODIDAE Sub-family: ANISOPODINAE

Anisopus punctatus (Fabricius) *(Sylvicola p. (Fabricius))* damp sites

BIBIONIDAE

Bibio ferruginatus (L.)

B. lanigerus Meigen		Occasional
B. marci (L.)	ST. MARK'S FLY	Very common
B. pomonae (Fabricius)	heather areas	Common
B. venosus (Meigen)		Occasional
Dilophus febrilis (L.)		Very common
D. femoratus Meigen		Very common

MYCETOPHILIDAE - FUNGUS GNATS Sub-family: BOLITOPHILINAE

Bolitophila cinerea Meigen	
B. saundersi (Curtis)	Common
B. hybrida (Meigen)	Common

Sub-family: DIADOCIDIINAE

Diadocidia ferruginosa (Meigen)

Sub-family: DITOMYIINAE

Symmerus annulatus (Meigen)

Sub-family: SCIOPHILINAE

Mycomya cinerascens (Macquart)	
M. marginata (Meigen)	Common
Neuratelia nigricornis Edwards	Rare
Phthinia winnertzi Mik	Local
Acnemia nitidicollis (Meigen)	Common
Coelosia flava (Staeger)	Local
Boletina flaviventris Strobl	Local
B. trivittata (Meigen)	Common
Tetragoneura sylvatica (Curtis)	Common

FLIES

Anatella ciliata Winnertz	Sub-family: MYCETOPHILINAE	Common
Allodiopsis rustica (Edwards)		
Exechia fusca (Meigen)		Common
Exechiopsis unguiculata (Lundström)		Local
Allodiopsis cristata Staeger		
Pseudexechia trisignata (Edwards)		Local
Allodia lugens (Wiedemann)		Common
Brevicornu crassicorne (Stannius)		Common
Pseudobrachypeza helvetica (Walker)		
Brachypeza armata Winnertz		Very rare
Phronia basalis Winnertz		Common
P. biarcuata (Becker)		Common
P. cinerascens Winnertz		
P. conformis (Walker)		
P. humeralis Winnertz		Common
Dynatosoma fuscicornis (Meigen)		
Mycetophila adumbrata Mik		
M. alea (Laffoon)		
M. britannica Laštovka & Kidd		Common
M. curviseta Lundström		
M. finlandica Edwards		
M. forcipata Lundström		
M. formosa Lundström		
M. fraterna Winnertz		
M. lastovkai Caspers		Very rare
M. marginata Winnertz		
M. ocellus Walker		
M. ornata Stephens		
M. perpallida Chandler		
M. sygnatoides Dziedzicki		
M. unipunctata Meigen		Common
M. vittipes Zetterstedt		
KEROPLATIDAE - FUNGUS GNATS		
Macrocera angulata Meigen		Common
M. fasciata Meigen		Common
M. parva Lundström		
M. phalerata Meigen		
M. stigma Curtis		Common
M. stigmoides Edwards		Common

FLIES

Macrocera tusca Loew		Rare
M. vittata Meigen		Common
Macrorrhyncha flava Winnertz		
Orfelia fasciata (Meigen)		
O. nemoralis (Meigen)		Common
O. unicolor (Staeger)		

SCIARIDAE

Sciara thomae (L.)	on Heracleum umbels	Common
Lycoriella bruckii (Winnertz)		Uncommon
Phytosciara flavipes (Meigen)	deciduous woodland	Common

CECIDOMYIIDAE – GALL MIDGES Sub-family: CECIDOMYIINAE

Bayeria capitigena (Bremi)	Fasciation on garden Spurge (Euphorbia)	
Craneiobia corni (Giraud)	Galls on Swida	
Cystiphora sonchi (Bremi)	Galls on Sonchus arvensis	Fairly common
Dasineura acrophila (Winnertz)	Galls on Fraxinus	Frequent
D. crataegi (Winnertz)	Galls on Crataegus	Common
D. filicina (Kieffer)	Galls on Pteridium	Frequent
D. fraxinea Kieffer	Galls on Fraxinus	Fairly common
D. galiicola (Löw)	Galls on Galium palustre	Rare
D. glechomae (Kieffer)	Galls on Glechoma	Frequent
D. kiefferiana (Rübsaamen)	Galls on Epilobium	Uncommon
D. pustulans (Rübsaamen)	Galls on Filipendula ulmaria	Common
(D. rosarum (Hardy) – see Wachtliella r.)		
D. tympani (Kieffer)	Galls on Acer pseudoplatanus	Common
D. ulmaria (Bremi)	Galls on Filipendula ulmaria	Frequent
D. urticae (Perris)	Galls on Urtica dioica	Common
D. viciae (Kieffer)	Galls on Vicia sepium	Frequent
Hartigiola annulipes (Hartig)	Galls on Fagus	Very common
Iteomyia capreae (Winnertz)	Galls on Salix	Frequent
Jaapiella veronicae (Vallot)	Galls on Veronica chamaedrys	Very common
Janetiella lemei (Kieffer)	Galls on Ulmus	Uncommon
Oligotrophus betulae (Winnertz)	Galls on Betula	Uncommon
O. fagineus Kieffer	Galls on Fagus	Common
Rhabdophaga marginemtorquens (Bremi)	Galls on Salix	Common
R. salicis (Schrank)	Stem-gall on Salix cinerea	Frequent
Rondaniola bursaria (Bremi)	Galls on Glechoma	Uncommon
Taxomyia taxi (Inchbald)	Galls on Taxus	Frequent
Wachtliella rosarum (Hardy)	Galls on Rosa	Uncommon
Anisostephus betulinum (Kieffer)	Galls on Betula	Uncommon

FLIES

Contarinia jacobaeae (Loew)	Galls on flowers of Senecio	Fairly common
C. steini (Karsch)	Galls on flower bud of Silene dioica	Frequent
C. tiliarum (Kieffer)	Galls on Tilia	Fairly common
Macrodiplosis dryobia (Löw)	Galls on Quercus	Common
M. volvens Kieffer	Galls on Quercus	Common

Sub-Order: BRACHYCERA (SHORTHORNS)

STRATIOMYIDAE - SOLDIER FLIES   Sub-family: BERIDINAE

Beris chalybata (Forster)		
B. fuscipes Meigen	Larvae in decaying vegetable matter	Rare
B. geniculata Curtis		Occasional
B. morrisii Dale		Occasional
B. vallata (Forster)		Common
Chorisops nagatomi Rozkonski		Rare
C. tibialis (Meigen)		Local

Sub-family: CLITELLARIINAE

Nemotelus uliginosus (L.)	in marshes	Local

Sub-family: PACHYGASTRINAE

Pachygaster atra (Panzer)	dead wood	Local
P. leachii Curtis	from beetle burrows especially in oak	

Sub-family: SARGINAE

Chloromyia formosa (Scopoli)	Common
Microchrysa cyaneiventris (Zetterstedt)	Common
M. flavicornis Meigen	Common
M. polita (L.)	Common
Sargus bipunctatus (Scopoli)	Occasional

Sub-family: STRATIOMYINAE

Odontomyia viridula (Fabricius)	marshes

RHAGIONIDAE - SNIPE FLIES   Sub-family: CHRYSOPILINAE

Chrysopilus asiliformis Preyssler *(C. aurea (Meigen))*		
C. cristatus (Fabricius)	by streams	Common
C. erythrophthalmus Loew	larvae aquatic	Very rare

Sub-family: RHAGIONINAE

Atherix ibis (Fabricius)	river banks and damp vegetation	
A. marginata (Fabricius)		Common
Rhagio lineola Fabricius		Common
R. scolopacea (L.)		Common
R. tringarius (L.)		Common

FLIES

TABANIDAE – HORSE FLIES, GADFLIES AND CLEGS Sub-family: TABANINAE

Haematopota pluvialis (L.)		Common
Tabanus autumnalis L.		Occasional
T. bromius L.		Occasional

ASILIDAE – ROBBER FLIES

Asilus crabroniformis L.	on heaths and unimproved grassland	Rare
Epitriptus cingulatus (Fabricius)		Occasional
Machimus atricapillus (Fallén)		Common
Pamponerus germanicus (L.)	mainly coastal	Rare
Leptogaster cylindrica (DeGeer)	grassland	Common
L. guttiventris Zetterstedt	grassland	Local
Dioctria atricapilla Meigen	grassland	Local
D. baumhaueri Meigen		Local
D. oelandica (L.)	tree foliage	Very rare
D. rufipes (DeGeer)		Local
Leptarthrus brevirostris (Meigen)	grassland	Local

BOMBYLIIDAE – BEE FLIES Sub-family: BOMBYLIINAE

Bombylius major L.	Parasitises solitary bees	

EMPIDIDAE – ASSASSIN FLIES Sub-family: TACHIDROMINAE

Platypalpus ciliaris (Fallén)		Common

Sub-family: OCYDROMIINAE

Bicellaria nigra (Meigen)	damp sites	
Ocydromia glabricula (Fallén)		Common
Oropezella sphenoptera (Loew)	among Vaccinium	Local

Sub-family: EMPIDINAE

Rhamphomyia crassirostris (Fallén)	Local
R. tarsata Meigen	Common
R. nitidula Zetterstedt	Local
R. longipes (Meigen)	Common
R. flava (Fallén)	Common
Empis aemula Loew	Local
E. lutea Meigen	
E. scutellata Curtis	
E. livida L.	Common
E. grisea Fallén	Common
E. tessellata Fabricius	Common
E. aestiva Loew	Fairly common
E. nuntia Meigen	
E. pennipes L.	

FLIES

Hillara anglodanica Lundbeck		
H. chorica (Fallén)		Common
H. cornicula Loew	by streams	Local
H. lurida (Fallén)	by streams	Local
H. maura (Fabricius)		
H. quadrivittata Meigen		Common
H. rejecta Collin	by streams	Local
H. thoracica Macquart	by streams	Local

Sub-family: HEMERODROMIINAE

Phyllodromia melanocephala (Fabricius)		Common
Chelifera precatoria (Fallén)	near water	Common
Hemerodromia sp.	near water	

Sub-family: CLINOCERINAE

Trichopeza longicornis (Meigen)		Locally common
Clinocera fontinalis (Haliday)	seepages	Common
C. stagnalis (Haliday)		Common
C. bipunctata (Haliday)	bare sediment	Local
Wiedemannia sp.	near water	

HYBOTIDAE

Hybos culiciformis (Fabricius)		Common

DOLICHOPODIDAE – LONG-HEADED FLIES Sub-family: Sciapodinae

Sciapus longulus (Fallén)		Local
Sciapus platypterus (Fabricius)		Common

Sub-family: DOLICHOPODINAE

Dolichopus brevipennis Meigen		Common
D. discifer Stannius	upland areas	Common
D. festivus Haliday		Common
D. griseipennis Stannius		Common
D. pennatus Meigen		Common
D. plumipes (Scopoli)		Common
D. popularis Wiedemann		Common
D. trivialis Haliday		Very common
D. ungulatus (L.)		Very common
D. urbanus Meigen		Common
D. ventripennis Meigen	upland areas	Fairly common
Hercostomus aerosus (Fallén)	seepages	Locally common
H. brevicornis (Staeger)	seepages	Local
H. cupreus (Fallén)	seepages	Local
H. metallicus (Stannius)		Occasional

FLIES

Hercostomus nanus (Macquart)	seepages	Local
H. nigripennis (Fallén)		Local
Hypophyllus obscurellus (Fallén)		Local
Poecilobothrus nobilitatus (L.)		Local

Sub-family: RHAPHIINAE

Rhaphium appendiculatum (Zetterstedt)		Common
R. caliginosum Meigen	near water	Local
R. monotrichum Loew		Common
Syntormon monilis (Haliday)	near water	Local
S. pallipes (Fabricius)	near water	Common

Sub-family: NEURIGONINAE

Neurigona pallida (Fallén)		Common

Sub-family: DIAPHORINAE

Chrysotus blepharosceles Kowarz		
C. gramineus (Fallén)		Occasional
C. neglectus (Wiedemann)		Common
C. varians Kowarz		Occasional
Argyra leucocephala (Meigen)	marshy areas	

Sub-family: CAMPSICNEMINAE

Campsicnemus curvipes (Fallén)	near water	Common
C. loripes (Haliday)		Common
C. scambus (Fallén)	near water	Common
Anepsiomyia flaviventris (Meigen)	seepages	Local
Xanthochlorus ornatus (Haliday)		Local

Sub-order: CYCLORRHAPHA

PHORIDAE – SCUTTLE FLIES   Sub-family: PHORINAE

Triphleba gracilis (Wood)	woodland	

LONCHOPTERIDAE – POINTED-WINGED FLIES

Lonchoptera lutea Panzer	damp woodland	
L. tristis Meigen	woodland litter	Locally common

PIPUNCULIDAE – LARGE-HEADED FLIES   Sub-family: PIPUNCULINAE

Eudorylas zonellus Collin	woodland glades	Local

SYRPHIDAE – HOVERFLIES   Sub-family: SYRPHINAE

Syrphus ribesii (L.)		Common
S. torvus Osten-Sacken		Common
S. vitripennis Meigen		Common
Epistrophe eligans (Harris)		

FLIES

Epistrophe grossulariae (Meigen)		Uncommon
Metasyrphus latifasciatus (Macquart)	open or wet areas	Common
Scaeva pyrastri (L.)		Uncommon
Dasysyrphus lunulatus (Meigen)	woodland margins	Local
Leucozona glaucius (L.)	woodland margins	Uncommon
L. laternarius (Müller)	lush vegetation	Uncommon
Melangyna labiatarum (Verrall)		
Parasyrphus annulatus (Zettersedt)		Uncommon
Didea fasciata Macquart		Uncommon
Meliscaeva auricollis (Meigen)		
Episyrphus balteatus (DeGeer)		Very common
Sphaerophoria philanthus (Meigen)	woodland margins	Common
S. scripta (L.)		Common
Chrysotoxum bicinctum (L.)		Common
C. cautum (Fabricius)		Common
Baccha elongata (Fabricius)	in flowers of Hedera	
B. obscuripennis Meigen		Uncommon
Xanthandrus comtus (Harris)	meadows and scrub	
Melanostoma mellinum (L.)	woodland margins	Common
M. scalare (Fabricius)	grassland	Very common
Platycheirus angustatus (Zettersedt)	damp grassland	Common
P. clypeatus (Meigen)		Very common
P. cyaneus (Müller)		Very common
P. manicatus (Meigen)		
P. scutatus (Meigen)		Common
Pyrophaena granditarsa (Forster)	meadows	
P. rosarum (Fabricius)	meadows	
Paragus haemorrhous Meigen	dry heath grassland	Very local

Sub-family: MILESIINAE

Pipiza austriaca Meigen	damp sites	
Cheilosia albipila Meigen		Local
C. fraterna (Meigen)	damp meadows	
C. illustrata (Meigen)		
C. longula (Zettersedt)		
C. scutellata (Fallén)	woodland	Frequent
Rhingia campestris Meigen		Common
Ferdinandea cuprea (Scopoli)	sap-runs	Local
Chrysogaster cemiteriorum (L.) *(C. chalybeata Meigen)*	lush meadows	Local
C. solstitialis (Fallén)	damp sites	Common

FLIES

Melanogaster hirtella (Loew) *(C. hirtella Loew)*	marshes	Common
Lejogaster metallina (Fabricius)	wet meadows	Frequent
Orthonevra splendens (Meigen)	wet sites	Local
Sphegina clunipes (Fallén)	wet dead wood	Local
S. kimakowiczi Strobl	in old woodland	Rare
S. elegans Schummel	wet dead wood	Locally frequent
S. verecunda Collin	wet dead wood	Very rare
Neoascia geniculata (Meigen)		Fairly common
N. podagrica (Fabricius)	lush herbage	Common
Callicera aenea (Fabricius)		Local
Microdon mutabilis (L.)	marshy glades	Rare
Volucella bombylans (L.)		Common
V. inanis (L.)		Local
V. pellucens (L.)	woods and copses	Common
Sericomyia lappona (L.)	seepages	Local
S. silentis (Harris)		Common
Arctophila fulva (Harris)		Uncommon
Xylota florum (Fabricius)		Local
X. segnis (L.)		Common
X. xanthocnema Collin	dead wood	Very rare
Brachypalpoides lenta (Meigen)	rotting wood	Local
Brachypalpus laphriformis (Fallén)	dead wood	Very rare
Syritta pipiens (L.)		Common
Criorhina berberina (Fabricius)	rotting wood	Local
Merodon equestris f. narcissi (Fabricius)	NARCISSUS FLY	
Helophilus pendulus (L.)		Common
H. trivittatus (Fabricius)		Fairly common
Parhelophilus versicolor (Fabricius)		Local
Eristalis abusivus Collin	usually coastal	Local
E. arbustorum (L.)		Very common
E. horticola (DeGeer)		Locally common
E. interrupta (Poda) *(E. nemorum auctt. nec L.)*		Common
E. pertinax (Scopoli)		Common
E. tenax (L.)		Very common
Myanthropa florea (L.)		Common

CONOPIDAE   Sub-family: **CONOPINAE**

Conops flavipes L.	Uncommon
C. quadrifasciata DeGeer	Uncommon

FLIES

Sub-family: MYOPINAE

Zodion notatum (Meigen)		Rare
Myopa strandi Duda		Rare
Thecophora atra (Fabricius)	grassland	Local
Sicus ferrugineus (L.)		Fairly common

TEPHRITIDAE – PICTURE-WINGED FLIES Sub-family: TRYPETINAE

Euleia cognata (Wiedemann)	Blotch mines on Petasites fragrans	Rare
E. heraclei (L.) CELERY FLY	mines leaves of Smyrnium, etc.	Common
Trypeta artemisiae (Fabricius)	mines leaves of Artemisia vulgaris	Uncommon
Xyphosia miliaria (Schrank)	by streams	

Sub-family: UROPHORINAE

Urophora solstitialis (L.)	gall on Cirsium	
U. stylata (Fabricius)	gall on Cirsium	

PLATYSTOMATIDAE

Platystoma seminationis (L.)	rank vegetation in varied habitats	

OTITIDAE   Sub-family: ULIDIINAE

Physiphora alceae (Preyssler) *(Chrysomyza demandata (Fabricius))*		
	most numerous in hot summers	Local

Sub-family: OTITINAE

Melieria omissa (Meigen)	on vegetation by ponds and streams	

MICROPEZIDAE – STILT-LEGGED FLIES   Sub-family: CALOBATINAE

Calobata cibaria (L.)	Common

PSILIDAE   Sub-family: LOXOCERINAE

Chamaepsila rosae (Fabricius)	CARROT FLY in carrot roots	Occasional

LAUXANIIDAE

Minettia inusta (Meigen)	
Sapromyza sordida Haliday	
Peplomyza litura (Meigen)	Local
Lyciella rorida (Fallén)	Common
L. stylata Papp	Local
Tricholauxania praeusta (Fallén)	Common
Homoneura thalhammeri Papp	Local

COELOPIDAE – KELP FLIES

Coelopa frigida (Fabricius)	breeds in rotting seaweed	Locally frequent

HELEOMYZIDAE   Sub-family: SUILLIINAE

Suillia dumicola (Collin)	on fungi	Rare
S. fuscicornis (Zetterstedt)		Common
Allophyla atricornis (Meigen)		Common
Neoleria ruficeps (Zetterstedt)	moorland fringes	Local

FLIES

SEPSIDAE

Themira putris (L.)	decomposing animal matter	

SCIOMYZIDAE - SNAIL-KILLING FLIES Sub-family: SCIOMYZINAE

Pherbellia albocostata (Fallén)		Common
P. dubia (Fallén)	damp areas in woodland	Common
Tetanura pallidiventris Fallén	damp areas in woodland	Local
Elgiva cucularia (L.)		Occasional
Renocera pallida (Fallén)	seepages in alder-carr	Very local
Tetanocera hyalipennis Von Roser	seepages in alder-carr	Locally common
T. phyllophora Melander	damp sites	
Trypetoptera punctulata (Scopoli)		Common

SPHAEROCERIDAE

Copromyza similis (Collin)	decomposing animal matter	
Leptocera fontinalis (Fallén)	decomposing animal matter	

PALLOPTERIDAE

Palloptera umbellatarum (Fabricius)	grazed river meadows	Common

LONCHAEIDAE

Lonchaea chorea (Fabricius)

L. laticornis Meigen

OPOMYZIDAE

Geomyza tripunctata Fallén		
Opomyza germinationis (L.)		Common

CLUSIIDAE

Clusia flava (Meigen)	dead wood		Local
Paraclusia tigrina (Fallén)	old or diseased trees	(RDB 2)	Very rare

ANTHOMYZIDAE

Anthomyza gracilis Fallén		Common

DIASTATIDAE

Diastata fuscula (Fallén)		Common

DROSOPHILIDAE - FRUIT FLIES Sub-family: DROSOPHILINAE

Scaptomyza flava (Fallén)	mines leaves of Tropaeolum majus	Very local
S. graminum (Fallén)	mines leaves of Chenopodium album	
Drosophila confusa Staeger		
D. funebris (Fabricius)	in decaying vegetable refuse	

BRAULIDAE - BEE LOUSE

Braula coeca Nitzsch	in bee-hives	

AGROMYZIDAE - LEAF-MINING FLIES Sub-family: AGROMYZINAE

Ophiomyia cunctata (Hendel)	on Sonchus spp.	Very common
O. pulicaria (Meigen)	on Sonchus spp.	Fairly common

FLIES

Agromyza abiens Zetterstedt	on Symphytum officinale	Rare
A. albipennis Meigen	on Phalaris arundinacea	Local
A. alnibetulae Hendel	on Betula spp.	Common
A. alnivora Spencer	on Alnus glutinosa	Occasional
A. anthracina Meigen	on Urtica dioica	Common
A. bicophaga Hering	on Vicia sepium	Rare
A. demeijerei Hendel	on Laburnum	Common
A. felleri Hering	on Vicia sepium	Rare
A. filipendulae Spencer	on Filipendula vulgaris	Common
A. flaviceps Fallén	on Humulus lupulus	Very local
A. frontella Rondani	on Medicago lupulina	Rare
A. igniceps Hendel	on Humulus lupulus	Very local
A. lathyri Hendel	on Lathyrus latifolius	Common
A. nana Meigen	on Trifolium spp.	Common
A. potentillae (Kaltenbach)	on Potentilla reptans	Common
A. pseudoreptans Nowakowski	on Urtica dioica	Rare
A. reptans Fallén	on Urtica dioica	Frequent
A. rufipes Meigen	on Artemisia vulgaris	Very rare
A. sulfuriceps Strobl	on Rubus idaeus	Common
A. varicornis Strobl	on Lathyrus latifolius	Common
A. vicifoliae Hering	on Vicia cracca	Rare

Sub-family: PHYTOMYZINAE

Calycomyza artemisiae (Kaltenbach)	on Artemisia and Eupatorium	Uncommon
Amauromyza flavifrons (Meigen)	on Saponaria or Silene spp.	Common
A. labiatarum (Hendel)	on Ajuga or Stachys betonica	Rare
A. morionella (Zetterstedt)	on Stachys sylvatica	Rare
A. verbasci (Bouché)	on Scrophularia and Verbascum	Uncommon
Liriomyza amoena (Meigen)	on Sambucus nigra	Fairly common
L. artemisicola de Meijere	on Artemisia vulgaris	Common
L. centaureae Hering	on Centaurea nigra	Rare
L. cicerina (Rondani)	on Ononis repens	Very local
L. congesta (Becker)	on Galega officinalis	Very local
L. demeijerei Hering	on Artemisia vulgaris	Fairly common
L. eupatoriana Spencer	on Eupatorium cannabinum	Common
L. eupatorii (Kaltenbach)	on Eupatorium cannabinum	Common
L. flaveola (Fallén)	on Holcus mollis	Frequent
L. graminivora Hering	on Arrhenatherum elatius	Frequent
L. hieracii (Kaltenbach)	on Hieracium sabaudum	Very local
L. ptarmicae de Meijere	on Achillea millefolium	Rare

L. pusilla (Meigen)	on Bellis perennis	Uncommon
L. sonchi Hendel	on Sonchus spp.	Common
L. strigata (Meigen)	on Eupatorium cannabinum	Common
Metopomyza violiphaga (Hendel)	on Viola riviniana	Very rare
Phytoliriomyza hilarella (Zetterstedt)	on Pteridium aquilinum	Common
P. melampyga (Loew)	on Impatiens glandulifera	Rare
Nemorimyza posticata (Meigen)	on Solidago virgaurea	Locally common
Paraphytomyza fulvicornis (Hendel)	on Salix caprea	Very rare
P. hendeliana (Hering)	on Lonicera and Symphoricarpos	Very common
P. heringi (Hendel)	on Fraxinus excelsior	Very rare
P. populi (Kaltenbach)	on Populus nigra	Uncommon
P. populicola (Walker)	on Populus nigra	Rare
P. tridentata (Loew)	on Salix fragilis	Rare
Phytomyza argromyzina Meigen	on Swida sanguinea	Very local
P. angelicastri Hering	on Angelica sylvestris	Rare
P. aprilina Goureau	on Lonicera and Symphoricarpos	Very common
P. aquilegiae Hardy	on Aquilegia vulgaris	Rare
P. artemisivora Spencer	on Artemisia vulgaris	Occasional
P. bipunctata Loew	on Echinops sp.	Very local
P. calthivora Hendel	on Caltha palustris	Rare
P. calthophila Hering	on Caltha palustris	Rare
P. chaerophylli Kaltenbach	on Anthriscus and Chaerophyllum	Very common
P. cirsii Hendel	on Cirsium spp.	Common
P. conyzae Hendel	on Pulicaria dysenterica	Uncommon
P. crassiseta Zetterstedt	on Veronica chamaedrys	Fairly common
P. cytisi Brischke	on Laburnum	Common
P. eupatorii Hendel	on Eupatorium cannabinum	Common
P. fallaciosa Brischke	on Ranunculus spp.	Rare
P. fulgens Hendel	on Clematis vitalba	Common
P. glechomae Kaltenbach	on Glechoma hederacea	Uncommon
P. horticola Goureau	on many herbaceous plants	Very common
P. ilicis Curtis	on Ilex aquifolium	Abundant
P. lappae Goureau	on Arctium minus	Common
P. leucanthemi Hering	on Leucanthemum vulgare	Local
P. lonicerae Robineau-Desvoidy	on Lonicera and Leycesteria	Common
P. marginella Fallén	on Taraxacum and Hieracium	Fairly common
P. milii Kaltenbach	on Milium effusum	Very local
P. minuscula Goureau	on Aquilegia vulgaris	Common
P. nigra Meigen	on Holcus and Brachypodium	Common

FLIES

Phytomyza obscura Hendel	on Calamintha ascendens	Rare
P. obscurella Fallén	on Aegopodium podagraria	Very local
P. periclymeni de Meijere	on Lonicera and Leycesteria	Common
P. petoei Hering	on Mentha x villosa	Rare
P. plantaginis Robineau-Desvoidy	on Plantago spp.	Uncommon
P. primulae Robineau-Desvoidy	on Primula vulgaris	Very common
P. pullula Zetterstedt	on Matricaria chamomilla	Rare
P. ranunculi (Schrank)	on Ranunculus ficaria and repens	Very common
P. ranunculicola Hering	on Ranunculus acris	Rare
P. ranunculivora Hering	on Ranunculus repens	Uncommon
P. scolopendri Robineau-Desvoidy	on Phyllitis scolopendrium	Common
P. solidaginis Hendel	on Solidago virgaurea	Common
P. spinaciae Hendel	on Cirsium arvense	Occasional
P. spondylii Robineau-Desvoidy	on Heracleum sphondylium	Very common
P. syngenesiae (Hardy)	on Sonchus spp.	Common
P. tanaceti Hendel	on Tanacetum vulgare	Rare
P. tetrasticha Hendel	on Mentha x villosa	Rare
P. tussilaginis Hendel	on Tussilago and Petasites	Fairly common
P. virgaureae Hering	on Solidago virgaurea	Rare
P. vitalbae Kaltenbach	on Clematis vitalba	Common
Cerodontha ireos (Goureau)	on Iris pseudacorus	Uncommon
C. iridis (Hendel)	on Iris foetidissima	Fairly common
C. flavocingulata (Strobl)	on Dactylis glomerata	Rare
C. phalaridis Nowakowski	on Phalaris arundinacea	Rare

CHLOROPIDAE   Sub-family: **OSCINELLINAE**

Lipara lucens Meigen	gall on Phragmites	Frequent

Sub-family: **CHLOROPINAE**

Platycephala planifrons (Fabricius)	waterside vegetation and reed-beds	Local
Thaumatomyia notata (Meigen)	marshland	Common

OESTRIDAE   Sub-family: **OESTRINAE**

Oestrus ovis L.	SHEEP NOSTRIL FLY	Uncommon

Sub-family: **HYPODERMATINAE**

Hypoderma bovis (L.)	WARBLE FLY	May now be eradicated on Exmoor. No recent records.

GASTEROPHILIDAE

Gasterophilus intestinalis (DeGeer)	BOT-FLY	Fairly common

TACHINIDAE - PARASITIC FLIES   Sub-family: **PHASIINAE**

Alophora hemiptera (Fabricius)	Parasite of Hemiptera	Rare

Specimen in Reading Museum collected Doone Valley 1988 B.R.Baker

FLIES

Sub-family: TACHININAE

Eriothrix rufomaculatus (DeGeer)		
Gymnocheta viridis (Fallén)		Common
Tachina fera (L.)		Occasional

Sub-family: GONIINAE

Cyzenis albicans (Fallén)		
Masicera pavoniae (Robineau-Desvoidy)		Occasional

Sub-family: DEXIINAE

Dexia rustica (Fabricius)

RHINOPHORIDAE

Rhinophora lepida (Meigen)

SARCOPHAGIDAE   Sub-family: MILTOGRAMMINAE

Metopia grandii Venturi	Record from Dunster 1953 (D'Assis Fonseca)	Very rare

Sub-family: AGRIINAE

Nyctia halterata (Panzer)

Sub-family: SARCOPHAGINAE

Sarcophaga (sensu stricto) sp.

CALLIPHORIDAE - BLUEBOTTLES, GREENBOTTLES and BLOW-FLIES

Sub-family: CALLIPHORINAE

Calliphora vomitoria (L.)	BLUEBOTTLE	Very common
Lucilia ampullacea Villeneuve	woodland	Local
L. caesar (L.)	GREENBOTTLE	Common
L. illustris (Meigen)		

SCATHOPHAGIDAE - DUNG FLIES

Sub-family: SCATHOPHAGINAE

Scathophaga stercoraria (L.)	on cow-dung	Very common
S. suilla (Fabricius)		Common

ANTHOMYIIDAE

Anthomyia sp.	woodland fringe	
Chirosia betuleti (Ringdahl)	galling of Athyrium felix-foemina	Very local
C. grossicauda (Strobl) *(C. parvicornis (Zetterstedt))*	gall on Pteridium (Bracken)	Common
C. histricina Rondani	mines on Pteridium (Bracken)	Very common
Delia brassicae (Hoffmannsegg in Wiedemann)	CABBAGE ROOT-FLY	Frequent
Paradelia intersecta (Meigen) *(Pseudonupedia intersecta (Meigen))*		
Hylemya variata (Fallén)		Common
Pegoplata infirma (Meigen) *(Nupedia infirma (Meigen))*		
Pegomya flavifrons (Walker) *(P. albimargo (Pandellé))*	mines on Silene dioica	Common
P. hyoscyami (Panzer)	mines on Atriplex prostrata	Rare
P. pulchripes (Loew)		

FLIES

Pegomya solennis (Meigen)	large blotch-mines on Rumex spp.	Very common

FANNIIDAE - LESSER HOUSE FLIES

Fannia canicularis (L.)	Very common
F. scalaris (Fabricius)	Common

MUSCIDAE - HOUSE FLIES etc. Sub-family: MUSCINAE

Polietes lardaria (Fabricius)	light woodland	Frequent
Mesembrina meridiana (L.)	woods and hedgerows	Frequent
Eudasyphora cyanella (Meigen) *(Dasyphora cyanella (Meigen))*		
Morellia hortorum (Fallén)	woodland	
Musca domestica L. COMMON HOUSE FLY	in houses	Abundant
Eumusca autumnalis DeGeer	hibernates in large swarms in attics	Common
Azelia sp.		Common
Thricops semicinerea (Wiedemann)		Common
Hydrotaea cyrtoneurina (Zetterstedt)		
H. irritans (Fallén)	sips human perspiration	Common

Sub-family: PHAONIINAE

Phaonia basalis (Zetterstedt)	Common
P. incana (Wiedemann)	Common
P. pallida (Fabricius)	Common
P. subventa (Harris) *(P. variegata (Meigen))*	
Helina impuncta (Fallén)	Common

Sub-family: LIMNOPHORINAE

Limnophora riparia (Fallén)	by streams

Sub-family: COENOSIINAE

Coenosia tigrina (Fabricius)	Common

Sub-family: STOMOXYINAE

Stomoxys calcitrans (L.) STABLE FLY	bites animals and humans	Fairly common

HIPPOBOSCIDAE - LOUSE FLIES   Sub-family: ORNITHOMYINAE

Ornithomya avicularia (L.)	most frequent on owls and pigeons	Common
Crataerina pallida (Latreille)	ectoparasite of swifts	Common

Sub-family: LIPOPTENINAE

Lipoptena cervi (L.) DEER FLY	newly emerged adults on tree foliage	
Melophagus ovinus (L.) SHEEP KED		Uncommon

Note:-
Members of the following families have also been observed on Exmoor but have not so far been determined to genera:
SCATOPSIDAE, DRYOMYZIDAE, PIOPHILIDAE, EPHYDRIDAE, MILICHIIDAE and **TETHINIDAE.**

FLEAS

References:-

Audcent (1927) *Notes on the Diptera of Somerset* VI Procs SANHS LXXIII

Charbonnier (1915-1919) *Notes on the Diptera of Somerset* I to VI Procs SANHS LXI to LXV

Collin, J.E. (1961) *British Flies (Empididae)* 3 vols. CUP

Freeman P. & Lane, R.P. (1985) *Bibionid and Scatopsid Flies* Handbooks for the Identification of British Insects IX 7 RESL

Fonseca, E.C.M. d'Assis (1978) *Dolichopodidae* Handbooks for the Identification of British Insects IX 5 RESL

Oldroyd (1969) *Tabanoidea and Asiloidea* Handbooks for the Identification of British Insects IX 4 RESL

Kloet & Hincks (1976) *Checklist of British Insects* (2nd edn.) Handbooks for the Identification of British Insects XI 5 RESL

Robbins, J. (1991) *The Leaf-Miners of Warwickshire.* Warwick Museum Service

Smith, K.G.V. (1969) *Conopidae* Handbooks for the Identification of British Insects X 3(a) RESL

Spencer, K.A. (1976) *The Agromyzidae of Fennoscandia & Denmark* 2 vols. Scandinavian Science Press Ltd.

Stubbs, A. & Falk, S. (1983) *British Hoverflies* BENHS London

Stubbs, F. (ed.) (1986) *Provisional* Key to British Plant Galls. BPGS

Wilson, M. (1986) *Somerset Plant Gall Records.* Cecidology I p27.

Order: SIPHONAPTERA — FLEAS

HYSTRICHOPSYLLIDAE Sub-family: CTENOPHTHALMINAE

Palaeopsylla soricis soricis (Dale) — Very common on pygmy and common shrews

CERATOPHYLLIDAE

Paraceras melis melis (Walker) — Common on badgers, also foxes. Occasional stray on dogs

Orchopeas howardi howardi (Baker) — Its main host is the grey squirrel with which it was introduced

Dasypsyllus gallinulae gallinulae (Dale) — A common nest parasite of passerines that build their nests in low positions

Ceratophyllus garei Rothschild — Prefers nests in damp places or a little above the ground

C. gallinae gallinae (Schrank) — The commonest nest parasite throughout the country. Prefers relatively dry nests

PULICIDAE Sub-family: PULICINAE

Pulex irritans L. — HUMAN FLEA   Much less common than formerly due to general improvement in standards of hygiene

Ctenocephalides canis (Curtis) — DOG FLEA   Common

C. felis felis (Bouché) — CAT FLEA   Common

Spilopsyllus cuniculi (Dale) — RABBIT FLEA Strays found on other mammals. It is the vector of myxomatosis.

Order: HYMENOPTERA
(WASPS, ANTS, BEES)

The order Hymenoptera found within the U.K. is represented by 66 families, culminating in a total of 6641 species which were listed by 1978. This number of species is gradually increasing with time. In spite of present day environmental problems, Hymenoptera, as an entire group, is extremely successful in its survival. Hyperparasites in particular are noticeably absent in the following data and parasites are very under recorded. Some have yet to be observed and others are difficult to identify in the absence of published keys, so those seen have been listed by family only. Hymenoptera which cause distinct symptoms to develop on plants, or have unpleasant effects on man, or are well-known beneficial insects, tend to be noticed and are subsequently recorded.

The original list of 80 species which appeared in the first edition of the *Fauna & Flora* was prepared by T.J. 'Bill' Richards. The present list now totals 194 species and thanks are due to David Boyce, Heather Bristow, John Hollier, John Robbins and Stuart Roberts for their assistance.

New additions are always welcomed. Nomenclature follows Kloet and Hincks (1975).

Sub-order: SYMPHYTA (SAWFLIES)

SIRICIDAE - WOOD WASPS

Urocerus gigas (L.)	GREAT HORNTAIL	Locally common

CEPHIDAE - STEM SAWFLIES

Cephus cultratus Eversmann

ARGIDAE

Arge clavicornis Fabricius

CIMBICIDAE

Cimbex femoratus (L.)	BIRCH SAWFLY	Larvae on birch (Betula)
Trichiosoma tibiale Stephens	HAWTHORN SAWFLY	Adult reared from cocoon

TENTHREDINIDAE

Strombocerus delicatulus (Fallén)

Strongylogaster lineata (Christ)

Dolerus madidus (Klug)

Heterarthrus aceris (Kaltenbach)	JERKING DISC SAWFLY	Mines on sycamore (Acer pseudoplatanus)
H. healyi Altenhofer & Zambori		Mines on field maple (Acer campestre)
H. microcephalus (Klug)		Mines on willow (Salix spp.) Adult bred
H. nemoratus (Fallén)		Mines on birch (Betula)
H. vagans (Fallén)		Mines on alder (Alnus)

Monostegia abdominalis (Fabricius)
Monosoma pulverata (Retzius)   ALDER SAWFLY   Adult bred from larva on alder (Alnus)
Allantus cinctus (L.)   Fairly common on flowers
Phymatocera aterrima (Klug)   SOLOMON'S-SEAL SAWFLY   On solomon's-seal (Polygonatum multiflorum)

Blennocampa pusilla (Klug)   LEAF-ROLLING SAWFLY   On roses (Rosa spp.)
Metallus gei Brischke   Mines on wood avens (Geum urbanum)
M. pumilus (Klug)   Mines on raspberry (Rubus idaeus)
Scolioneura betuleti (Klug)   Mines on birch (Betula)
Messa nana (Klug)   Mines on birch (Betula)
Profenusa pygmaea (Klug)   Mines on sessile oak (Quercus petraea)
P. thomsoni (Konow)   Mines on birch (Betula)
Fenusa dohrnii (Tischbein)   Mines on alder (Alnus)
F. ulmi (Sundewall)   Mines on elm (Ulmus spp.)
Fenella nigrita Westwood   Mines on agrimony (Agrimonia eupatorium)
Tenthredopsis nassata (L.) *(Aglaostigma n.)*
Rhogogaster viridis (L.)
Tenthredo balteata Klug
T. celtica Benson
T. mesomelas L.
Trichiocampus viminalis (Fallén)   POPLAR SAWFLY
Pristiphora mollis (Hartig)   Larvae on Vaccinium
Euura venusta (Zaddach)   Galls on leaf-stalks of willow (Salix spp.)
Pontania pedunculi (Hartig)   Galls on grey willow (Salix cinerea)
P. proxima (Lepeletier)   Galls on willow (Salix spp.)
P. vesicator (Bremi-Wolf)   Galls on willow (Salix spp.)
P. viminalis (L.)   GOAT WILLOW SAWFLY   Galls on goat willow (Salix caprea)
Croesus septentrionalis (L.)   BIRCH SAWFLY   On birch (Betula)
Nematus ribesii (Scopoli)   GOOSEBERRY SAWFLY   Common on gooseberry (Ribes uva-crispa)

Sub-order: APOCRITA
Section: PARASITICA

ICHNEUMONIDAE

Pimpla instigator (Fabricius)   On flowers of ivy (Hedera helix)
Perithous divinator (Rossius)
Rhyssa persuasoria (L.)   SABRE WASP

WASPS/ANTS/BEES

Netelia opaculus (Thomson)		Occasional in light-trap
Lissonota setosa (Geoffroy)		Parasite of Goat Moth (Cossus)
Perispuda bignellii (Bridgman)		
P. facialis (Gravenhorst)		
Ophion costatus Ratzeburg		Parasite of Noctuid moths
O. luteus (L.)		Very common
Enicospilus ramidulus (L.)		Parasite of Hawk-moths and Noctuids
Mesochorus politus Gravenhorst		
Syspasis lineator (Fabricius)		Parasite of Heterarthrus vagans
Amblyteles armatorius (Forster)		Grazed water meadows; common

BRACONIDAE

Apanteles glomeratus (L.) Parasite of Pieris butterflies

APHIDIIDAE

Praon spp. Parasites of aphids

GASTERUPTIIDAE

Gasteruption assectator (L.) HUNGER WASP Parasite of various bees

CYNIPIDAE - GALL WASPS

Phanacis hypochoeridis (Kieffer)		Galls on cats-ear (Hypochoeris)
Liposthenus latreillei (Kieffer)		Galls on ground-ivy (Glechoma)
Diastrophus rubi (Bouché)	BRAMBLE STEM GALL	Galls on brambles (Rubus)
Synergus apicalis Hartig		Inquiline in oak galls
S. rotundiventris Mayr		Inquiline in oak galls
Diplolepis eglanteriae (Hartig)	SMOOTH PEA-GALL	Galls on wild rose (Rosa spp.)
D. nervosa (Curtis)	SPUTNIK PEA-GALL	Galls on wild rose (Rosa spp.)
D. rosae (L.)	BEDEGUAR GALL	Galls on wild rose (Rosa spp.)
Neuroterus albipes (Schenck)		Galls on oak (Quercus spp.)
N. numismalis (Geoffroy)	SILK-BUTTON SPANGLE-GALL	Galls on oak (Quercus spp.)
N. quercusbaccarum (L.)	COMMON SPANGLE-GALL	Galls on oak (Quercus spp.)
Andricus anthracinus (Hartig)		Galls on oak (Quercus spp.)
A. curvator Hartig		Galls on oak (Quercus spp.)
A. fecundator (Hartig)	ARTICHOKE GALL	Galls on oak (Quercus spp.)
A. kollari (Hartig)	MARBLE GALL	Galls on oak (Quercus spp.)
A. lignicola (Hartig)		Galls on oak (Quercus spp.)
A. quadrilineatus Hartig		Galls on oak (Quercus spp.)
A. quercuscalicis (Burgsdorf)	KNOPPER GALL	Galls on oak (Quercus spp.)
A. quercusradicis (Fabricius)		Galls on oak (Quercus spp.)
A. solitarius (Fonscolombe)		Galls on oak (Quercus spp.)

WASPS/ANTS/BEES

Cynips divisa Hartig	RED PEA-GALL	Galls on oak (Quercus spp.)
C. quercusfolii L.	CHERRY GALL	Galls on oak (Quercus spp.)
Biorhiza pallida (Olivier)	OAK-APPLE GALL	Galls on oak (Quercus spp.)

CHALCIDIDAE spp. — Parasites of Lepidoptera and Diptera

TORYMIDAE
Megastigmus dorsalis (Fabricius) — Parasitoid in oak marble galls
Torymus nitens (Walker) — Parasitoid in oak marble galls

PTEROMALIDAE
Pteromalus puparum (L.) — Parasite of Lepidoptera

EULOPHIDAE
Chrysocharis polyzo (Walker) — Parasite of Cerodontha ireos fly

TRICHOGRAMMATIDAE
Prestwichia aquatica Lubbock — Parasite in eggs of aquatic bugs and beetles

MYMARIDAE - FAIRY FLIES
spp. — Parasites in eggs of bugs and dragonflies

PROCTOTRUPIDAE
Codrus niger Panzer — Parasite of Carabid beetles

PLATYGASTRIDAE
spp. — Parasites of gall-midges

Sub-order: **APOCRITA**
Section: **ACULEATA**

DRYINIDAE
spp. — Parasites of leaf-hopper bugs

BETHYLIDAE
Epyris niger (Westwood)

CHRYSIDIDAE
Chrysis angustula Schenck
C. ignita (L.) — RUBY-TAILED WASP Parasite of other Hymenoptera
C. rutiliventris Abeille de Perrin — Mainly coastal
Chrysis schencki Linsenmaier — **Notable**
Trichrysis cyanea (L.) — Kleptoparasite of wood-boring aculeates

TIPHIIDAE
Tiphia femorata Fabricius — Parasite of dung-beetles

MUTILLIDAE
Mutilla europaea L. — LARGE VELVET ANT — Parasite of Bombus spp. Females wingless

WASPS/ANTS/BEES

FORMICIDAE

Myrmica lobicornis Nylander		Nests in open woodland or moorland
M. ruginodis Nylander	RED ANT	Nests under stones in woods & moorland
M. scabrinodis Nylander		Nests in varying sites; very common
M. sulcinodis Nylander		Nests under flat stones on heather moorland
Leptothorax acervorum (Fabricius)	SLENDER ANT	Nests in tree stumps under bark
Tetramorium caespitum (L.)	TURF ANT	Nests under stones on heaths and cliffs
Tapinoma erraticum (Latreille)		Nests in heathland
Formica cunicularia Latreille		Nests under stones and in dry turf banks
F. fusca L.		Nests under stones and tree stumps
F. lemani Bondroit		Nests in upland areas
F. rufa L.	WOOD ANT	Very common in woodland
Lasius alienus (Förster)		On heather moorland
L. flavus (Fabricius)	YELLOW MEADOW ANT	Very common in fields and gardens
L. fuliginosus (Latreille)	JET-BLACK ANT	Nests in varying sites
L. niger (L.)	COMMON BLACK ANT	Abundant in gardens

POMPILIDAE – SPIDER-HUNTING WASPS

Anoplius concinnus (Dahlbom)		Parasite of Lycosid spiders
A. viaticus (L.)	BLACK-BANDED SPIDER WASP	Parasite of various spiders

EUMENIDAE – POTTER-WASPS

Odynerus spinipes (L.)	MASON WASP	Parasite of larvae of Coleoptera
Ancistrocerus nigricornis (Curtis)		Nests in cavities; parasite of Tortricid larvae
A. parietinus (L.)	WALL MASON WASP	Parasite of Lepidopterous larvae
Symmorphus connexus (Curtis)		Nests in plant stems
S. gracilis (Brullé)		Visits flowers of Scrophularia

VESPIDAE

Vespa crabro L.	HORNET	Nests in tree holes; locally common
Dolichovespula norwegica (Fabricius)	NORWEGIAN WASP	Fairly common
D. sylvestris (Scopoli)	TREE WASP	Nests in trees; fairly common
D. media Retzius		Nests in bushes; very rare. A recent arrival in Britain; first Exmoor record early 1990s
Vespula rufa (L.)	RED WASP	Nests usually in ground; uncommon
V. vulgaris (L.)	COMMON WASP	Nests in varying sites; abundant

SPHECIDAE

Miscophus concolor Dahlbom	Nests on heaths; parasite of small spiders
Trypoxylon attenuatum Smith, F.	Parasite of various spiders

WASPS/ANTS/BEES

Crabro cribrarius (L.)	SLENDER-BODIED DIGGER WASP	On sandy heathland; parasite of Diptera
Crossocerus capitosus (Shuckard)		Parasite of Diptera and Hymenoptera
C. cetratus (Shuckard)		Nests in hollow stems and dead wood; parasite of Diptera and Homoptera
C. megacephalus (Rossius)		Nests in rotten wood; parasite of Diptera
C. pusillus Lepeletier & Brullé		Nests in soil; parasite of small Diptera
C. quadrimaculatus (Fabricius)		Nests in soil; parasite of Diptera
C. dimidiatus (Fabricius)		Nests in rotten wood; parasite of Diptera
Ectemnius continuus (Fabricius)		Nests in dead wood; parasite of Muscids and Syrphids
E. cephalotes (Olivier)		Nests in dead wood; parasite of Muscids and Syrphids
E. lituratus (Panzer)		Nests in dead wood; parasite of Muscids
Oxybelus uniglumis (L.)	COMMON SPINY DIGGER WASP	Nests in sandy soils; parasite of Diptera
Psen bicolor Jurine		Nests in sandy soils; parasite of Homoptera
Diodontus tristis (Vander Linden)		Nests in sand or mortar; parasite of aphids
Passaloecus gracilis (Curtis)		Nests in beetle burrows; parasite of same
Ammophila sabulosa (L.)	SAND WASP	Nests in sandy soil; parasite of Lepidoptera
Mellinus arvensis (L.)	FIELD DIGGER WASP	Nests in light soils; parasite of Diptera
Nysson spinosus (Forster)		Kleptoparasite of Argogorytes spp.
Gorytes bicinctus (Rossius)		Nests in light soil; parasite of Homoptera
Argogorytes mystaceus (L.)		Nests in light soil; parasite of Homoptera

COLLETIDAE

Colletes marginatus Smith,F.	Nests in loose sand; a coastal species
C. succinctus (L.)	Nests in ground; visits flowers of Calluna and Erica

ANDRENIDAE - SOLITARY BEES

Andrena fucata Smith,F.	Visits many different flowers
A. lapponica Zetterstedt	Visits flowers of Vaccinium
A. jacobi Perkins, R.C.L.	Visits many different flowers
A. bicolor Fabricius	Visits many different flowers
A. nigroaenea (Kirby)	Visits many different flowers
A. haemorrhoa (Fabricius)	Nests in ground; visits flowers of Crataegus and Salix
A. coitana (Kirby)	Visits floweers of Rubus and Malvus
A. subopaca Nylander	Visits many different flowers
A. ovatula (Kirby)	Visits many different flowers
Panurgus banksianus (Kirby)	Nests in sandy ground; visits flowers of Taraxacum

HALICTIDAE - SOLITARY BEES

Halictus rubicundus (Christ)	Nests in ground, often in large colonies

WASPS/ANTS/BEES

Halictus tumulorum (L.)	Often stylopised
Lassioglossum laevigatum (Kirby)	Visits flowers of Scrophulara
L. xanthopum (Kirby)	Visits various flowers
L. albipes (Fabricius)	Visits flowers of Senecio, etc.
L. calceatum (Scopoli)	Visits flowers of Senecio and Umbelliferae
L. fratellum (Pérez)	A moorland species; visits flowers of Senecio
L. malachurus (Kirby)	Visits flowers of Trifolium
L. villosulum (Kirby)	Visits flowers of yellow Composites
L. cupromicans (Pérez)	Visits flowers of yellow Composites
L. leucopum (Kirby)	Nests in sandy ground; visits flowers
L. morio (Fabricius)	Nests in wall mortar; common in gardens
Specodes crassus Thomson	Visits various flowers

MELITTIDAE

Dasypoda altercator (Harris)	HAIRY-LEGGED MINING BEE	In sandy localities

MEGACHILIDAE

Anthidium manicatum (L.)	CARDER BEE	Nests in woodland; visits flowers of Labiates
Osmia fulviventris (Kirby)		
Megachile centuncularis (L.)	LEEF-CUTTER BEE	Nests in wood or soil; visits flowers of Rubus
M. willughbiella (Kirby)	Nests in pre-existing holes in wood, walls or soil	

ANTHOPHORIDAE

Nomada fabriciana (L.)	Kleptoparasite of Andrena spp.	Visits flowers
N. flava Panzer	Kleptoparasite of Andrena spp.	Visits flowers
N. flavoguttata (Kirby)	Kleptoparasite of Andrena spp.	Visits flowers
Nomada goodeniana (Kirby)	Kleptoparasite of Andrena spp.	Visits flowers
N. marshamella (Kirby)	Kleptoparasite of Andrena spp.	Visits flowers
N. rufipes Fabricius	Kleptoparasite of Andrena spp.	Visits flowers
Eucera longicornis (L.)	LONG-HORNED BEE	Nests in ground, often in large colonies
Anthophora plumipes (Pallas)		Nests in walls and in ground; visits Labiates

APIDAE

Bombus lucorum (L.)	SMALL EARTH BUMBLEBEE	Nests subterranean; visits various flowers
B. terrestris (L.)	BUFF-TAILED BUMBLEBEE	Nests subterranean; visits various flowers
B. lapidarius (L.)	LARGE RED-TAILED BUMBLEBEE	Nests subterranean; visits various flowers
B. jonellus (Kirby)	HEATH BUMBLEBEE	Nests subterranean; heathland
B. pratorum (L.)	EARLY BUMBLEBEE	Nests early in season in various sites; visits blossom of fruit-trees

WASPS/ANTS/BEES

Bombus hortorum (L.)	SMALL GARDEN BUMBLEBEE	Nests among tree roots and in banks
B. pascuorum (Scopoli)	COMMON CARDER BEE	Nests on surface; widespread
Psithyrus vestalis (Geoffroy)		Social parasite of B. lucorum and B. terrestris
Apis mellifera L.	HONEY BEE	Commercially maintained but wild colonies sometimes found; very common on flowers

References:

Burton, J. (1968) *The Oxford Book of Insects* O.U.P.

Chinery, M. (1973) *A Field Guide to the Insects of Britain and Northern Europe.* Collins.

Darlington, A. (1968) *Plant Galls* Blandford Press.

Davis, B.N.K. (1983) *Insects on Nettles.* Naturalists' Handbook No.1. C.U.P.

Eady, R.D. & Quinlan, J. (1963) Handbooks for the Identification of British Insects, *Hymenoptera, Cynipoidea.* Royal Entomological Society.

Kloet, G.S. and Hincks, W.D. (1975) A Check List of British Insects Vol XI Part 4 *Hymenoptera.* Royal Entomological Society.

National Trust Surveys 1982-93. (Unpublished)

Prys-Jones, O.E. & Corbet, S.A. (1987) *Bumble Bees* Naturalists' Handbook No.6. C.U.P.

Richards, O.W. (1956) Handbooks for the Identification of British Insects, *Hymenoptera.* Royal Entomological Society.

Step, E. (1932) *Bees, Wasps & Allied Insects of the British Isles.* Warne.

Willmer P. (1985) *Bees, Ants and Wasps* A Key to the genera of the British Aculeates, No. 7. Field Studies Council.

Yeo P.F. & Corbet, S.A. (1983) *Solitary Wasps* Naturalists' Handbook No.3. C.U.P.

Order: COLEOPTERA – BEETLES

This checklist covers the entirety of Exmoor National Park, and additionally, the small area of flat, coastal land that runs from Minehead in the west to Dunster Beach in the east. The latter lies immediately to the north-east of the National Park boundary and has been traditionally included by the Exmoor Natural History Society in its area of search. It includes rich habitats such as coastal marsh and sand which are very scarce in the National Park proper.

The number of beetle species listed below is 1,198 which represents a very considerable increase over the 277 species included in the previous checklist (Exmoor Natural History Society, 1988). However, I would predict that in the region of 2,000 species of beetle should occur in such an area, so clearly many more exciting discoveries remain to be made.

The majority of the records included in this checklist have previously been published in the excellent work of Duff (1994) on the beetles of Somerset. The considerable area of the National Park that lies within Devon has been neglected by comparison, but the recent survey of Watersmeet (National Trust, 1994) has added many useful records. The author also wishes to acknowledge the contributions of Heather Bristow, John Robbins and Peter Hodge to this report.

Nomenclature follows Kloet and Hincks (Pope, 1977), with recent additions and revisions following Duff (1994). The emboldened letters (e.g. **RDB, Notable, Nb.** etc.) indicate nationally rare and threatened species as defined by Hyman and Parsons (1992 and 1994). These gradings are as follows:

RDB1 - Endangered: Taxa in danger of extinction and whose survival is unlikely if causal factors continue operating.

RDB2 - Vulnerable: Taxa believed likely to move into the endangered category in the near future if the causal factors continue operation.

RDB3 - Rare: Taxa with small populations that are not at present Endangered or Vulnerable, but are at risk.

RDBI - Indeterminate: Taxa considered to be Endangered, Vulnerable or Rare, but where there is not enough information to say which of the three categories are appropriate.

RDBK - Insufficiently Known: Taxa that are suspected but not definitely known to belong to any of the above categories, because of lack of information.

Na - Notable A: Taxa which do not fall within RDB categories but which are none-the-less uncommon in Great Britain and thought to occur in 30 or fewer 10 km. squares of the National Grid, or for less well-recorded groups, in seven or fewer vice-counties.

Nb - Notable B: Taxa which do not fall within RDB categories but which are none-the-less uncommon in Great Britain and thought to occur in between 31 and 100 10 km. squares of the National Grid or, for less well-recorded groups between 8 and 20 vice-counties.

Notable - Notable: Taxa considered to be Na or Nb, but where there is not enough information to say which of the two categories is appropriate.

An asterisk (*) before the species name indicates a beetle last recorded in the Exmoor area before 1950.

David C. Boyce
Coleoptera Recorder, ENHS; Ecologist, Exmoor National Park

BEETLES

CARABIDAE - GROUND BEETLES

Cincindela campestris L.	GREEN TIGER BEETLE	Local on moorland and Coastal heath
Cychrus caraboides (L.)		Local in woodland
C. arvensis Herbst		Local on moorland
C. granulatus L.		Scarce in wet woodland, fens and bogs
C. problematicus Herbst		Common in a range of habitats
C. violaceus L.	VIOLET GROUND BEETLE	Common in a range of habitats
Leistus ferrugineus (L.)		Local in woodland
L. fulvibarbis Dejean		Local in wet woodland
L. rufescens (Fabricius)		Rare on moorland
L. spinibarbis (Fabricius)		Local in a range of habitats
Nebria brevicollis (Fabricius)		Common in a range of habitats
N. salina Fairmaire & Laboulbène		Local on moorland and coastal heath
Notiophilus aquaticus (L.)		Scarce in dry habitats
N. biguttatus (Fabricius)		Common in a range of habitats
N. palustris (Duftschmid)		Scarce in damp places
*N. rufipes Curtis		Rare in woodland
N. substriatus Waterhouse G.R.		Scarce in dry habitats
Elaphrus cupreus Duftschmid		Local on open, muddy substrates, in wetlands
E. riparius (L.)		Rare on open, muddy substrates in fens
Loricera pilicornis (Fabricius)		Common in a range of habitats
*Dyschirius luedersi Wagner		Rare in coastal marshes
D. salinus Schaum		Rare in coastal marshes
Clivina fossor (L.)		Local in a range of habitats
Broscus cephalotes (L.)		Scarce on sandy substrates on the coast
Patrobus atrorufus (Ström)		Scarce in humid woodland
Aepus marinus (Ström) **Nb**		Rare under stones on sand at around high water mark
Trechus obtusus Erichson		Common on moorland and sometimes in other habitats
T. quadristriatus (Schrank)		Common in a range of habitats
Bembidion lampros (Herbst)		Common in a range of habitats
B. punctulatum Drapiez		Scarce on shingle and gravel banks by streams and rivers
B. varium (Olivier)		Scarce on coastal marshes
B. atrocoeruleum Stephens		Rare on damp, sandy soils at the coast
B. tibiale (Duftschmid)		Common on shingle and gravel banks by streams and rivers
B. decorum (Zenker)		Scarce on shingle and gravel banks by streams and rivers
B. nitidulum (Marsham)		Rare in humid woodland
B. tetracolum Say		Common in a range of habitats
*B. laterale (Samouelle) **Nb**		Rare in salt-marshes

BEETLES

Bembidion quadrimaculatum (L.)	Rare on damp, sparsely vegetated soils
B. assimile Gyllenhal	Scarce; generally occurring in reedbeds
B. minimum (Fabricius)	Rare on sparsely vegetated, brackish soils by the coast
B. articulatum (Panzer)	Rare on banks of streams and rivers
B. obtusum Serville	Rare on open, cultivated land
B. harpaloides Serville	Common in a range of habitats
B. quinquestriatum Gyllenhal	Rare in old walls
B. aeneum Germar	Local on muddy riverbanks and in coastal marshes
B. biguttatum (Fabricius)	Scarce in coastal marshes
B. guttula (Fabricius)	Local in fens
B. lunulatum (Fourcroy)	Rare in coastal marshes
B. unicolor Chaudoir	Local in a range of habitats
Pogonus chalceus (Marsham)	Rare in salt-marshes
Stomis pumicatus (Panzer)	Rare in coastal marshes
Pterostichus aethiops (Panzer) **Nb**.	Scarce in upland woodland and on moorland
P. cupreus (L.)	Scarce in a range of habitats
P. diligens (Sturm)	Scarce in moorland bogs and fens
P. longicollis (Duftschmid) **Nb**.	Scarce in coastal marshes
P. madidus (Fabricius)	Common in a range of habitats
P. melanarius (Illiger)	Local in a range of habitats
P. niger (Schaller)	Common in woodland
P. nigrita sensu lato.	Common in a range of wet habitats
P. oblongopunctatus (Fabricius) **Nb**.	Common in ancient oak woodland
P. strenuus (Panzer)	Common in a range of habitats
P. vernalis (Panzer)	Scarce in a range of habitats
P. versicolor (Sturm)	Common in a range of open habitats
Abax parallelepipedus (Piller & Mitterpacher)	Common in woodland
Calathus erratus Sahlberg C.R.	Scarce on coastal sand
C. fuscipes (Goeze)	Local in a range of open habitats
C. melanocephalus sensu lato.	Common in a range of open habitats
*C. mollis (Marsham)	Rare on sand at the coast
C. piceus (Marsham)	Local in deciduous woodland
Synuchus nivalis (Panzer)	Rare on dry sandy soil
Olisthopus rotundatus (Paykull)	Local in a range of dry, open habitats
Agonum albipes (Fabricius)	Common in a range of habitats near water
A. assimile (Paykull)	Scarce under bark in deciduous woodland
*A. dorsale (Pontoppidan)	Rare on cultivated ground
A. fuliginosum (Panzer)	Scarce in a range of wet habitats
A. gracile Sturm	Local in fens

BEETLES

Agonum marginatum (L.)	Local on open muddy substrates in wetlands
A. muelleri (Herbst)	Scarce in a range of open habitats
A. obscurum (Herbst)	Scarce in coastal fens
A. piceum (L.)	Local in fens
A. thoreyi Dejean	Rare in coastal marshes
Amara aenea (DeGeer)	Common in a range of open habitats
A. apricaria (Paykull)	Scarce on open weedy ground
A. aulica (Panzer)	Scarce on open weedy ground
A. communis (Panzer)	Scarce in a range of habitats
A. convexiuscula (Marsham)	Rare on sandy soils at the coast
A. familiaris (Duftschmid)	Local in a range of dry open habitats
A. lucida (Duftschmid) **Nb**.	Local on sandy soil at the coast
A. lunicollis Schiödte	Common on moorland
A. ovata (Fabricius)	On open weedy ground
A. plebeja (Gyllenhal)	Scarce in a range of habitats
A. similata (Gyllenhal)	On open weedy ground
A. tibialis (Paykull)	On dry sandy soils
Harpalus rufipes (DeGeer)	Common in a range of habitats
H. rufibarbis (Fabricius)	Local in a range of open habitats
H. affinis (Schrank)	Common in dry open habitats
H. anxius (Duftschmid)	Scarce on dry sandy soils at the coast
H. attenuatus Stephens	Local on dry sandy soils at the coast
H. latus (L.)	Local in a range of open habitats
H. rubripes (Duftschmid)	Scarce on dry sandy soils at the coast
H. rufitarsis (Duftschmid)	Local in dry open habitats
H. tardus (Panzer)	Local on dry sandy soils at the coast
Dicheirotrichus gustavi Crotch	Rare in salt-marshes
Bradycellus harpalinus (Serville)	Local in a range of dry open habitats
B. ruficollis (Stephens)	Common on heather moorland
B. sharpi Joy	Rare in moss
*B. verbasci (Duftschmid)	Rare on dry sandy soils
*Stenolophus mixtus (Herbst)	Rare in coastal marshes
Acupalpus dubius Schilsky	Rare in coastal marshes
A. exiguus Dejean **Nb**.	Rare in coastal marshes
A. meridianus (L.)	Local in a range of habitats
Badister bipustulatus (Fabricius)	Rare on dry, open ground
Panagaeus bipustulatus (Fabricius) **Nb**.	Rare on sand at the coast
Oodes helopioides (Fabricius) **Nb**.	Rare in wetlands
Demetrias atricapillus (L.)	Local in a range of open habitats

BEETLES

*Dromius agilis (Fabricius)	Rare under bark
D. linearis (Olivier)	Local in a range of open habitats
D. melanocephalus Dejean	Scarce in dry grassland
D. meridionalis Dejean	Rare under bark
D. quadrimaculatus (L.)	Scarce on tree trunks and branches and under bark
D. quadrinotatus (Zenker)	Local on tree trunks and branches and under bark
Microlestes maurus (Sturm)	Scarce on dry grassland
Metabletus foveatus (Fourcroy)	Local in dry open habitats

HALIPLIDAE – WATER BEETLES

*Brychius elevatus (Panzer)	Rare in rivers and streams
Peltodytes caesus (Duftschmid) **Nb**.	Rare in coastal marshes
*Haliplus fluviatilis Aubé	Rare in coastal marshes
H. fulvus (Fabricius)	Rare in moorland pools
H. lineatocollis (Marsham)	Scarce in standing and flowing freshwater

NOTERIDAE

*Noterus clavicornis (DeGeer)	Rare in coastal marshes

DYTISCIDAE – WATER BEETLES

*Laccophilus minutus (L.)	Rare in coastal marshes
Hyphydrus ovatus (L.)	Rare in freshwater
Hygrotus inaequalis (Fabricius)	Rare in coastal marshes
Hydroporus gyllenhali Schiödte	Local in moorland pools
H. longulus Mulsant & Rey **Nb**.	Status and habitat unknown
H. nigrita (Fabricius)	Scarce in moorland pools
H. obscurus Sturm	Rare in moorland pools
H. palustris (L.)	Scarce in coastal marshes
H. pubescens (Gyllenhal)	Local in standing and flowing freshwater
H. tristis (Paykull)	Rare in moorland pools
Stictonectes lepidus (Olivier) **Nb**.	Rare in moorland pools
Oreodytes sanmarkii (Sahlberg C.R.)	Common in gravelly streams and rivers
O. davisi (Curtis)	Rare in freshwater
O. septentrionalis (Sahlberg C.R.)	Scarce in gravelly streams and rivers
Platambus maculatus (L.)	Rare in fast-flowing streams
*Agabus biguttatus (Olivier) **Nb**.	Rare in small streams and springs
Agabus bipustulatus (L.)	Scarce in standing and flowing freshwater
A. conspersus (Marsham) **Nb**.	Rare in brackish coastal ditches
A. guttatus (Paykull)	Common in streams and springs
*Colymbetes fuscus (L.)	Rare in coastal marshes
Dytiscus marginalis L. GREAT DIVING BEETLE	Rare in moorland pools
D. dimidiatus Bergstraesser	Rare in freshwater

BEETLES

GYRINDAE - WATER BEETLES, WHIRLIGIGS

Gyrinus aeratus Stephens	Status and habitat unknown
G. substriatus Stephens	Scarce in standing freshwater
Orectochilus villosus (Müller O.F.) HAIRY WHIRLIGIG	Local in streams and rivers

HYDROPHILIDAE

Helophorus aequalis Thomson C.G.	Rare in coastal marshes
H. aquaticus sensu lato.	Scarce in coastal marshes
H. brevipalpis Bedel	Common in a range of freshwater habitats
H. flavipes (Fabricius)	Common in a range of freshwater habitats
H. fulgidicollis Motschulsky **Nb**.	Rare in brackish coastal ditches
*H. griseus Herbst **Nb**.	Rare in coastal marshes
H. minutus Fabricius	Local in a range of wetland habitats
H. nubilus Fabricius	Rare in dry grassland
H. obscurus Mulsant	Rare in upland pools
Coelostoma orbiculare (Fabricius)	Local in a range of freshwater habitats
Sphaeridium lunatum Fabricius	Rare in herbivore dung
S. marginatum Fabricius	Rare in dung
S. scarabaeoides (L.)	Rare in dung
Cercyon analis (Paykull)	Local in vegetable detritus
C. atomarius (Fabricius)	Scarce in dung and vegetable detritus
C. haemorrhoidalis (Herbst)	Rare in herbivore dung
C. melanocephalus (L.)	Scarce in herbivore dung
C. pygmaeus (Illiger)	Scarce in herbivore dung
*C. tristis (Illiger) **Nb**.	Rare in coastal marshes
C. unipunctatus (L.)	Rare in compost
C. ustulatus (Preyssler) **Nb**.	Rare in coastal marshes
Megasternum obscurum (Marsham)	Common in dung and vegetable detritus
Cryptopleurum minutum sensu lato.	Scarce in dung and vegetable detritus
Hydrobius fuscipes (L.)	Local in coastal marshes
*Anacaena bipustulata (Marsham) **Nb**.	Rare in coastal marshes
A. globulus (Paykull)	Common in a range of freshwater and wetland habitats
A. limbata sensu lato	Scarce in coastal marshes
A. lutescens Stephens	Rare in upland pools
Laccobius atratus (Rottemburg) **Nb**.	Scarce in moorland streams
L. bipunctatus (Fabricius)	Common in a range of freshwater habitats
*L. striatulus (Fabricius)	Rare in coastal marshes
Helochares lividus (Forster) **Nb**.	Scarce in a range of wetland habitats
H. punctatus Sharp **Nb**.	Rare in moorland pools

BEETLES

Enochrus bicolor (Fabricius) **Nb.** — Scarce in brackish coastal marshes
E. melanocephalus (Olivier) **Nb.** — Rare in coastal marshes
E. testaceus (Fabricius) — Scarce in coastal marshes
Cymbiodyta marginella (Fabricius) — Scarce in coastal marshes
*Chaetarthria seminulum (Herbst) **Nb.** — Rare in coastal marshes
*Berosus affinis Brullé **Nb.** — Rare in coastal marshes

HISTERIDAE

Abraeus globosus (Hoffmann J.) — Local in decaying wood
Saprinus aeneus (Fabricius) — Rare in carrion
S. semistriatus (Scriba) — Scarce in carrion
Kissiter minimus (Aubé) — Rare on sandy soil at the coast
Paromalus flavicornis (Herbst) — Scarce under bark of decaying wood, in parkland
Onthophilus striatus (Forster) — Rare in dung and vegetable detritus
Hister striola Sahlberg C.R. — Rare in vegetable detritus
H. unicolor L. — Rare in dung and vegetable detritus
Paralister carbonarius (Hoffman J.) — Rare in dung and vegetable detritus
Atholus duodecimstriatus (Schrank) — Rare in dung and vegetable detritus

HYDRAENIDAE

Ochthebius bicolon Germar. **Nb.** — Rare in coastal marshes
O. dilatatus Stephens — Scarce in coastal marshes
O. exsculptus Germar **Nb.** — Rare in wet valley woodland
O. marinus (Paykull) **Nb.** — Rare in brackish coastal ditches
O. minimus (Fabricius) — Scarce in coastal marshes
Hydraena gracilis Germar — Common in gravel-bottomed streams and rivers
H. minutissima Stephens **Nb.** — Rare in gravel-bottomed streams and rivers
*H. nigrita Germar **Nb.** — Rare in gravelly streams in woodland
*H. pygmaea Waterhouse G.R. **RDB3.** — Rare in gravelly rivers
H. testacea Curtis **Nb.** — Rare in coastal marshes
Limnebius truncatellus (Thunberg) — Common in a range of freshwater and wetland habitats

PTILIIDAE

Ptenidium nitidum (Heer) — Rare in vegetable detritus
Acrotrichis atomaria (DeGeer) — Rare in vegetable detritus
A. rosskotheni Sundt — Rare in ancient valley woodland

LEPTINDAE

Leptinus testaceus Müller P.W.J. Scarce in nests of small mammals in woodland & parkland

LEIODIDAE

Leiodes polita (Marsham) — Rare in woodland

BEETLES

Anisotoma humeralis (Fabricius)	Local in decaying wood in woodland and parkland
*Agathidium rotundatum Gyllenhal	Rare in fungi on dead wood
A. seminulum (L.)	Rare under bark of decaying oak
A. varians Beck	Rare in leaf litter in woodland
Ptomaphagus subvillosus (Goeze)	Scarce in vegetable detritus
Nargus velox (Spence)	Scarce in leaf litter in woodland
Sciodrepoides watsoni (Spence)	Rare in carrion
Catops coracinus Kellner	Rare in carrion
C. fuscus (Panzer)	Rare in carrion and vegetable detritus
*C. grandicollis Erichson	Scarce in carrion and vegetable detritus
C. morio (Fabricius)	Scarce in carrion and vegetable detritus
C. nigricans (Spence)	Rare in carrion and vegetable detritus
C. tristis (Panzer)	Scarce in carrion and vegetable detritus

SILPHIDAE - BURYING and CARRION BEETLES

Nicrophorus humator (Gleditsch)	BLACK BURYING BEETLE	Local in carrion
N. investigator Zetterstedt		Rare at mercury vapour light
N. vespillo (L.)	SEXTON BEETLE	Scarce in carrion
N. vespilloides Herbst		Local in carrion
Necrodes littoralis (L.)		Rare in carrion
Thanatophilus rugosus (L.)		Rare in carrion
T. sinuatus (Fabricius)		Local in carrion
Oiceoptoma thoracicum (L.)		Local in carrion
Silpha atrata L.		Local in a range of habitats
S. laevigata Fabricius		
*S. obscura L. **RDB2**.		Rare on coastal grassland
S. tristis Illiger		Scarce on coastal grassland

SCYDMAENIDAE

*Cephennium gallicum Ganglbauer	Rare in woodland
*Neuraphes elongatulus (Müller P.W.J. & Kunze)	Rare in woodland
Stenichnus bicolor (Denny)	Rare under bark of old parkland trees
S. collaris (Müller P.W.J. & Kunze)	Local in woodland
S. poweri (Fowler) **RDBK**.	Rare on shingle beach
Scydmaenus tarsatus Müller P.W.J. & Kunze	Scarce in vegetable detritus

SCAPHIDIIDAE

Scaphidium quadrimaculatum Olivier	Local in woodland
*Scaphisoma agaricinum (L.)	Rare in rotten wood in old parkland
S. boleti (Panzer) **Nb**.	Local in rotten wood

BEETLES

STAPHYLINIDAE - ROVE BEETLES

Micropeplus fulvus Erichson	Rare in vegetable detritus
Metopsia retusa (Stephens)	Rare in vegetable detritus
Megarthrus affinis Miller	Rare in vegetable detritus
M. depressus (Paykull)	Scarce in dung and vegetable detritus
M. sinuatocollis (Boisduval & Lacordaire)	Scarce in vegetable detritus
Proteinus brachypterus (Fabricius)	Local in woodland
P. ovalis Stephens	Rare in grassland
Olophrum piceum (Gyllenhal)	Local in woodland and moorland
Lesteva heeri Fauvel	Scarce in various wetland habitats
L. longoelytrata (Goeze)	Local on stream banks in woodland
*Lesteva pubescens Mannerheim	Scarce on stream banks in woodland
Lesteva punctata Erichson	Scarce on stream banks
Eusphalerum luteum (Marsham)	Scarce in woodland and wetland habitats
E. minutum (Fabricius)	Rare in woodland
E. sorbi (Gyllenhal)	Rare in woodland
E. torquatum (Marsham)	Rare in woodland
Acrulia inflata (Gyllenhal)	Rare in old parkland
Phyllodrepa floralis (Paykull)	Rare in woodland
Omalium caesum Gravenhorst	Rare in vegetable detritus
*O. excavatum Stephens	Rare in vegetable detritus
*O. laeviusculum Gyllenhal	Scarce under strandline litter on the coast
O. oxyacanthae Gravenhorst	Rare in vegetable detritus
O. rivulare (Paykull)	Rare in vegetable detritus, carrion, etc.
Phloeonomus punctipennis Thomson C.G.	Scarce under bark in woodland
*Phloeostiba plana (Paykull)	Rare under sappy bark
*Micralymma marina (Ström)	Rare in intertidal rock crevices
Philorinum sordidum (Stephens)	Local on gorse flowers
Siagonium quadricorne Kirby	Scarce under bark
Phloeocharis subtilissima Mannerheim	Rare in old woodland
Pseudopsis sulcata Newman **Notable**	Rare in vegetable detritus
Deleaster dichrous (Gravenhorst) **Nb.**	Rare at mercury-vapour light
Bledius limicola Tottenham	Rare in brackish mud
B. unicornis (Germar)	Local on the coast
*Ochthephilus aureus (Fauvel)	Rare on banks of streams and rivers
Carpelimus corticinus (Gravenhorst)	Rare in coastal marshes
*C. pusillus (Gravenhorst)	Rare in coastal marshes
Platystethus arenarius (Fourcroy)	Scarce in vegetable detritus and dung
P. cornutus (Gravenhorst)	Rare in wetlands

BEETLES

Platystethus nitens (Sahlberg C.R.)	Rare in coastal marshes
Anotylus complanatus (Erichson)	Scarce in vegetable detritus
A. inustus (Gravenhorst)	Rare in vegetable detritus and dung
A. rugosus (Fabricius)	Local in a range of habitats
A. sculpturatus (Gravenhorst)	Local in a range of habitats
A. tetracarinatus (Block)	Local in a range of habitats
Oxytelus laqueatus (Marsham)	Scarce in herbivore dung
*O. sculptus Gravenhorst	Rare in coastal marshes
*Stenus aceris Stephens	Rare in woodland/heathland
S. bimaculatus Gyllenhal	Rare in wetlands
S. brunnipes Stephens	Scarce in a range of dry habitats
S. canescens Rosenhauer **Nb**.	Rare in coastal marshes
S. clavicornis (Scopoli)	Rare in open country
*S. exiguus Erichson **Nb**.	Rare under stones
Stenus flavipes Stephens	Rare in wetlands
*Stenus fuscipes Gravenhorst	Rare in coastal marshes
S. geniculatus Gravenhorst	Scarce on moorland
S. guttula Müller P.W.J.	Local on stream and river banks
S. guynemeri Jacquelin du Val	Local on stream banks in woodland
S. impressus Germar	Local in a range of habitats
*S. juno (Paykull)	Rare in wetlands
Stenus latifrons Erichson	Rare in wetlands
*S. lustrator Erichson	Rare in valley fen
*S. nanus Stephens	Rare in coastal marshes
S. nigritulus Gyllenhal **Nb**.	Rare in wetlands
S. nitidiusculus Stephens	Local in a range of wetland habitats
S. ossium Stephens	Rare in coastal marshes
S. pallipes Gravenhorst	Local in a range of wetland habitats
S. pallitarsis Stephens	Scarce in coastal marshes
S. picipes Stephens	Rare in wetlands
*S. rogeri Kraatz	Rare in valley fen
S. similis (Herbst)	Local in wetlands
S. tarsalis Ljungh	Rare in wetlands
Dianous coerulescens (Gyllenhal)	Common in stream banks
*Euaesthetus bipunctatus (Ljungh)	Rare in nests of ants
Paederus littoralis Gravenhorst	Common in a range of open habitats
P. riparius (L.)	Rare in coastal marshes
Lathrobium brunnipes (Fabricius)	Local in a range of habitats
L. fulvipenne (Gravenhorst)	Rare in woodland

BEETLES

*Lathrobium quadratum (Paykull)	Rare in wetlands
L. terminatum Gravenhorst	Rare in upland bogs
*Medon brunneus (Erichson)	Local in woodland and parkland leaf litter
*M. piceus (Kraatz) **RDBI**	Rare in woodland leaf litter
*Sunius melanocephalus (Fabricius) **Notable**.	Rare in moss
Lithocharis ochracea (Gravenhorst)	Rare in vegetable detritus
Astenus lyonessius (Joy)	Rare in vegetable detritus
A. pulchellus (Heer)	Rare in vegetable detritus
*Rugilus erichsoni (Fauvel)	Rare in vegetable detritus
R. orbiculatus (Paykull)	Scarce in vegetable detritus
*R. rufipes Germar	Rare in vegetable detritus
Othius angustus Stephens	Status and habitat unknown
O. laeviusculus Stephens	Scarce in a range of habitats
O. myrmecophilus Kiesenwetter	Rare in woodland
O. punctulatus (Goeze)	Scarce in woodland
Atrecus affinis (Paykull)	Local under bark in woodland
Leptacinus batychrus (Gyllenhal)	Rare in vegetable detritus
*Gauropterus fulgidus (Fabricius)	Rare in compost
Gyrohypnus angustatus Stephens	Rare in vegetable detritus
*G. atratus (Heer) **Nb**.	Rare in nests of the red wood ant
G. fracticornis sensu lato.	Rare. Habitat unknown
Xantholinus glabratus (Gravenhorst)	Rare in grassland
X. linearis (Olivier)	Scarce in open country
X. longiventris Heer	Local in a range of habitats
Erichsonius signaticornis (Mulsant & Rey) **Nb**.	Rare in coastal marshes
*Philonthus addendus Sharp	Rare in woodland
*P. albipes (Gravenhorst)	Rare in dung and compost
P. cephalotes (Gravenhorst)	Rare in vegetable detritus
P. cognatus Stephens	Local in a range of habitats
*P. cruentatus (Gmelin)	Rare under stones and in moss
P. decorus (Gravenhorst)	Scarce in a range of habitats
P. fimetarius (Gravenhorst)	Scarce in a range of habitats
*P. intermedius (Boisduval & Lacordaire)	Rare in vegetable detritus and dung
*P. laminatus (Creutzer)	Rare in vegetable detritus and dung
*P. longicornis Stephens	Rare in grassland
P. marginatus (Ström)	Local in a range of habitats
*P. micans (Gravenhorst)	Rare in coastal marshes
P. politus (L.)	Scarce in a range of habitats
P. puella von Nordmann	Rare in woodland

BEETLES

Philonthus quisquiliaris (Gyllenhal)	Scarce in coastal marshes
P. rectangulus Sharp	Rare in vegetable detritus
P. rubripennis Stephens **Nb**.	Rare on gravelly river bank
P. splendens (Fabricius)	Local in a range of habitats
P. succicola Thomson C.G.	Rare in rotten fungi in woodland
P. varians (Paykull)	Local in a range of habitats
P. varius (Gyllenhal)	Local in a range of habitats
P. ventralis (Gravenhorst)	Scarce in vegetable detritus
Gabrius nigritulus (Gravenhorst)	Local in vegetable detritus
*G. pennatus Sharp	Rare in wetlands
G. splendidulus (Gravenhorst)	Local under bark in woodland and parkland
*Cafius fucicola Curtis	Rare in strandline litter at the coast
*C. xantholoma (Gravenhorst)	Scarce in strandline litter at the coast
Platydracus fulvipes (Scopoli) **Nb**.	Rare on moorland
Staphylinus dimidiaticornis Gemminger	Rare on coastal grassland
S. olens Müller O.F. DEVIL'S COACH HORSE	Open sites in woods and gardens
S. erythropterus L.	Common on moorland
*Ocypus ater (Gravenhorst)	Local in a range of coastal habitats
*O. brunnipes (Fabricius)	Local in grassland
O. fortunatarum (Wollaston) **Nb**.	Rare on coastal grassland
O. melanarius (Heer)	Scarce in grassland
O. morsitans (Rossi)	Local in a range of habitats
*O. nero (Faldermann) **Na**.	Rare in woodland
Creophilus maxillosus (L.)	Rare in carrion
Ontholestes murinus (L.)	Scarce in dung and carrion
*O. tessellatus (Fourcroy)	Rare in dung and carrion
Heterothops dissimilis sensu lato	Rare in vegetable detritus
*Quedius aridulus Jansson	Rare on dry sandy soils at the coast
Q. auricomus Kiesenwetter **Nb**.	On stream banks in woodland
*Q. boops (Gravenhorst)	Rare on gravelly river banks
*Q. brevicornis (Thomson C.G.) **Nb**.	Rare in bird nests
Q. cinctus (Paykull)	Rare in vegetable detritus
Q. cruentus (Olivier)	Local in vegetable detritus
*Q. fuliginosus (Gravenhorst)	Rare in wetlands
Q. invreae Gridelli **Nb**.	Rare in mammal nests
*Q. maurorufus (Gravenhorst)	Rare in wetlands
Q. maurus (Sahlberg C.R.)	Rare under bark
Q. mesomelinus (Marsham)	Rare in vegetable detritus
*Q. microps Gravenhorst J.L.C. **Nb**.	Rare in dead wood in old parkland

BEETLES

Quedius nemoralis Baudi	Rare in dead wood in woodland
Q. nigriceps Kraatz	Rare. Habitat unknown
Q. nitipennis (Stephens)	Scarce on stream banks in woodland
Q. pallipes Lucas	Rare in strandline litter
Q. picipes (Mannerheim)	Scarce in a range of habitats
Q. riparius Kellner **RDBK**	Rare on banks of small streams
*Q. semiaeneus (Stephens)	Rare in coastal marshes
Q. tristis (Gravenhorst)	Scarce in open country
Q. umbrinus Erichson	Local, on stream banks in woodland
Q. xanthopus Erichson **Nb**.	Local under bark in old woodland and parkland
Habrocerus capillaricornis (Gravenhorst)	Scarce in woodland
Mycetoporus angularis Mulsant & Rey	Rare. Habitat unknown
*M. splendidus (Gravenhorst)	Rare in litter
Lordithon lunulatus (L.)	Scarce in fungi in woodland
L. thoracicus (Fabricius)	Rare in fungi in woodland
L. trinotatus (Erichson)	Rare in fungi in woodland
Bolitobius analis (Fabricius)	Rare in grass tussocks
*B. cingulatus (Mannerheim)	Rare in moss
Sepedophilus littoreus (L.)	Status and habitat unknown
S. lusitanicus Hammond	Rare in dead wood in conifer woodland
Tachyporus chrysomelinus sensu lato	Common in a range of habitats
T. formosus Matthews A.H. **Na**.	Rare in litter
T. hypnorum (Fabricius)	Common in a range of habitats
T. nitidulus (Fabricius)	Local in a range of habitats
T. obtusus (L.)	Rare. Habitat unknown
T. pallidus Sharp	Rare in coastal marshes
T. solutus Erichson	Local in a range of habitats
Tachinus humeralis Gravenhorst	Scarce in woodland
T. laticollis Gravenhorst	Rare in vegetable detritus
T. marginellus (Fabricius)	Rare in vegetable detritus
T. signatus Gravenhorst	Scarce in vegetable detritus
T. subterraneus (L.)	Rare in decaying fungi and carrion
Cilea silphoides (L.)	Rare in compost heaps
Cypha longicornis (Paykull)	Local in vegetable detritus
Oligota apicata Erichson **Notable**.	Rare in woodland
*Myllaena brevicornis (Matthews A.H.)	Scarce in a range of wet habitats
*M. elongata (Matthews A.H.) **Notable**.	Rare in wetlands
M. infuscata Kraatz	Rare in upland bogs
*M. minuta (Gravenhorst)	Rare in valley fen

BEETLES

*Diglotta submarina (Fairmaire & Laboulbène) **Notable**.	Rare on coastal sand
Gyrophaena affinis Mannerheim.	Rare in bracket fungi in woodland
G. angustata (Stephens)	Rare in bracket fungi in woodland
G. fasciata (Marsham)	Rare in bracket fungi in woodland
G. gentilis Erichson	Rare in bracket fungi in woodland
Homalota plana (Gyllenhal)	Rare under bark
Leptusa fumida Kraatz	Local under bark
*L. pulchella (Mannerheim)	Rare under bark
*L. ruficollis (Erichson)	Rare under bark
Bolitochara bella Märkel	Scarce on fungi in woodland and parkland
*B. lucida (Gravenhorst)	Rare on fungi in old parkland
B. mulsanti Sharp **Nb**.	Rare on bracket fungi in woodland
Autalia impressa sensu lato	Rare in decaying fungi
A. longicornis Scheerpeltz	Rare in decaying fungi
A. rivularis (Gravenhorst)	Scarce in vegetable detritus
Falagria caesa Erichson	Rare in vegetable detritus
Myrmecopora uvida (Erichson)	Rare in strandline litter
*Gnypeta caerulea (Sahlberg C.R.) **Notable**.	Scarce in flood litter
G. rubrior Tottenham	Rare on muddy river banks
*Callicerus obscurus Gravenhorst	Rare in flood litter
*Hydrosmecta eximia (Sharp)	Rare on river shingle
*Aloconota cambrica (Wollaston)	Rare in flood litter
*Aloconota currax (Kraatz)	Rare in flood litter
A. gregaria (Erichson)	Rare in wetlands
*A. sulcifrons (Stephens)	Scarce on river shingle and in flood litter
Amischa analis (Gravenhorst)	Common in a range of habitats
*A. cavifrons (Sharp)	Rare in moss
A. decipiens (Sharp)	Scarce in woodland
A. forcipata Mulsant & Rey	Rare in flood litter
*Nehemitropia sordida (Marsham)	Rare in vegetable refuse
Notothecta flavipes (Gravenhorst)	Rare in nests of the red wood ant
*Lyprocorrhe anceps (Erichson)	Rare in nests of the red wood ant
*Geostiba circellaris (Gravenhorst)	Local in moss
*Dinaraea angustula (Gyllenhal)	Rare in leaf litter
*Liogluta longiuscula (Gravenhorst)	Scarce in wet litter
L. microptera Thomson C.G.	On banks of streams and rivers in woodland
*Atheta elongatula (Gravenhorst)	Scarce in litter
*A. luridipennis (Mannerheim)	Rare in flood litter
*A. melanocera (Thomson C.G.)	Rare in flood litter

BEETLES

A. divisa (Märkel)	Rare in rotting fungi in woodland
*A. liturata (Stephens)	Rare in fungi in woodland
*A. trinotata (Kraatz)	Rare in vegetable detritus
A. melanaria (Mannerheim)	Rare in vegetable detritus and dung
A. amplicollis (Mulsant & Rey)	Rare in vegetable detritus
A. fungi sensu lato	Common in vegetable detritus
*A. orbata (Erichson)	Rare in wet litter
*A. subsinuata (Erichson)	Rare in vegetable detritus
A. nigra (Kraatz)	Rare in vegetable detritus
*A. aquatica (Thomson C.G.)	Rare in vegetable detritus
*A. hypnorum (Kiesenwetter)	Scarce in litter in woodland
A. pertyi (Heer)	Rare in rotting fungi
*A. xanthopus (Thompson C.G.)	Rare in moss
A. crassicornis (Fabricius)	Rare in rotting fungi
A. laticollis (Stephens)	Rare in vegetable detritus
A. ravilla (Erichson)	Rare in rotting fungi
A. atramentaria (Gyllenhal)	Local in vegetable detritus and dung
A. longicornis (Gravenhorst)	Local in vegetable detritus
A. vestita (Gravenhorst)	Scarce in strandline litter
*Thamiaraea cinnamomea (Gravenhorst)	Rare at sap runs on trees
Drusilla canaliculata (Fabricius)	Local in coastal grassland
*Zyras funestus (Gravenhorst)	Rare in ant nests
Lomechusa emarginata (Paykull) **Notable**.	Local in ant nests on coastal heath
Dinarda maerkeli Kiesenwetter	Rare in nests of the red wood ant
*Phloeopora testacea (Mannerheim)	Rare under bark
Ilyobates nigricollis sensu lato	Rare. Habitat unknown
*Ocalea picata (Stephens)	Scarce in woodland
*O. rivularis sensu lato	Rare. Habitat unknown
*Meotica exilis (Erichson)	Rare on banks of streams
*Oxypoda alternans (Gravenhorst)	Rare in rotting fungi
*O. annularis Mannerheim	Rare in vegetable detritus
O. elongatula Aubé	Scarce in a range of wetland habitats
*O. haemorrhoa (Mannerheim)	Rare in nests of the red wood ant
O. opaca (Gravenhorst)	Rare in vegetable detritus
*O. spectabilis Märkel	Rare in mole nests
O. umbrata (Gyllenhal)	Rare in vegetable detritus
*Ischnoglossa prolixa (Gravenhorst)	Scarce under bark
Aleochara bilineata Gyllenhal	Rare in vegetable detritus
A. bipustulata sensu lato	Scarce in dung

BEETLES

*Aleochara cuniculorum Kraatz — Rare in rabbit burrows
*A. curtula (Goeze) — Scarce in carrion
*A. grisea Kraatz — Rare in strandline litter
*A. intricata Mannerheim. — Rare in vegetable detritus
*A. maculata Brisout **RDB2**. — Rare in old valley woodland

PSELAPHIDAE
*Euplectus fauveli Guillebeau **Notable**. — Rare in dead wood
*E. sanguineus Denny — Rare in vegetable detritus
E. signatus (Reichenbach) — Rare in vegetable detritus
*Trichonyx sulcicollis (Reichenbach) **RDB2**. — Rare under oak bark in old parkland
*Bythinus burrellii (Denny) — Rare in moss
Bryaxis curtisii (Leach) — Rare in coastal marshes
*B. puncticollis (Denny) — Scarce in woodland
Tychus niger (Paykull) — Local in a range of habitats
Brachygluta haematica (Reichenbach) — Rare in wet woodland
B. helferi (Schmidt-Gobel) — Rare in salt-marshes
B. simplex (Waterhouse G.R.) **Notable**. — Scarce in salt-marshes
*Reichenbachia juncorum (Leach) — Rare in wetlands
*Pselaphus heisei (Herbst) — Rare in wetlands
Claviger testaceus Preyssler **Notable**. — Local in coastal grassland with ants

LUCANIDAE - STAG BEETLES
Lucanus cervus (L.) **Nb**.   STAG BEETLE   Scarce in rotten wood in old woodlands
Dorcus parallelopipedus (L.)   LESSER STAG BEETLE   Common in rotten wood
Sinodendron cylindricum (L.) — Common in rotten wood

TROGIDAE
Trox scaber (L.) — Rare in bird nests

GEOTRUPIDAE
Typhaeus typhoeus (L.)   MINOTAUR BEETLE   Common on moorland & coastal heath
*Geotrupes mutator (Marsham) **Nb**. — Rare in dung
G. spiniger (Marsham) — Scarce in dung
G. stercorarius (L.)   DOR BEETLE   Common in dung
G. stercorosus (Scriba) — Common in dung
G. vernalis (L.) **Nb**. — Local in dung on dry heathland

SCARABAEIDAE - DUNG BEETLES, SCARABS & CHAFERS
Aegialia arenaria (Fabricius) — Rare on sandy soils at the coast
Aphodius ater (DeGeer) — Local on dung in open country
A. coenosus (Panzer) **Nb**. — Local in dung on dry heathland
A. contaminatus (Herbst) — Rare in dung
A. depressus (Kugelann) — Scarce in dung

BEETLES

Aphodius equestris (Panzer)	Local on dung in woodland
*A. erraticus (L.)	Rare in dung
A. fimetarius (L.)	Local in dung
A. foetidus (Herbst)	Rare in dung
A. fossor (L.)	Scarce in dung and at mercury-vapour light
A. granarius (L.)	Scarce in dung
A. haemorrhoidalis (L.)	Rare in dung
A. ictericus (Laicharting)	Rare in vegetable detritus
*A. luridus (Fabricius)	Rare in dung
*A. merdarius (Fabricius)	Rare in dung
*A. obliteratus Panzer	Rare in dung
A. plagiatus (L.) **Nb**.	Rare in coastal marshes
*A. prodromus (Brahm)	Rare in dung and vegetable detritus
A. pusillus (Herbst)	Scarce in dung
A. rufipes (L.)	Scarce in dung and at light
A. sphacelatus (Panzer)	Scarce in dung
Onthophagus coenobita (Herbst)	Local in dung
*O. joannae Goljan	Rare in dung
*O. nuchicornis sensu lato	Scarce in dung
O. similis (Scriba)	Common in dung on dry sandy soils
*O. vacca (L.) **Nb**.	Rare on grassland in dung
*Hoplia philanthus (Fuessly)	Rare. Habitat unknown
Serica brunnea (L.)	Rare at mercury-vapour light
Amphimallon solstitialis (L.) SUMMER CHAFER	Scarce. Habitat unknown
Melolontha melolontha (L.) COCKCHAFER or MAYBUG	Local on shrubs and trees and at light
Phyllopertha horticola (L.) GARDEN CHAFER	Common on grassland and moorland
Cetonia aurata (L.) ROSE CHAFER	Rare on coastal slopes

DASCILLIDAE

Dascillus cervinus (L.)	Scarce on grassland

CLAMBIDAE

Calyptomerus dubius (Marsham)	Rare in vegetable detritus
*Clambus pubescens Redtenbacher	Rare in vegetable detritus

SCIRTIDAE

Elodes marginata (Fabricius)	Common in a range of habitats
E. minuta sensu lato	Local in a range of habitats
Microcara testacea (L.)	Rare in valley fens
Cyphon coarctatus Paykull	Status and habitat unknown
C. hilaris Nyholm	Rare in valley fens

BEETLES

Cyphon palustris Thomson C.G.	Rare. Habitat unknown
C. variabilis sensu lato	Scarce in coastal marshes
Prionocyphon serricornis (Müller P.W.J.) **Nb**.	Scarce in rotholes in old parkland beeches
Hydrocyphon deflexicollis (Müller P.W.J.) **Nb**.	Rare on river banks
Scirtes hemisphaericus (L.)	Local in coastal marshes

BYRRHIDAE - PILL BEETLES

Simplocaria semistriata (Fabricius)	Scarce in a range of habitats
Cytilus sericeus (Forster)	Common in a range of habitats
*Byrrhus fasciatus (Forster)	Rare in coastal heathland
*B. pilula (L.)	Rare. Habitat unknown
B. pustulatus (Forster)	Scarce in a range of habitats

HETEROCERIDAE

Heterocerus fenestratus (Thunberg)	Rare in coastal marshes
*H. flexuosus Stephens	Rare in salt-marshes
*H. fossor Kiesenwetter	Rare in coastal marshes

DRYOPIDAE

*Dryops auriculatus (Fourcroy) **Nb**.	Rare in coastal marshes
*D. ernesti des Gozis	Rare in coastal marshes
D. luridus (Erichson)	Scarce in coastal marshes

ELMIDAE

Elmis aenea (Müller P.W.J.)	Common in fast-flowing streams and rivers
Esolus parallelopipedus (Müller P.W.J.)	Common in fast-flowing streams and rivers
Limnius volckmari (Panzer)	Local in fast-flowing streams and rivers
Oulimnius troglodytes (Gyllenhal)	Rare in freshwater
O. tuberculatus (Müller P.W.J.)	Common in freshwater

ELATERIDAE - CLICK BEETLES

Agrypnus murinus (L.)		Local on coastal grassland
*Ampedus balteatus (L.)		Rare in rotten birch
*Ischnodes sanguinicollis (Panzer) **Na**.		Rare in dead wood in old woodland
Fleutiauxellus quadripustulatus (Fabricius) **Na**.		Rare on stream banks in woodland
Melanotus villosus (Geoffroy)		Common in dead wood
Kibunea minuta (L.)		Common in a range of habitats
Athous bicolor (Goeze)		Local in a range of habitats
A. haemorrhoidalis (Fabricius)	RED-BROWN SKIPJACK	Common in a range of habitats
A. hirtus (Herbst)		Rare in woodland
A. vittatus (Fabricius)		Rare in old woodland

BEETLES

Ctenicera cuprea (Fabricius)		Local on moorland
C. pectinicornis (L.) **Nb**.		Local on moorland
Actenicerus sjaelandicus (Müller O.F.)		Rare on wet moorland
Selatosomus aeneus (L.)		Common on moorland and coastal heath
*S. bipustulatus (L.) **Nb**.		In dead wood in old parkland
S. incanus (Gyllenhal)		Rare in wetlands
Prosternon tessellatum (L.)		
*Agriotes acuminatus (Stephens)		Rare in woodland
A. lineatus (L.)	Larvae known as WIREWORMS	Local in open habitats on the coast
A. obscurus (L.)		Scarce in a range of open habitats
A. pallidulus (Illiger)		Common in a range of habitats
*A. sordidus (Illiger) **RDB3**.		Rare in strandline litter
A. sputator (L.)		Local in a range of open habitats
Dalopius marginatus (L.)	BORDERED SKIPJACK	Local in woodland
*Adrastus pallens (Fabricius)		Rare in woodland
Denticollis linearis (L.)		Local in rotten wood

THROSCIDAE

Trixagus dermestoides (L.)		Rare in woodland

CANTHARIDAE - SOLDIER and SAILOR BEETLES

Podabrus alpinus (Paykull)		Rare. At mercury-vapour light
Cantharis cryptica Ashe	COMMON SOLDIER	Local in a range of habitats
C. decipiens Baudi		Common in a range of habitats
C. fusca L. **RDB3**.	DARK SAILOR	Local in a range of wetland habitats
C. lateralis L.		Scarce in coastal marshes
C. livida L.		Scarce in woodland
C. nigra (DeGeer)		Common in a range of habitats
*C. nigricans (Müller O.F.)	GREY SAILOR	Rare in woodlands
Cantharis pallida Goeze	PALE SOLDIER	Rare in old woodland
C. pellucida Fabricius	WOOD SAILOR	Scarce in old woodland
*C. rufa L.		Rare. Habitat unknown
C. rustica Fallén	RUSTIC SAILOR	Common in a range of habitats
Rhagonycha femoralis (Brullé)		Rare. Habitat unknown
R. fulva (Scopoli)	THE 'BLOODSUCKER'	Common in a range of habitats
R. lignosa (Müller O.F.)		Common in a range of habitats
R. testacea (L.)		
Malthinus flaveolus (Herbst)	YELLOW-TIPPED MALTHENE	Scarce in woodland
M. balteatus Suffrian **Nb**.		Status and habitat unknown
M. seriepunctatus Kiesenwetter		Common in woodland
Malthodes flavoguttatus Kiesenwetter		Rare in wet woodland

BEETLES

Malthodes fuscus (Waltl)	Scarce in woodland
M. guttifer Kiesenwetter **Nb**.	Status and habitat unknown
M. marginatus (Latreille)	Common in woodland
M. minimus (L.)	Rare in woodland
*M. mysticus Kiesenwetter	Rare in woodland
*M. pumilus (Brébisson)	Rare. Habitat unknown

LAMPYRIDAE
Lampyris noctiluca (L.)   GLOW-WORM   Common in a range of habitats

DERMESTIDAE - SKIN BEETLES

Dermestes murinus L.	Rare in carrion
Attagenus pellio (L.)	Rare. Found in houses and outdoors
Ctesias serra (Fabricius) **Nb**.	Local in spider webs on bark of old parkland trees
Anthrenus fuscus Olivier	Rare. Habitat not known
A. verbasci (L.) VARIED CARPET BEETLE	Scarce in houses

ANOBIIDAE - WOOD-BORING BEETLES

Ptinomorphus imperialis (L.) **Nb**.	Rare in dead wood
Grynobius planus (Fabricius)	Local in dead wood
Dryophilus pusillus (Gyllenhal)	Rare, on larch (Larix)
Ochina ptinoides (Marsham)	Scarce in dead ivy branches (Hedera)
Xestobium rufovillosum (DeGeer) DEATH-WATCH	Local in dead wood and in old buildings
Ernobius mollis (L.)	Local in dead wood and in old buildings
Hemicoelus fulvicornis (Sturm)	Rare in dead wood
Anobium punctatum (DeGeer) FURNITURE BEETLE	Rare in dead wood and in old buildings
Ptilinus pectinicornis (L.)	Rare in dead wood
Dorcatoma flavicornis (Fabricius) **Nb**.	Rare in dead wood

PTINIDAE
Ptinus fur (L.) SPIDER BEETLE	Rare. Habitat may be indoors or out
P. subpilosus Sturm **Nb**.	Rare under bark in old oak tree (Quercus)

PHLOIOPHILIDAE
Phloiophilus edwardsi Stephens **Nb**.   On fungi in woodland

PELTIDAE
Thymalus limbatus (Fabricius) **Nb**.   Scarce in dead wood in old woodland and parkland

CLERIDAE
Thanasimus formicarius (L.)	Scarce in dead wood
Necrobia violacea (L.)	Rare in carrion on the coast

MELYRIDAE
Dasytes aeratus Stephens	Scarce in woodland
Malachius bipustulatus (L.) RED-TIPPED FLOWER BEETLE	Local in a range of habitats
M. viridis Fabricius	Rare. Habitat unknown

BEETLES

NITIDULIDAE - SAP BEETLES

Kateretes rufilabris (Latreille)	Common in a range of wet habitats
Brachypterus glaber (Stephens)	Local, on stinging nettle (Urtica dioica)
B. urticae (Fabricius)	Scarce on stinging nettle (U. dioica)
Brachypterolus pulicarius sensu lato	Rare on toadflax (Linaria)
Carpophilus hemipterus (L.)	Rare in food stores
C. marginellus Motschulsky	Rare in food stores
Pria dulcamarae (Scopoli)	Rare on bittersweet (Solanum dulcamara)
Meligethes aeneus (Fabricius)	Local on a range of flowering plants
*M. atratus (Olivier)	Local on a range of flowering plants
M. brunnicornis Sturm	Scarce on flowers of hedge woundwort (Stachys sylvatica)
M. flavimanus Stephens	
M. obscurus Erichson	Local on flowers of wood sage (Teucrium scorodonia) etc.
M. ovatus Sturm	Local on a range of flowering plants
M. planiusculus (Heer)	Rare on flowers of viper's bugloss (Echium vulgare)
M. viridescens (Fabricius)	Scarce on a range of flowering plants
Epuraea aestiva (L.)	Local on trees and shrubs
E. deleta Sturm	Rare in woodland
E. florea Erichson	Scarce. On flowers of hawthorn (Crataegus)
*E. longula Erichson **Notable**.	In parkland and woodland
E. melanocephala (Marsham)	Local in woodland
E. melina Erichson	Rare in woodland
E. pusilla (Illiger)	Rare in fungi
*E. unicolor (Olivier)	Rare in woodland
Nitidula rufipes (L.)	Rare in carrion
Omosita colon (L.)	Scarce in carrion
O. depressa (L.)	Rare in carrion
O. discoidea (Fabricius)	Scarce in carrion
*Soronia grisea (L.)	Rare in vegetable detritus
S. punctatissima (Illiger)	In sappy old oak trees
Pocadius ferrugineus sensu lato	In decaying fungi
Cychramus luteus (Fabricius)	Rare in woodland
Glischrochilus quadriguttatus (Fabricius)	Scarce in dead wood under bark

RHYZOPHAGIDAE

Rhyzophagus bipustulatus (Fabricius)	Scarce under tree bark
R. dispar (Paykull)	Local under tree bark
R. ferrugineus (Paykull)	Scarce under tree bark
R. perforatus Erichson	Rare under tree bark
*Monotoma angusticollis Gyllenhal **RDB3**.	Rare in nests of the red wood ant

BEETLES

Monotoma bicolor Villa	Rare in vegetable detritus
*M. conicicollis Aubé	Rare in nests of the red wood ant
M. longicollis Gyllenhal	Rare in vegetable detritus
M. picipes Herbst	Rare in vegetable detritus

SPHINDIDAE

Aspidiphorus orbiculatus (Gyllenhal)	Rare in fungi

CUCUJIDAE

Pediacus dermestoides (Fabricius)	Scarce under bark of old trees in parkland

CRYPTOPHAGIDAE

Telmatophilus caricis (Olivier)	Scarce in coastal marshes
T. typhae (Fallén)	Rare in coastal marshes
*Henoticus serratus (Gyllenhal)	Rare in coastal marshes
*Cryptophagus dentatus (Herbst)	Rare. Habitat unknown
C. distinguendus Sturm	Rare, in small mammal nests
C. lycoperdi (Scopoli)	Local in earth-ball fungi
C. pilosus Gyllenhal	Rare in haystack refuse
*C. ruficornis Stephens **Notable**.	In cramp-ball fungi *(Daldinia)* on dead wood
C. scanicus (L.)	Rare in vegetable detritus
Micrambe villosus (Heer)	Rare in gorse flowers
M. vini (Panzer)	Scarce in gorse flowers
Antherophagus nigricornis (Fabricius)	Scarce. Thought to be associated with humble bees
A. pallens (L.)	Scarce. Thought to be associated with humble bees
*Atomaria atricapilla Stephens	Scarce in vegetable detritus
*A. gutta Stephens	Rare in coastal marshes
A. pusilla (Paykull)	Rare in vegetable detritus
A. rubida Reitter	Rare in dung
A. linearis Stephens	Scarce in haystack refuse
Ootypus globosus (Waltl)	Rare in dung
Ephistemus globulus (Paykull)	Rare in vegetable detritus

BIPHYLLIDAE

Biphyllus lunatus (Fabricius)	Local in cramp-ball fungi *(Daldinia)* on dead wood

BYTURIDAE

Byturus tomentosus (DeGeer) RASPBERRY BEETLE	Local on bramble & raspberry flowers

EROTYLIDAE

Triplax aenea (Schaller)	Rare in fungi on dead wood
Dacne bipustulata (Thunberg)	Rare in fungi on dead wood and amongst lichens
D. rufifrons (Fabricius)	Rare in fungi on dead wood

PHALACRIDAE

*Phalacrus brunnipes Brisout	Rare on smutted sedges

BEETLES

Phalacrus corruscus (Panzer)	Local on smutted grasses
Olibrus aeneus (Fabricius)	Rare on flowering composites
O. corticalis (Panzer)	Local on flowering composites
O. liquidus Erichson	Rare on flowering composites
*O. pygmaeus (Sturm) **Nb**.	Rare on flowering composites
Stilbus oblongus (Erichson)	Rare on coastal marshes

CERYLONIDAE

Anommatus duodecimstriatus (Müller P.W.J.) **Na**.	Rare in vegetable detritus
Cerylon fagi Brisout **Nb**.	Rare in dead wood in old woodland
C. ferrugineum Stephens	Common under bark
C. histeroides (Fabricius)	Local under bark

COCCINELLIDAE - LADYBIRD BEETLES

Subcoccinella vigintiquattuorpunctata (L.) 24-SPOT LADYBIRD Local in a range of habitats
Coccidula rufa (Herbst) Local in coastal marshes
*C. scutellata (Herbst) Rare in coastal marshes
Rhyzobius litura (Fabricius) Common in a range of habitats
Scymnus frontalis (Fabricius) Rare. Habitat unknown
S. auritus Thunberg. Rare. Habitat unknown
*S. limbatus Stephens **Nb**. Rare in coastal marshes
Chilocorus bipustulatus (L.) HEATHER LADYBIRD Rare on coastal heaths
C. renipustulatus (Scriba) KIDYEY-SPOT LADYBIRD Rare. Habitat unknown
Exochomus quadripustulatus (L.) 4-SPOT LADYBIRD Scarce on trees and shrubs
Anisosticta novemdecimpunctata (L.) WATER LADYBIRD Local on coastal marshes
Aphidecta obliterata (L.) LARCH LADYBIRD Local on coniferous trees
Tytthaspis sedecimpunctata (L.) 16-SPOT LADYBIRD Local on coastal grassland
Adalia bipunctata (L.) 2-SPOT LADYBIRD Rare. Usually very common in range of habitats
A. decempunctata (L.) 10-SPOT LADYBIRD Local in a range of habitats
Coccinella septempunctata L. 7-SPOT LADYBIRD Common in a range of habitats
C. undecimpunctata L. 11-SPOT LADYBIRD Scarce in coastal habitats
Propylea quattuordecimpunctata (L.) 14-SPOT LADYBIRD Local in a range of habitats
Anatis ocellata (L.) EYED LADYBIRD Rare on conifers
Myrrha octodecimguttata (L.) 18-SPOT LADYBIRD Rare on Scots Pine *(Pinus sylvestris)*
Calvia quattuordecimguttata (L.) CREAM-SPOT LADYBIRD Scarce in woodland
Halyzia sedecimguttata (L.) ORANGE LADYBIRD Local on sycamore in woodland
Thea vigintiduopunctata (L.) 22-SPOT LADYBIRD Scarce in a range of habitats

ENDOMYCHIDAE

Mycetaea hirta (Marsham)	Rare in haystack refuse
Lycoperdina bovistae (Fabricius) **RDB3**.	Rare in puff-ball fungi
Endomychus coccineus (L.) FALSE LADYBIRD	Local in fungi on dead wood

BEETLES

LATRIDIIDAE - MOULD BEETLES

Aridius bifasciatus (Reitter)	Scarce in a range of habitats
A. nodifer (Westwood)	Local in a range of habitats
Latridius minutus sensu lato	Rare. Habitat unknown
Enicmus transversus (Olivier)	Common in a range of habitats
*Dienerella elongata (Curtis)	Rare in vegetable detritus
D. ruficollis (Marsham)	Rare in haystack refuse
Corticaria elongata (Gyllenhal)	Rare in vegetable detritus
C. ferruginea Marsham	Rare in moss
*C. impressa (Olivier)	Rare in flood litter
Corticarina fuscula (Gyllenhal)	Common in a range of habitats
*C. similata (Gyllenhal)	Rare on spruce
Cortinicara gibbosa (Herbst)	Scarce in a range of habitats

CISIDAE

Octotemnus glabriculus (Gyllenhal)	Local in fungi on dead wood
Cis bidentatus (Olivier)	Rare in fungi on dead wood
C. bilamellatus Wood	Scarce on fungi in woodland
C. boleti (Scopoli)	Local in fungi on dead wood
C. fagi Waltl	Rare in fungi on dead wood
C. hispidus (Paykull)	Rare in fungi on dead wood
C. nitidus (Fabricius)	Local in fungi on dead wood
C. vestitus Mellié	Rare in fungi on old parkland trees
Ennearthron cornutum (Gyllenhal)	Rare in fungi on dead wood

MYCETOPHAGIDAE

Pseudotriphyllus suturalis (Fabricius)	Rare in bracket fungi on old parkland trees
Triphyllus bicolor (Fabricius)	Rare in bracket fungi on old parkland trees
*Litargus connexus (Fourcroy)	Rare in fungi on dead wood
Mycetophagus atomarius (Fabricius)	Local in fungi on old parkland trees
M. quadripustulatus (L.)	Local in fungi on dead wood
Typhaea stercorea (L.)	Local in haystack refuse

COLYDIIDAE

Bitoma crenata (Fabricius)	Local under bark of beech

TENEBRIONIDAE - DARKLING BEETLES

Blaps mucronata Latreille CHURCHYARD BEETLE	Scarce in buildings
Phylan gibbus (Fabricius)	Scarce on sandy soil at the coast
Melanimon tibialis (Fabricius)	Scarce on sandy soil at the coast
*Opatrum sabulosum (L.) **Nb**.	Rare on sand at the coast
Eledona agricola (Herbst) **Nb**.	Scarce on sulphur polypore fungus *(Laetiporus sulphureus)*
Scaphidema metallicum (Fabricius) **Nb**.	Scarce in fungi on dead wood

BEETLES

*Corticeus linearis (Fabricius)	Rare in bark beetle burrows on conifers
Tenebrio molitor L. YELLOW MEALWORM	Rare in buildings
Helops caeruleus (L.) **Nb.**	Rare in dead wood
Cylindrinotus laevioctostriatus (Goeze)	Common in a range of habitats
Lagria hirta (L.)	Scarce in a range of habitats
Gonodera luperus (Herbst)	Rare on the coast
Pseudocistela ceramboides (L.) **Nb.**	Rare in dead wood in old parkland
Isomira murina (L.)	Local in a range of habitats

SALPINGIDAE

Salpingus castaneus (Panzer)	Rare on scots pine *(Pinus sylvestris)*
S. reyi (Abeille)	Scarce on burnt gorse
Vincenzellus ruficollis (Panzer)	Rare under bark
Rhinosimus planirostris (Fabricius)	Local under bark
R. ruficollis (L.)	Rare under bark

PYROCHROIDAE - CARDINAL BEETLES

Pyrochroa coccinea (L.) **Nb.**	Rare in dead wood on coastal marshes
P. serraticornis (Scopoli)	Local in dead wood

MELANDRYIDAE - FALSE DARKLING BEETLES

Orchesia micans (Panzer) **Nb.**	Rare on fungi in old woodland
O. minor Walker **Nb.**	Rare on fungi in old woodland
O. undulata Kraatz	Rare under bark of trees in old parkland
Phloiotrya vaudoueri Mulsant **Nb.**	Rare in dead wood of beech in old parkland
Melandrya caraboides (L.) **Nb.**	Local in dead wood

SCRAPTIIDAE - FLOWER BEETLES

Anaspis costai Emery	Rare on hawthorn (Crataegus) flowers in woodland
A. frontalis (L.)	Local on hawthorn (Crataegus) blossom
*A. garneysi Fowler	Rare on hawthorn (Crataegus) blossom
A. humeralis (Fabricius)	Rare on hawthorn (Crataegus) blossom
A. lurida Stephens	Scarce in woodlands
A. maculata Fourcroy	Local on hawthorn (Crataegus) blossom
A. pulicaria Costa, A.	Local on hawthorn (Crataegus) blossom
A. regimbarti Schilsky	Local on hawthorn (Crataegus) blossom
A. rufilabris (Gyllenhal)	Rare on hawthorn (Crataegus) blossom

MORDELLIDAE

*Mordellistena pumila (Gyllenhal)	Rare in old parkland

RHIPIPHORIDAE

Metoecus paradoxus (L.)	Rare at mercury-vapour light

OEDEMERIDAE

Nacerdes melanura (L.)	Rare in coastal driftwood

BEETLES

Ischnomera caerulea sensu lato	Local in dead wood
I. cyanea (Fabricius) **Nb**.	Rare in dead wood
Oncomera femorata (Fabricius) **Nb**.	Local in woodland
Oedemera lurida (Marsham)	Scarce in grassland
O. nobilis (Scopoli)	Common in a range of habitats

MELOIDAE - OIL BEETLES
Meloe proscarabaeus L.	Scarce on dry grassland and heathland
M. violaceus Marsham **Nb**.	Local on dry grassland and heathland

ANTHICIDAE
Notoxus monoceros (L.)	Scarce on sandy soils at the coast
Anthicus antherinus (L.)	Rare in hedges
A. floralis (L.)	Rare in vegetable detritus
A. tobias Marseul	Rare on rubbish dumps

CERAMBYCIDAE - LONGHORN BEETLES
Arhopalus tristis (Fabricius)		Rare in coniferous timber in houses
*Asemum striatum (L.)		Rare on coniferous logs
Rhagium bifasciatum Fabricius	2-BANDED LONGHORN	Common in dead wood
R. mordax (DeGeer)		Common in dead wood
Stenocorus meridianus (L.)	VARIABLE LONGHORN	Local in dead wood
Grammoptera ruficornis (Fabricius)		Local in hawthorn blossom
Alosterna tabacicolor (DeGeer)		Common in woodland
Leptura sexguttata Fabricius **RDB3**.		Rare in dead wood in old valley woodland
Judolia cerambyciformis (Schrank)		Scarce in woodland
Strangalia maculata (Poda)	SPOTTED LONGHORN	Common in woodland
*S. melanura (L.)		Rare in woodland
*S. quadrifasciata (L.)		Rare in woodland
Phymatodes testaceus (L.)		Rare in dead wood in old parkland
Clytus arietis (L.)	WASP BEETLE	Common in woodland
Anaglyptus mysticus (L.) **Nb**.		Rare in woodland
Pogonocherus hispidus (L.)		Local in woodland
Leiopus nebulosus (L.)		Common in woodland
Saperda populnea (L.)		Status and habitat unknown

BRUCHIDAE
Bruchus loti Paykull	Local on vetches
*B. rufimanus Boheman	Rare in grassland

CHRYSOMELIDAE - LEAF and FLEA BEETLES
Donacia marginata Hoppe		Scarce in coastal marshes
D. simplex Fabricius	PLAIN REED BEETLE	Local in coastal marshes

BEETLES

Donacia thalassina Germar **Na**.	Rare in moorland valley fen
D. versicolorea (Brahm)	Rare on upland pools
Oulema lichenis Voet	Common in a range of habitats
O. melanopa (L.)	Common in a range of habitats
Cryptocephalus fulvus Goeze	Local in heath and grassland
C. pusillus Fabricius	Local in birch (Betula) woodland
Lamprosoma concolor (Sturm) **Nb**.	Common in woodland
Timarcha goettingensis (L.)	Scarce on dry grassland
T. tenebricosa (Fabricius) BLOODY-NOSED BEETLE	Common in a range of habitats
Chrysolina banksi (Fabricius)	Local in a range of habitats
C. haemoptera (L.) **Nb**.	Local in coastal grassland
C. hyperici (Forster)	Rare on St. John's-worts (Hypericum)
C. oricalcia (Müller O.F.) **Nb**.	Scarce. Habitat not known
C. polita (L.) TWO-COLOURED LEAF BEETLE	Common in a range of habitats
*C. staphylaea (L.)	Rare on buttercups (Ranunculus)
C. varians (Schaller)	Scarce on St. John's-wort (Hypericum)
C. violacea (Müller O.F.) **Nb**.	Local on dry grassland
Gastrophysa polygoni (L.)	Common in a range of habitats
G. viridula (DeGeer) DOCK LEAF BEETLE	Common on docks in a range of habitats
Phaedon armoraciae (L.)	Scarce in coastal marshes
P. cochleariae (Fabricius) WATERCRESS BEETLE	Rare. On crucifers
P. tumidulus (Germar)	Local in a range of habitats
Hydrothassa marginella (L.)	Rare in wet meadows
Prasocuris junci (Brahm)	Common in a range of wetland habitats
P. phellandrii (L.)	Scarce in coastal marshes
Phyllodecta laticollis Suffrian	Rare on poplars (Populus)
P. vitellinae (L.)	Rare on willows (Salix)
Galerucella grisescens (Joannis)	Rare on coastal marshes
G. lineola (Fabricius)	Status and habitat unknown
G. sagittariae (Gyllenhal)	Status and habitat unknown
G. tenella (L.)	Status and habitat unknown
Lochmaea caprea (L.)	Rare on willows (Salix)
L. crataegi (Forster)	Rare on hawthorn blossom (Crataegus)
L. suturalis (Thomson C.G.)	Common on heather moorland
Luperus longicornis (Fabricius)	Local in birch woodland
Calomicrus circumfusus (Marsham) **Na**.	Scarce on heath and moorland
Sermylassa halensis (L.)	Scarce on dry grassland
*Phyllotreta atra (Fabricius)	Rare on crucifers
P. consobrina (Curtis)	Rare on crucifers

BEETLES

*Phyllotreta cruciferae (Goeze) **Nb**.		Rare on crucifers
*P. diademata (Foudras)		Rare on scurvy-grass (Cochlearia)
P. flexuosa (Illiger)		Rare on crucifers
P. nemorum (L.)	TURNIP FLEA BEETLE	Rare on crucifers
P. nigripes (Fabricius)		Rare on crucifers
P. ochripes (Curtis)		Local on garlic mustard (Alliaria petiolata)
*P. tetrastigma (Comolli)		Rare on crucifers on wetlands
P. undulata Kutschera		Local on crucifers
P. vittula Redtenbacher		Scarce on crucifers
Aphthona nonstriata (Goeze)		Scarce on yellow flag (Iris pseudacorus)
Longitarsus atricillus (L.)		Rare on leguminous plants
*L. curtus (Allard) **Na**.		Rare on Boraginaceae
L. exoletus (L.)		Rare on Boraginaceae
L. holsaticus (L.)		Rare in valley fens on lousewort (Pedicularis sylvatica)
*L. jacobaeae sensu lato		Rare on ragwort (Senecio jacobaea)
L. luridus (Scopoli)		Local in a range of habitats
*L. melanocephalus (DeGeer)		Rare on plantain (Plantago)
L. membranaceus (Foudras)		Rare on wood sage (Teucrium scorodonia)
*L. nigrofasciatus (Goeze) **Na**.		Rare on mullein (Verbascum)
*L. parvulus (Paykull) **Na**.		Rare on flax (Linum)
L. pratensis (Panzer)		Scarce on plantain (Plantago)
L. succineus (Foudras)		Status and habitat unknown
L. tabidus (Fabricius) **Nb**.		Rare on mullein (Verbascum)
*Altica lythri Aubé		Rare on coastal marshes
A. oleracea (L.)		Common on moorland and heathland
Hermaeophaga mercurialis (Fabricius)		Rare on dog's mercury (Mercurialis perennis)
Batophila rubi (Paykull)		Scarce on brambles (Rubus)
Ochrosis ventralis (Illiger) **RDB3**.		Scarce on mayweed (Tripleurospermum)
Crepidodera ferruginea (Scopoli)		Local on thistles
C. transversa (Marsham)		Scarce on thistles
Derocrepis rufipes (L.)		Scarce on vetches
*Chalcoides aurea (Fourcroy)		Rare on poplars (Populus)
C. fulvicornis (Fabricius)	SALLOW FLEA BEETLE	Scarce on willows (Salix)
Mantura rustica (L.) **Nb**.		Scarce on docks at the coast
Chaetocnema concinna (Marsham)	MANGOLD FLEA BEETLE	Common in a range of habitats
C. hortensis (Fourcroy)		Rare on grassland
Apteropeda globosa (Illiger)		Rare on white deadnettle (Lamium album)
Apteropeda orbiculata (Marsham)		Rare in woodland
Mniophila muscorum (Koch J.D.W.) **Nb**.		Rare on foxglove (Digitalis purpurea)

BEETLES

Psylliodes affinis (Paykull)	POTATO FLEA BEETLE	Local on bittersweet (Solanum dulcamara)
P. attenuata (Koch J.D.W.) **RDB1.**		Rare on hops (Humulus lupulus)
P. chrysocephala (L.)		Local on crucifers
P. cuprea (Koch J.D.W.)		Status and habitat unknown
P. napi sensu lato.		Local in a range of habitats
Cassida flaveola Thunberg		Local in a range of wetland habitats
C. rubiginosa Müller O.F.	COMMON TORTOISE BEETLE	Local on thistles
C. viridis L.	GREEN TORTOISE BEETLE	Scarce on water mint (Mentha aquatica)
C. vittata de Villers		Local on coastal grassland

ANTHRIBIDAE - WEEVILS

*Platyrhinus resinosus (Scopoli) **Nb.**		On cramp-ball fungi (Daldinia concentrica) in woods

ATTELABIDAE - WEEVILS

Attelabus nitens (Scopoli)	RED OAK ROLLER	Rare in old woodland
Apoderus coryli (L.)		Local on hazel (Corylus) in woodlands
*Rhynchites caeruleus (DeGeer)		Rare on poplar bark (Populus)
R. aeneovirens (Marsham)	RED & BRONZE WEEVIL	Rare on oak in woodland
*R. aequatus (L.)		Rare on hawthorn (Crataegus)
R. germanicus Herbst		Local on rosaceous plants
R. tomentosus Gyllenhal **Nb.**		Rare on birch (Betula)
Deporaus betulae (L.)		Local on birch (Betula)
D. mannerheimi (Hummel)		Rare on birch (Betula)

APIONIDAE - WEEVILS

Apion curtirostre Germar	Common on dock (Rumex)
A. hydrolapathi (Marsham)	Scarce on dock (Rumex)
A. marchicum Herbst	Rare on sheep's sorrel (Rumex acetosella)
A. violaceum Kirby	Scarce on dock (Rumex)
A. malvae (Fabricius)	Rare on mallow (Malva)
A. rufirostre (Fabricius)	Scarce on mallow (Malva)
*Apion aeneum (Fabricius)	Rare on mallow (Malva)
A. radiolus (Marsham)	Scarce on mallow (Malva)
A. semivittatum Gyllenhal **Na.**	Rare on annual mercury (Mercurialis annua)
A. urticarium (Herbst)	Rare on nettle (Urtica dioica)
Apion ulicis (Forster)	Common on gorse (Ulex)
A. frumentarium (Paykull)	Local on dock (Rumex)
A. haematodes Kirby	Scarce on sheep's sorrel (Rumex acetosella)
A. rubens Stephens	Rare on sheep's sorrel (Rumex acetosella)
A. pubescens Kirby **Nb.**	Rare on clover (Trifolium)
A. seniculus Kirby	Scarce on clover (Trifolium)
A. confluens Kirby	Rare on mayweed (Tripleurospermum)

BEETLES

*Apion stolidum Germar **Nb**.	Rare on ox-eye daisy (Leucanthemum vulgare)
A. carduorum Kirby	Rare on thistles
*A. carduorum sensu lato	Local on thistles
A. onopordi Kirby	Scarce on thistles
A. hookeri Kirby	Rare on mayweed (Tripleurospermum)
*A. sorbi (Fabricius) **RDBI**.	Rare on mayweed (Tripleurospermum)
A. atratulum Germar	Scarce on gorse (Ulex)
*A. aethiops Herbst	Rare on vetch
A. pisi (Fabricius)	Scarce on medick (Medicago)
A. punctigerum (Paykull) **Nb**.	Scarce on vetch
A. ervi Kirby	Local on vetches
A. loti Kirby	Scarce on common bird's-foot trefoil (Lotus corniculatus)
A. scutellare Kirby	Scarce on western gorse (Ulex gallii)
A. tenue Kirby	Rare on medick (Medicago)
A. viciae (Paykull)	Rare on tufted vetch (Vicia cracca)
A. virens Herbst	Rare on clover (Trifolium)
*Apion vorax Herbst	Rare on vetch
A. craccae (L.)	Common on tufted vetch (Vicia cracca)
A. pomonae (Fabricius)	Local on common vetch (Vicia sativa)
*A. assimile Kirby	Rare on red clover (Trifolium pratense)
A. dichroum Bedel	Local on clover (Trifolium)
*A. difforme Ahrens **Nb**.	Rare on clover (Trifolium)
A. nigritarse Kirby	Local on clover (Trifolium)
A. schoenherri Boheman **Na**.	Rare on coastal grassland
A. trifolii (L.)	Common on white clover (Trifolium repens)
*A. varipes Germar **Nb**.	Rare on clover (Trifolium)

CURCULIONIDAE - WEEVILS

Otiorhynchus ovatus (L.)		Rare on sandy soils
O. rugifrons (Gyllenhal)		Rare on dry grassland
O. rugosostriatus (Goeze)		Rare on dry grassland
O. singularis (L.)		Common in a range of habitats
O. sulcatus (Fabricius)		Local in a range of habitats
Caenopsis waltoni (Boheman)		Rare in moss
Trachyphloeus bifoveolatus (Beck)		Scarce on dry grassland
*T. laticollis Boheman **Na**.		Rare on dry grassland
Phyllobius argentatus (L.)	GOLD-GREEN LEAF WEEVIL	Local on trees
*P. calcaratus (Fabricius)		Rare on alder (Alnus)
P. oblongus (L.)		Scarce on trees
P. pomaceus Gyllenhal		Scarce on nettles

BEETLES

Phyllobius pyri (L.)		Local on trees
*P. roboretanus Gredler		Scarce on trees
P. viridiaeris (Laicharting)		Status and habitat unknown
*Polydrusus cervinus (L.)	SPECKLED LEAF WEEVIL	Rare in woodland
P. confluens Stephens **Nb**.		Scarce on gorse (Ulex)
P. pterygomalis Boheman		Scarce on trees
P. sericeus (Schaller) **Na**.		Rare on birch (Betula) and alder (Alnus)
P. undatus (Fabricius)		Rare on oak in woodland
*Barypeithes araneiformis (Schrank)		Local in a range of habitats
*B. duplicatus Keys		Rare on low vegetation
B. pellucidus (Boheman)		Common in a range of habitats
Sciaphilus asperatus (Bonsdorff)		Local on shrubs
Strophosomus melanogrammus (Forster)		Local in woodland
S. nebulosus Stephens		Local on moorland and coastal heath
*Philopedon plagiatus (Schaller)		Scarce on sand at the coast
Liophloeus tessulatus (Müller O.F.)		Common on ivy (Hedera helix)
Barynotus obscurus (Fabricius)		Local in woodland
Sitona cambricus Stephens		Local in a range of habitats
S. hispidulus (Fabricius)		Local on clover (Trifolium)
S. lepidus Gyllenhal		Local on clover (Trifolium)
S. lineatus (L.)	PEA WEEVIL	Common on leguminous plants
*S. puncticollis Stephens		Rare on clover (Trifolium)
S. regensteinensis (Herbst)		Local on gorse (Ulex)
S. striatellus Gyllenhal		Common on gorse (Ulex)
S. sulcifrons (Thunberg)		Common on clover (Trifolium)
S. suturalis Stephens		Local on vetch (Vicia)
S. waterhousei Walton J. **Nb**.		Scarce on common bird's-foot trefoil (Lotus corniculatus)
*Lixus vilis (Rossi) **RDB1**.		Rare on common storksbill on sandy soils
Larinus planus (Fabricius) **Nb**.		Scarce on thistles
Hypera adspersa (Fabricius)		Scarce in coastal marshes
H. arator (L.)		Rare on leguminous plants
H. meles (Fabricius) **Na**.		Rare on lucerne (Medicago) and red clover (Trifolium)
H. nigrirostris (Fabricius)		Scarce on restharrow (Ononis) on sand at the coast
H. plantaginis (DeGeer)		Local in a range of habitats
H. postica (Gyllenhal)		Local on leguminous plants
H. punctata (Fabricius)	SANDY CLOVER WEEVIL	Scarce on clover
*H. rumicis (L.)		Rare on dock (Rumex)
H. venusta (Fabricius)		Rare on western gorse (Ulex gallii)
Cionus alauda (Herbst)		Rare on figwort (Scrophularia)

BEETLES

Cionus hortulanus (Fourcroy)	FIGWORT WEEVIL	Common on figwort (Scrophularia)
C. scrophulariae (L.)		Common on figwort (Scrophularia)
Cleopus pulchellus (Herbst)		Local on mullein (Verbascum) and figwort (Scrophularia)
Alophus triguttatus (Fabricius) **Nb**.		Rare on grassland
Hylobius abietis (L.)	LARGE PINE WEEVIL	Local in conifer plantations
Leiosoma deflexum (Panzer)		Common on buttercups (Ranunculus)
Pissodes castaneus (DeGeer)		Rare in houses
Magdalis armigera (Fourcroy)		Local on elm (Ulmus)
*Magdalis carbonaria (L.) **Nb**.		Rare on birch (Betula)
Anoplus plantaris (Naezen)		Rare on birch (Betula)
A. roboris Suffrian **Nb**.		Rare on alder (Alnus)
Tanysphyrus lemnae (Paykull)		Rare on coastal marshes
Euophryum confine (Broun)		Scarce under bark
Pentarthrum huttoni (Wollaston)		Scarce under bark
Rhopalomesites tardii (Curtis) **Nb**.		Scarce in dead wood
Rhyncolus chloropus (L.)		Rare in dead wood
Phloeophagus lignarius (Marsham)		Scarce in dead wood
Caulotrupodes aeneopiceus (Boheman)		Scarce in dead wood
*Pselactus spadix (Herbst) **Nb**.		Rare in dead wood at the coast
*Trachodes hispidus (L.) **Nb**.		Rare in oak woodland
Orobitis cyaneus (L.)		Rare on violets (Viola)
Acalles ptinoides (Marsham) **Nb**.		Scarce in dead wood
Hydronomus alismatis (Marsham) **Nb**.		Scarce on coastal marshes on water-plantain (Alisma plantago-aquatica)
Dorytomus longimanus (Forster)		Local on poplar (Populus)
D. melanophthalmus (Paykull)		Scarce on willow (Salix)
D. taeniatus (Fabricius)		Local on willow (Salix) and poplar (Populus)
Notaris acridulus (L.) **Nb**.		Rare on coastal marshes
N. scirpi (Fabricius) **Nb**.		Rare on coastal marshes
Thryogenes nereis (Paykull)		Rare on coastal marshes
Smicronyx jungermanniae (Reich) **Nb**.		Local on dodder (Cuscuta epithymum) on coastal heath
Pelenomus olssoni Israelson **RDB3**.		Rare on water-purslane (Lythrum portula)
P. quadrituberculatus (Fabricius)		Scarce on Polygonaceae
Rhinoncus castor (Fabricius)		Rare on sheep's sorrel (Rumex acetosella)
R. inconspectus (Herbst)		Rare on amphibious bistort (Polygonum amphibium)
R. pericarpius (L.)		Common on Polygonaceae
R. perpendicularis (Reich)		Rare on bistort and persicaria (Polygonum)
Amalorrhynchus melanarius (Stephens)		Local on water-cress (Rorippa nasturtium-aquaticum)
Drupenatus nasturtii (Germar) **Nb**.		Local on water-cress (Rorippa nasturtium-aquaticum)

BEETLES

*Coeliodes dryados (Gmelin)	Local in oak (Quercus) woodland
*C. ruber (Marsham) **Nb**.	Rare in oak (Quercus) woodland
C. rubicundus (Herbst)	Scarce on birch (Betula)
Micrelus ericae (Gyllenhal)	Common on coastal heath and moorland
Parethelcus pollinarius (Forster)	Local on nettle (Urtica)
Datonychus angulosus (Boheman) **Na**.	Rare on marsh woundwort (Stachys palustris) in valley fen
D. melanostictus (Marsham)	Scarce in coastal marshes
*Microplontus campestris Gyllenhal **Nb**.	Rare on ox-eye daisy (Leucanthemum vulgare)
M. rugulosus (Herbst)	Local on mayweed (Tripleurospermum)
Hadroplontus litura (Fabricius)	Rare on thistles
Ceutorhynchus assimilis (Paykull)	Scarce on crucifers
C. constrictus (Marsham) **Nb**.	Rare on garlic mustard (Alliaria petiolata)
C. contractus (Marsham)	Rare on crucifers
C. erysimi (Fabricius)	Scarce on shepherd's-purse (Capsella bursa-pastoris)
C. floralis (Paykull)	Rare on crucifers
C. pallidactylus (Marsham)	Local on crucifers
C. pectoralis Weise **Na**.	Rare on bitter-cress (Cardamine)
*C. picitarsis Gyllenhal	Rare on hedge mustard (Sisymbrium officinale)
C. sulcicollis (Paykull)	Scarce on hedge mustard (Sisymbrium officinale)
Sirocalodes mixtus (Mulsant & Rey) **Nb**.	Scarce on fumitory (Fumaria)
Trichosirocalus troglodytes (Fabricius)	Local in grassland
*Stenocarus ruficornis (Stephens) **Nb**.	Rare on poppy (Papaver)
Nedyus quadrimaculatus (L.)	Common on nettle (Urtica)
Limnobaris t-album (L.)	Rare on sedges (Carex)
Anthonomus pedicularius (L.)	Rare on hawthorn (Crataegus)
A. rubi (Herbst)	Local on rosaceous plants
A. ulmi (DeGeer) **Nb**.	Local on elm (Ulmus)
Curculio glandium Marsham	Rare on oak (Quercus)
C. pyrrhoceras Marsham	Local on oak (Quercus)
C. salicivorus Paykull	Rare on willow (Salix)
C. venosus (Gravenhorst)	Rare on oak (Quercus)
*C. villosus Fabricius **Nb**.	Rare on oak (Quercus)
Tychius junceus (Reich)	Rare on medick and clover
T. pusillus Germar **Nb**.	Rare on gorse (Ulex)
T. stephensi Gyllenhal	Rare on common bird's-foot trefoil (Lotus corniculatus)
T. tibialis Boheman **Na**.	Scarce on coastal grassland on clovers
Miccotrogus picirostris (Fabricius)	Common on clover (Trifolium)

BEETLES

Sibinia primitus (Herbst) **Nb**.	Rare on sweet alison (Lobularia maritima)
Mecinus pyraster (Herbst)	Common on plantain (Plantago)
Gymnetron antirrhini (Paykull)	Common on toadflax (Linaria)
G. melanarium (Germar)	Rare on wall speedwell (Veronica arvensis)
G. veronicae (Germar) **Nb**.	Rare on brooklime (Veronica beccabunga)
Rhynchaenus alni (L.)	Local on elm (Ulmus)
R. avellanae (Donovan)	Scarce on hazel (Corylus) and oak (Quercus)
R. fagi (L.)	Common on beech (Fagus)
R. pilosus (Fabricius)	Rare on oak (Quercus)
R. quercus (L.)	Common on oak (Quercus)
R. rusci (Herbst)	Local on birch (Betula)
R. salicis (L.)	Rare on willow (Salix)
*R. stigma (Germar)	Rare on willow (Salix)
Ramphus oxyacanthae (Marsham)	Common on hawthorn (Crataegus)
R. pulicarius sensu lato	Rare. On birch (Betula)

SCOLYTIDAE - BARK BEETLES

Scolytus intricatus (Ratzeburg)		Scarce under oak (Quercus) bark
S. multistriatus (Marsham)		Scarce on elm (Ulmus)
S. scolytus (Fabricius)	LARGE ELM BARK BEETLE	Local on elm (Ulmus) Carrier of Dutch elm disease
*Hylesinus crenatus (Fabricius)		Rare under ash (Fraxinus) bark
H. varius (Fabricius)		Scarce under ash (Fraxinus) bark
Kissophagus hederae (Schmitt) **Nb**.		Rare under ivy (Hedera helix) bark
Hylastinus obscurus (Marsham)		Scarce under gorse (Ulex) bark
Phloeophthorus rhododactylus (Marsham)		Rare under gorse (Ulex) bark
Hylurgops palliatus (Gyllenhal)		Rare under conifer bark
Hylastes ater (Fabricius)	BLACK PINE BEETLE	Rare under conifer bark
*H. attenuatus (Erichson)		Rare under pine (Pinus) bark
H. opacus (Erichson)		Rare under pine (Pinus) bark
*Tomicus piniperda (L.)	PINE SHOOT BEETLE	Rare on conifers
Dryocoetinus villosus (Fabricius)		Local under oak (Quercus) bark
*Trypodendron domesticum (L.)		Rare under oak (Quercus) bark
*T. signatum (Fabricius) **Nb**.		Rare under oak (Quercus) bark
Pityophthorus pubescens (Marsham)		Rare on conifer twigs
*Pityogenes bidentatus (Herbst)		Scarce on conifer twigs
Orthotomicus laricis (Fabricius)		Rare under conifer bark

PLATYPODIDAE

Platypus cylindrus (Fabricius) **Nb**. PINHOLE BORER   Rare under oak bark in old parkland

References:
Duff, A.G. (1993). *The Beetles of Somerset*. Somerset Archaeological and Natural History Society, Taunton.

Exmoor Natural History Society (1988). *The Flora and Fauna of Exmoor National Park*. ENHS, Minehead.

Hyman, P.S. and Parsons, M.S. (1992). *A Review of the Scarce and Threatened Coleoptera of Great Britain*. Part 1. UK Nature Conservation Series No. 3. Joint Nature Conservation Committee, Peterborough.

Hyman, P.S. and Parsons, M.S. (1994). *A Review of the Scarce and Threatened Coleoptera of Great Britain*. Part 2. UK Nature Conservation Series No. 12. Joint Nature Conservation Committee, Peterborough.

National Trust (1994). Biological Survey, Watersmeet, Devon. National Trust, Cirencester.

Pope, R.D. (1977). *A Checklist of British Insects*. Part 3: Coleoptera and Strepsiptera. Second Revised Edition. Handbooks for the Identification of British Insects Vol. XI, Part 3. Royal Entomological Society, London.

SPIDERS, HARVESTMEN, PSEUDOSCORPIONS, TICKS & MITES.

The following list of Arachnids is a record of the species which have been found on Exmoor so far, and further work would undoubtedly reveal the presence of many more. It is hoped however, that it will provide a foundation on which other workers on these groups of animals will be able to build in the future.

I would like to thank Dr. Peter Merrett of Swanage and Rowley Snazell of the Institute of Terrestrial Ecology's research station at Furzebrook, Dorset for providing a list of spiders from the heathlands of Exmoor and helping with the identification of the more critical species. The late Mr John Sankey of Mickleham, Dorking, Surrey very kindly assisted with the more problematical harvestmen. Dr Peter Gabbutt of the Dept. of Zoology at Manchester University identified all of the pseudoscorpions for which I am most grateful. Mr Francis Farr-Cox of Burnham-on-Sea has very generously allowed me to incorporate his list of arachnids for the area, and he has my grateful thanks. Finally, my thanks to fellow members of the Exmoor Natural History Society who have provided specimens or records in the past.

The nomenclature of the spiders follows that of Merrett, P., Locket, G.H., and Millidge, A.F., (1985) *Bulletin British Arachnological Society* 6(9) pp.381-403. That of the harvestmen follows Martens, J. (1978) *'Die Tierwelt Deutschlands'* 64 Tiel, and the pseudoscorpions follows Legg, G. and Jones, R.E. (1988) *Synopses of the British Fauna* (New Series), The Linnean Society.

A.E. Cooper
Recorder of Arachnida, ENHS

Class: ARACHNIDA

Order: ARANEAE
Sub-order: MYGALOMORPHAE

ATYPIDAE

Atypus affinis Eichwald   Constructs a finger-like tube which is usually supported by surrounding vegetation, the 'retreat' portion of tube is built into the ground

Sub-order: ARANEOMORPHAE

AMAUROBIIDAE

Amaurobius fenestralis (Ström)	Under bark of trees, etc.
A. similis (Blackwall)	Widespread in crevices around buildings
A. ferox (Walckenaer)	Under stones and logs

DICTYNIDAE

Dictyna arundinacea (L.)   Web built in heads of heather, gorse, etc.

SPIDERS

Lathys humilis (Blackwall)	Amongst bushes and dead leaves

OONOPIDAE

Oonops domesticus de Dalmas	Found indoors

DYSDERIDAE

Dysdera erythrina (Walckenaer)	Under stones
D. crocata C.L.Koch	Under stones
Harpactea hombergi (Scopoli)	In dry, matted vegetation

SEGESTRIIDAE

Segestria senoculata (L.)	Crevices in walls, under stones, etc.

PHOLCIDAE

Pholcus phalangioides (Fuesslin)	The 'daddy-longlegs' spider in the corners of rooms

GNAPHOSIDAE

Drassodes lapidosus (Walckenaer)	Under stones in various habitats
D. cupreus (Blackwall)	Under stones in various habitats
D. pubescens (Thorell)	Under stones in various habitats
Haplodrassus signifer (C.L. Koch)	On open heaths under stones
Scotophaeus blackwalli (Thorell)	In houses, active at night
Zelotes apricorum (L.Koch)	Under stones etc. Widespread
Micaria pulicaria (Sundevall)	Active in sunshine, on open ground; ant mimic

CLUBIONIDAE

Clubiona reclusa O.Pickard-Cambridge	Marshy places in grass and herbage
C. stagnatilis Kulczynski	In damp, marshy places
C. terrestris Westring	On trees, shrubs, etc.
C. compta C.L. Koch	On trees and bushes
C. trivialis C.L. Koch	Heathy places under stones
C. diversa O.Pickard-Cambridge	On low plants in damp places
Phrurolithus festivus (C.L. Koch)	Running in sunshine, or under stones; ant mimic

LIOCRANIDAE

Agroeca brunnea (Blackwall)	An egg-cocoon, probably of this species, found on Agrostis
A. proxima (O.Pickard-Cambridge)	In woods and dry places
Scotina gracilipes (Blackwall)	On heaths
Liocranum rupicola (Walckenaer)	Under stones in dry places

THOMISIDAE - CRAB SPIDERS

Misumena vatia (Clerck)	Found on flower heads, and low plants
Xysticus cristatus (Clerck)	Common in undergrowth
X. audax (Schrank)	On furze bushes
X. kochi Thorell	On bushes and in undergrowth
X. erraticus (Blackwall)	Under stones
X. sabulosus (Hahn)	On dry, sandy heaths

SPIDERS

Oxyptila trux (Blackwall)	In undergrowth, grass, etc.
O. simplex (O.Pickard-Cambridge)	In undergrowth
O. atomaria (Panzer)	In short grass, undergrowth, etc.

PHILODROMIDAE

Philodromus dispar Walckenaer	Found on low trees and bushes
P. aureolus (Clerck)	On bushes and shrubs
P. cespitum (Walckenaer)	On bushes etc.

SALTICIDAE

Salticus scenicus (Clerck)	ZEBRA SPIDER	Sunny walls
Heliophanus cupreus (Walckenaer)		Undergrowth and low vegetation
Neon reticulatus (Blackwall)		In detritus in woods
Euophrys frontalis (Walckenaer)		In grass and low herbage

LYCOSIDAE

Pardosa agricola (Thorell)	On coasts and riverbanks
P. arenicola (O.Pickard-Cambridge)	Amongst shingle; also inland
P. palustris (L.)	On open heaths
P. pullata (Clerck)	Widespread in many habitats
P. prativaga (L.Koch)	Less widespread, but in many habitats
P. amentata (Clerck)	Widespread in open, sunny sites
P. nigriceps (Thorell)	On heathland and open sites
P lugubris (Walckenaer)	Usually in woods
P. proxima (C.L. Koch)	In marshy areas
Alopecosa pulverulenta (Clerck)	Widespread in many habitats
A. cuneata (Clerck)	A heath and grassland species
A. accentuata (Latreille)	Mainly on open heaths
Trochosa ruricola (DeGeer)	Under stones, etc.; nocturnal
T. terricola Thorell	Widespread in many habitats
Arctosa leopardus (Sundevall)	In detritus in wet habitats
Pirata piraticus (Clerck)	Marshes and damp habitats
P. uliginosus (Thorell)	Marshes and damp habitats
P. latitans (Blackwall)	Marshes and damp habitats
P. piscatorius (Clerck)	Marshes and damp habitats
*Aulonia albimana (Walckenaer)	Probably now extinct on Exmoor due to change of its one known habitat

PISAURIDAE

Pisaura mirabilis (Clerck)	Widespread in tall grass etc.

ARGYRONETIDAE

Argyroneta aquatica (Clerck)	WATER SPIDER	Entirely aquatic

SPIDERS

AGELENIDAE
Agelena labyrinthica (Clerck)	In tall grass, gorse bushes, etc.
Tegenaria saeva Blackwall	In houses and outhouses, quarries, trees, etc.
T. domestica (Clerck)	In houses and outhouses, etc.
Coelotes atropus (Walckenaer)	Under stones, bark and holes in walls
Cryphoeca silvicola (C.L. Koch)	In detritus in woods and heather
*Tuberta macrophthalma Kulczynski	No current records for this Red Data Book species but there is a record from 1911 when it was found as a 'guest' in an ant's nest

HAHNIIDAE
Antistea elegans (Blackwall)	In vegetation in wet places
Hahnia montana (Blackwall)	Widespread in undergrowth
H. nava (Blackwall)	Under stones and in low vegetation

MIMETIDAE
Ero cambridgei Kulczynski	Predatory on other spiders
E. furcata (Villers)	Predatory on other spiders

THERIDIIDAE
Euryopis flavomaculata (C.L.Koch)	Damp places, in moss, etc.
Steatoda bipunctata (L.)	In houses, sheds etc., rarely outdoors
Theridion sisyphium (Clerck)	Widespread and common on bushes
T. simile C.L.Koch	Bushes and low vegetation
T. pallens Blackwall	A tiny spider, common on trees
Enoplognatha ovata (Clerck)	In low vegetation, especially nettles
Robertus lividus (Blackwall)	Widespread in detritus
R. arundineti (O. Pickard-Cambridge)	Undergrowth in woods
Theonoe minutissima (O. Pickard-Cambridge)	Widespread under stones, etc.

NESTICIDAE
Nesticus cellulanus (Clerck)	In damp and dark situations, cellars, etc.

TETRAGNATHIDAE
Tetragnatha extensa (L.)	Reeds and rushes close to water
T. pinicola L.Koch	On trees
Pachygnatha clercki Sundevall	Amongst long grass
P. listeri Sundevall	Amongst low plants and shrubs
P. degeeri Sundevall	Amongst shrubs and long grass

METIDAE
Metellina segmentata (Clerck)	Widespread in late summer and autumn
M. mengei (Blackwall)	Widespread in spring and early summer
M. merianae (Scopoli)	In damp holes and caves
Meta menardi (Latreille)	In caves and damp cellars
Zygiella x-notata (Clerck)	Common, window-frames and eaves of buildings

SPIDERS

ARANEIDAE

Araneus diadematus Clerck	GARDEN SPIDER	Widespread and common on bushes, etc.
A. quadratus Clerck		Widespread on heather and gorse
Larinioides cornutus (Clerck)		Widespread, especially in rank vegetation near water
Nuctenea umbratica (Clerck)		Widespread under bark of trees
Atea sturmi (Hahn) *(Araneus sturmi Hahn)*	Bushes & trees.	(Horner Woods, 1953 SANHS)
Araniella cucurbitina (Clerck)		Widespread on bushes and trees
Cercidia prominens (Westring)		Amongst low plants, bracken, etc.
Mangora acalypha (Walckenaer)		Widespread on heathland
Cyclosa conica (Pallas)	Evergreen shrubs and trees.	(Dunster 1953 SANHS)

LINYPHIIDAE

Ceratinella brevipes (Westring)	Widespread in detritus etc.
C. brevis (Wider)	Widespread in detritus etc.
Walckenaeria acuminata Blackwall	Widespread in woodland detritus
W. antica (Wider)	In sunny habitats
W. atrotibialis (O.Pickard-Cambridge)	Amongst low grass and heather
W. dysderoides (Wider)	In woodland detritus
W. nudipalpis (Westring)	Widespread in wet habitats
W. cuspidata Blackwall	In detritus in woods
W. vigilax (Blackwall)	Moss etc., in wet places
Dicymbium brevisetosum Locket	In a variety of habitats
D. tibiale (Blackwall)	Moss and leaves in wet areas
Entelecara erythropus (Westring)	Widespread in moss, etc.
Gnathonarium dentatum (Wider)	By streams and wet, marshy areas
Dismodicus bifrons (Blackwall)	Widespread in many habitats
Hypomma bituberculatum (Wider)	In wet marshy places
Metopobactrus prominulus (O.Pickard-Cambridge)	In undergrowth, moss etc.
Hybocoptus decollatus (Simon)	Gorse bushes
Gonatium rubens (Blackwall)	Widespread in many habitats
G. rubellum (Blackwall)	Undergrowth in woods
Maso sundevalli (Westring)	Widespread in many habitats
Pedponocranium ludicrum (O.Pickard-Cambridge)	Widespread in a variety of habitats
Pocadicnemis pumila (Blackwall)	Widespread in many habitats
P. juncea Locket & Millidge	Widespread in many habitats
Hypselistes jacksoni (O.Pickard-Cambridge)	In marshy areas
Oedothorax gibbosus (Blackwall)	Widespread in various habitats
O. tuberosus (Blackwall)	Widespread in various habitats
O. fuscus (Blackwall)	Widespread in various habitats
O. retusus (Westring)	Widespread in various habitats

SPIDERS

Pelecopsis mengei (Simon)	In detritus in damp places
Silometopus elegans (O. Pickard-Cambridge)	Undergrowth in wet areas
S. reussi (Thorell)	In undergrowth
Cnephalocotes obscurus (Blackwall)	Widespread amongst detritus
Evansia merens O.Pickard-Cambridge	In nests of ants
Tiso vagans (Blackwall)	In detritus etc.
Minyriolus pusillus (Wider)	In undergrowth and on low bushes
Tapinocyba praecox (O.Pickard-Cambridge)	Widespread in grass
Monocephalus fuscipes (Blackwall)	In detritus in woods, especially coniferous
Lophomma punctatum (Blackwall)	Moss and grass in swampy areas
Gongylidiellum vivum (O.Pickard-Cambridge)	In detritus in moist places
Micrargus apertus (O.Pickard-Cambridge)	In detritus, etc.
Erigonella hiemalis (Blackwall)	In detritus in woods
Savignia frontata (Blackwall)	In various habitats
Diplocephalus permixtus (O.Pickard-Cambridge)	Widespread in various habitats
D. latrifrons (O.Pickard-Cambridge)	Widespread in various habitats
D. picinus (Blackwall)	Widespread in various habitats
Typhochrestus digitatus (O.Pickard-Cambridge)	On moors and sandhills
Erigone dentipalpis (Wider)	Widespread in many habitats
E. atra (Blackwall)	Widespread in many habitats
E. promiscua (O.Pickard-Cambridge)	Widespread in many habitats
Drepanotylus uncatus (O.Pickard-Cambridge)	Widespread in marshy areas
Leptothrix hardyi (Blackwall)	In marshy areas and on high ground
Hilaira excisa (O.Pickard-Cambridge)	Amongst vegetation in wet habitats
Jacksonella falconeri (Jackson)	In detritus in coniferous woods
Porrhomma convexum (Westring)	In shady, damp situations
P. pallidum Jackson	In detritus in woods
P. campbelli F.O.Pickard-Cambridge	Under stones, very rare
P. egeria Simon	In caves, cellars, etc.
Agyneta subtilis (O.Pickard-Cambridge)	In undergrowth
A. conigera (O.Pickard-Cambridge)	In low vegetation
A. decora (O. Pickard-Cambridge)	Found in moss and grass
A. ramosa Jackson	Vegetation in marshy areas
Meioneta rurestris (C.L.Koch)	Widespread in many habitats
M. saxatilis (Blackwall)	Widespread in low vegetation
Microneta viaria (Blackwall)	Widespread in detritus
Maro minutus O.Pickard-Cambridge	Under stones and in low vegetation
Centromerus sylvaticus (Blackwall)	In low vegetation in woods
C. prudens (O.Pickard-Cambridge)	In grass and heather

SPIDERS

Centromerus arcanus (O.Pickard-Cambridge)	In low vegetation on high ground
C. dilutus (O.Pickard-Cambridge)	In detritus in woods, widespread
Tallusia experta (O. Pickard-Cambridge)	Moss and grass in woods
Centromerita concinna (Thorell)	In low vegetation
Sintula cornigera (Blackwall)	Wet and swampy habitats
Saaristoa abnormis (Blackwall)	Moss, grass etc. in woods
Macrargus rufus (Wider)	Grass and leaves in woods
Bathyphantes approximatus (O.Pickard-Cambridge)	In marshy areas
B. gracilis (Blackwall)	Widespread in undergrowth
B. parvulus (Westring)	Widespread in undergrowth
B. nigrinus (Westring)	On low plants
Kaestneria pullata (O.Pickard-Cambridge)	Amongst grass and heather
Diplostyla concolor (Wider)	Widespread, under stones
Poeciloneta globosa (Wider)	Under stones etc.
Tapinopa longidens (Wider)	In detritus in woods and damp areas
Floronia bucculenta (Clerck)	Amongst low vegetation
Taranucnus setosus (O.Pickard-Cambridge)	In marshy places
Labulla thoracica (Wider)	In holes in trees, holes in the ground, etc.
Stemonyphantes lineatus (L.)	Widespread in many habitats
Bolyphantes luteolus (Blackwall)	In grass, heather and low vegetation
Lepthyphantes minutus (Blackwall)	Around buildings, holes in trees, etc.
L. alacris (Blackwall)	In detritus in woods
L. obscurus (Blackwall)	In undergrowth
L. tenuis (Blackwall)	Widespread in many habitats
L. zimmermanni Bertkau	Widespread in many habitats
L. cristatus (Menge)	In undergrowth, grass, etc.
L. mengei Kulczynski	Widespread in undergrowth
L. flavipes (Blackwall)	Widespread in undergrowth
L. tenebricola (Wider)	In detritus in woods
L. ericaeus (Blackwall)	In low vegetation in dry habitats
L. insignis O.Pickard-Cambridge	In undergrowth. Rare
Helophora insignis (Blackwall)	In moss and grass in damp areas
Linyphia triangularis (Clerck)	Widespread on bushes in late summer
L. hortensis Sundevall	In low undergrowth in woods
L. *(Neriene)* clathrata Sundevall	Widespread in low undergrowth
L. *(Neriene)* peltata Wider	Widespread in woods
Microlinyphia pusilla (Sundevall)	On low vegetation
Allomengea scopigera (Grube)	Wet fresh- and salt-water marshes

Order: OPILIONES – HARVESTMEN
Sub-order: PALPATORES

NEMASTOMATIDAE

Nemastoma bimaculatum (Fabricius)	Widespread in herbage, under logs, etc.

PHALANGIIDAE

Phalangium opilio L.	Widespread and frequent
Megabunus diadema (Fabricius)	Widespread in moss, also in heather
Rilaena triangularis (Herbst)	In low vegetation in woods
Lophopilio palpinalis (Herbst)	Vegetation in open woodland
Paroligolophus agrestis (Meade)	Common in various habitats
Lacinius ephippiatus (C.L. Koch)	In low vegetation; not common
Mitopus morio (Fabricius)	Widespread, often abundant
Leiobunum rotundum (Latrielle)	Widespread in low vegetation, etc.
L. blackwalli R.H. Meade	Widespread in low vegetation, etc.

Order: PSEUDOSCORPIONES

CHTHONIIDAE

Chthonius (Chthonius) ischnocheles (Hermann) Chamberlin	Under stones, logs, etc.
Chthonius (Chthonius) orthodactylus (Leach) L.Koch	In leaf litter, moss, etc.

NEOBISIIDAE

Neobisium (Neobisium) muscorum (Leach) Chamberlin	Widespread in various habitats
Roncocreagris cambridgei (L.Koch) Mahnert	In detritus, under stones, etc.

CHERNETIDAE

Pselaphochernes scorpioides (Hermann) Beier	In compost, straw, gardens, etc.

Sub-Class: ACARI (TICKS & MITES)

Order: METASTIGMATA – TICKS

IXODIDAE

Ixodes canisuga Johnston *(I.autumnalis Leach)*   Common parasite of badgers, foxes, dogs
I. arboricola Schulze & Schlottke *(I. passericola Schulze)* Around the eyes of small passerine birds.   Rather common
I. ricinus (L.)   CASTOR-BEAN TICK (SHEEP (or DEER) TICK)   A ubiquitous species on Exmoor affecting many animals including man. Notorious as the vector of Lyme disease.

Order: **PROSTIGMATA (MITES)**

Evans, et al (1961) give the figure of 1600 species of mite (in six Orders) on the British List, adding that many more undoubtedly remain to be discovered! Mites occur in a very wide range of habitats, many species being present in the soil and in leaf-litter in woodland. Some are predatory while others feed on a wide variety of plant matter such as algae and fungi. Some species are notorious for being the causative agents of a number of animal and human diseases.

Many mites of the family Eriophyidae feed on living plants producing various types of gall characteristic of each species and these are well represented in the following list. Included are a mere handful of others which are either of medical or economic importance. Almost everyone is familiar with the notorious ticks, especially the Sheep-tick, but there are many others of this group to be found as ectoparasites of birds, reptiles and mammals.

Identification of mites presents many problems and is really a matter for specialists.

ERIOPHYIDAE

Aceria brevitarsa brevitarsa (Fockeu)	Erineum on Alnus (Alder)	Common
A. calycophthira (Nalepa)	Bud-galls on Betula (Birch)	Common
A. erinea (Nalepa)	Erineum on Juglans (Walnut)	Common
A. eriobia eriobia (Nalepa)	Erineum on Acer campestre (Field Maple)	Frequent
A. fraxinivora (Nalepa)	Galls on inflorescence of Fraxinus (Ash)	
A. genistae (Nalepa)	'Bushy-bud' on garden Cytisus (Broom)	Local
A. geranii (Nalepa)	Leaf-galls on Geranium lucidum (Shining Cranesbill)	
A. iteina Nalepa	Leaf-galls on Salix (Sallow)	
A. macrochela macrochela (Nalepa)	Leaf-galls on Acer campestre (Field Maple)	Common
A. macrorhyncha macrorhyncha (Nalepa)	Pustules on leaves of Acer pseudoplatanus (Sycamore)	Common
A. macrorhyncha cephalonea (Nalepa)	Pustules on Acer campestre (Field Maple)	Common
A. nervisequa nervisequa (Canestrini)	Tomentum on upperside of leaves of Fagus (Beech)	Very common
A. nervisequa faginea (Nalepa)	Tomentum on underside of leaves of Fagus (Beech)	Very common
A. pseudoplatani (Nalepa)	Erineum on Acer pseudoplatanus (Sycamore)	Frequent
A. rudis (Canestrini)	Erineum on leaves of Betula (Birch)	Common
A. tetanothrix laevis (Nalepa)	Leaf-galls on Salix (Sallow)	Fairly common
A. ulmicola ulmicola (Nalepa)	Pustules on leaves of Ulmus (Elm)	Uncommon
Cecidophyes galii (Karpelles)	Thickened and rolled leaves on Galium (Cleavers)	Very common
Epitrimerus trilobus (Nalepa)	Leaf-galls on Sambucus (Elder)	Common
Eriophyes convolvens Nalepa	Leaf-galls on Euonymus (Spindle)	Frequent
E. crataegi Nalepa	Small pustules on leaves of Crataegus (Hawthorn)	Rare
E. goniothorax Nalepa	Rolled leaf-edges on Crataegus (Hawthorn)	Abundant
E. inangulis Nalepa	Pustules on leaves of Alnus (Alder)	Common
E. laevis laevis Nalepa	Pustules on leaves of Alnus (Alder)	Common

MITES

Eriophyes lateannulatus Schulze	Short nail-galls on Tilia (Lime)	Uncommon
E. leionota Nalepa	Leaf-galls on Betula (Birch)	
E. leiosoma Nalepa	Erineum on leaves of Tilia (Lime)	Common
E. padi prunianus Nalepa	Leaf-galls on Prunus spinosa (Blackthorn)	Common
E. similis prunispinosa Nalepa	Galls leaf-margins of Prunus spinosa (Blackthorn)	Very common
E. sorbi (Canestrini)	Leaf-galls on Sorbus acucparia (Rowan)	
E. stenaspis stenaspis Nalepa	Inrolled leaf-margins on Fagus (Beech)	Common
E. tiliae tiliae (Pagenstecher)	Long nail-galls on of Tilia (Lime)	Very common
Phytopus avellanae Nalepa	Bud-galls on Corylus (Hazel)	Very common

The names of the Eriophyidae follow Buhr. H. (see references)

TROMBICULIDAE

Trombicula autumnalis (Shaw)	HARVEST MITE	Often afflicts humans

TROMBIDIIDAE

Eutrombidium rostratus (Scopoli)	RED VELVET MITE	On garden paths in spring

TETRANYCHIDAE

Panonychus ulmi (C.L.Koch)	RED SPIDER MITE	A pest of fruit trees

Order: ASTIGMATA

PSOROPTIDAE

Psoroptes equi (Raspail) f.ovis	SHEEP SCAB	A curse of Exmoor sheep farmers

SARCOPTIDAE

Sarcoptes scabiei (L.)	SCABIES ITCH-MITE	Afflicts humans

References:

Buhr, H. (1964/5) *Bestimmungstabellen der Gallen an Pflanzen Mittel- und Nordeuropas* Fischer, Jena.

Evans, G.O., Sheals, J.G. & Macfarlane, D. (1961) *Terrestrial Acari of the British Isles* Volume 1. British Museum (Natural History).

Robbins, J. (1994) *A Provisional Atlas of the Gall-Mites of Warwickshire* Warwick Museum Service.

Stubbs, F.B. Ed. (1986) *Provisional Keys to British Plant Galls* British Plant Gall Society.

VERTEBRATES
Phylum: **CHORDATA**
Sub-Phylum: **VERTEBRATA**

MARINE AND FRESHWATER FISH (PISCES)

This list has been compiled from records held by our Maritime Recorder, Fred Porter, from information gathered from local fishermen, and from a list of fish caught by members of the Minehead and District Sea Angling Club. We are grateful to Mr Steve Pilbrow, their Club Secretary, for checking through this list. The classification follows that of Nelson, J. (1976) *Fishes of the World*.

Sea fishing takes place from the quays at Minehead, Porlock Weir, Lynmouth and Combe Martin; off the various short sandy beaches, and from rock marks all along the coast. Careful attention must be paid to tides at all times to avoid difficulties and dangers. Local Angling Clubs and tackle shops can help and advise new-comers to Exmoor. In recent years catches off the Exmoor coast include tope to 65 lbs., conger to 42 lbs., cod to 36 lbs., monkfish to 38 lbs., ling to 15 lbs., bull huss to 17 lbs., bass to 14 lbs. Other fish caught regularly include mackerel, pollack, pouting, whiting and lesser spotted dogfish.

Most reservoirs are stocked with rainbow trout, and native brown trout occur in all the rivers and streams. There are summer runs of salmon and sea trout in the East Lyn and to a lesser extent in the Exe and Barle.

N.V. Allen,
Editor of Vertebrates

Super-Class: **AGNATHA**; Class: **CEPHALASPIDOMORPHI**

Order: **PETROMYZONIFORMES (LAMPREYS)**

PETROMYZONIDAE

Lampetra fluviatilis (L.)	RIVER LAMPREY	Scarce
L. planeri (Bloch)	BROOK LAMPREY	Rare
	Larvae trapped at Aller/Horner junction 1994/5	

Super-Class: **GNATHOSTOMATA**; Class: **CHONDRICHTHYES**
Sub-Class: **ELASMOBRANCHII**

Order: **LAMNIFORMES (SHARKS & DOGFISH)**

SCYLIORHINIDAE

Scyliorhinus stellaris (L.)	BULL HUSS or GREATER SPOTTED DOGFISH	Common
S. canicula (L.)	LESSER SPOTTED DOGFISH	Very common

FISHES

LAMNIDAE
Lamna nasus (Bonnaterre)	PORBEAGLE	Rare

CARCHARINIDAE
Galeorhinus galeus (L.)	TOPE	Common in summer
Mustelus mustelus (L.)	SMOOTH HOUND	Scarce

Order: SQUALIFORMES

SQUALIDAE
Squalus acanthias L.	SPUR DOGFISH	Common in season

SQUATINIDAE
Squatina squatina (L.)	MONKFISH	Rare

Order: RAJIFORMES (RAYS & SKATES)

RAJIDAE
Raja batis L.	COMMON or BLUE SKATE	Rare
R. undulata Lacepede	UNDULATE RAY	Scarce
R. montagui Fowler	SPOTTED RAY	Fairly common
R. clavata L.	THORNBACK RAY	Common
R. microocellata Montagu	SMALL-EYED or PAINTED RAY	Fairly common
R. brachyura Lafont	BLONDE RAY	Fairly common

DASYATIDAE
Dasyatis pastinaca (L.)	STING RAY	Rare

Class: OSTEICHTHYES Sub-Class: ACTINOPTERYGII

Super-Order: TELEOSTEI Order: CLUPEIFORMES

CLUPEIDAE
Alosa alosa (L.)	ALLIS SHAD	Legally protected.	Rare
Clupea harengus L.	HERRING		Scarce

Order: ANGUILLIFORMES

ANGUILLIDAE
Anguilla anguilla (L.)	EEL	Common

CONGRIDAE
Conger conger (L.)	CONGER EEL	Common

FISHES

Order: SALMONIFORMES

THYMALLIDAE

Thymallus thymallus (L.)	GRAYLING	Scarce

SALMONIDAE

Salmo salar L.	SALMON	Locally common
S. trutta fario L.	BROWN TROUT	Abundant
S. trutta trutta L.	SEA TROUT	Locally common
S. gairdneri Richardson	RAINBOW TROUT	Escapes from fish farms and reservoir stock

Order: CYPRINIFORMES

CYPRINIDAE

Cyprinus carpio (L.)	KOI CARP	Released domestic Dunster Hawn pond
Leuciscus idus (L.)	GOLDEN ORFE	Released domestic Dunster Hawn pond
Phoxinus phoxinus (L.)	MINNOW	Frequent in slow-moving water
Scardinus erythrophthalmus (L.)	RUDD	Uncommon in slow-moving water
Tinca tinca (L.)	TENCH	Scarce

COBITIDAE

Noemacheilus barbatulus (L.)	STONE LOACH	Rare

Order: GOBIESOCIFORMES

GOBIESOCIDAE

Lepadogaster lepadogaster (Bonnaterre)	CORNISH SUCKER or SHORE CLINGFISH	Scarce

Order: GADIFORMES

GADIDAE

Merlangius merlangus (L.)	WHITING	Common in season
Trisopterus luscus (L.)	POUTING	Fairly common
Pollachius pollachius (L.)	POLLACK	Common
P. virens (L.)	COALFISH or COLEY	Scarce
Gadus morhua L.	COD	Common
Melanogrammus aeglefinus (L.)	HADDOCK	Scarce
Molva molva (L.)	LING	Fairly common in season
Gaidropsarus vulgaris (Cloquet)	THREE-BEARDED ROCKLING	Common

FISHES

Ciliata mustela (L.)	FIVE-BEARDED ROCKLING	Scarce
MERLUCCIIDAE		
Merluccius merluccius (L.)	HAKE	Scarce

Order: LOPHIIFORMES

LOPHIIDAE

Lophius piscatorius L.	ANGLER or FROGFISH	Rare

Order: ATHERINIFORMES

BELONIDAE

Belone belone (L.)	GARFISH	Scarce

Order: SYNGNATHIFORMES

SYNGNATHIDAE

Syngnathus acus L.	GREAT PIPEFISH	Scarce

Order: ZEIFORMES

ZEIDAE

Zeus faber L.	JOHN DORY or ST. PETER'S FISH	Rare

Order: GASTEROSTEIFORMES

GASTEROSTEIDAE

Gasterosteus aculeatus L.	THREE-SPINED STICKLEBACK	Scarce
Pungitius pungitius (L.)	TEN-SPINED STICKLEBACK	Fairly common
Spinachia spinachia (L.)	SEA or FIFTEEN-SPINED STICKLEBACK	Rare

Order: SCORPAENIFORMES

TRIGLIDAE

Aspitrigla cuculus (L.)	RED GURNARD	Rare
AGONIDAE		
Agonus cataphractus (L.)	POGGE or ARMED BULLHEAD	Rare
COTTIDAE		
Cottus gobio L.	BULLHEAD or MILLER'S THUMB	Common

FISHES

CYCLOPTERIDAE
Cyclopterus lumpus L.   LUMPSUCKER   Uncommon

Order: PERCIFORMES

SERRANIDAE
Dicentrarchus labrax (L.)   BASS   Scarce
CARANGIDAE
Trachurus trachurus (L.)   SCAD or HORSE MACKEREL   Common in season
SPARIDAE
Pagellus bogaraveo (Brunnich)   RED SEA-BREAM   Scarce
Spondyliosoma cantharus (L.)   BLACK SEA-BREAM   Rare
MULLIDAE
Mullus surmuletus L.   RED MULLET   Scarce
MUGILIDAE
Liza ramada (Risso)   THIN-LIPPED GREY MULLET   Scarce in season
LABRIDAE
Labrus bergylta Ascanius   BALLAN WRASSE   Scarce
TRACHINIDAE
Trachinus vipera Cuvier   LESSER WEEVER   Scarce
AMMODYTIDAE
Ammodytes tobianus L.   LESSER SAND EEL   Common
GOBIIDAE
Chapparudo flavescens (Fabricius)   TWO-SPOT GOBY   Rare; rockpools
Pomatoschistus minutus (Pallas)   SAND or COMMON GOBY   Common; rockpools
SCOMBRIDAE
Scomber scombrus L.   MACKEREL   Common in season

Order: PLEURINECTIFORMES

BOTHIDAE
Scophthalmus maximus (L.)   TURBOT   Common in season
S. rhombus (L.)   BRILL   Scarce
PLEURONECTIDAE
Limanda limanda (L.)   DAB   Common
Platichthys flesus (L.)   FLOUNDER   Common
Pleuronectes platessa L.   PLAICE   Common
Hippoglossus hippoglossus (L.)   HALIBUT   Scarce

FISHES

SOLEIDAE

Solea solea (L.)   DOVER SOLE   Scarce

Order: TETRAODONTIFORMES

BALISTIDAE

Balistes carolinensis (Gmelin)   GREY TRIGGER-FISH   Rare in British waters (several caught 1995)

MOLIDAE

Mola mola (L.)   SUN FISH   Scarce (several seen 1994 and 1995)

References:

Nelson, J. (1976) *Fishes of the World* J. Wiley & Sons.

Muus, Bent J. (1971) *The Freshwater Fishes of Britain and Europe* Collins.

Nixon, M. (1982) *The Oxford Book of Vertebrates* O.U.P.

AMPHIBIANS & REPTILES

There are in Britain six native species of amphibians and six of reptiles. On Exmoor three of the species of amphibian are fairly common: the common frog, the common toad and the palmate newt. The crested newt and the smooth newt tend to be lowland species and there have been no recent records of them on Exmoor, although they occur in other parts of Somerset.

Exmoor has four of the six British species of reptiles. Slow-worm, common lizard and adder are quite frequent, while the grass snake is more rarely seen. The reptiles are particularly vulnerable to the many heath fires, but their populations seem fairly constant.

All British reptiles and amphibians have some degree of protection under the Wildlife Act; Crested Newts and Adders have full protection.

Beryl Lappage
Recorder of Herpetology, E.N.H.S.

Class: AMPHIBIA
Order: CAUDATA (NEWTS)

SALAMANDRIDAE

Triturus helveticus (Razoumowski)   PALMATE NEWT   Common
  Breeds in shallow water, puddles, ponds and garden pools, also in brackish water. Occurs on the moor and on coastal marsh. Adults found in various habitats near breeding sites.

  (T. cristatus (Laurenti)   CRESTED or WARTY NEWT   No recent records)
    May be found in water at any time of year, or hiding beneath nearby stones.

  (T. vulgaris (L.)   SMOOTH NEWT   No recent records)
    More terrestrial than other species. Easily confused with Palmate Newt.

Order: ANURA (FROGS & TOADS)

BUFONIDAE

Bufo bufo (L.)   COMMON TOAD   common in various fairly dry places
                                  except in breeding season when it seeks ponds and pools

RANIDAE

Rana temporaria L.   COMMON FROG   very common in damp places

Class: REPTILIA

Order: SQUAMATA (LIZARDS & SNAKES)

ANGUIDAE
Anguis fragilis L.   SLOW-WORM   common; heaths, hedgebanks, gardens
LACERTIDAE
Lacerta vivipara Jacquin   COMMON or VIVIPAROUS LIZARD   common
COLUBRIDAE
Natrix natrix (L.)   GRASS SNAKE   scarce
                                            usually near water; swims well
VIPERIDAE
Vipera berus (L.)   ADDER or VIPER   common on damp or dry moorland
   also in hedgerows and walls. Varied coloration: grey, brown, greenish, cinnamon and black (melanistic) forms have been recorded on Exmoor. A legally protected species.

References:

Arnold, E.N. and Burton, J.A. *A Field Guide to the Reptiles and Amphibians of Britain and Europe* (1978) Collins.

Beebee, Trevor *Frogs and Toads* (1989) Whittet Books Ltd.

Langton, Tom *Snakes and Lizards* (1989) Whittet Books Ltd.

Class: AVES (BIRDS)

This check-list covers 272 species of birds recorded from the Exmoor area since 1970, i.e. 26 additions since the first edition of *The Flora and Fauna* in 1988. The wide variety of habitats occurring within the National Park provide for a diverse and rich bird life. These habitats include the rugged North Devon cliffs stretching from Lynmouth to Heddon's Mouth with colonies of auks, gulls and other nesting seabirds. Porlock Marsh and the few coastal beaches are favourite spots for spring and autumn passage waders and terns, and for the occasional rarity such as spoonbill, long-billed dowitcher, and grey and Wilson's phalaropes. Birds of prey are well represented with buzzard, sparrowhawk, kestrel, merlin and peregrine all nesting, and possibly the hobby. The high moorland ranging from 1200 to 1700 feet above sea level attracts ring ouzel, wheatear, whinchat, curlew, snipe and raven. The filling of the 370 acres of Wimbleball Lake in 1977 has provided a winter refuge for many species of wildfowl and a nesting site for great crested grebe, coot, Canada goose and tufted duck. Spring migrants such as pied flycatchers and warblers inhabit the large areas of broadleaved woodland together with the resident woodpeckers, nuthatch and treecreeper. The conifer plantations attract siskin and crossbill and when felled provide open spaces for nightjars.

Classification in this Check-list follows that of *The Birds of the Western Palearctic* (1977-1994) 9 vols.

Roger Butcher,
Recorder, E.N.H.S.

Order: GAVIIFORMES

GAVIIDAE - DIVERS

Gavia stellata (Pontoppidan)   RED-THROATED DIVER
   Winter and passage visitor to coastal waters; occasional Wimbleball Lake

G. arctica (L.)   BLACK-THROATED DIVER
   Scarce winter visitor to coastal waters. Two Wimbleball, February 1985

G. immer (Brünnich)   GREAT NORTHERN DIVER   Rare off shore winter visitor

Order: PODICIPEDIFORMES

PODICIPEDIDAE - GREBES

Tachybaptus ruficollis (Pallas)   LITTLE GREBE   Winter visitor: reservoirs, coast, ponds

Podiceps cristatus (L.)   GREAT CRESTED GREBE   Nests
   Resident, winter visitor. First nested Wimbleball, 1982

P. grisegena (Boddeart)   RED-NECKED GREBE   Very rare winter visitor
   One, Wimbleball, March 1993

P. auritus (L.)   SLAVONIAN GREBE   Very rare winter visitor
   One, Dunster Hawn, October 1972

P. nigricollis Brehm   BLACK-NECKED GREBE   Rare winter visitor
   Recorded Porlock Marsh, Feb. 1985 and Wimbleball, Apr. 1995

BIRDS

Order: PROCELLARIIFORMES

PROCELLARIIDAE - FULMARS, PETRELS, SHEARWATERS

Fulmarus glacialis (L.)   FULMAR   Nests
Mainly spring/summer visitor. First bred Devon Exmoor 1958; Somerset 1981
About 400 nesting pairs Lynmouth to Heddon's Mouth, 1994

Calonectris diomedea (Scopoli)   CORY'S SHEARWATER   Rare vagrant
Off-shore records 1986, 1987 and 1994

Puffinus gravis (O'Reilly)   GREAT SHEARWATER   Rare vagrant
Two off Lynmouth, August 1986

P. griseus (Gmelin)   SOOTY SHEARWATER   Rare off-shore passage migrant

P. puffinus (Brünnich)   MANX SHEARWATER   Passage visitor
Feeding parties in coastal waters, spring to autumn

P. yelkouan mauretanicus (Acerbi & Lowe) MEDITERRANEAN SHEARWATER   Vagrant
Race of Manx Shearwater breeding in the Mediterranean and only recently split from
P. puffinus.   One off Minehead, April 1994

HYDROBATIDAE - STORM PETRELS

Hydrobates pelagicus (L.)   STORM PETREL   Vagrant; coastal waters summer/autumn

Oceanodroma leucorhoa (Vieillot) LEACH'S STORM PETREL   Rare storm vagrant

Order: PELECANIFORMES

SULIDAE - BOOBIES, GANNETS

Sula bassana (L.)   GANNET Regular summer and passage visitor off the coast

PHALACROCORACIDAE - CORMORANTS, SHAGS

Phalacrocorax carbo (L.)   CORMORANT   Nests
Resident, winter visitor. Coasts and inland on reservoirs

P. aristotelis (L.)   SHAG   Nests
Resident. A few breeding pairs on the North Devon cliffs

Order: CICONIIFORMES

ARDEIDAE - BITTERNS, HERONS

Botaurus stellaris (L.)   BITTERN   Rare winter visitor to coastal marshes

Egretta garzetta (L.)   LITTLE EGRET   Rare visitor
Regular at Porlock Marsh 1993 and 1994, occasional inland

Ardea cinerea L.   GREY HERON   Nests
Resident. About 25 breeding pairs at five heronries

THRESKIORNITHIDAE - IBISES, SPOONBILLS

Platalea leucorodia L.   SPOONBILL   Vagrant. One Porlock Marsh 1994

BIRDS

Order: ANSERIFORMES

ANATIDAE - WILDFOWL

Cygnus olor (Gmelin)	MUTE SWAN	Nests
	Resident. Minehead/Dunster Marshes, rare elsewhere	
C. columbianus bewickii (Yarrell)	BEWICK'S SWAN	
	Rare winter visitor to Minehead and Porlock Marshes	
C. cygnus (L.)	WHOOPER SWAN	Rare winter visitor to the coast
Anser fabalis (Latham)	BEAN GOOSE	Vagrant. One Porlock Marsh spring 1993
A. brachyrhynchus Baillon	PINK-FOOTED GOOSE	Vagrant. One Wimbleball Dec.1991
A. albifrons (Scopoli)	WHITE-FRONTED GOOSE	
	Irregular winter visitor to Minehead and Porlock Marshes and Wimbleball	
A. anser (L.)	GREYLAG GOOSE	Rare winter visitor
Branta canadensis (L.)	CANADA GOOSE	Nests
	Resident. Breeds Wimbleball and Minehead. Up to 400 in winter	
B. canadensis minima Delacour	CACKLING CANADA GOOSE	
	Single birds occasional with flocks of nominate race; probable escapes	
B. leucopsis (Bechstein)	BARNACLE GOOSE	Winter visitor
	A few most years with Canada flocks	
B. bernicla (L.)	BRENT GOOSE Scarce winter visitor, usually dark breasted	
Alopochen aegyptiacus (L.)	EGYPTIAN GOOSE	Resident and local
	Feral breeder at Wimbleball, 1982-1986	
Tadorna tadorna (L.)	SHELDUCK	Nests
	Resident and winter visitor. Breeds Porlock Marsh	
Aix galericulata (L.)	MANDARIN	Vagrant or feral resident
Anas penelope L.	WIGEON	Winter visitor
	Common on the coastal marshes and Wimbleball	
A. americana Gmelin	AMERICAN WIGEON	Vagrant
	Male, Wimbleball, winters 1987 and 1988	
A. strepera, L.	GADWALL Scarce winter visitor Wimbleball/Dunster Beach	
A. crecca L.	TEAL Regular winter visitor, coastal marshes & Wimbleball	
A. platyrhynchos L.	MALLARD	Nests
	Resident and winter visitor. Widespread and common	
A. acuta L.	PINTAIL	Rare winter visitor
A. querquedula L.	GARGANEY	Vagrant. Male Porlock Marsh, April 1972
A. discors L.	BLUE-WINGED TEAL Vagrant. Male Porlock Marsh, 1981	
A. clypeata L.	SHOVELER	Regular winter visitor; coast and Wimbleball
Netta rufina (Pall.)	RED-CRESTED POCHARD Five Nutscale, November, 1995	
Aythya ferina (L.)	POCHARD	Winter visitor Wimbleball, rarely the coast
A. collaris (Donovan)	RING-NECKED DUCK	Vagrant
	Wintering male, Wimbleball, 1988, 1989 and 1990	
A. fuligula (L.)	TUFTED DUCK	Winter visitor and scarce resident
	Bred Wimbleball, 1989	
A. marila (L.)	SCAUP Scarce winter visitor to Wimbleball, occ. the coast	

BIRDS

Somateria mollissima (L.)	EIDER	Rare winter visitor to coastal waters
Clangula hyemalis (L.)	LONG-TAILED DUCK	Vagrant. One, Nutscale, Mar. 1995
Melanitta nigra (L.)	COMMON SCOTER	Scarce

Passage and winter visitor to coastal waters. Recorded Wimbleball 1983

M. fusca (L.)	VELVET SCOTER	Vagrant

Male, Dunster Beach, December 1985; two Minehead Beach, November 1994

Bucephala clangula (L.)	GOLDENEYE	Regular winter visitor to Wimbleball; occasional elsewhere
Mergus albellus L.	SMEW	Rare winter visitor

Single birds Wimbleball 1984, 1986 and 1987

M. serrator L.	RED-BREASTED MERGANSER	Rare winter visitor mainly to the coast
M. merganser L.	GOOSANDER	Rare resident. First bred Exmoor 1993

Regular winter visitor to Wimbleball, occasionally to Nutscale and the coast

Oxyura jamaicensis (Gmelin)	RUDDY DUCK	Rare winter visitor to Wimbleball First recorded 1985

Order: ACCIPITRIFORMES

ACCIPITRIDAE - HAWKS

Pernis apivorus (L.)	HONEY BUZZARD	Vagrant

Single birds: Robber's Bridge, May 1990; Selworthy, Aug. 1994; Barna Barrow, Aug. 1995

Milvus milvus (L.)	RED KITE	Most frequent as spring passage visitor One or two over Exmoor in most years
Circus aeruginosus (L.)	MARSH HARRIER	Rare passage migrant usually to coastal areas
C. cyaneus (L.)	HEN HARRIER	Scarce but regular winter visitor to moors
C. pygargus (L.)	MONTAGU'S HARRIER	Rare passage migrant

Recent records from Exford Common and Porlock Marsh

Accipiter gentilis (L.)	GOSHAWK	Rare resident

A few breeding season records since 1990

A. nisus (L.)	SPARROWHAWK	Resident and fairly common. Nests
Buteo buteo (L.)	BUZZARD	Resident, widespread and common. Nests
B. lagopus (Pontoppidan)	ROUGH-LEGGED BUZZARD	Vagrant

Recorded in the winters of 1973, 1974 and 1987

PANDIONIDAE - OSPREY

Pandion haliaetus (L.)	OSPREY	Irregular spring and autumn passage visitor

Order: FALCONIFORMES

FALCONIDAE - FALCONS AND ALLIES

Falco tinnunculus L.	KESTREL	Resident and common. Nests
F. columbarius L.	MERLIN	Resident but scarce with only a few breeding pairs
F. subbuteo L.	HOBBY	Scarce summer visitor, may breed occasionally

BIRDS

Falco rusticolus L.   GYRFALCON   Vagrant. One Foreland Point, March 1972
F. peregrinus Tunstall   PEREGRINE   Nests
                                      Resident. Locally frequent on coast, also hunts inland

Order: GALLIFORMES

TETRAONIDAE - GROUSE

Lagopus lagopus (L.)   RED GROUSE   Scarce, mainly on Dunkery slopes. Nests
Tetrao tetrix (L.)   BLACK GROUSE   Probably now extinct on Exmoor
                                                                     Last recorded in 1981

PHASIANIDAE - PARTRIDGES, QUAILS, PHEASANTS

Alectoris rufa (L.)   RED-LEGGED PARTRIDGE   Nests
                              Resident, locally common, usually where reared and released
Perdix perdix (L.)   GREY PARTRIDGE   Nests
                             Resident, scarce. Some records may refer to hand-reared birds
Coturnix corturnix (L.)   QUAIL   May nest
               Scarce and irregular summer visitor. About 20 calling males, summer 1989
Phasianus colchicus L.   PHEASANT   Nests
                                        Resident and common but rare on the moors

Order: GRUIFORMES

RALLIDAE - RAILS

Rallus aquaticus L.   WATER RAIL   Regular but scarce winter visitor
                                                     to marshy habitats on coast and inland
Porzana porzana (L.)   SPOTTED CRAKE   Vagrant. One Porlock Marsh Aug.1971
Crex crex (L.)   CORNCRAKE   Rare passage visitor. Last recorded 1982
Gallinula chloropus (L.)   MOORHEN   Nests
                                         Resident and local around reservoirs and ponds
Fulica atra L.   COOT   Nests
                                   Resident and winter visiter. Main winter refuge is Wimbleball

Order: CHARADRIIFORMES

HAEMATOPODIDAE - OYSTERCATCHERS

Haematopus ostralegus L.   OYSTERCATCHER   Nests
                                        Resident and winter visitor. Breeds Devon Exmoor

RECURVIROSTRIDAE - AVOCETS

Recurvirostra avosetta L.   AVOCET Vagrant. Records include 8 Porlock Bay,Dec.1987

CHARADRIIDAE - PLOVERS, LAPWINGS

Charadrius dubius Scopoli   LITTLE RINGED PLOVER   Rare passage visitor
                                          Recorded Dunster Beach, Porlock Marsh, Wimbleball

BIRDS

Charadrius hiaticula L.	RINGED PLOVER	Resident, passage and winter visitor Bred Dunster Beach, 1993
C. morinellus (L.)	DOTTEREL	Scarce passage visitor, usually seen on moors
Pluvialis apricaria (L.)	GOLDEN PLOVER	Winter, spring and autumn passage visitor. Coasts and inland
P. squatarola (L.)	GREY PLOVER	Winter visitor Small numbers Minehead and Dunster Beach
Vanellus vanellus (L.)	LAPWING	Resident, winter and passage visitor. Nests

SCOLOPACIDAE - SANDPIPERS AND ALLIES

Calidris canutus (L.)	KNOT	Scarce autumn passage visitor to the beaches
C. alba (Pallas)	SANDERLING	Regular passage/winter visitor along coast
C. minuta (Leisler)	LITTLE STINT	Rare autumn passage visitor
C. temminckii (Leisler)	TEMMINCK'S STINT	Vagrant. One Porlock Marsh Sep.1972
C. fuscicollis (Vieillot)	WHITE-RUMPED SANDPIPER	Rare visitor; one Dunster Beach, Aug./Sept. 1995
C. bairdii (Coues)	BAIRD'S SANDPIPER	Vagrant. One Porlock Marsh Sep.1973
C. melanotos (Vieillot)	PECTORAL SANDPIPER	Vagrant. Porlock Marsh May 1974
C. ferruginea (Pontoppidan)	CURLEW SANDPIPER	Rare passage visitor to coast
C. maritima (Brünnich)	PURPLE SANDPIPER	Rare winter visitor Mainly between Lynmouth and Heddon's Mouth. One Dunster Beach, Aug. 1994
C. alpina (L.)	DUNLIN	Regular winter and passage visitor. Rarely > 200
Philomachus pugnax (L.)	RUFF	Scarce spring and autumn passage visitor to coast and Wimbleball. 15 Porlock Marsh, April 1987
Lymnocryptes minimus (Brünnich)	JACK SNIPE	Scarce winter visitor to freshwater marshes, lakes and ponds
Gallinago gallinago (L.)	SNIPE	Nests Resident, winter visitor. Breeds moorland bogs
Limnodromus scolopaceus (Say)	LONG-BILLED DOWITCHER	Vagrant One Porlock Marsh, Sept/Oct 1973
Scolopax rusticola L.	WOODCOCK	Regular autumn/winter visitor. Nested 1981
Limosa limosa (L.)	BLACK-TAILED GODWIT	Scarce spring/autumn passage
L. lapponica (L.)	BAR-TAILED GODWIT	Small numbers spring/autumn passage, occasional in winter
Numenius phaeopus (L.)	WHIMBREL	Regular spring and autumn visitor to coast and Wimbleball
N. arquata (L.)	CURLEW	Nests Resident, common passage and winter visitor. Breeds on the moorland
Tringa erythropus (Pallas)	SPOTTED REDSHANK	Scarce autumn passage visitor
T. totanus (L.)	REDSHANK	Resident/winter visitor. Breeds Porlock Marsh
T. nebularia (Gunnerus)	GREENSHANK	Scarce but regular spring/autumn passage visitor
T. ochropus L.	GREEN SANDPIPER	Regular, mainly autumn, passage visitor to reservoirs and marshes

BIRDS

Tringa glareola L.	WOOD SANDPIPER	Scarce autumn passage visitor
Xenus cinereus (Güldenstädt)	TEREK SANDPIPER	Vagrant.One Porlock Marsh May 1987
Actitis hypoleucos (L.)	COMMON SANDPIPER	Regular spring/autumn passage visitor. Sometimes winters
Arenaria interpres (L.)	TURNSTONE	Common passage and winter visitor Recorded most months
Phalaropus tricolor (Vieillot)	WILSON'S PHALAROPE	Vagrant Female, Porlock Marsh, June 1995
P. lobatus (L.)	RED-NECKED PHALAROPE	Vagrant One Porlock Marsh, Sept. 1970
P. fulicarius (L.)	GREY PHALAROPE	Rare passage visitor to coast

STERCORARIIDAE - SKUAS

Stercorarius pomarinus (Temminck)	POMARINE SKUA	Rare autumn passage visitor Exceptional, 33 off Dunster Beach, November 1985
S. parasiticus (L.)	ARCTIC SKUA	Scarce autumn passage visitor coastal waters
S. longicaudus Vieillot	LONG-TAILED SKUA	Vagrant Recorded autumn 1991, 1993 and 1994
S. skua (Brünnich)	GREAT SKUA	Rare autumn passage visitor A few off-shore most years

LARIDAE - GULLS

Larus melanocephalus Temminck	MEDITERRANEAN GULL	Scarce passage and winter visitor recorded annually
L. atricilla L.	LAUGHING GULL	Vagrant. Bossington Beach Sept.1980
L. minutus Pallas	LITTLE GULL	Rare passage visitor, recorded most years
L. sabini Sabine	SABINE'S GULL	Vagrant Four autumn coastal records since 1985
L. ridibundus L.	BLACK-HEADED GULL	Common winter visitor present spring and summer
L. delawarensis Ord	RING-BILLED GULL	Vagrant One Dunster Beach April 1991
L. canus L.	COMMON GULL	Common passage and winter visitor coasts and inland
L. fuscus graellsii Brehm	LESSER BLACK-BACKED GULL	Scarce passage and winter visitor. Has bred on Devon cliffs
L. fuscus fuscus L.	Scandinavian race	Vagrant. One, Hurlstone Point Jul.1989
L. argentatus Pontoppidan	HERRING GULL	Nests Resident and common visitor. Notable decline in breeding population since early 1980's
L. glaucoides Meyer	ICELAND GULL	Vagrant. Five, mainly winter, since 1981
L. hyperboreus Gunnerus	GLAUCOUS GULL	Vagrant Three records, Dunster Beach to Porlock Bay, 1991 and 1993
L. marinus L.	GREAT BLACK-BACKED GULL	Nests Resident and winter visitor. A few cliff-nesting pairs
Rissa tridactyla (L.)	KITTIWAKE	Breeds Devon Exmoor Declined since 1985; fairly common passage and winter visitor in coastal waters

BIRDS

STERNIDAE - TERNS

Sterna sandvicensis Latham	SANDWICH TERN	Small numbers on spring/autumn passage most years
Sterna dougallii Montagu	ROSEATE TERN	Rare autumn passage visitor Three Minehead Beach Aug. 1971
S. hirundo L.	COMMON TERN	Regular spring and autumn passage visitor
S. paradisaea Pontoppidan	ARCTIC TERN	Fairly frequent on autumn passage
S. albifrons Pallas	LITTLE TERN	A few most years on autumn passage
Chlidonias niger (L.)	BLACK TERN	Rare passage visitor, mainly coastal Recorded Wimbleball, May 1989 and Sept. 1994
C. leucopterus (Temminck)	WHITE-WINGED BLACK TERN	Vagrant One Porlock Marsh, August 1986

ALCIDAE - AUKS

Uria aalge (Pontoppidan)	GUILLEMOT	Nests

About 500 nesting pairs, Lynmouth to Heddon's Mouth, 1994. Not uncommon passage and winter visitor off-shore.

Alca torda L.	RAZORBILL	Nests

About 450 pairs breed North Devon cliffs. Passage and winter visitor off-shore

Cepphus grylle (L.)	BLACK GUILLEMOT	Vagrant One, Dunster Beach, Aug. 1991
Alle alle (L.)	LITTLE AUK	Rare storm vagrant
Fratercula arctica (L.)	PUFFIN	Storm vagrant on the coast

Order: COLUMBIFORMES

COLUMBIDAE - PIGEONS

Columba livia (Gmelin)	ROCK DOVE (FERAL FORM)	Fairly common. Nests
C. oenas L.	STOCK DOVE	Resident and fairly common. Nests
C. palumbus L.	WOODPIGEON	Nests Resident and common passage and winter visitor
Streptopelia decaocto (Frivaldszky)	COLLARED DOVE	Nests Resident. Common in towns and villages
S. turtur (L.)	TURTLE DOVE	Nests Scarce summer visitor, recorded most years

Order: PSITTACIFORMES

PSITTACIDAE - PARROTS

Psittacula krameri (Scopoli)	RING-NECKED PARAKEET	One presumed this species, Dunkery area 1985 (possible escape)

BIRDS

Order: CUCULIFORMES

CUCULIDAE - CUCKOOS

Cuculus canorus L.   CUCKOO   Breeds
Fairly common summer visitor. Meadow Pipit is the commonest host on the moors

Order: STRIGIFORMES

TYTONIDAE - BARN OWLS

Tyto alba (Scopoli)   BARN OWL   Nests
Resident. Now very scarce with only a few breeding pairs

STRIGIDAE - TYPICAL OWLS

Athene noctua (Scopoli)   LITTLE OWL   Resident and scarce. Nests
Strix aluco L.   TAWNY OWL   Nests
Resident. Widespread and common - woods, farmland
Asio otus (L.)   LONG-EARED OWL   Vagrant, one Porlock Feb. 1984
A. flammeus (Pontoppidan)   SHORT-EARED OWL   Winter visitor
occurring annually, usually on moorland

Order: CAPRIMULGIFORMES

CAPRIMULGIDAE - NIGHTJARS

Caprimulgus europaeus L.   NIGHTJAR   Nests
Summer visitor. Breeds locally at about five sites

Order: APODIFORMES

APODIDAE - SWIFTS

A. apus (L.)   SWIFT   Common summer visitor. Nests
Exceptionally late sighting: One, Porlock Marsh, 29 November 1995
Apus melba (L.)   ALPINE SWIFT   Vagrant. One Dunkery Beacon May 1980

Order: CORACIIFORMES

ALCEDINIDAE - KINGFISHERS

Alcedo atthis (L.)   KINGFISHER   Resident. Nests
Breeds on a few rivers. Frequent coasts, reservoirs in winter

UPUPIDAE - HOOPOES

Upupa epops L.   HOOPOE   Rare passage visitor, usually in spring

BIRDS

Order: PICIFORMES

PICIDAE - WRYNECKS, WOODPECKERS AND ALLIES

Jynx torquilla L.	WRYNECK	Rare autumn passage visitor
Picus viridis L.	GREEN WOODPECKER	Resident and fairly common. Nests
Dendrocopos major (L.)	GREAT SPOTTED WOODPECKER	Nests
	Resident and common. Breeds in all suitable woods	
D. minor (L.)	LESSER SPOTTED WOODPECKER	Nests
	Resident, locally common in the larger deciduous woods	

Order: PASSERIFORMES

ALAUDIDAE - LARKS

Lullula arborea (L.)	WOODLARK	Irregular visitor. No recent breeding records
Alauda arvensis L.	SKYLARK	Nests
	Resident and common passage and winter visitor	
Eremophila alpestris (L.)	SHORE LARK	Rare winter visitor to coastal beaches

HIRUNDINIDAE - SWALLOWS AND MARTINS

Riparia riparia (L.)	SAND MARTIN	Nests
	Summer and passage visitor. Scarce as a breeding bird	
Hirundo rustica L.	SWALLOW	Nests
	Common summer visitor and passage migrant	
H. daurica L.	RED-RUMPED SWALLOW	Vagrant
	One Porlock, October 1987	
Delichon urbica (L.)	HOUSE MARTIN	Nests
	Common summer visitor and passage migrant	

MOTACILLIDAE - PIPITS AND WAGTAILS

Anthus novaeseelandiae (Gmelin)	RICHARD'S PIPIT	Vagrant
	Single birds, Minehead and Dunster area, 1977, 1980 and 1991	
A. campestris (L.)	TAWNY PIPIT	Vagrant
	One Dunster beach Aug. 1993	
A. trivialis (L.)	TREE PIPIT	Nests
	Summer visitor. Scattered trees along hillsides, woodland fringes	
A. pratensis (L.)	MEADOW PIPIT	Nests
	Common resident, passage and winter visitor	
A. spinoletta petrosus (Montagu)	ROCK PIPIT	Resident. Nests rocky shores
A. spinoletta spinoletta (L.)	WATER PIPIT	Very rare passage and winter visitor
	Only recorded at Porlock Marsh	
Motacilla flava flavissima (Blyth)	YELLOW WAGTAIL	Spring/autumn passage visitor
	Mainly on the coast	
M. flava flava L.	BLUE-HEADED WAGTAIL	Very rare passage visitor
	Recent records only from Porlock Marsh	

BIRDS

Motacilla cinerea Tunstall	GREY WAGTAIL	Nests
	Resident and fairly common on streams and rivers	
M. alba yarrellii Gould	PIED WAGTAIL	Resident, common. Nests
M. alba alba L.	WHITE WAGTAIL	Spring and autumn passage visitor along the coast

BOMBYCILLIDAE – WAXWINGS

Bombycilla garrulus (L.)	WAXWING	Rare and irregular winter visitor

CINCLIDAE – DIPPERS

Cinclus cinclus (L.)	DIPPER	Nests
	Common resident of fast flowing streams and rivers	

TROGLODYTIDAE – WRENS

Troglodytes troglodytes (L.)	WREN	Resident, common. Nests

PRUNELLIDAE – ACCENTORS

Prunella modularis (L.)	DUNNOCK	Common resident. Nests

TURDIDAE – THRUSHES

Erithacus rubecula (L.)	ROBIN	Common resident. Nests
Luscinia megarhynchos Brehm	NIGHTINGALE	Passage visitor
	Nests on outskirts of Exmoor National Park	
Phoenicurus ochruros (Gmelin)	BLACK REDSTART	Scarce
	Mainly autumn passage and winter visitor	
P. phoenicurus (L.)	REDSTART	Regular summer visitor and passage migrant. Nests
Saxicola rubetra (L.)	WHINCHAT	Nests
	Summer visitor. Very common in moorland combes	
S. torquata (L.)	STONECHAT	Resident. Nests
	Frequent on gorse/heather moorland	
Oenanthe oenanthe (L.)	WHEATEAR	Nests
	Common summer visitor and passage migrant. Stony outcrops, walls, coast & moors	
O. oenanthe leucorhoa (Gmelin)	GREENLAND WHEATEAR	Small numbers of this larger race on passage most years
Turdus torquatus L.	RING OUZEL	Summer visitor to moorland combes. Nests
T. merula L.	BLACKBIRD	Resident and very common. Nests
T. pilaris L.	FIELDFARE	Winter visitor, fairly common
T. philomelos Brehm	SONG THRUSH	Common resident; nests. Also autumn and winter visitor
T. iliacus L.	REDWING	Regular winter visitor
T. viscivorus L.	MISTLE THRUSH	Common resident. Nests

SYLVIIDAE – WARBLERS

Cettia cetti (Temminck)	CETTI'S WARBLER	Very scarce, probably now resident and breeding
Locustella naevia (Boddaert)	GRASSHOPPER WARBLER	Nests
	Scarce summer visitor to marshes, moorland slopes etc.	

BIRDS

Acrocephalus schoenobaenus (L.)	SEDGE WARBLER	Nests
	Scarce summer visitor to the coastal marshes, rare elsewhere	
A. scirpaceus (Hermann)	REED WARBLER	Nests
	Scarce but regular summer visitor to Porlock and Dunster Marshes	
Hippolais icterina (Vieillot)	ICTERINE WARBLER	Vagrant
	One Heddon Valley 1972; Withypool 1975	
Sylvia undata (Boddaert)	DARTFORD WARBLER	Bred on Exmoor in 1995
		Rare visitor prior to 1995
S. curruca (L.)	LESSER WHITETHROAT	Scarce summer visitor
		No recent breeding records
S. communis, Latham	WHITETHROAT	Nests
		Common summer visitor
S. borin (Boddaert)	GARDEN WARBLER	Nests
	Summer visitor, fairly common in open woodland, thickets	
S. atricapilla (L.)	BLACKCAP	Nests
	Common summer visitor, with some overwintering birds	
Phylloscopus inornatus (Blyth)	YELLOW-BROWED WARBLER	Vagrant
	Recorded spring 1970 and 1990 and autumn 1993	
P. sibilatrix (Bechstein)	WOOD WARBLER	Nests
	Common summer visitor of mature deciduous (mainly oak) woodlands	
P. collybita (Vieillot)	CHIFFCHAFF	Nests
	Fairly common summer visitor, occasionally winters	
P. trochilus (L.)	WILLOW WARBLER	Nests
	Summer visitor - the commonest warbler	
Regulus regulus (L.)	GOLDCREST	Resident and fairly common. Nests
R. ignicapillus (Temminck)	FIRECREST	Scarce winter visitor
		Usually recorded near the coast

MUSCICAPIDAE - FLYCATCHERS

Muscicapa striata (Pallas)	SPOTTED FLYCATCHER	Nests
		Summer visitor, fairly common
Ficedula hypoleuca (Pallas)	PIED FLYCATCHER	Nests
	Summer visitor, locally common in mature oak woodland	
	A regular occupant of ENHS nest boxes in Exmoor woodlands	

TIMALIIDAE - REEDLINGS

Panurus biarmicus (L.)	BEARDED TIT	Vagrant
	Three Porlock Marsh, October 1972; One Dunster Beach, October, 1990	

AEGITHALIDAE LONG-TAILED TITS

Aegithalos caudatus (L.)	LONG-TAILED TIT	Resident and fairly common. Nests

PARIDAE - TITS

Parus palustris L.	MARSH TIT	Resident and common. Nests
P. montanus Conrad	WILLOW TIT	Nests
	Resident and local, often breeding in damp woodland	
P. ater L.	COAL TIT	Resident and common. Nests
P. caeruleus L.	BLUE TIT	Resident, abundant and widespread. Nests
P. major L.	GREAT TIT	Resident and common. Nests

BIRDS

SITTIDAE - NUTHATCHES
Sitta europaea L.   NUTHATCH   Nests
Resident and common in deciduous woodland

CERTHIIDAE - TREECREEPERS
Certhia familiaris L.   TREECREEPER   Resident and fairly common. Nests

ORIOLIDAE - ORIOLES
Oriolus oriolus (L.)   GOLDEN ORIOLE   Rare spring and summer passage visitor

LANIIDAE - SHRIKES
Lanius isabellinus Hemprich & Ehrenberg   ISABELLINE SHRIKE   Minehead 1989. Vagrant
Lanius collurio L.   RED-BACKED SHRIKE   Rare passage visitor
Most recent record, male Hoar Moor, June 1995

L. excubitor L.   GREAT GREY SHRIKE   Irregular autumn and winter
visitor, usually to moorland areas

CORVIDAE - CROWS
Garrulus glandarius (L.)   JAY   Common resident of wooded areas. Nests
Pica pica (L.)   MAGPIE   Resident and common. Nests
Nucifraga caryocatactes (L.)   NUTCRACKER   Vagrant
One West Luccombe August 1985

Pyrrhocorax pyrrhocorax (L.)   CHOUGH   Vagrant
Ten records since 1970, mainly coastal Devon, but three inland Somerset 1991
Corvus monedula L.   JACKDAW   Resident and very common. Nests
C. frugilegus L.   ROOK   Resident and common. Nests
C. corone corone L.   CARRION CROW   Resident and very common. Nests
C. corone cornix L.   HOODED CROW   Vagrant
Single birds recorded a few times since 1970

C. corax L.   RAVEN   Nests
Resident and fairly common. Flocks of over 100 recorded

STURNIDAE - STARLINGS
Sturnus vulgaris L.   STARLING   Nests
Resident, passage and an abundant winter visitor

S. roseus (L.)   ROSE-COLOURED STARLING   Vagrant
One Wootton Courtenay and Dunster, autumn 1975

PASSERIDAE - SPARROWS
Passer domesticus (L.)   HOUSE SPARROW   Resident and common. Nests
P. montanus (L.)   TREE SPARROW   Rare visitor
Recorded Carhampton 1984 and Porlock Marsh 1989

FRINGILLIDAE - FINCHES
Fringilla coelebs L.   CHAFFINCH   Abundant resident and winter visitor. Nests
F. montifringilla L.   BRAMBLING   Scarce winter visitor
Carduelis chloris (L.)   GREENFINCH   Resident and common. Nests
C. carduelis (L.)   GOLDFINCH   Resident and fairly common. Nests
C. spinus (L.)   SISKIN   Resident winter visitor. Nests
First recorded nesting in 1979

BIRDS

Carduelis cannabina (L.)	LINNET	Resident and common. Nests
C. flavirostris (L.)	TWITE	Rare winter visitor
	Recorded at Porlock Marsh, 1975 and 1984 and Molland 1994	
C. flammea (L.)	REDPOLL	Scarce resident. Nests
Loxia curvirostra L.	CROSSBILL	Irregular visitor, occasionally breeds
Pyrrhula pyrrhula (L.)	BULLFINCH	Resident and fairly common. Nests
Coccothraustes coccothraustes (L.)	HAWFINCH	Very rare visitor to Exmoor
	One Webber's Post July 1983; One Dunster 1995	

EMBERIZIDAE – BUNTINGS

Calcarius lapponicus (L.)	LAPLAND BUNTING	Very rare passage visitor usu.coast
Plectrophenax nivalis (L.)	SNOW BUNTING	Scarce passage/winter visitor to the coast, occasionally the moors
Emberiza citrinella L.	YELLOWHAMMER	Resident and fairly common. Nests
E. cirlus L.	CIRL BUNTING	Rare resident, previously bred
E. schoeniclus (L.)	REED BUNTING	Resident and fairly common. Nests
Miliaria calandra (L.)	CORN BUNTING	Vagrant. One, Minehead Sept. 1989

References:

Allen, N.V. *The Birds of Exmoor* Revised edn. Exmoor Press (1976) Dulverton.

Allen, N.V. & Butcher, R.J. *Birds in Exmoor National Park* Alcombe Books (1984) Minehead.

Cramp, S. et al. (eds.) *The Birds of the Western Palearctic* 9 vols. (1977-1994)

Roger, M.J. (Rarities Committee) *Report of Rare Birds in Great Britain in 1980, British Birds*, (1981)

White, Jonathan *Exmoor Birds* Exmoor Books (1994) Dulverton

Annual Reports: Devon Bird-Watching and Preservation Society

        Somerset Ornithological Society

        Exmoor Natural History Society *(Exmoor Naturalist)*

MAMMALS

Out of a possible total of 63 species of British mammals, we have a list of 39 land mammals ranging from the Red Deer, the largest, down to the tiny Pygmy Shrew, plus four sea mammals occasionally seen from the coast of Exmoor. If further effort is put into recording, with our increased conservation knowledge and application, this will undoubtedly produce a more positive approach and hope for future generations who should enjoy and nurture our wildlife.

These days, new fields of modern recording equipment enable us to observe more accurately, and new ways to study the behaviour patterns of mammals have opened up. Radio tagging and tracking; release trapping and captive breeding of protected endangered species for release in suitable habitats are all progress factors. Although many of these fields of study are specialised and usually require a licence, they are open to those who genuinely wish to learn to study mammals, provided correct procedure is followed.

In 1994 a countrywide study was made under the direction of English Nature, to collect hazel nut shells in the autumn, and pick out those that had been opened by dormice. On Exmoor we found ten sites, there could be more as we could not cover every wood and hedgerow. For many years our members have studied the deer population on the moor, particularly the pride of the moor, the Red Deer. Others have made small mammals their speciality while some people delight in bats. Exmoor has such a varied terrain it is up to us all to protect and encourage those mammals which thrive in this beautiful area. Let's try, let's be positive about it.

Nomenclature follows Corbett & Harris (1991). **RDB** = Endangered species listed in *A Red Data Book for British Mammals* P.A. Morris (1993). The Mammal list for the first edition was compiled by Jan Rance and for this present list I acknowledge with very many thanks, the help I have received from Mr Doug Woods of the Mammal Society.

Tina Cattley
Mammal Recorder, E.N.H.S.

Class: **MAMMALIA**
Order: **INSECTIVORA (INSECTIVORES)**

ERINACEIDAE

Erinaceus europaeus L.	**RDB.**	HEDGEHOG	Fairly common

TALPIDAE

Talpa europaea L.		MOLE	Common, in low and high ground

SORICIDAE

Sorex araneus L.	**RDB.**	COMMON SHREW	Common
S. minutus L.	**RDB.**	PYGMY SHREW	Common
Neomys fodiens (Pennant)	**RDB.**	WATER SHREW	Scarce

Order: **CHIROPTERA (BATS)**

RHINOLOPHIDAE

Rhinophus ferrumequinum (Schreber)	**RDB**	GREATER HORSESHOE BAT	Scarce
Rhinolophus hipposideros (Bechstein)	**RDB**	LESSER HORSESHOE BAT	Fairly scarce

MAMMALS

VESPERTILIONIDAE

Myotis mystacinus (Kuhl)	RDB	WHISKERED BAT	Rare
M. nattereri (Kuhl)	RDB	NATTERER'S BAT	Scarce
M. daubentoni (Kuhl) RDB		DAUBENTON'S BAT (WATER BAT)	Rather scarce
Eptesicus serotinus (Schreber)	RDB	SEROTINE	Scarce
Nyctalus noctula (Schreber)	RDB	NOCTULE	Fairly common
Pipistrellus pipistrellus (Schreber)	RDB	PIPISTRELLE	Common
Barbastella barbastellus (Schreber)	RDB	BARBASTELLE	Scarce and local
Plecotus auritus (L.)	RDB	BROWN LONG-EARED BAT	Common

Order: LAGOMORPHA
LEPORIDAE – RABBITS & HARES

Oryctolagus cuniculus (L.)		RABBIT	Very common
Lepus europaeus Pallas	RDB	BROWN HARE	Scarce; has declined

Order: RODENTIA
SCIURIDAE – SQUIRRELS

(Sciurus vulgaris L. RED SQUIRREL Formerly common, but none on Exmoor since ^{c}1947)

Sciurus carolinensis Gmelin	GREY SQUIRREL	Common

MURIDAE – VOLES, MICE, etc.
Sub-family: ARVICOLINAE – VOLES

Clethrionomys glareolus (Schreber)		BANK VOLE	Common
Microtus agrestis (L.)		FIELD VOLE	Common
Auvicola terrestris (L.)	RDB	WATER VOLE	Numbers declining

Sub-family: MURINAE – RATS & MICE

Apodemus sylvaticus (L.)		WOOD MOUSE	Very common
A. flavicollis (Melchior)	RDB	YELLOW-NECKED MOUSE	Rare and local
Micromys minutus (Pallas)		HARVEST MOUSE	Scarce
Mus domesticus (L.)		HOUSE MOUSE	Common
Rattus norvegicus (Berkenhout)		COMMON BROWN RAT	Common

GLIRIDAE – DORMICE

Muscardinus avellanarius (L.) **RDB** COMMON or HAZEL DORMOUSE		Local

Order: CETACEA (DOLPHINS, PORPOISES)
DELPHINIDAE – DOLPHINS

Delphinus delphis L.	RDB	COMMON DOLPHIN	Rare
		Dead specimens occasionally washed up on beaches	
Tursiops truncatus (Montagu)	RDB	BOTTLE-NOSED DOLPHIN	Occasional

MAMMALS

PHOCOENIDAE – PORPOISES

Phocoena phocoena (L.)	**RDB**	HARBOUR PORPOISE	Occasional sightings

Order: CARNIVORA

CANIDAE – DOGS

Vulpes vulpes (L.)		FOX	Very common

MUSTELIDAE

Mustela erminea L.		STOAT	Fairly common
M. nivalis L.		WEASEL	Fairly common
M. vison Schreber		MINK	Scarce; not increasing
Meles meles (L.)	**RDB**	BADGER	Common
Lutra lutra (L.)	**RDB**	OTTER	Rare

Order: PINNIPEDIA – SEALS etc.

PHOCIDAE – SEALS

Halichoerus grypus (Fabricius)	GREY SEAL	Occasional sightings

Order: PERISSODACTYLA

EQUIDAE

Equus sp.   EXMOOR PONY
There are no truly wild ponies on Exmoor but it has long been a contention that the small herds of free ranging Exmoor ponies are relicts of the late glacial Equus ferus Boddaert. A specific scientific name has not been allocated.

Order: ARTIODACTYLA

CERVIDAE – DEER

Cervus elaphus L.   RED DEER   Common, especially in heart of Exmoor. Population estimate 2500; many more hinds than stags

Dama dama (L.)   FALLOW DEER   Fairly common but restricted to east part of Exmoor National Park. Population estimate 600

Capreolus capreolus (L.)   ROE DEER scarce but widespread; increasing

Muntiacus reevesi (Ogilby)   CHINESE MUNTJAC   A few recent reports

BOVIDAE – GOATS

Capra sp.   FERAL GOAT   Valley of Rocks, Lynton
The present herd was introduced in 1980's to replace feral goats of the Saarien breed introduced in 19th century. They are the only wild Cheviot herd in Southern England. Feral goats were common on the Exmoor coast in previous centuries.

References:
Corbet, Gordon B. & Harris, Stephen Eds. *The Handbook of British Mammals* 3rd Edn. (1991) Blackwell Scientific Publications, Oxford.

Morris, P.A. (1993) *A Red Data Book for British Mammals*. The Mammal Society.

APPENDIX I. ADDITIONS TO THE DIPTERA.

BOLITHOPHILIDAE
Bolitophila occulusa Edwards

KEROPLATIDAE: Macrocerinae
Macrocera centralis Meigen
M. lutea Meigen
    Keroplatinae
Cerotelion lineatus (Fabricius)
Platyura marginata Meigen
Neoplatyura biumbrata (Edwards)
N. nigricauda (Strobl)
Orfelia nigricornis (Fabricius)
Antlemon servulum (Walker)

MYCETOPHILIDAE Mycomyinae
Mycomya annulata (Meigen)
M. winnertzi (Dziedzicki)
M. circumdata (Staeger)
M. fimbriata (Meigen)
M. trilineata (Zetterstedt)
M. pectinifera Edwards
    Sciophilinae
Polylepta guttiventris (Zetterstedt)
Neuratelia nemoralis (Meigen)
Speolepta leptogaster (Winnertz)
    Gnoristinae
Palaeodocosta janickii (Dziedzicki)
Apolephthisa subincana (Curtis)
Boletina basalis (Meigen)
B. dubia (Meigen)
B. gripha Dziedzicki
B. plana Walker
Synapha fasciata Meigen
S. vitripennis (Meigen)
    Leiinae
Leia crucigera Zetterstedt
Docosia moravica Landrock

    Mycetophilinae
Rymosia bifida Edwards
R. fasciata (Meigen)
R. placida Winnertz
R. virens Dziedzicki
Tarnania fenestralis (Meigen)
T. nemoralis (Edwards)
Synplasta excogitata (Dziedzicki)
Allodia lundstroemi Edwards
A. ornaticollis (Meigen)
A. pyxidiiformis Zaizev
A truncata Edwards
Exechiopsis leptura (Meigen)
E. subulata (Winnertz)
Exechia contaminata Winnertz
E. dorsalis (Staeger)
E. parvula (Zetterstedt)
Brevicornu auriculatum (Edwards)
B. foliatum (Edwards)
B. griseicolle (Staeger)
B. sericoma (Meigen)
Cordyla brevicornis (Staeger)
C. fissa Edwards
C. murina Winnertz
Trichonta vitta (Meigen)
Phronia exigua (Zetterstedt)
P. flavipes Winnertz
P. forcipata Winnertz
P. nigricornis (Zetterstedt)
P. nitidiventris (Wulp)
P. notata Dziedzicki
P. stignata Winnertz
P. strenua Winnertz
P. contanica Chandler
Mycetophila cingulum Meigen
M. edwardsi Lundström
M. fungorum (DeGeer)
M. inchneumonea Say
M. pumila Winnertz
Zygomyia vara (Staeger)
Sceptonia membranacea Edwards

68 species.

The above records have been kindly supplied by Mr Peter Chandler, Curator of the British Entomological & Natural History Society based at Dinton Pastures Country Park in Berkshire.

S.S.S.I.'s Within Exmoor National Park

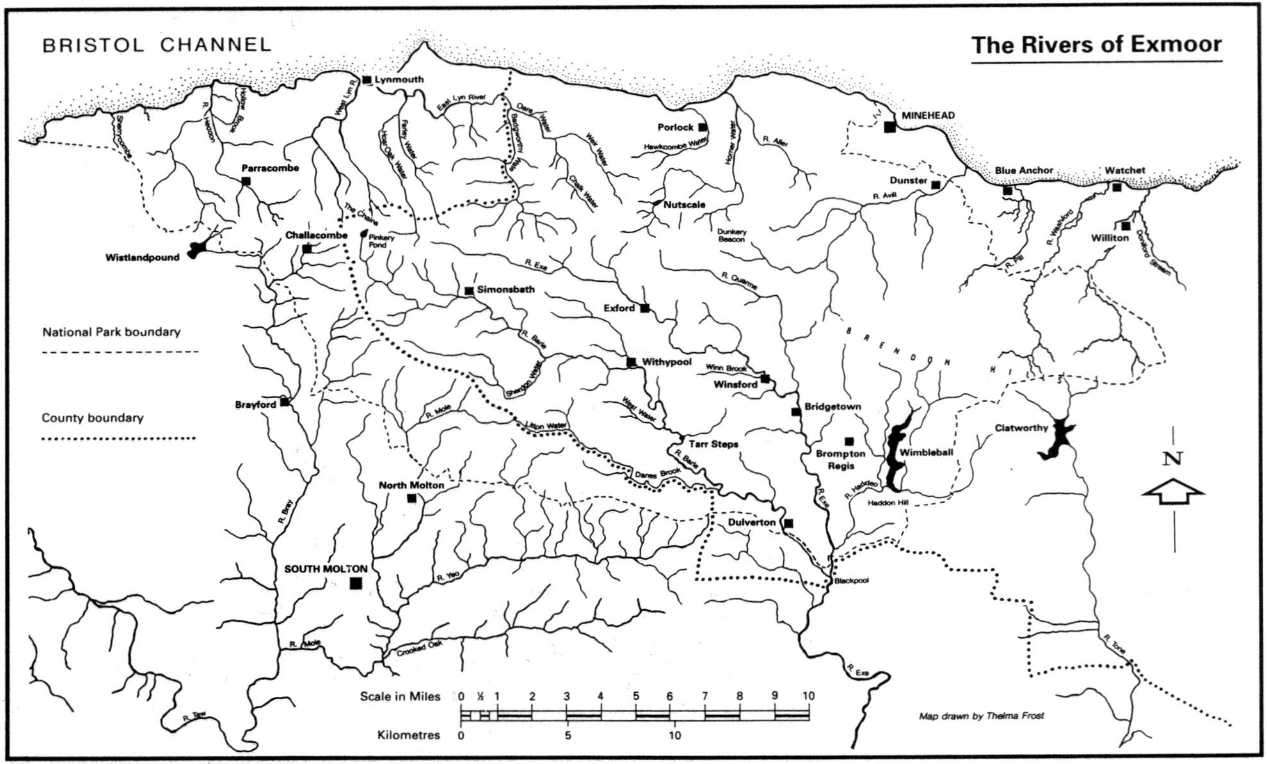

The Rivers of Exmoor National Park

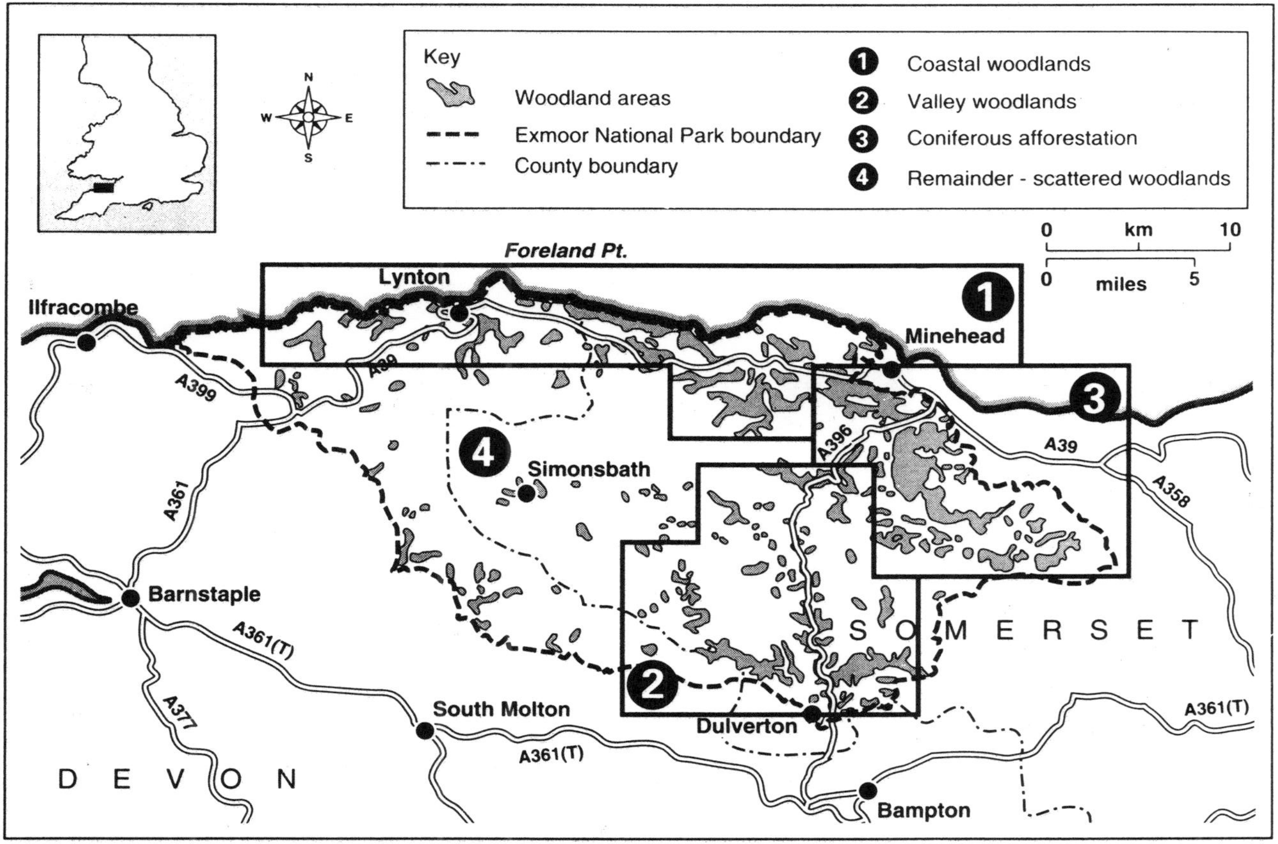

Woodland Areas Within Exmoor National Park

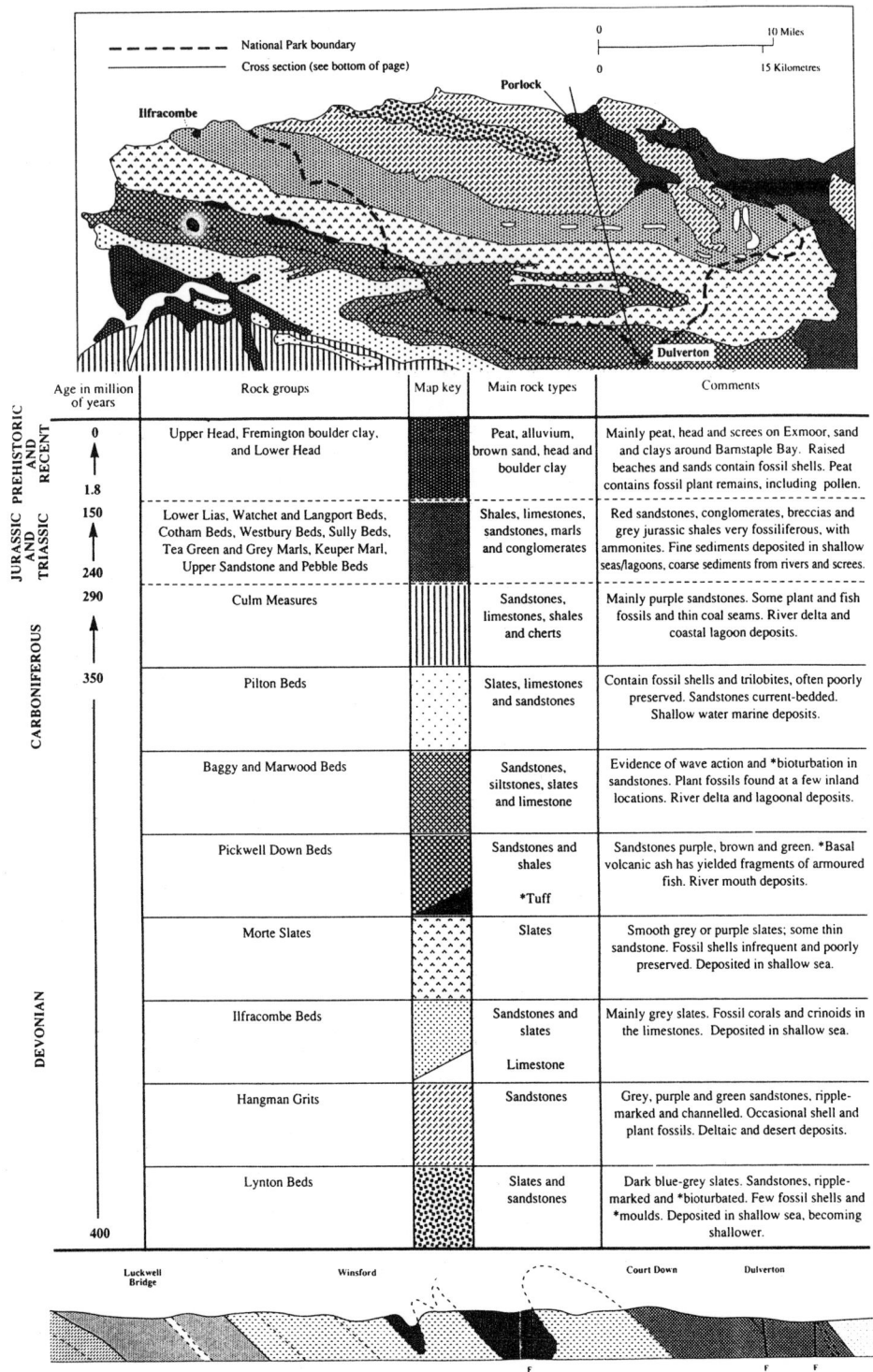

Age in million of years	Rock groups	Map key	Main rock types	Comments
JURASSIC PREHISTORIC AND RECENT 0 ↑ 1.8	Upper Head, Fremington boulder clay, and Lower Head		Peat, alluvium, brown sand, head and boulder clay	Mainly peat, head and screes on Exmoor, sand and clays around Barnstaple Bay. Raised beaches and sands contain fossil shells. Peat contains fossil plant remains, including pollen.
JURASSIC AND TRIASSIC 150 ↑ 240	Lower Lias, Watchet and Langport Beds, Cotham Beds, Westbury Beds, Sully Beds, Tea Green and Grey Marls, Keuper Marl, Upper Sandstone and Pebble Beds		Shales, limestones, sandstones, marls and conglomerates	Red sandstones, conglomerates, breccias and grey jurassic shales very fossiliferous, with ammonites. Fine sediments deposited in shallow seas/lagoons, coarse sediments from rivers and screes.
CARBONIFEROUS 290 ↑ 350	Culm Measures		Sandstones, limestones, shales and cherts	Mainly purple sandstones. Some plant and fish fossils and thin coal seams. River delta and coastal lagoon deposits.
	Pilton Beds		Slates, limestones and sandstones	Contain fossil shells and trilobites, often poorly preserved. Sandstones current-bedded. Shallow water marine deposits.
	Baggy and Marwood Beds		Sandstones, siltstones, slates and limestone	Evidence of wave action and *bioturbation in sandstones. Plant fossils found at a few inland locations. River delta and lagoonal deposits.
DEVONIAN	Pickwell Down Beds		Sandstones and shales *Tuff	Sandstones purple, brown and green. *Basal volcanic ash has yielded fragments of armoured fish. River mouth deposits.
	Morte Slates		Slates	Smooth grey or purple slates; some thin sandstone. Fossil shells infrequent and poorly preserved. Deposited in shallow sea.
	Ilfracombe Beds		Sandstones and slates Limestone	Mainly grey slates. Fossil corals and crinoids in the limestones. Deposited in shallow sea.
	Hangman Grits		Sandstones	Grey, purple and green sandstones, ripple-marked and channelled. Occasional shell and plant fossils. Deltaic and desert deposits.
400	Lynton Beds		Slates and sandstones	Dark blue-grey slates. Sandstones, ripple-marked and *bioturbated. Few fossil shells and *moulds. Deposited in shallow sea, becoming shallower.

Geological Map of Exmoor Region

BIBLIOGRAPHY

PUBLISHED NATURAL HISTORY WORKS RELATING TO EXMOOR NATIONAL PARK

Allen, N.V. *The Birds of Exmoor.* Exmoor Press (1976)
Allen, N.V. *Exmoor's Wild Red Deer.* Exmoor Press (1990)
Allen, N.V. and Butcher, R.J. *Birds of Exmoor National Park.* Alcombe Books (1984)
Allen, N.V. and Giddens C. *Exmoor Wildlife.* Exmoor Press (1989)
Baker, Sue *Survival of the Fittest - A Natural History of the Exmoor Pony.* Exmoor Books (1993)
Bonham-Carter, V. *The Essence of Exmoor.* Exmoor Press (1991)
Boyden, Crothers, Little & Mettam. *The Intertidal Invertebrate Fauna of the Severn Estuary.* Reprinted from *Field Studies* (1977)
Curtis, L.F. *Soils of Exmoor Forest.* Rothampsted Experimental Station (1971)
Devon Bird Watching & Preservation Society. *Annual Reports* since 1928
Devon Trust for Nature Conservation. *Annual Reports* since 1961
Duff, A.G. *The Beetles of Somerset.* S.A.N.H.S. Taunton. (1993)
Exmoor Natural History Society. *Exmoor Naturalist.* Annual Report since 1974.
Exmoor Society. *Exmoor Review.* Issued Annually since 1959
Giddens, C.J. *Flowers of Exmoor.* Alcombe Books (1979)
Giddens, C.J. *Atlas to the Flowers of Exmoor.* Alcombe Books (1984)
Ilfracombe Field Club. Palmer, M.G. Editor *Ilfracombe Fauna and Flora.* (1946)
Ivimey-Cook, R.B. *Atlas of the Devon Flora.* Devonshire Association (1984)
Lloyd, E.R. *The Wild Red Deer of Exmoor.* Exmoor Press (1970)
Martin, W.K. & Fraser, G.T. *The Flora of Devon.* Devonshire Association (1939)
Marshall, E.S. *A Supplement to the Flora of Somerset.* S.A.N.H.S. Taunton (1914)
Maund, H.B. *The Fish of Exmoor.* Exmoor Press (1970)
Miles, R.O. *The Trees and Woods of Exmoor.* Exmoor Press (1972)
Moore,R. *The Birds of Devon.* David & Charles, Newton Abbot (1969)
Murray, R.P. *The Flora of Somerset.* Barnicott & Pearce, Taunton (1896)
Palmer & Ballance *The Birds of Somerset.* Longmans (1968)
Robbins, J. *The Moths and Butterflies of Exmoor National Park.* E.N.H.S.Minehead (1990)
Roe, R.G.B. *The Flora of Somerset.* S.A.N.H.S. Taunton (1981)
Sinclair, G. *The Vegetation of Exmoor.* Exmoor Press (1970)
Somerset Archaeological & Natural History Society. Taunton. *Proceedings.* Since 1849.
Somerset Ornithological Society. *Annual Reports* since 1974.
" " " *Birds of Somerset* (1988)
Somerset Wildlife Trust. *Annual Reports* since 1964.
Swanton, E.W. *The Mollusca of Somerset.* S.A.N.H.S. (1912)
Turner, A.H. *Lepidoptera of Somerset.* S.A.N.H.S. (1955)
Watts, Mrs J., *The Handbook of the Exmoor Pony.* Exmoor Pony Society (1979)
White, J. *Exmoor Birds.* Exmoor Books (1994)
Wilson, W.A. *Coleoptera of Somerset.* S.A.N.H.S. Taunton (1950)

Other publications are listed under 'References' at the end of each section throughout the book.

SUMMARY OF SPECIES
recorded in this book

FLORA:

Algae/Stoneworts	174
Ferns & Allies	41
Conifers	23
Flowering Plants	1187
Liverworts	96
Hornworts	2
Mosses	241
Lichens	611
Slime Moulds	113
Ascomycetes	71
Rust Fungi	98
Larger Fungi	650
	3307

FAUNA:
VERTEBRATES:

Fish	74
Amphibians/Reptiles	7
Birds	272
Mammals	43
	396

FAUNA:
INVERTEBRATES:

Coastal invertebrates	333
Freshwater invertebrates	193
Snails & Slugs	46
Earthworms	15
Bristletails, etc.	7
Centipedes/Millipedes	17
Woodlice	9
Lice, etc.	18
Grasshoppers/Crickets	15
Dragonflies/Damselflies	22
Lacewings, etc.	28
Bugs	332
Moths/Butterflies	1203
Flies	632*
Fleas	10
Bees/Wasps/Ants	194
Beetles	1198
Spiders & Allies	228
Ticks	3
Mites	38
	4541*

GRAND TOTAL: <u>8,244*</u> species

*Plus Appendex I.

INDEX TO SCIENTIFIC NAMES

Note: Due to the large number of records it is not possible to include a full index of the Genera, but as the lists are arranged in systematic order the reader should have little difficulty in turning up the section required. The following index is therefore to Phylum for sections which cover just one or two pages and to Orders/Families for the longer sections.

FLORA:

ALGAE:
  FRESHWATER ALGAE:
  Bryopsidaceae, 8
  Chamaeosiphonaceae, 10
  Characeae, 9
  Chlorococcaceae, 7
  Chroococcaceae, 10
  Cladophoraceae, 8
  Desmidiaceae, 8
  Dictyosphaeriaceae, 8
  Euglenaceae, 11
  Fragilariaceae, 10
  Glaucocystaceae, 10
  Helminthocladiaceae, 11
  Lemaneaceae, 11
  Melosiraceae, 10
  Microsporaceae, 8
  Nostocaceae, 11
  Oedogoniaceae, 9
  Oocystaceae, 7
  Oscillatoriaceae, 10
  Palmellaceae, 7
  Pleurococcaceae, 8
  Prasiolaceae, 9
  Rivulariaceae, 11
  Scytonemaceae, 11
  Selenastraceae, 8
  Sphaerellaceae, 7
  Stigonemaceae, 11
  Trentepohliaceae, 8
  Tribonemaceae, 9
  Ulothricaceae, 9
  Vaucheriaceae, 8
  Zygnemaceae, 8
  MARINE ALGAE:
  Bangiaceae, 12
  Ceramiaceae, 13
  Chaetangiaceae, 11
  Cladostephaceae, 15
  Corallinaceae, 12
  Corynophloeaceae, 14
  Delesseriaceae, 12
  Desmarestiaceae, 14
  Dictyotaceae, 15
  Dumontiaceae, 12
  Ectocarpaceae, 14
  Elachistaceae, 14
  Fucaceae, 15

  Gelidiaceae, 12
  Gigartinaceae, 13
  Grateloupiaceae, 12
  Laminariaceae, 15
  Myrionemaceae, 14
  Nemastomaceae, 12
  Punctariaceae, 15
  Rhizophyllidaceae, 12
  Rhodomelaceae, 13
  Rhodophyllidaceae, 14
  Rhodymeniaceae, 14
  Sphacelariaceae, 15
  Sphaerococcaceae, 14
  Stypocaulaceae, 15
  Ulvaceae, 9
  Wrangelliaceae, 12

**ANGIOSPERMAE
(FLOWERING PLANTS)**
  Aceraceae, 97
  Adoxaceae, 106
  Agavaceae, 118
  Alismataceae, 110
  Amaranthaceae, 84
  Apiaceae, 98
  Apocynaceae, 99
  Aponogetonaceae, 110
  Aquifoliaceae, 97
  Araceae, 110
  Araliaceae, 98
  Asteraceae, 106
  Balsaminaceae, 98
  Berberidaceae, 82
  Betulaceae, 83
  Boraginaceae, 100
  Brassicaceae, 88
  Buddlejaceae, 103
  Buxaceae, 97
  Callitrichaceae, 102
  Campanulaceae, 105
  Cannabaceae, 83
  Caprifoliaceae, 105
  Caryophyllaceae, 84
  Celastraceae, 96
  Chenopodiaceae, 84
  Clusiaceae, 87
  Compositae, 106

  Convolvulaceae, 100
  Cornaceae, 96
  Crassulaceae, 91
  Cuscutaceae, 100
  Cyperaceae, 111
  Dioscoreaceae, 118
  Dipsacaceae, 106
  Droseraceae, 87
  Elaeagnaceae, 96
  Empetraceae, 90
  Ericaceae, 90
  Euphorbiaceae, 97
  Fabaceae, 94
  Fagaceae, 83
  Fumariaceae, 82
  Gentianaceae, 99
  Geraniaceae, 98
  Gramineae, 113
  Grossulariaceae, 91
  Gunneraceae, 96
  Haloragaceae, 96
  Hippocastanaceae, 97
  Hydrangeaceae, 91
  Hydrocharitaceae, 110
  Hydrophyllaceae, 100
  Iridaceae, 118
  Juglandaceae, 83
  Juncaceae, 111
  Juncaginaceae, 110
  Lamiaceae, 101
  Lauraceae, 81
  Lemnaceae, 110
  Lentibulariaceae, 104
  Liliaceae, 116
  Linaceae, 97
  Lythraceae, 96
  Malvaceae, 87
  Menyanthaceae, 100
  Moraceae, 83
  Myricaceae, 83
  Nymphaeaceae, 81
  Oleaceae, 103
  Onagraceae, 96
  Orchidaceae, 118
  Orobanchaceae, 104
  Oxalidaceae, 97
  Papaveraceae, 82

327

ANGIOSPERMAE Cont....
(FLOWERING PLANTS)
Papilionaceae, 94
Phytolaccaceae, 84
Pittosporaceae, 91
Plantaginaceae, 102
Platanaceae, 82
Plumbaginaceae, 87
Poaceae, 113
Polemoniaceae, 100
Polygalaceae, 97
Polygonaceae, 86
Portulacaceae, 84
Potamogetonaceae, 110
Primulaceae, 90
Ranunculaceae, 81
Resedaceae, 90
Rhamnaceae, 97
Rosaceae, 92
Rubiaceae, 105
Ruppiaceae, 110
Salicaceae, 88
Scrophulariaceae, 103
Solanaceae, 100
Sparganiaceae, 116
Tamaricaceae, 88
Thymelaeaceae, 96
Tiliaceae, 87
Typhaceae, 116
Ulmaceae, 83
Umbelliferae, 98
Urticaceae, 83
Valerianaceae, 106
Verbenaceae, 101
Violaceae, 87
Viscaceae, 96
Vitaceae, 97
Zannichelliaceae, 110

BRYOPHYTA:
ANTHOCEROTALES
(HORNWORTS)
Anthocerotaceae, 65
HEPATICAE (LIVERWORTS)
Aneuraceae, 64
Aytoniaceae, 64
Blasiaceae, 64
Calypogeiaceae, 61
Cephaloziaceae, 62
Cephaloziellaceae, 62
Codoniaceae, 64
Conocephalaceae, 64
Frullaniaceae, 63
Geocalycaceae, 63
Gymnomitriaceae, 62
Jungermanniaceae, 62
Lejeuneaceae, 63
Lepidoziaceae, 61

Lophoziaceae, 62
Lunulariaceae, 64
Marchantiaceae, 64
Metzgeriaceae, 64
Pelliaceae, 64
Plagiochilaceae, 63
Porellaceae, 63
Pseudolepicoleaceae, 61
Ptilidiaceae, 63
Radulaceae, 63
Ricciaceae, 64
Scapaniaceae, 62
Trichocoleaceae, 61
Wiesnerellaceae, 64
MUSCI (MOSSES)
Amblystegiaceae, 72
Andreaeaceae, 65
Aulacomniaceae, 70
Bartramiaceae, 70
Brachytheciaceae, 73
Bryaceae, 69
Buxbaumiaceae, 66
Climaciaceae, 71
Cryphaeaceae, 71
Dicranaceae, 67
Ditrichaceae, 66
Encalyptaceae, 68
Fissidentaceae, 67
Fontinalaceae, 71
Funariaceae, 69
Grimmiaceae, 69
Hedwigiaceae, 71
Hookeriaceae, 72
Hypnaceae, 73
Leucobryaceae, 67
Leucodontaceae, 71
Mniaceae, 70
Neckeraceae, 72
Orthotrichaceae, 71
Plagiotheciaceae, 73
Polytrichaceae, 66
Pottiaceae, 68
Ptychomitriaceae, 69
Schistostegaceae, 69
Sphagnaceae, 65
Tetraphidaceae, 66
Thamniaceae, 72
Thuidiaceae, 72

EQUISETOPSIDA:
(HORSETAILS)
Equisetaceae, 75

FUNGI:
ASCOMYCETES, 19-20
A-Z in list
BASIDIOMYCETES, 25-42
A-Z in list

MYXOMYCETES, 18
A - Z in list
UREDINALES, 21-24
A - Z in list
USTILAGINALES, 24

LICHENES, 43-60
A - Z in list

LYCOPODIOPSIDA
(CLUBMOSSES)
Lycopodiaceae, 75
Selaginellaceae, 75

PINOPSIDA (CONIFERS)
Cupressaceae, 79
Pinaceae, 78
Taxaceae, 79

PTEROPSIDA (FERNS)
Adiantaceae, 76
Aspleniaceae, 76
Azollaceae, 77
Blechnaceae, 77
Dennstaedtiaceae, 76
Dryopteridaceae, 77
Hymenophyllaceae, 76
Ophioglossaceae, 76
Osmundaceae, 76
Polypodiaceae, 76
Thelypteridaceae, 76
Woodsiaceae, 77

FAUNA - INVERTEBRATA

ANNELIDA:
Archiannelida, 126
Hirundinea, 147
Myzostomaria, 128
Oligochaeta, 128, 146, 157
Polychaeta, 126

ARTHROPODA:
ARACHNIDA:
Acari, 147, 292
Araneae, 285
Opiliones, 292
Pseudoscorpiones, 292
CRUSTACEA:
Brachiopoda, 148
Branchiura, 149
Cirripedia, 129
Copepoda, 129, 148
Isopoda, 130, 149, 158
Malacostraca, 130, 149
Myriapoda, 159
Pycnogonida, 133
INSECTA:
ANOPLURA, 165
BLATTODEA, 164
COLEOPTERA, 250-284
Anobiidae, 269
Anthicidae, 275
Anthribidae, 278
Apionidae, 278
Attelabidae, 278
Biphyllidae, 271
Bruchidae, 275
Byrrhidae, 267
Byturidae, 271
Cantharidae, 268
Carabidae, 251
Cerambycidae, 275
Cerylonidae, 272
Chrysomelidae, 275
Cisidae, 273
Clambidae, 266
Cleridae, 269
Coccinellidae, 272
Colydiidae, 273
Cryptophagidae, 271
Cucujidae, 271
Curculionidae, 279
Dascillidae, 266
Dermestidae, 269
Dryopidae, 267
Dytiscidae, 254
Elateridae, 267
Elmidae, 267
Elminthidae, 267

Endomychidae, 272
Erotylidae, 271
Geotrupidae, 265
Gyrinidae, 255
Haliplidae, 254
Helodidae, 256
Heteroceridae, 267
Histeridae, 256
Hydraenidae, 256
Hydrophilidae, 255
Lampyridae, 269
Lathridiidae, 273
Leiodidae, 256
Leptinidae, 256
Lucanidae, 265
Melandryidae, 274
Meloidae, 275
Melyridae, 269
Mordellidae, 274
Mycetophagidae, 273
Nitidulidae, 270
Noteridae, 254
Oedemeridae, 274
Peltidae, 269
Phalacridae, 271
Phloiophilidae, 269
Platypodidae, 283
Pselaphidae, 265
Ptiliidae, 256
Ptinidae, 269
Pyrochroidae, 274
Rhipiphoridae, 274
Rhyzophagidae, 270
Salpingidae, 274
Scaphidiidae, 257
Scarabaeidae, 265
Scirtidae, 266
Scraptiidae, 274
Scolytidae, 283
Scydmaenidae, 257
Silphidae, 257
Sphindidae, 271
Staphylinidae, 258
Tenebrionidae, 273
Throscidae, 268
Trogidae, 265
COLLEMBOLA, 160
DERMAPTERA, 164
DIPLURA, 160
DIPTERA, 221-240
Agromyzidae, 235
Anisopodidae, 225
Anthomyiidae, 239
Anthomyzidae, 235
Asilidae, 229

Bibionidae, 225
Bombyliidae, 229
Braulidae, 235
Calliphoridae, 239
Cecidomyiidae, 227
Ceratopogonidae, 224
Chaoboridae, 223
Chironomidae, 224
Chloropidae, 238
Clusiidae, 235
Coelopidae, 234
Conopidae, 233
Culicidae, 223
Diastatidae, 235
Dixidae, 223
Dolichopodidae, 230
Drosophilidae, 235
Dryomyzidae, 240
Empididae, 229
Ephydridae, 240
Fanniidae, 240
Gasterophilidae, 238
Heleomyzidae, 234
Hippoboscidae, 240
Hybotidae, 230
Keroplatidae, 226
Lauxaniidae, 234
Limoniidae, 221
Lonchaeidae, 235
Lonchopteridae, 231
Micropezidae, 234
Milichiidae, 240
Muscidae, 240
Mycetophilidae, 225
Oestridae, 238
Opomyzidae, 235
Otitidae, 234
Pallopteridae, 235
Phoridae, 231
Piophilidae, 240
Pipunculidae, 231
Platystomatidae, 234
Psilidae, 234
Psychodidae, 223
Ptychopteridae, 223
Rhagionidae, 228
Rhinophoridae, 239
Sarcophagidae, 239
Scathophagidae, 239
Scatopsidae, 240
Sciaridae, 227
Sciomyzidae, 235
Sepsidae, 235
Simuliidae, 225
Sphaeroceridae, 235
Stratiomyidae, 228
Syrphidae, 231

INSECTA:
DIPTERA cont....
Tabanidae, 229
Tachinidae, 238
Tephritidae, 234
Tethinidae, 240
Thaumaleidae, 224
Tipulidae, 221
Trichoceridae, 221
EPHEMERATA: 149
HEMIPTERA: 166-176
Acanthosomatidae, 166
Adelgidae, 176
Aleyrodidae, 176
Alydidae, 167
Aphididae, 176
Berytinidae, 167
Callaphididae, 176
Cercopidae, 171
Cicadellidae, 172
Cimicidae, 168
Cixiidae, 174
Coreidae, 167
Corixidae, 171
Cydnidae, 166
Delphacidae, 175
Gerridae, 171
Hydrometridae, 171
Issidae, 175
Lachnidae, 176
Lygaeidae, 167
Membracidae, 172
Microphysidae, 169
Miridae, 169
Nabidae, 168
Naucoridae, 171
Nepidae, 171
Notonectidae, 171
Pemphigidae, 176
Pentatomidae, 166
Psyllidae, 175
Reduviidae, 168
Rhopalidae, 167
Saldidae, 171
Tingidae, 168
Triozidae, 175
Veliidae, 171
HYMENOPTERA 242-249
Andrenidae, 247
Anthophoridae, 248
Aphidiidae, 244
Apidae, 248
Argidae, 242
Bethylidae, 245
Braconidae, 244
Cephidae, 242
Chalcididae, 245

Chrysididae, 245
Cimbicidae, 242
Colletidae, 247
Cynipidae, 244
Dryinidae, 245
Eulophidae, 245
Eumonidae, 246
Formicidae, 246
Gasteruptiidae, 244
Halictidae, 247
Ichneumonidae, 243
Megachilidae, 248
Mellitidae, 248
Mutillidae, 245
Mymaridae, 245
Platygastridae, 245
Pompilidae, 246
Proctotrupidae, 245
Pteromalidae, 245
Siricidae, 242
Sphecidae, 246
Tenthredinidae, 242
Tiphiidae, 245
Torymidae, 245
Trichogrammatidae, 245
Vespidae, 246
LEPIDOPTERA 179-220
MICRO-MOTHS:
Alucitidae, 198
Blastobasidae, 192
Bucculatricidae, 184
Choreutidae, 186
Coleophoridae, 188
Cosmopterigidae, 193
Cossidae, 183
Elachistidae, 189
Epermeniidae, 188
Eriocraniidae, 180
Gelechiidae, 191
Glyphipterigidae, 186
Gracillariidae, 185
Heliozelidae, 183
Hepialidae, 180
Incurvariidae, 182
Lyonetiidae, 184
Micropterigidae, 180
Momphidae, 192
Nepticulidae, 180
Ochsenheimeriidae, 184
Oecophoridae, 189
Psychidae, 183
Pterophoridae, 201
Pyralidae, 198
Schreckensteiniidae, 188
Scythrididae, 193
Sesiidae, 186
Tineidae, 183

Tischeriidae, 182
Tortricidae, 193
Yponomeutidae, 187
Zygaenidae, 183
BUTTERFLIES:
Hesperiidae, 202
Lycaenidae, 202
Pieridae, 202
MACRO-MOTHS:
Arctiidae, 212
Drepanidae, 205
Geometridae, 205
Lasiocampidae, 204
Lymantriidae, 212
Noctuidae, 213
Nolidae, 213
Notodontidae, 212
Saturniidae, 205
Sphingidae, 211
Thyatiridae, 205
MALLOPHAGA, 165
MECOPTERA, 178
MEGALOPTERA, 177
NEUROPTERA, 177
ODONATA, 161
ORTHOPTERA, 163
PLECOPTERA, 150
PROTERA, 160
PSOCOPTERA, 164
RAPHIDIOPTERA, 177
SIPHONAPTERA, 241
THYSANOPTERA,177
THYSANURA, 160
TRICHOPTERA, 151

BRYOZOA:
Gymnolaemata, 139
Stenolaemata, 139

CHORDATA:
Ascidiacea, 142

COELENTERATA:
Anthozoa, 125
Hydrozoa, 124, 143
Scyphozoa, 124

CTENOPHORA:
Nuda, 125

ECHINODERMATA:
Asteroidea, 141
Crinoidea, 141
Echinoidea, 142
Holothuroidea, 142
Ophiuroidea, 141

MOLLUSCA:
Gastropoda, 134, 145, 154
Bivalvia, 137, 145
Cephalopoda, 138
Polyplacophora, 134

NEMATODA: 129
NEMATOMORPHA, 144

NEMATINA:
Anopla, 125
Enopla, 126

OLIGOCHAETA: 128,146,157
PLATYHELMINTHES:
Turbellaria, 125, 144

PORIFERA, 123
PROTOZOA, 122
ROTIFERA:
Bdelloidea, 144
Monogononta, 144

SIPUNCULA, 129

VERTEBRATA

AMPHIBIA:
Bufonidae, 301
Ranidae, 301
Salamandridae, 301

AVES (BIRDS)
Accipitridae, 306
Aegithalidae, 314
Alaudidae, 312
Alcedinidae, 311
Alcidae, 310
Anatidae, 305
Apodidae, 311
Ardeidae, 304
Bombycillidae, 313
Caprimulgidae, 311
Certhiidae, 315
Charadriidae, 307
Cinclidae, 313
Columbidae, 310
Corvidae, 315
Cuculidae, 311
Emberizidae, 316
Falconidae, 306
Fringillidae, 315
Gaviidae, 303
Haematopodidae, 307
Hirundinidae, 312
Hydrobatidae, 304
Laniidae, 315
Laridae, 309
Motacillidae, 312
Muscicapidae, 314
Oriolidae, 315
Pandionidae, 306
Paridae, 314
Passeridae, 315
Phalacrocoracidae, 304
Phasianidae, 307
Picidae, 312
Podicipedidae, 303
Procellariidae, 304
Prunellidae, 313
Psittacidae, 310
Rallidae, 307
Recurvirostridae, 307
Scolopacidae, 308
Sittidae, 315
Stercorariidae, 309
Sternidae, 310
Strigidae, 311
Sturnidae, 315
Sulidae, 304
Sylviidae, 313
Tetraonidae, 307
Threskiornithidae, 304
Timaliidae, 314
Troglodytidae, 313
Turdidae, 313
Tytonidae, 311
Upupidae, 311

MAMMALIA:
Bovidae, 319
Canidae, 319
Cervidae, 319
Delphinidae, 318
Equidae, 319
Erinaceidae, 317
Gliridae, 318
Leporidae, 318
Muridae, 318
Mustelidae, 319
Phocidae, 319
Phocoenidae, 319
Rhinolophidae, 317
Sciuridae, 318
Soricidae, 317
Talpidae, 317
Vespertilionidae, 318

PISCES (FISH):
Agonidae, 298
Ammodytidae, 299
Anguillidae, 296
Balistidae, 300
Belonidae, 298
Bothidae, 299
Carangidae, 299
Carcharinidae, 296
Clupeidae, 296
Cobitidae, 297
Congridae, 296
Cottidae, 298
Cyclopteridae, 299
Cyprinidae, 297
Dasyatidae, 296
Gadidae, 297
Gasterosteidae, 298
Gobiesocidae, 297
Gobiidae, 299
Labridae, 299
Lamnidae, 296
Lophiidae, 298
Merlucciidae, 298
Molidae, 300
Mugilidae, 299
Mullidae, 299
Petromyzonidae, 295
Pleuronectidae, 299
Rajidae, 296
Salmonidae, 297
Scombridae, 299
Scyliorhinidae, 295
Serranidae, 299
Soleidae, 300
Sparidae, 299
Squalidae, 296
Squatinidae, 296
Syngnathidae, 298
Thymallidae, 297
Trachinidae, 299
Triglidae, 298
Zeidae, 298

REPTILIA:
Anguidae, 302
Colubridae, 302
Lacertidae, 302
Viperidae, 302

INDEX OF ENGLISH NAMES

ADDER, 302
ALDERFLIES, 177
ALGAE:
　Blanket Weed, 8
　Carragheen, 13
　Dabberlocks, 15
　Diatoms, 10
　Dulse, 14
　Furbelows, 15
　Irish Moss, 13
　Laver, 12
　Oarweed, 15
　Pepper Dulse, 13
　Sea Belt, 15
　Sea Lettuce, 9
　Sea-oak, 16
　Stoneworts, 9
　Wracks, 15
ANTS: 245
BEES: 247
BEETLES: Bark, 283
　Bloodsucker, 268
　Bloody-nosed, 276
　Burying, 257
　Cardinal, 274
　Carpet, 269
　Carrion, 257
　Chafers, 266
　Click, 267
　Cockchafer, 266
　Darkling, 273
　Death-watch, 269
　Devils Coach-horse, 261
　Dor, 265
　Dung, 265
　Elm bark, 283
　False Darkling, 274
　Flea, 275, 277-8
　Flower, 269, 274
　Furniture, 269
　Glow-worm, 269
　Great Diving, 254
　Green Tiger, 251
　Ground, 251
　Ladybird Mimic, 272
　Ladybirds, 272
　Leaf, 275, 276
　Longhorn, 275
　Malthene, 268
　Maybug, 266
　Minotaur, 265
　Mould, 273
　Oil, 275
　Pill, 267
　Pine, 283
　Pinhole borer, 283
　Raspberry, 271
　Reed, 275
　Rove, 258
　Sailor, 268
　Sap, 270
　Scarabs, 265
　Sexton, 257　Skin, 269
　Skipjack, 267, 268
　Soldier, 268
　Spider, 269
　Stag, 265
　Tortoise, 278
　Violet Ground, 251
　Wasp, 275
　Water, 254, 255
　Watercress, 276
　Weevils, 278-283
　Whirligig, 255
　Wireworm, 268
　Wood-boring, 269
BIBLIOGRAPHY, 325
BIRDS:
　Auks, 310
　Avocet, 307
　Bittern, 304
　Blackbird, 313
　Blackcap, 314
　Brambling, 315
　Bullfinch, 316
　Buntings, 316
　Buzzard, 306
　Chaffinch, 315
　Chiffchaff, 314
　Chough, 315
　Coot, 307
　Cormorant, 304
　Corncrake, 307
　Crake, 307
　Crossbill, 316
　Crows, 315
　Cuckoo, 311
　Curlew, 308
　Dipper, 313
　Divers, 303
　Dotterel, 308
　Doves, 310
　Dowitcher, 308
　Ducks, 305, 306
　Dunlin, 308
　Dunnock, 313
　Egret, 304
　Eider, 306
　Fieldfare, 313
　Firecrest, 314
　Flycatchers, 314
　Fulmar, 304
　Gadwall, 305
　Gannet, 304
　Garganey, 305
　Geese, 305
　Godwit, 308
　Goldcrest, 314
　Goldeneye, 306
　Golden Oriel, 315
　Goldfinch, 315
　Goosander, 306
　Goshawk, 306
　Grebes, 303
　Greenfinch, 315
　Greenshank, 308
　Grouse, 307
　Guillemot, 310
　Gulls, 309
　Gyrfalcon, 307
　Harriers, 306
　Hawfinch, 316
　Heron, 304
　Hobby, 306
　Hoopoe, 311
　Jackdaw, 315
　Jay, 315
　Kestrel, 306
　Kingfisher, 311
　Kite, 306
　Kittiwake, 309
　Knot, 308
　Lapwing, 308
　Larks, 312
　Linnet, 316
　Long-tailed Duck, 306
　Magpie, 315
　Mallard, 305
　Martins, 312
　Merganser, 306
　Merlin, 306
　Moorhen, 307
　Nightingale, 313
　Nightjar, 311
　Nutcracker, 315
　Nuthatch, 315
　Osprey, 306
　Owls, 311
　Oystercatcher, 307
　Parakeet, 310
　Partridge, 307
　Peewit, 308
　Peregrine, 307
　Petrels, 304
　Phalarope, 309

BIRDS cont..
Pheasant, 307
Pigeon, 310
Pintail, 305
Pipits, 312
Plovers, 308
Pochard, 305
Puffin, 310
Quail, 307
Raven, 315
Razorbill, 310
Redpoll, 316
Redshank, 308
Redstarts, 313
Redwing, 313
Ringed Plover, 307, 308
Ring Ouzel, 313
Robin, 313
Rook, 315
Ruff, 308
Sanderling, 308
Sandpipers, 308, 309
Scaup, 305
Scoter, 306
Shag, 304
Shearwaters, 304
Shelduck, 305
Shoveler, 305
Shrikes, 315
Siskin, 315
Skua, 309
Skylark, 312
Smew, 306
Snipe, 308
Sparrowhawk, 306
Sparrows, 315
Spoonbill, 304
Starling, 315
Stint, 308
Stonechat, 313
Swallows, 312
Swans, 305
Swifts, 311
Teal, 305
Terns, 310
Thrushes, 313
Tits, 314
Treecreeper, 315
Turnstone, 309
Twite, 316
Wagtails, 312, 313
Warblers, 313, 314
Water Rail, 307
Waxwing, 313
Wheatear, 313
Whimbrel, 308
Whinchat, 313
Whitethroat, 314

Wigeon, 305
Woodcock, 308
Woodlark, 312
Woodpeckers, 312
Wren, 313
Wryneck, 312
Yellowhammer, 316
BRISTLE-TAILS, 160
BUGS:
  Aphids, 176
  Assassin bugs, 168
  Damsel bugs, 168
  F/water shore bugs, 171
  Flower bugs, 168
  Froghoppers, 171
  Groundbugs, 167
  Lacebugs, 168
  Leafhoppers, 172
  Plant lice, 175
  Plantbugs, 169
  Planthoppers, 174
  Pond skaters, 171
  Saucer bug, 171
  Shieldbugs, 166
  Squashbugs, 167
  Stiltbugs, 167
  Tree hoppers, 172
  Water boatmen, 171
  Water crickets, 171
  Water measurers, 171
  Water scorpion, 171
  Whiteflies, 175/6
BUSH-CRICKETS, 163
BUTTERFLIES:
  Blues, 203
  Brimstone, 202
  Brown Argus, 203
  Clouded Yellow, 202
  Comma, 203
  Duke of Burgundy, 203
  Fritillaries, 203-4
  Gatekeeper, 204
  Grayling, 204
  Hairstreaks, 202-3
  Marbled White, 204
  Meadow Brown, 204
  Monarch, 204
  Orange Tip, 202
  Painted Lady, 203
  Peacock, 203
  Red Admiral, 203
  Ringlet, 204
  Skippers, 202
  Small Copper, 203
  Small Heath, 204
  Speckled Wood, 204
  Tortoiseshells, 203
  Wall, 204

  White Admiral, 203
  Whites, 202
  Wood White, 202
CAMEL-CRICKET, 163
CENTIPEDES, 159
CLIMATE, 4
CLUBMOSSES, 75
COAST - see MARITIME
COCKROACH, 164
CONEHEAD, 163
CONIFERS, 78
DAMSELFLIES, 161
DRAGONFLIES, 161
EARTHWORMS, 157
EARWIG, 164
FERNS, 76
FIREBRAT, 160
FISH:
  Allis Shad, 296
  Angler, 298
  Bass, 299
  Brill, 299
  Bullhead, 298
  Coalfish, 297
  Cod, 297
  Coley, 297
  Cornish Sucker, 297
  Dab, 299
  Dogfish, 295
  Dover Sole, 300
  Eels, 296
  Flounder, 299
  Frogfish, 298
  Garfish, 298
  Goby, 299
  Golden Orfe, 297
  Grayling, 297
  Gurnard, 298
  Haddock, 297
  Hake, 298
  Halibut, 299
  Herring, 296
  Horse Mackerel, 299
  John Dory, 298
  Koi Carp, 297
  Lampreys, 295
  Ling, 297
  Lumpsucker, 299
  Mackerel, 299
  Miller's Thumb, 298
  Minnow, 297
  Monkfish, 296
  Mullet, 299
  Pipefish, 298
  Plaice, 299
  Pogge, 298
  Pollack, 297
  Porbeagle, 296

Pouting,297
Rays,296
Rockling,297/8
Rudd,297
Salmon,297
Sand Eel,299
Sea Bream,299
Shore Clingfish,297
Skate,296
Smooth Hound,296
Spur Dogfish,296
St.Peter's Fish,298
Sticklebacks,298
Stone Loach,297
Sun Fish,300
Tench,297
Tope,296
Trigger Fish,300
Trout,297
Turbot,299
Weever,299
Whiting,297
Wrasse,299
FLEAS: 241
FLIES: Assassin Flies,229
Bee Flies,229
Bee Louse,235
Black Flies,225
Blowflies,239
Bluebottles,239
Bot-fly,238
Cabbage Root-fly,239
Carrot Fly,234
Celery Fly,234
Clegs,229
Crane-flies,221
Deer Fly,240
Dung Flies,239
Fruit Flies,235
Fungus Gnats,225/6,320
Gadflies,229
Gall Midges,227
Greenbottles,239
Horse Flies,229
House Flies,240
Hoverflies,231
Kelp Flies,234
Large-headed Flies,231
Leaf-mining Flies,235
Long-headed Flies,230
Louse Flies,240
Meniscus Midges,223
Midges,224
Mosquitoes,223
Narcissus Fly,233
Owl Midges,223
Parasitic Flies,238
Phantom Midges,223

Picture-winged Flies,234
Pointed-winged Flies,231
Robber Flies,229
Scuttle Flies,231
Sheep Ked,240
Sheep Nostril Fly,238
Snail-killing Flies,235
Snipe Flies,228
Soldier Flies,228
St.Mark's Fly,225
Stable Fly,240
Stilt-legged Flies,234
Warble Fly,238
Winter Gnats,221
FLOWERS:
Abraham-Isaac-Jacob,101
Acaena,93
Agrimony,92/3
Alder,83
Alder Buckthorn,97
Alexanders,98
Alison,89
Alkanet,101
Almond,93
Amaranth,84
Anemones,81
Angelica,99
Apple,93
Apple of Peru,100
Arrowgrass,110
Ash,103
Asparagus,117
Aspen,88
Aubrietia,89
Aunt Eliza,118
Avens,92
Azaelea,90
Balm,101,102
Balm of Gilead,88
Balsam,Indian,98
Barberry,82
Basil,102
Bastard Balm,101
Bay,81
Beach Aster,108
Bedstraw,105
Beech,83
Beet,84
Bellflower,105
Betony,101
Bilberry,90
Bindweed,86,100
Birch,83
Bird's-foot,94
Bistort,86
Bittercress,89
Bittersweet,100
Bitter-vetch,95

Blackthorn, 93
Black Bryony,118
Black Mustard,89
Bleeding Heart,82
Blinks,84
Blood-drop-emlets,103
Bluebell,117
Blue-eyed-grass,118
Bog Asphodel,116
Bogbean,100
Bog Myrtle,83
Borage,101
Box,97
Brambles,92
Bridewort,92
Brooklime,104
Brookweed,91
Broom,95
Broomrape,104
Buckwheat,86
Bugle,102
Bugloss,100
Bullace,93
Bullwort,99
Bulrush,116
Bur-reed,116
Burdock,106
Bur Marigold,109
Burnet,93
Burnet Saxifrage,99
Bur Parsley,98
Butcher's-broom,117
Butterbur,109
Buttercups,81
Butterfly-bush,103
Butterwort,104/5
Calamint,102
Campions,85
Canterbury Bell,105
Carrot,99
Catchfly,85
Catmint,102
Cat's-ear,107
Celandine,81,82
Celery,99
Centaury,99
Chamomile,109
Charlock,90
Checkerberry,90
Cherry Laurel,93
Cherry,93 -Plum,93
Chervil,98
Chickweed,85
Chicory,107
Chives,117
Cinquefoil,92
Clary,102
Cleavers,105

FLOWERS cont....
Clovers, 95
Club-rushes, 111
Coltsfoot, 109
Columbine, 82
Comfrey, 100
Corncockle, 85
Cornflower, 107
Cornish Moneywort, 104
Corn Marigold, 109
Corn Parsley, 99
Cornsalad, 106
Corydalis, 82
Cotoneaster, 94
Cottongrass, 111
Cow Parsley, 98
Cowslip, 90
Cow-wheat, 104
Cranberry, 90
Crane's-bill, 98
Creeping Jenny, 90
Cress, 88/89
Crocus, 118
Crosswort, 105
Crowberry, 90
Crow-foot, 81-82
Cuckooflower, 89
Cudweed, 108
Currants, 91
Cyclamen, 90
Daffodil, 117
Daisy, 108, 109
Dame's-violet, 88
Dandelion, 107
Danewort, 105
Day Lily, 116
Dead-nettle, 101
Deergrass, 80, 111
Deptford Pink, 86
Dewberry, 92 Docks, 86
Dodder, 100
Dogwood, 96
Dropwort, 92
Duckweed, 110
Duke of Argyll's Tea, 100
Eastern Rocket, 88
Elder, 105
Elecampane, 108
Elephant's-ears, 91
Elms, 83
Enchanter's Nightshade, 96
Escallonia, 91
Evening Primrose, 96
Everlasting Pea, 95
Eyebright, 104
False Acacia, 94
False Buck's-beard, 91
Fat-hen, 84

Fennel, 99
Feverfew, 108
Field Gentian, 99
Field Madder, 105
Fig, 83
Figwort, 103
Firethorn, 94
Firs, 78
Flax, 97
Fleabane, 108
Flixweed, 88
Fluellen, 103
Fool's Parsley, 99
Fool's Water-cress, 99
Forget-me-not, 100, 101
Forsythia, 103
Fox & Cubs, 107
Foxglove, 103
Fringecups, 92
Fringed Water-lily, 100
Fritillary, 116
Fuchsia, 96
Fumitory, 82
Furze, 95
Galingale, 112
Garlic, 117
Giant Rhubarb, 96
Gipsywort, 102
Gladiolus, 118
Glasswort, 84
Glory-of-the-snow, 117
Goat's-beard, 107
Goat's Rue, 94
Goldenrod, 108
Golden-saxifrage, 92
Good-King-Henry, 84
Gooseberry, 91
Goosefoot, 84
Gorse, 95
Grape Hyacinth, 117
Grasses, 113-116
Gromwell, 100
Ground-elder, 99
Ground Ivy, 102
Groundsel, 109
Guelder-rose, 105
Harebell, 105
Hawkbit, 107
Hawk's-beard, 107
Hawkweeds, 107/8
Hawthorn, 94
Hazel, 84
Heath, 90
Heather, 90
Hebe, 104
Hedge-parsley, 99
Heliotrope, 109
Hellebore, 81

Helleborine, 118
Hemlock, 99
Hemp Agrimony, 109
Hemp-nettle, 101
Henbane, 100
Herb Robert, 98
Hogweed, 99
Holly, 97
Hollyhock, 87
Honesty, 89
Honeysuckle, 105/106
Hop, 83
Hop Trefoil, 95
Horehound, 101
Hornbeam, 84
Horse Chestnut, 97
Horse-radish, 89
Houndstongue, 101
Houseleek, 91
Iris, 118
Ivy, 98
Jacob's Ladder, 100
Jerusalem Sage, 101
Juneberry, 94
Kangaroo Apple, 100
Kerria, 92
Kingcup, 81
Knapweed, 107(Knawel, 85)
Knotgrass, 86
Knotweeds, 86
Kohuhu, 91
Koromiko, 104
Laburnum, 95
Lady's-mantle, 93
Lady's-tresses, 118
Larch, 78
Laurustinus, 105
Leek, 117
Lenten Rose, 81
Leopard's-bane, 109
Lettuce, 107
Lilac, 103
Lily, Pyrenean, 116
Lily-of-the-valley, 116
Lime, 87
Ling, 90
Lobelia, 105
Londonpride, 91
Loosestrife, 90, 91, 96
Lords & Ladies, 110
Lousewort, 104
Love-in-a-mist, 81
Lucerne, 95
Lungwort, 100
Madder, 105
Mallow, 87
Maple, 97
Marigold, Pot, 109

FLOWERS cont....
Marjoram,102
May Lily,116
Mayweed,109
Meadow Rue,82
Meadowsweet,92
Medick,95
Medlar,94
Melilot,95
Mercury,97
Michaelmas Daisy,108
Milkwort,97
Mind-your-own-business,83
Mints,102
Mistletoe,96
Mock Orange,91
Monkey-flower,103
Monkshood,81
Montbretia,118
Moor-grass,115
Moschatel,106
Motherwort,101
Mouse-ear,85
Mugwort,108
Mullein,103
Musk,103
Mustard,88-90
Navelwort,91
Nettles,83
Nightshade,100
Nipplewort,107
Oaks,83
Onion,117
Orache,84
Orchids,118
Oregon Grape,82
Orpine,91
Osier,88
Oxeye,109
Oxtongue,107
Palm,Cabbage,118
Pansy,88
Parsley Piert,93
Parsnip,99
Pear,93
Pearlworts,85
Pearly Everlasting,108
Pellitory,83
Pennycress,89
Pennyroyal,102
Pennywort,Marsh, 98
Pennywort,Wall,91
Pepper Saxifrage,99
Pepperwort,89
Periwinkle,99
Persicaria,86
Pettywhin,95
Phacelia,100

Pick-a-back plant,91
Pignut,99
Pimpernel,Scarlet,91
Pimpernel,Bog,91
Pimpernel,Yellow,90
Pine,78
Pineappleweed,109
Pink Purslane,84
Pink Sorrel,97/8
Plane tree,82
Plantains,102
Ploughman's-spikenard,108
Plum,93
Pokeweed,84
Pondweed,110
Poplar,88
Poppies,82
Portugal Laurel,93
Potato,100
Prickly-heath,90
Primrose,90
Privet,103
Pygmy-weed,91
Quince,93
Radish,90
Ragged Robin,85
Ragwort,109
Ramsons,117
Rape,89
Raspberry,92
Red Bartsia,104
Red Rattle,104
Redshank,86
Reed,115
Restharrow,95
Rhododendron,90
Roble,83
Rockcress,89
Rocket,88,89,90
Rock Samphire,99
Rosebay,96
Rosemary,102
Rose-of-Sharon,87
Roses,93
Rowan,93
Rushes,111
Russian-vine,86
Salsify,107
Saltwort,84
Sand Catchfly,85
Sandwort,84
Sanicle,98
Saw-wort,106
Saxifrage,91
Scabious,106
Scurvygrass,89
Sea-blite,84
Sea Aster,108

Sea Buckthorn,96
Sea Milkwort,91
Sea Purslane,84
Sedges,111,112
Self-heal,102
Shaggy-soldier,109
Sheepsbit,105
Shepherd's-needle,98
Shepherd's-purse,89
Shoreweed,102
Silverweed,92
Skullcap,101
Skunk Cabbage,110
Snap-dragon,103
Sneezewort,108
Snowberry,105
Snowdrop,117
Snowflake,117
Snow-in-summer,85
Soapwort,85
Solomon's-seal,116
Sorrel,86,97,98
Sowthistle,107
Spearwort,81
Speedwell,103-4
Spikerushes,111
Spindle,96
Spring-beauty,84
Spurge,97
Spurge Laurel,96
Spurrey,85
Squill,117
St.John's-wort,87
Star-of-Bethlehem,117
Star Thistle,107
Stinkweed,89
Stitchwort, 84,85
Stock,Hoary,88
Stonecrop,91
Stone Parsley,99
Stork's-bill,98
Strawberry,92
Strawberry-tree,90
Sundew,87
Sunflower,109
Sweet Cicely,98
Sweet-briar,93
Sweet Chestnut,83
Sweet William,86
Swinecress,89
Sycamore,97
Tamarisk,88
Tansy,108
Tare,94
Tasselweed,110
Teasel,106
Thalecress,88
Thistles,106

FLOWERS cont....
Thornapple, 100
Thorow-wax, 99
Thrift, 87
Thyme, 102
Toadflax, 103
Toadrush, 111
Tomato, 100
Toothwort, 104
Tormentil, 92
Traveller's Joy, 81
Tree Lupin, 95
Trefoil, 95
Tulip, 116
Turnip, 89
Tutsan, 87
Twayblade, 118
Valerian, 106
Vervain, 101
Vetches, 94
Vetchlings, 95
Violets, 87
Viper's Bugloss, 100
Virginia Creeper, 97
Wallflower, 88
Wall Rocket, 89
Walnut, 83
Water-cress, 89
Water Dropwort, 99
Water-lily, 81, 100
Water-milfoil, 96
Water Parsnip, 99
Water Pepper, 86
Water Plantain, 110
Water Purslane, 96
Water-starwort, 102
Waterweed, 110
Wayfaring Tree, 105
Weasel's-snout, 103
Weld, 90
Whitebeam, 93
Whitlowgrass, 89
Whortleberry, 90
Willowherb, 96
Willows, 88
Wineberry, 92
Winter-cress, 88
Wolf's-bane, 81
Wood-sorrel, 97
Woodruff, 105
Woodrushes, 111
Wood Sage, 102
Wormwood, 108
Woundworts, 101
Yarrow, 108
Yellow-cress, 89
Yellow-rattle, 104
Yellow-sorrel, 97

Yellow Archangel, 101
Yellow-eyed-grass, 118
Yellow-wort, 99
FRESHWATER LIFE: 143
Caddis flies, 151
Cockle, 145
Cyclops, 148
Damselflies, 161
Dragonflies, 161
Fish lice, 149
Hydra, 143
Leeches, 147
Limpet, 145
Mayflies, 149/150
Mussel, 145
Polyps, 143
Pond Skaters, 171
Shrimps, 149
Snails, 145
Springtails, 160
Stoneflies, 150
Water Beetles, 254, 255
Water Boatmen, 171
Water Crickets, 171
Water Fleas, 148
Water Measurer, 171
Water Mites, 147
Water Scorpion, 171
Water Slater, 149
Water Spider, 287
Wheel Animalcules, 144
Worm, Square-tailed, 146
Worms, Blood, 146
Worms, Flat, 144
Worms, Pot, 146
Worms, Thread, 144
Worms, True, 146
FROG, 301
FUNGI: 17
Amethyst Deceiver, 33
Aniseed Toadstool, 28
Artist's Fungus, 31
Beef-steak, 31
Birch Polypore, 38
Bird's Nest, 30
Bitter Bolete, 42
Black Bulgar, 19
Blewits, 35
Blusher, 26
Blushing Bracket, 30
Boletes, 26, 27, 42
Bonnet Mycena, 36
Brain Fungus, 40
Brick Cap, 33
Brown Cup, 20
Brown Roll-rim, 37
Butter Cap, 28
Candle-snuff, 20

Cauliflower, 40
Cep, 26
Champignon, 35
Chanterelle, 27
Charcoal Burner, 40
Chicken-of-the-woods, 34
Clouded Agaric, 28
Club Foot, 27
Clubs, 27
Coral Spot, 20
Corals, 27
Cramp Ball, 19
Dead Man's Fingers, 20
Death Cap, 26
Deceiver, 33
Devil's Snuff-box, 40
Dog Stinkhorn, 36
Dryad's Saddle, 39
Dung Roundhead, 41
Dutch Elm disease, 19
Earthball, 40
Earth Fan, 41
Earth Stars, 31
Earth tongue, 20
Elf-cup, 20
Ergot, 19
Eyelash, 20
Fairies' Bonnets, 29
Fairy Umbrella, 36
Fairy-ring, 35
False Chanterelle, 33
False Death Cap, 25
False Truffle, 19
Fly Agaric, 26
Funnel Cap, 28, 35
Galerina, 31
Giant Polypore, 36
Goblet, 39
Green Oak, 19
Heath Fungus, 37
Hedgehog, 32
Helvella, 19
Honey Fungus, 26
Horn-of-Plenty, 30
Horse-hair, 35
Ink Caps, 29
Jelly Babies, 20
Jelly Tongue, 39
Jew's Ear, 26
King Alfred's Cakes, 19
Lacquered Bracket, 31
Lawyer's Wig, 29
Liberty Cap, 39
Magpie Fungus, 29
Many-zoned Polypore, 29
Maze Fungus, 30
Milk Caps, 34
Miller, 28

FUNGI cont....
Mock Oyster, 26
Morel, 19
Mottlegill, 37
Mushrooms, 25
Nut Cup, 19
Orange Peel, 19
Oyster, 38
Panther Cap, 26
Parasols, 35
Pick-a-back, 26
Pine Fire, 20
Pinecone Fungus, 26
Plums & Custard, 41
Poached Egg, 37
Poison Pie, 31
Porcelain, 37
Prince, 25
Puffballs, 27, 31, 35
Razor Strop, 38
Root Fomes, 32
Rooting Shank, 37
Russulas, 39, 40
Rust Fungi, 21-24
Scaly Polypore, 39
Scarlet Caterpillar, 19
Sedge Fungus, 20
Shaggy Pholiota, 38
Shield Lepiota, 34
Sickener, 40
Silver Leaf, 27
Slime Moulds, 18
Slippery Jack, 26
Smut Fungi, 24
Snow Bonnet, 32
Soap Tricholoma, 41
Spindle Shank, 28
Spindles, 27
Split-gill, 40. Stags-horn, 27
Stereum, 41
Stinkhorn, 36, 38
Sulphur Polypore, 34
Sulphur Tuft, 33
Tar Spot, 20
Tawny Funnel-cap, 35
Tawny Grisette, 26
Tough Shanks, 28
Tripe Fungus, 26
Upright Ramaria, 39
Velvet Shank, 31
Verdigris Agaric, 41
Wax Caps, 32
Weeping Widow, 34
White Brain, 31
White Lead, 27
Winter Fungus, 31
Witches' Broom, 20
Witches' Butter, 31

Wood Woolly-foot, 28
Yellow Brain, 41
Yellow Stainer, 25
GALL-WASPS, 244
GRASSHOPPERS, 163
GRASS-SNAKE, 302
GROUNDHOPPERS, 163
HARVESTMEN, 292
HORNWORTS, 65
HORSETAILS, 75
LACEWINGS, 177
LICE, 164, 175
LICHENS: 43-60
  Dog Lichen, 54
  Lungwort, 51
LIVERWORTS, 61
LIZARD, 302
MAMMALS:
  Badger, 319
  Bats, 317/318
  Deer, 319
  Dolphins, 318
  Exmoor Pony, 319
  Fox, 319
  Goat, 319
  Hare, 318
  Hedgehog, 317
  Mice, 318
  Mink, 319
  Mole, 317
  Muntjac, 319
  Otter, 319
  Porpoise, 319
  Rabbit, 318
  Rat, 318
  Seal, 319
  Shrews, 317
  Squirrel, 318
  Stoat, 319
  Voles, 318
  Weasel, 319
MARITIME CREATURES:
  Barnacles, 129
  Chink-shells, 135
  Chitons, 134
  Cockles, 138
  Cowrie, 135
  Crabs, 132, 133
  Crawfish, 132
  Cuttlefish, 138
  Fish, 295-300
  Jelly-fish, 124
  Limpets, 134, 135
  Lobsters, 132
  Mussels, 137
  Nut shells, 137
  Octopus, 138
  Oysters, 137

Peppery Furrow, 138
Pheasant Shell, 134
Piddock, 138
Portuguese Man-O'War, 124
Prawns, 132
Pullet, 138
Razor, 138
Rock Borer, 138
Sandhoppers, 131
Scallops, 137
Sea Anemones, 125
Sea-cucumber, 142
Sea-firs, 124
Sea Gooseberries, 125
Sea Hare, 136
Sea-mats, 139
Sea Slugs, 136
Sea-spiders, 133
Sea-squirt, 142
Sea Urchin, 142
Shipworm, 138
Shrimps, 131, 132
Slaters, 130
Spire Shell, 136
Sponges, 123
Squid, 138
Starfish, 141
Tellin, 138
Top-shells, 134
Whelks, 135, 136
Winkles, 135
Worms, 125-129
MILLIPEDES, 159
MITES, 293
MOSSES: 65
  Apple-moss, 70
  Bristle-moss, 71
  Cave moss, 69
  Cord-moss, 69
  Feather-moss, 72
  Fern-moss, 67
  Fork-moss, 67
  Hair-moss, 66
  Screw-moss, 68
  Sphagnum, 65
  Thread-moss, 69
  Tree-moss, 71
  Willow-moss, 71
MOTHS:
  Alder, 217
  Angle-striped Sallow, 217
  Angle Shades, 217
  Annulet, 211
  Anomalous, 218
  Antler, 215
  Apple, 194
  Argent & Sable, 206, 207
  Ash-bud, 187

MOTHS cont....
Autumnal, 208
Barred Red, 211
Barred Straw, 207
Barred Umber, 210
Barred Yellow, 207
Beautiful Hook-tip, 220
Bee Moth, 200
Belles, 206
Black Arches, 212, 213
Black-neck, 219
Black Rustic, 216
Blood-vein, 206
Blossom Underwing, 215
Bordered Beauty, 210
Bordered Sallow, 219
Bordered Straw, 219
Bordered White, 211
Brick, 216
Bright-line Brown-eye, 215
Brimstone, 210
Brindle, 209, 217, 218
Brindled Beauty, 210
Brindled Green, 216
Brindled Ochre, 216
Broad-barred White, 215
Brocade, 214, 215
Broom-tip, 209
Broom Moth, 215
Brown-line Bright-eye, 215
Brown-spot Pinion, 216
Brown Rustic, 217
Brussels Lace, 211
Bud, 197
Buff Arches, 205
Burnets, 183
Burnished Brass, 219
Cabbage, 214
Cacao, 201
Campion, 215
Carpets, 206-211
Cherry Bark, 197
Chestnut, 216
Chevron, 207
Chimney Sweeper, 209
China Mark, 199
Chinese Character, 205
Chocolate Tip, 212
Cinnabar, 213
Clay, 214, 215
Clay Triple-lines, 205
Clearwings, 186
Clouded Buff, 213
Clouded Drab, 215
Clouded Silver, 211
Codling, 197
Common Heath, 211
Common Wave, 211

Copper Underwings, 217
Cork, 184
Corn-borer, 199
Coronet, 215, 217
Crescent, 218
Crescent-striped, 217
Crimson Speckled, 213
Dark Arches, 217
Dark Brocade, 216
Dark Dagger, 217
Dark Sword-grass, 213
Darts, 213, 214
December, 204
Delicate, 215
Diamond-back, 188
Dingy Shell, 209
Dingy Shears, 217
Dog's-tooth, 215
Dot, 214
Dotted Border, 210
Double-line, 215
Double Kidney, 217
Double Lobed, 218
Drinker, 204
Dun-bar, 217
Dusky Brocade, 217
Dusky Sallow, 218
Ear-moth, 218
Early, 211
Early Grey, 216
Eggars, 204
Emeralds, 205
Emperor, 205
Engrailed, 211
Ermines, 213
Fan-foot, 220
Feathered Gothic, 215
Fern, 207
Figure of Eight, 212
Figure of Eighty, 205
Flame, 213
Footmen, 212, 213
Forester, 183
Fox, 204
Frosted Green, 205
Frosted Orange, 218
Garden Pebble, 199
Gem, 206
Ghost, 180. Goat, 183
Gold Spangle, 219
Gold Triangle, 200
Gold-spot, 219
Golden Plusia, 219
Golden Twin-spot, 219
Golden Y 219
Gothic, 214
Grass Wave, 211
Green-brindled Crescent, 216

Green Arches, 214
Grey Arches, 214
Grey Birch, 211
Grey Dagger, 217
Grey Scalloped Bar, 211
Hawk-moths, 211, 212
Haworth's Minor, 218
Heart & Club, 213
Heart & Dart, 213
Hebrew Character, 214, 215
Hedge Rustic, 215
Highflyers, 207
Hook-tips, 205
Horse-chestnut, 210
Kittens, 212
Knot-grass, 217
Lackey, 204
Lappet, 204
Large Ear, 218
Large Nutmeg, 217
Latticed Heath, 210
Leopard, 183
Light Arches, 217
Light Emerald, 211
Lilac Beauty, 210
Little Thorn, 210
Lobster, 212
Lunar Underwing, 216
Lutestring, 205
Lychnis, 215
Magpies, 199, 209
Maiden's Blush, 205
Mallow, 206
Marbled Beauty, 217
Marbled Brown, 212
Marbled Clover, 219
Marbled Green, 217
Marbled White-spot, 219
March, 205
Meal Moth, 200
Merveille du Jour, 216
Miller, 217
Minors, 218
Mocha, 205
Mother Shipton, 219
Mottled Grey, 207
Mottled Beauty, 211
Mottled Willow, 218
Mouse Moth, 217
Mullein, 216
Muslin, 213
Ni, 219
Northern Drab, 215
November, 208
Nut-tree Tussock, 219
Nut-bud, 196
Nutmeg, 214
Oak Nycteoline, 219

339

MOTHS cont....
Oak Beauty, 210
Old Lady, 217
Olive, 217
Olive-tree Pearl, 200
Orange, 210
Pale Tussock, 212
Pea, 197
Peach Blossom, 205
Peacocks, 210
Pearly Underwing, 214
Peppered, 210
Phoenix, 207
Pine Beauty, 215
Pine Shoot, 197
Pinion, 216, 217
Pinion-spotted, 211
Plain Clay, 213
Plum Fruit, 197
Poplar Grey, 217
Portland, 213
Prominents, 212
Pugs, 208-9
Purple-bar, 207
Purple Marbled, 219
Puss Moth, 212
Quakers, 215, 216
Ranunculus, 216
Red Chestnut, 214
Red Sword-grass, 216
Red Underwing, 219
Rivulet, 208, 209
Rustic, 213, 214, 218
Sallows, 216, 219
Saltern Ear, 218
Satellite, 216
Satin Beauty, 211
Scallop, 206
Scallop Shell, 207
Scalloped Hazel, 210
Scalloped Oak, 210
Scorched Carpet, 210
Scorched Wing, 210
Seraphim, 209
Shaded Broad-bar, 206
Sharks, 216
Shears, 214
Shell, 206
Short-cloaked, 213
Shoulder-stripe, 207
Shoulder-knot, 216, 217
Silver Cloud, 215
Silver Hook, 219
Silver Y, 219
Silver-line, 210
Silver-lines, 219
Small Dotted Buff, 218
Small Marbled, 219

Small Purple-barred, 220
Small Rufous, 218
Small Waved Umber, 207
Small Yellow Underwing, 218
Snout, 220
Speckled Yellow, 210
Spectacle, 219
Spinach, 207
Spotted Shoot, 197
Sprawler, 216
Square-spot, 214
Straw Underwing, 217
Straw-dot, 220
Streak, 209
Streamer, 207
Suspected, 217
Swallow-tail, 210
Swifts, 180
Tawny-barred Angle, 210
Tawny Shears, 215
The Herald, 220
Thorns, 210
Tigers, 213
Tissue, 207
Tooth-striped, 209
Tortrix, 193-7
Treble-bar, 209
Treble Brown-spot, 206
Treble-lines, 218
True-lover's Knot, 214
Turnip Moth, 213
Twenty-plume, 198
Umber, 210-211
Uncertain, 218
Underwings, 205, 214, 218
Usher, 210
V-moth, 210
Vapourer, 212
Vestal, 206
Wainscots, 215, 218
Water Veneer, 199
Waves, 206
Wax Moth, 200
White Colon, 214
White-marked, 214
White Wave, 211
White-speck, 215
Willow Beauty, 211
Winter, 208
Wormwood, 215
Yellow Belle, 211
Yellow-horned, 205
Yellow-tail, 212
Yellow Underwings, 214, 218
NEWTS, 301
PSEUDOSCORPIONS, 292
PROTURANS, 160
ROCKHOPPERS, 160

SAWFLIES, 242
SCORPION FLY, 178
SEAWEEDS - see algae
SILVERFISH, 160
SLOW-WORM, 302
SLUGS, 155
SNAILS, 154-156
SNAKEFLIES, 177
SOILS, 1
SPIDERS, 285
SPRINGTAILS, 160
STONEWORTS, 9
SUMMARY of SPECIES, 336
THRIPS, 177
TICKS, 292
TOAD, 301
VIPER, 302
WASPS, 243, 245, 246
WEEVILS, 278-283
WHITEFLY, 175
WOODLICE, 158

- NOTES -

- NOTES -